The machinery question and the making of
political economy 1815–1848

The machinery question and the making of political economy

1815–1848

MAXINE BERG

CAMBRIDGE UNIVERSITY PRESS

CAMBRIDGE

LONDON   NEW YORK   NEW ROCHELLE

MELBOURNE   SYDNEY

Published by the Press Syndicate of the University of Cambridge
The Pitt Building, Trumpington Street, Cambridge CB2 1RP
32 East 57th Street, New York, NY 10022, USA
296 Beaconsfield Parade, Middle Park, Melbourne 3206, Australia

First published 1980

Printed in Great Britain by The Anchor Press Ltd
Tiptree, Essex

Library of Congress Cataloguing in Publication Data

Berg, Maxine, 1950–
The machinery question and the making of
political economy, 1815–1848.

Revision of the author's thesis, Oxford, 1976.
Bibliography: p.
Includes index.
1. Economics – History – 19th century.
2. Machinery in industry – History – 19th century.
3. Technological innovations – History – 19th century.
I. Title.
HB85.B35   1980   338'.06'09034   79–15271

ISBN 0 521 22782 8

For my parents
Frederick and Gwendoline Berg

The hoary sage, that first did raise
Slow steaming from his faggot's blaze,
The subtle vapour, – instant hail'd
Alcides, in his cradle veil'd;

Reason and Force, too oft opposed,
For once their hands resistless closed,
Combined to rear – and pledged their troth –
This full epitome of both.

Then limb by limb, the giant rose,
A Sampson – e'en in swaddling clothes;
Matured – he changed Earth's form and face,
And half subjected time and space;

Pierced through the mountain's bowels deep,
Where sunless, countless treasures sleep,
And like a Nero, ripp'd the womb
From whence his iron sinews came.

.   .   .

Still foot by foot, and year by year,
This giant gains in growth and gear;
But what he shall be none can say
But those that bide the judgment day.

'Steam Power', *The New Moral World*, 28 May 1836

CONTENTS

ILLUSTRATIONS

PREFACE

This book is a revision of my Oxford D.Phil. thesis presented in June 1976. I am grateful to my former supervisor, Peter Mathias, who provided constant enthusiasm and encouragement while I was working on my thesis, and who gave me the perceptive and constructive criticism I needed to transform it into a book. I would also like to thank my examiners, Angus MacIntyre and R. D. Collison Black, the readers for the Cambridge University Press and Robert M. Young for their criticisms and the suggestions they made for revision of the manuscript.

The following people read and criticised parts of my work in various stages and I am most grateful: A. W. Coats, Nathan Rosenberg, the late Ronald Meek, Michael Lebowitz, Ronald Robinson, D. N. Winch, J. R. Hays, Andrew Glyn, Everett Mendelsohn, and Michael Sonenscher. Paul Sturges gave me useful advice on manuscript collections, and A. N. Whitelegge of Goldsmiths' Library was always very helpful. I appreciate the meticulous care with which my manuscript was treated through the various stages of publication by my editor William Davies and especially by my sub-editor, Rosemary Dooley. Mark Robertson gave generous and painstaking labour to the difficult tasks of helping me to proofread and provide an index for this book.

This research was dependent on funding provided by the Canada Council and by Balliol College's Sir Lewis Namier Junior Research Fellowship. I am grateful to Christopher Hill, Thomas Hodgkin, John Prest, and the fellows and students of Balliol College who helped to make the research post I held there while writing my thesis and book such an enjoyable one.

I would like particularly to thank my parents, my first teacher in economic history, Michael Lebowitz, and an old friend, Ruth Pearson, for the encouragement they each gave me many years ago. My greatest debt, however, is to John Robertson, my husband. In addition to the great happiness he has brought me over the years of research and writing of this book, he has provided the day-by-day argument and unremitting criticism which helped to create and to sustain my work.

Maxine Berg
University of Warwick
Coventry

January 1979

INTRODUCTION

In the eighteenth century there was no Machinery Question. The machine was then simply a material contrivance which demonstrated the culmination and success of the division of labour. It was but one of the many novel indications of industry in a largely rural landscape. The technical innovation of the eighteenth century certainly evoked a sense of excitement among contemporaries, and contributed to their belief in economic progress. The intellectuals of the Enlightenment welcomed it as an indicator of economic expansion which they believed would contribute to the general 'improvement' of society. But in the early nineteenth century this prospect of a harmonious integration of economic and social improvement was thrown into question. The face of industrialisation now appeared concentrated in the machine. It was the machine which seemed to be responsible for the disharmony of rapidly expanding cotton towns, unprecedented population growth and the economic crisis of the post-Napoleonic years. The eighteenth-century vision of improvement had become the machinery question of the early nineteenth century.

For contemporaries the Industrial Revolution meant steam power and rapid mechanisation in the cotton textile industry. Yet in reality such mechanisation directly affected only a small number of industries and regions, and even in these its permanence might be questioned. For rapid technical change was not the universal experience of the Industrial Revolution; elsewhere it appeared rather as an expansion on the basis of traditionally organised trades and manual labour. But if the economy of early- to mid-nineteenth-century Britain continued to display many traditional features, the discontinuity with the eighteenth century was none the less fundamental. The traditional crafts and manual labour might continue, but they now did so within the circuit of industrial capital. The economic cycle of a cotton industry rapidly becoming mechanised – waves of industrial credit creation culminating in periodic financial panics and overcapacity in the Lancashire factories – rippled outwards to affect the old artisan trades. The trades, too, were now pursued by the rationalisation of production and the standardisation of the product. An ever expanding supply of labour made its contribution, making possible the intensification of the division of labour and the reduction of skill. But already manifest, and dwarfing in potential significance these other forms which technical change in an industry might take, was the ultimate, the most exciting and the most threatening development of all – the replacement of man by machine.

The economic uncertainty of the period meant that mechanisation presented a distinctly ambiguous face to contemporaries. It was far from clear whether it was a portent of inevitable economic revolution, or but one course of development among several, which might be adopted or rejected, in whole or in part, depending on the nation's goals and priorities. Its consequences were equally hard to determine. Would it bring wealth only to those who owned it, or to society as a whole? Would it make work or create unemployment? Would it unite society or foment class conflict? Such uncertainties about both the direction and the effects of mechanisation naturally yielded a wide variety of responses. The machine was to evoke both eulogy and resistance, and above all ambivalence.

The machinery question became in fact the hinge which connected the new economic relations of production with the wider culture and consciousness of the new bourgeoisie and working classes. With perhaps greater clarity than any other contemporary issue the machinery question defined the lines of division between these classes. Among almost all the working classes, many of the middle classes and many landowners the reception of the machine was decidedly equivocal. Faced with their resistance, however, the industrial bourgeoisie and their associates adopted an attitude of increasingly aggressive determinism and optimism. For them it became axiomatic that mechanical change was natural and evolutionary, the very motor of progress itself.

At the centre of this struggle over the interpretation of the future effects of the new technology was political economy. The period of intense debate on the machinery issue coincided with the making of this new discipline. Both internal intellectual and external social developments contributed to establishing its status. Internally, a unique object of inquiry and a specific intellectual framework of analysis were established. At the centre of this inquiry was the phenomenon of technical change, and it was one of the first concerns of economic analysis to provide an adequate theoretical explanation of this. Simultaneously, machinery helped to establish the social standing of the discipline. In defence of the machine, middle-class popularisers and politicians elevated the ideas and mode of analysis of political economy into unquestioned doctrine, and economic theorists came to be closely associated with the formulation of economic policy. The intellectual and social prestige of political economy was only reinforced when those opposed to machinery began also to criticise the theory which defended it : working-class radicals and even Tories were not slow to discover that the best critical tools were provided by political economy itself.

It was thus that the great debate over machinery simultaneously shaped the features of political economy while both stood at the centre of the stage of social, political and intellectual conflict in the early nineteenth century. Yet the significance of this relation between the machinery question and the making of political economy in the upheaval of the period has passed almost unnoticed by historians. The reason for this remarkable indifference lies, I believe, in the previous splintering of many fields of history – the history of economic thought, the history of science and social science, the history of social and economic policy, economic history, and political and social history.

Political and social historians, for their part, have repeatedly re-turned to the 'condition of England' debate. But their attention has been concentrated either on the standard of living, wages and prices, or on the impact of industrialisation on working-class culture and political consciousness. They have only begun to explore in detail the impact of rapid mechanisation on the actual organisation of production, the definition of skill and the structure of employment and unemploy-ment, let alone the intense contemporary debate over the issue. Still less have they investigated the significance of political economy in either its popularised classical form or its radical alternatives. The ascendancy and success of Ricardian economics have not been explained, nor do we yet have a satisfactory explanation of the way in which political economy was woven into the rising careers of William Huskisson,

Joseph Hume and Francis Place. We have still to learn the extent to which political economy formed a dimension of middle-class provincial culture, and its relationship to the contemporary scientific movement.

Social and political historians have also, for the most part, consigned the consideration of political economy to a separate domain : the history of political economy has been left to economists and specialist historians of economic thought. These specialists have indeed produced a major literature, but they have cut themselves off from and made little impact on the mainstream of economic, political and social history. Most histories of economic thought have, in fact, been written within an identifiable and deliberately restrictive framework. It was Joseph Schumpeter's *History of Economic Analysis* which did most to define the limits of the specialist histories of political economy. Although he conceded that economic thought must ultimately be ideological, Schumpeter believed that economic analysis proper could be treated as independent and objective. He regarded it as a hard core of formal techniques and instruments governed by supra-historical standards and rules. For this economic analysis he accordingly proclaimed a separate history which would ascertain the course of its scientific progress.[1] On the basis of this view of the history of economic thought Schumpeter himself proceeded through his book to apportion praise and blame to each economic thinker he came to according to how well they measured up to his own (heterodox) opinions. Schumpeter's approach was to be adopted by the great majority of writers on the classical economists. Mark Blaug's *Economic Theory in Retrospect*, D. P. O'Brien's *The Classical Economists*, and Marian Bowley's *Studies in the History of Economic Theory before 1870*[2] were representative of the received methods. Only a few have resisted the trend. In 1946, Hla Myint warned against 'theoretical anthropomorphism', and advocated an approach to the classical economists in the 'context of their own intellectual climate'.[3] But his was a lone voice.

An historical approach was, to be sure, also advocated by a number of Marxist and Sraffian economists claiming to use the method of

---

[1] Joseph Schumpeter, *History of Economic Analysis*, London, 1954, pp. 37–9.

[2] Mark Blaug, *Economic Theory in Retrospect*, 2nd edition, London, 1958; D. P. O'Brien, *The Classical Economists*, Oxford, 1975; Marian Bowley, *Studies in the History of Economic Theory before 1870*, London, 1973.

[3] Hla Myint, 'The Classical View of the Economic Problem', *Economica*, May 1946.

historical materialism. But their practice was actually little different from that of their neo-classical opponents. They interpreted their claim as historical, to mean the search for the origins of Marxism and latterly for the origins of the Sraffian interpretation of Marx. Maurice Dobb expressed the perspective succinctly in his *Theories of Value and Distribution since Adam Smith*: 'Apart from its special corollaries, what is particularly striking . . . about the Sraffa-system viewed as a whole is its rehabilitation of the Ricardo–Marx approach to problems of value and distribution from the side of production.'[4] Otherwise, the method of historical materialism appeared to involve little more than the simple ascription of bourgeois class interests and motivation to the concepts and theories of classical economics, examples of which were often taken directly from Marx's own denunciations of classical political economy.

The practical similarities in the methodology of both neo-classical and neo-Marxist approaches ended, in fact, in a common pessimistic interpretation of Ricardo and the classical economists. Schumpeter and Blaug from the neo-classical standpoint and Pasinetti from the Sraffian presented the classicals as dominated by Malthusian fears of over-population, Ricardian predictions of the advent of the stationary state, and an apparent indifference to the impact of technological change.[5]

These conventional conclusions are still to be found in Keith Tribe's *Land, Labour and Economic Discourse*, despite a considerable effort to elaborate a more substantial alternative to the Schumpeterian framework.[6] Tribe's avowed approach is structural – a study not of the text and the author, but of the discourse. Following broadly the methods of the French structuralist philosophers and historians of ideas, Althusser and Foucault, Tribe seeks to provide an anatomy of economic argument from the seventeenth to the nineteenth centuries. What this method appears to involve is abandoning the attempt to read texts as self-contained entities and to investigate the intentions of specific authors in favour of establishing a general, impersonal pattern of

4 Maurice Dobb, *Theories of Value and Distribution since Adam Smith*, Cambridge, 1973, p. 257.
5 Schumpeter, *History of Economic Analysis*, p. 571; Mark Blaug, 'The Empirical Content of Ricardian Economics', *Journal of Political Economy*, LXIV, 1956; L. Pasinetti, 'A Mathematical Formulation of the Ricardian System', *Review of Economic Studies*, XXVII, 1959–60, and 'From Classical to Keynesian Dynamics', in L. Pasinetti, ed., *Growth and Income Distribution*, Cambridge, 1974.
6 Keith Tribe, *Land, Labour and Economic Discourse*, London, 1978.

concepts and arguments. By these means Tribe would escape both from teleological interpretations of the evolution of ideas and from crude ascriptions of ideology. Nevertheless, the interpretation of Ricardo in particular and the developments of early nineteenth-century political economy in general does not substantially differ from the received views of neo-classicals and Sraffians.

My book is also an attempt to escape the presentation of historical arguments as anticipations of more recent theories. However, I believe that, while it is important to establish the internal structure of ideas, this alone is not sufficient for a history of political economy. In addition, the context provided by evidence of authors' intentions, by the social concerns and connections of the period, and by contemporary issues of economic policy, must also be considered in an historical approach to the classical economists. The contextual framework can contribute as much as the intellectual structure of the theory to an understanding of the making of political economy as a discipline.

This book is such an attempt to integrate economic thought into economic and social change. In doing so I have reached some different conclusions on the internal evolution of political economy, and have made some new connections between social and intellectual developments. I have been led to emphasise a profound interest in technical change pervading political economy in the early nineteenth century, an interest associated with a decidedly optimistic view of future economic growth. There was, furthermore, a noticeable shift of emphasis in these theories of technical change from concern with the division of labour and labour productivity to fixed capital formation, a shift which may be connected directly with new levels of social conflict from the early 1830s and indirectly with changes in real economic structure. This external context for theories of technical change can be established at a variety of levels from the mundane, practical world of factory organisation and control, through the popular cultural institutions of the Mechanics Institutes and the scientific and statistical societies, up to the political worlds of radicals, Tories and social reformers. At the same time, it can be seen that machinery was a major problem of economic policy, drawing the political economists into the political arena. Over the period, in fact, a marked improvement in their political standing can be seen : where Ricardo was but a respected independent commentator, Nassau Senior was a fully-fledged government expert. I conclude that the machinery question was never resolved, but that in the 1840s it lay at the heart of an irreconciliable schism in economics and politics. On the one hand, J. S. Mill's sceptical restatement of Ricardianism opened up a newly questioning and progressive path for liberalism, but failed to resolve now well-established differences among economists. On the other, radical and working-class resistance to industrialisation found an unprecedented revolutionary expression in Engel's *Condition of the Working Class in England* which analysed the capitalist basis of recent technical change, and predicted its eventual destruction at the hands of the class conflict it generated.

My emphasis on the centrality of machinery and industrialisation to the making of political economy is not in itself original. It does no more than recall the judgements of the first histories of economic thought. Perhaps the earliest of these was J. R. McCulloch's *Discourse on the Rise, Progress, Peculiar Objects and Importance of Political Economy*, published in 1824.[7] There, McCulloch insisted that the emergence of political economy must be explained in material terms. McCulloch himself produced only the very general argument that the science could only arise in a commercial, capitalist society. But his injunction was followed by Travers Twiss, whose *View of the Progress of Political Economy in Europe* of 1847 developed an interpretation tied explicitly to the rise of industrial capitalism. According to Twiss,

> The great motive power which the genius of Watt had first disciplined . . . was applied, about the year 1785 in furtherance of the discoveries of Arkwright, and the combination of the steam engine with the spinning frame, [not only] changed an aspect of production [but also] gave rise to a new class of problems, bearing upon the distribution of the produce.

Twiss proceeded to distinguish Adam Smith's economics from that of the later classicals by reference to industrialisation. In Smith's period, 'the operation of *industry*, properly so called in distinction from *labour*, had not assumed that importance which entitled [it] to a special analysis'.[8]

Twiss drew material for his history from an earlier French work, Jerome Blanqui's *Political Economy in Europe*, first published in 1837. Blanqui explicitly argued that the English classicals had given political

[7] J. R. McCulloch, *A Discourse on the Rise, Progress, Peculiar Objects and Importance of Political Economy*, London, 1824.
[8] Travers Twiss, *View of the Progress of Political Economy in Europe, since the Sixteenth Century*, London, 1847, pp. 226, 227.

economy a 'physiognomy and tendency exclusively industrial'. He believed that this had led them to consider manufactures and machines as 'too separate from the welfare of the labourers'; with the consequence that they 'manifested an insensibility to the sufferings of the working classes'.[9]

This book is not conceived as a simple return to these early histories of political economy, for they were often highly simplified or sectarian. However, it does aspire to follow a similar course to those early historians in connecting the origins of the discipline to a specific economic context. My starting point like theirs was the coincidence of industrialisation with the beginnings of political economy. But I have tried to go further in offering an analysis of the many different levels – political, social, intellectual – at which political economy was made and articulated. For this is the only way, I believe, that we can hope to arrive at some understanding of the complex connections between context and theory, and thus write neither a hagiography nor a teleology, but a *history* of political economy. This book will prove, I hope, a step in that direction.

---

[9] Jerome Blanqui, *History of Political Economy in Europe*, London 1880, p. 529 (translated by E. J. Leonard from the fourth edition of *Histoire de L'Economie Politique en Europe*).

1

The age of machinery

In the popular mind the Industrial Revolution has always been associated with the steam engine and the cotton mill. For a long time this was also the characteristic view of the economic historian: traditionally, the story of the Industrial Revolution was written as the triumph of new techniques, and the inevitable march of invention. In recent years economic historians have indeed attempted to displace this technological bias in their predecessors, offering broader accounts of the economics of 'take-off' or balanced growth, of capital accumulation or gains in labour productivity. Important though these new interpretations are, however, they can never entirely supplant the popular, traditional conception of the Industrial Revolution. For the traditional has the justification of being the contemporary view: to those who lived through it, the Industrial Revolution was not take-off, but, more equivocally, the machinery question.

The machine was not an impersonal achievement to those living through the Industrial Revolution; it was an issue. The machinery question in early nineteenth-century Britain was the question of the sources of technical progress and the impact of the introduction of the new technology of the period on the total economy and society. The question was central to everyday relations between master and workman, but it was also of major theoretical and ideological interest. The very technology at the basis of economy and society was a platform of challenge and struggle.

The machinery question was, furthermore, an issue which stimulated analysis in political economy during the key years of the formation of this new intellectual discipline. Political economists took up the theoretical debate on the introduction, diffusion and social impact of the radically new techniques of production associated with the era. Recognising that the machine formed the basis for an unprecedented economic transformation, political economists created new concepts and made the growth potential and technological advances of the British economy the new focus of their analysis. Breaking from the wider political and social concerns of their forebears, political economists of the early nineteenth century forged a new and distinct science of political economy. It was economic growth and its now limitless prospects created by technological advance which became the new centre, not just of the analysis of the economy, but of the analysis of politics and society as well. The economy was no longer conceived as subordinate to broader social and political ideals. It now played a distinct and a dominant role. The analysis of the machinery question was formative in the creation of a political economy which became the 'natural science' of economy and society in the second quarter of the nineteenth century.

The machine awakened the interest of early political economists, not just for the departure it evidently meant for the significance and speed of economic expansion, but for the pervasiveness of its social impact. For, as a subject which evoked an equivocal response, the machine was debated at length in all sectors of society. It provoked the village cleric as much as it did the cosmopolitan intellectual; it concerned the politician as much as the workman and employer; the social reformer as much as scientist and inventor. These groups contended over the costs and benefits of the new technology. They hailed the release it provided from limits to growth, but disagreed over the impact it would have on wages, employment, and skill. They speculated on, and then either welcomed or dreaded, the changes the machine would bring to social relations. The origins and the ownership of machinery even came up for question. There was excitement and fear at this unknown force which swept relentlessly onward, casting the old society in its wake.

The great range of contemporary writing on economic, social and intellectual aspects of the rapid industrialisation of early nineteenth-century Britain made the machinery question a national controversy. It claimed the status of an intellectual debate. It was formulated as a policy question and was an important element in the strategic thinking among the various social and political interest groups of the period.

Actual occurrences of anti-machinery activity or of eulogies to the new technology are only meaningful in the broader context. They were part of a wider issue in the early nineteenth century, unlike the individual and specific reactions characteristic of the years both before and after the period.

The machinery question was unique, for the British experience of industrialisation was the first. Never again and in no other country's industrial revolution would there be quite the same sense of struggle, apprehension, excitement and unpredictability. Though technology would continue to be an issue in later phases of Britain's industrial-isation, the experience of the early years of the nineteenth century would always stand as an example, if not as a model. For some who contemplated the prospects of wealth and power the machine might bring, the experience of technical change was a novelty and an excite-ment. But alongside an emergent industrial landscape large sectors of the economy remained traditional. And, to many, the implications of the new machines were not at all welcome. The first generation of factory labour and cast-off artisans were among those who regarded the new machinery as unnatural. In the uncertainty of the times it still seemed possible to halt the process of rapid technical change.

Depression scarred the economy for well over a decade after the Napoleonic Wars. Against this dispiriting background, the machine appeared to some to be a simple and obvious symbol of progress. Inculcating its message wordlessly, its meaning was inherent in its physical attributes. As John Stuart Mill expressed it, 'The more visible fruits of scientific progress . . . the mechanical improvements, the steam engine, the railroads, carry the feeling of admiration for the modern, and disrespect for ancient times, down even to the wholly uneducated classes.'[1] But this reaction to the machine was by no means typical, for the response to reconstruction after long years of war was an indecisive one. It was difficult to predict the outcome of such artificial times, and the ultimate direction of the fragile society of these years was a great unknown. The machine was a symbol of progress, but it could also evoke feelings of powerlessness and fear. Even Charles Babbage recalled such feelings when he visited an iron works with a hundred horsepower engine : 'The intensity of that fire was peculiarly impressive. It recalled the past, disturbed the present, and suggested the future . . .

---

1 [J. S. Mill], 'M. de Tocqueville on Democracy in America', *Edinburgh Review*, October 1840, cited in Leo Marx, *The Machine in the Garden*, Oxford, 1964, 192.

candour obliges me to admit that my speculations on the future were not entirely devoid of anxiety.'[2]

And equally a disconsolate radical could comment, 'One rarely finds anyone who ventures to deal frankly with the problem of machinery . . . it appears to infuse a certain fear. Everybody sees that machinery is producing the greatest of all revolutions between classes, but somehow nobody dares to interfere.'[3] The machine might overturn the old society, but some dreaded the prospects of clanking steam engines, 'the Scottish Brass-smith's IDEA',[4] as Thomas Carlyle characterised it.

> The huge demon of Mechanism smokes and thunders, panting at his great task, in all sections of English land; changing his *shape* like a very Proteus; and infallibly at every change of shape, *oversetting* whole multitudes of workmen, as if with the waving of his shadow from afar, hurling them asunder, this way and that, in their crowded march and curse of work or traffic.[5]

The cultural critique of the machine is indeed best expressed by Carlyle, who dubbed this period as the 'Age of Machinery'. He connected the machine as technical fact with the machine as metaphor, representing the overvaluation of all aspects of life that were calculable and open to manipulation. The machine was material and incorporeal. With its onset 'the living artisan' was replaced by an 'inanimate one'. The 'shuttle dropped from the fingers of the weaver and fell into iron fingers that ply it faster'.[6] But the 'machine of society'[7] was also 'despair and death of spirit', 'a huge, dead, immeasurable steam engine, rolling on, in its dead indifference'.[8] The cultural critics blamed the machine for bringing to England's new industrial towns a bleak, quantitative, utilitarian society. Charles Dickens, for example, portrayed life in a town of machinery as dictated by the piston of a steam engine which worked monotonously up and down, 'like the head of an elephant in a

---

2 Charles Babbage, *Passages in the Life of a Philosopher*, London, 1864, p. 231.
3 R. L. Hill, *Toryism and the People*, London, 1929, p. 172.
4 Thomas Carlyle, *Sartor Resartus, Collected Works*, vol. III, p. 82.
5 Thomas Carlyle, 'Chartism', *Critical and Miscellaneous Essays, Collected Works*, vol. XXIII, p. 24.
6 Thomas Carlyle, 'Signs of the Times', *Critical and Miscellaneous Essays, Collected Works*, vol. XV, p. 474.
7 *Ibid.* p. 486.
8 Carlyle, *Sartor Resartus*, p. 114.

state of melancholy madness'.[9] It was a society where everything was quantified, mechanised, calculated as 'so many hundred hands in this Mill; so many hundred horse steampower' – everything except the soul of man.[10]

Carlyle's criticisms of the cultural implications of the machine also extended to the social dislocation and economic precedents created by the new technology. The 'Inventive Genius of England' would have to create more than the 'whirr of bobbins and billy-rollers'. It would have to find the means for a fairer distribution of the products of machinery. The introduction of steam power 'into the social system' was productive, not just of greater total wealth, but of greater distance between the rich and the poor, and 'would be a question for political economists and a much more complex and important one than they have yet engaged with'.

This emphasis on the social disruption caused by the machine was to be the main factor making the machinery question an economic issue of widespread public concern. Carlyle's opinion that disparities in wealth had been revealed and even widened by mechanisation and industrialisation was echoed in the writings of playwrights and novelists throughout the first half of the nineteenth century. They epitomised the social disruption caused by the machine in their dramatic depiction of resistance to machinery among the poor. John Walker, an early nineteenth-century London playwright, was one of the first to do this. His play, *The Factory Lad*, produced at the Surrey in 1832, centred on an incident of industrial strife and machine breaking which had ensued on the decision of a factory owner to introduce new machinery and to make many of his workers redundant.[11] Disraeli's working people in *Sybil* blamed their troubles on machinery: 'As for rights of labour,' said Harriet, 'the people goes for nothing with this machinery . . . Fancy preferring a piece of iron or wood to your own flesh and blood. And they call that Christian like.'[12] Disraeli identified machine breaking among the poor, not with mindless mob violence, but with physical force Chartism. Reading about an attack on a local mill, Field, the character chosen to represent the physical force Chartist, suggests, 'perhaps we may contrive to gain admission, and then we can

9 Charles Dickens, *Hard Times* (1854), Harmondsworth, 1969, p. 65.
10 *Ibid.* p. 108.
11 See Sally Vernon, 'Trouble up at T'Mill: the Rise and Decline of the Factory Play in the 1830's and 1840's', *Victorian Studies*, Winter 1977.
12 Benjamin Disraeli, *Sybil; or the Two Nations* (1845), London, 1926, p. 391.

sack the whole affair, and let the people burn the machinery. It will be a great moral lesson.'[13]

Elizabeth Gaskell, George Eliot and Charlotte Brontë all portrayed the poor and the working people of their novels as anti-machinery advocates, though for different reasons. Gaskell and Eliot depicted a stereotyped resistance to machinery among the poor. In Gaskell's *Mary Barton*, John Barton, elected Chartist delegate to London, garnered the grievances of his poor neighbours: 'Bless thee, lad, do ask 'un to make tha' masters break th' machines. There's never been good times sin' spinning jennies came up . . . "Machines is the ruin of poor folk" chimed in several voices.'[14] Eliot had Brooke, her reforming landlord, speak to the people: 'I've gone a good deal into public questions – machinery, now, and machine breaking – you're many of you concerned with machinery, and I've been going into that lately. It won't do, you know, breaking machines.'[15]

Brontë, in contrast, went deeper, and depicted the machine as an alien force. It was, like the millowner Moore, foreign to the region: 'Not being a native, nor for any length of time a resident of this neighbourhood, he did not sufficiently care when the new invention threw the old workpeople out of employment.'[16] And the 'starving poor of Yorkshire' released their pent-up frustrations: 'Misery generates hate: these sufferers hated the machines which they believed took their bread from them: they hated the buildings which contained those machines; they hated the manufacturers who owned those buildings.'[17]

Whereas Brontë sympathised with her poor, Gaskell ignored their attitudes as the product of ignorance. Gaskell, therefore, introduced into her story the character Job Leigh, a self-educated worker–intellectual with more 'progressive' opinions: 'It's true it was a sore time for handloom weavers when power looms came in: these new fangled things make a man's life like a lottery; and yet I'll never mis-doubt that power looms, and railways, and all such like inventions, are the gifts of God. I have lived long enough, too, to see that it is part of his plan to send suffering to bring out a higher good.'[18]

The novelist and later their literary critics, such as Raymond Williams, knew that the issue was important to the early Victorian

13 *Ibid.* p. 403.
14 Elizabeth Gaskell, *Mary Barton* (1848), Everyman, London, 1967, p. 81.
15 George Eliot, *Middlemarch* (1861–2), Harmondsworth, 1965, p. 547.
16 Charlotte Brontë, *Shirley* (1849), Everyman, London, 1970, p. 21.
17 *Ibid.* pp. 22 and 24.
18 Gaskell, *Mary Barton*, p. 364.

society they sought to probe. Raymond Williams has described this centrality of technology for the contemporary mind : 'Again and again, even by the critics of society, the excitement of this extraordinary release of man's powers was acknowledged and shared. The society could not have been acceptable to anybody without that. "These are our poems," Carlyle said in 1842, looking at one of the new locomotives, and this element, now so easily overlooked, is central to the whole culture.'[19] But historians have thus far told us little about the machinery question as an integrated intellectual, political and social issue. Disputes over the impact of the machine have been mentioned by historians only obliquely as an aspect of the 'condition of England' question. Many historians have dealt with merely the cultural dimensions of the debate, stopping short at any serious discussion of economic, social and political aspects of the machine. We know a great deal, therefore, about the struggle between the mechanistic Benthamite philosophy and the romantic reaction in the formation of the general culture. The machine has also figured in histories of working-class revolt. Machine breaking among the Luddites, the agricultural labourers 'led by' Captain Swing, and the weavers has fascinated social historians interested in the origins of the British labour movement, in the collective violence of the crowd, and in the politically conscious activity of the poor. But machine breaking has been written of mainly in terms of generalisation about these areas of interest. Social historians have shown less interest in making connections between such resistance to the machine and the political and intellectual disputes over technological improvement taking place in the wider society. They have been reluctant to regard individual occurrences of resistance to the machine as a part of a more general phenomenon – a national debate on the machinery question.

The political positions adopted in this period were stamped with economic choices, and a major issue on which a distinctive stand was necessary to each social group was the debate on industrialisation. Perspectives on the new technology infused both Tory-landed ideas about the new society and radical working-class alternatives. Middle-class ideologues grasped at the progressive implications of the machine in their attempt to loose the bondage of landed and pre-industrial attitudes. But they had also to face the challenge created by conservative and working-class alternatives to an industrial capitalist society.

[19] Raymond Williams, *The Long Revolution*, Harmondsworth, 1965, p. 88.

Conservative or Tory opinion was distinguished by protest against the very existence of industrial society, and at the foundation of this there was a deep-seated prejudice against the machine. The Tory choice was not simply one of rural versus urban life; its dilemma was not just the fate of the agricultural sector in the face of industry. For methods and relations of production on the land were changing as fundamentally as were those in industry. The image of the threshing machine in Hardy's *Tess of the D'Urbervilles* as 'the red tyrant that the women had come to serve . . . which . . . kept up a despotic demand on the endurance of their muscles and nerves' is aptly perceived by Raymond Williams as a part of a deeper change going beyond the abstraction of industry against rural life.[20] Williams argues that the vision of the country must include the 'action of the real threshing machine. It stands in that field and works those hours because it has been hired, not by industrialism, but by a farmer.'[21] The issue of industry and the land was just one part of a more general discussion of the whole process of industrialisation.

However, Toryism was not by any means a single set of doctrines. The novelty of industrial society was, in fact, one of the factors which contributed to a split in the early nineteenth-century Tory party, between the progressive liberal Toryism of Lord Liverpool's administration from 1815 to 1830 and the Tory country party. The liberal Tories did not welcome the machine, but they did believe it was here to stay. Country Toryism, on the other hand, was a continued protest against the suppression of a rural England it knew by an industrialised England it knew not.[22]

The working class challenged the beneficence of the machine first by its own distress then by its relentless protest. This protest did not just flare up in sporadic occurrences of Luddism or Swing Riots. Such incidents only highlighted a day by day resistance to the machine evident in many workplace settings. Workers criticised the rapid and unplanned introduction of new techniques in situations where the immediate result would be technological unemployment. But they also went beyond this to challenge the uses and property relations of technology. They demanded an equitable distribution of the gains from technical progress. Rather than raising the profits of the few,

[20] Raymond Williams, *The Country and the City*, St Albans, 1973, p. 256.
[21] *Ibid.*
[22] Hill, *Toryism and the People*, p. 11.

the machine, they argued, might lighten the labour and increase the leisure of the many. They also demanded greater control over the direction of technological change. Mechanisation was unnecessary in industries where there was an abundance of labour, for it only further dragged down wages and led to greater overcrowding of labour markets in other industries. The machine and what went with it, the technical division of labour, should not be allowed to degrade and alienate labour. Rather it should allow man the possibility of developing his potentials in many fields. Technological progress should also be directed to changing the role of women in society, dispensing with the heavy manual labour and the household chores which prevented many women from claiming an equal position with men.

But, like the Tories, working-class leaders took up many contradictory positions on the machinery issue. Some embraced the machine as fundamental to their utopian dreams, but many more saw it as a cause of economic distress. More immediate than the utopian dreaming was the bitter experience of technological unemployment, long hours of alienated factory labour, and the smoking blight of rapidly expanding industrial towns.

Middle-class economic and political perspectives actively eulogised the progress of science and technology. But, challenged on both sides by Tory and radical working-class opinion, the middle class had to find an explanation for the economic and social impact of the machine. Expressions of wonder at the technical perfection of the machine were not adequate. It was thus that the middle class took to itself a 'scientific' theory, political economy. This theory was expected to provide answers by employers, politicians, and middle-class ideologists. It was no mere coincidence that industrialisation and the emergence of political economy occurred at virtually the same time. Political economy became a distinct discipline from the 1790s, breaking free from the place allotted it by previous writers, including Adam Smith, as a branch of legislation or statesmanship. The Industrial Revolution in cotton and iron concurred with this intellectual break. Since the very inception of political economy as an intellectual discipline, the conscious reflection on the processes of economic development could not be separated from the emerging class forces and social interests at stake in the changes. Political economy was expected to explain the effects of the new industrialism. It was to these intellectuals that the middle class looked for the affirmation of their attitudes. It was these expositors of the new science of wealth who provided the authority and guidance needed by the new industrial élites. Tory and radical leaders came to identify the mechanical age or the new industrialism with the doctrine of political economy and the interests of the middle class. The machinery question, therefore, became entwined with political economy. In the process, the terms of debate on the machinery issue were set by political economy.

But the analysis offered by political economy was also a complicated one. Political economy, though regarded by many as an arm of middle-class opinion, escaped the boundaries of mere opinion. For, as an intellectual discipline, it was expected to go beyond the attempts of factions and social groups to stabilise the transitory order in some way best suited to their own special interests. The projections made by individuals and political economists on the economy, and their opinions on the social impact of mechanisation, ranged widely. Where they attempted to offer a fundamentally optimistic prospect, they were also forced to admit some naggingly obvious disadvantages. This, in turn, reflected the ambivalences of middle-class opinion. The disruptions caused by mechanisation brought in train a legacy of fear, and led to the expression of doubts coupled with a polemical optimism. Such an optimism was, however, also based partly on ignorance. This is clearly demonstrated in the general incomprehension of poverty during the period, in the response to critiques of machinery, and in the cult of comparative growth studies of England, Europe, and America. It is notable too that by the 1830s this optimism was joining a new Victorian middle-class conscience for the amelioration of poverty. Optimism and conscience complemented each other in those projects characteristic of the early Victorian middle classes : philanthropy, urban reform, education and moral virtue.

This book will chart the issues which made machinery a question of national significance. As a preliminary, it will describe the actual diffusion of the machine in the early nineteenth-century economy. But its purpose is to go beyond this, to demonstrate that the political and intellectual circumstances culminating in the emergence of political economy as a new discipline were also the ones which made the machinery question such a vital issue to contemporaries. The book will describe the range of opinions and many ambivalences in the positions of Tory, working-class and middle-class groups. It will demonstrate just how the machinery question became an issue around which the early discipline of political economy was formulated. It will also show just how central the machinery question was to the Tory and working-class critiques of political economy. It will relate the development of this political economy to the immediate social and political context of the machinery issue in popular scientific and social reform movements, and in policy debates in Parliament over the machine. Finally it will demonstrate the intellectual legacy of the machinery question in nineteenth-century Britain in the work of two contrasting and idiosyncratic, but subsequently highly influential, theorists, John Stuart Mill and Frederick Engels. Their works, the *Principles of Political Economy*, and *The Condition of the Working Class in England*, both first published in the 1840s, represent the summing up and the reformulation of the machinery question in such a way as to create two new and contrasted roads for political economy which were to dominate the rest of the nineteenth century and beyond.

This book will maintain throughout that the machinery question existed as a truly national issue of debate only in the early nineteenth century. A special economic and social context and a particular intellectual basis gave it a very distinctive historical character. The challenge of the first experience of industrialisation and mechanisation, and the sharply focussed controversy over the impact of mechanisation made this an issue that was unprecedented both in its scale and in its social repercussions. A distinct intellectual context set the terms for the manner in which the issue was debated, for discussion of the introduction of the new technology was never very far from discussion of the new political economy. The intellectual context of the machinery question in the early nineteenth century was the development of the new discipline of political economy.

The progress of the machine

The phenomenon of the machine was vividly apparent. It is the purpose of this chapter to chart the spread of the machine in a variety of important industries in early nineteenth-century Britain, as a knowledge of the actual extent of mechanisation is a prerequisite to any critical analysis of the ideas and assumptions of the time. Whether the period between the end of the Napoleonic Wars and the 1840s was one which saw only the inception of an industrialised economic structure, whether it was a period of flux, or whether it was a society already mechanised on a wide scale, has important implications for the way in which contemporary attitudes are interpreted. On the one hand, ideas might have been related to warnings and hopes, to possibilities for manipulation and to the impossibilities of prediction. On the other hand, such ideas could be interpreted as feelings of despair and regret for lost opportunities of turning back, or at least of changing direction. Even if the latter formulation is the more correct, it is still important to ask in turn whether the apparently irrevocable process of industrialisation was marked by a mechanical revolution, or whether it took other forms, and whether it was a rapid or a long-drawn-out process.

For some time it has been fashionable to see the Industrial Revolution as a lengthy process reaching back to the early eighteenth century and continuing into the mid nineteenth century. It has also been fashionable to stress the labour-intensive bias of the Industrial Revolution in Britain. The continued use of traditional methods and hand techniques was caused, it is argued, by the abundance of British labour. The assessment of British industrialisation by strict quantitative estimates over the economy as a whole has yielded widely differing suggestions of the amount of capital tied up in machinery in the late eighteenth and early nineteenth centuries. Phyllis Deane and W. A. Cole calculated that machinery accounted for as little as $2\frac{1}{2}$ per cent of national capital in 1800 and 4 per cent in 1832, and this confirmed the views of a generation of historians. These estimates have, however, been challenged recently by C. H. Feinstein's new figures on capital formation[1] which indicate, not only that capital formation overall was much greater in this period than was previously imagined, but that the amount of capital tied up in machinery was much closer to 5 per cent of domestic fixed capital in 1750 and 17 per cent in 1850. We may not perhaps choose to accept aggregative valuations that give rise to such wide differences on both basic data and on its implications. But, even so, it must be admitted that the shocks of a rapid process of mechanisation were there, albeit confined to particular sectors and regions, and these pointed the way of future developments. It was also evident that the economic and technical transformations of the 1820s and 1830s happened at a much faster pace than any previous change.

The evidence of the 1851 census shows that agriculture and domestic service were still by far the most important occupations, and that most labour was engaged in industries of the old type, that is, the building trades, tailoring, shoemaking, and unskilled labour of all sorts.[2] But behind this still traditional face of the economy, there were many striking advances.

The most obvious mark of the age of machinery was the steam engine. G. N. von Tunzelman's recent book on the diffusion of the steam engine[3] gathers together available contemporary figures on the numbers of engines and the quantity of horsepower in the country in the eighteenth and the early nineteenth centuries. Von Tunzelman emphasises that evidence for the growth and diffusion of the steam engine is scrappy and often inaccurate. We can glean at most an approximate picture of the amount of steam power in early industrial Britain. The imprecision of evidence also vitiates other estimates of

---

[1] C. H. Feinstein, 'Capital Formation in Great Britain', *Cambridge Economic History of Europe*, vol. VII, Cambridge, 1978, p. 88.

[2] Phyllis Deane and W. A. Cole, *British Economic Growth*, 2nd edition, Cambridge, 1969, pp. 142–3.

[3] G. N. von Tunzelman, *Steam Power and British Industrialization to 1860*, Oxford, 1978.

mechanisation, both over the economy as a whole and within specific industries. The estimates gathered by von Tunzelman for the steam engine can only be complemented by the guesses and approximations made by several historians for a wide range of other industries.

Our picture of the progress of steam power by 1800 is an imprecise one. Von Tunzelman guesses that there were probably somewhat fewer than 490 Watt engines erected by 1800, with a total of 12,750 horse-power. J. R. Harris estimated that the number of engines of all types built at some stage in the eighteenth century was between 985 and 1,330, with a total horsepower of 25,000 to 30,000. These figures, however, do not tell us how many of these steam engines had survived and were actually at work in 1800.

Estimates for the nineteenth century are probably even less reliable. Mulhall guessed there were 350,000 horsepower in stationary engines in 1840 and 500,000 in 1850. His guess for the earlier part of the century was certainly too high.

More specific nineteenth-century data exist for specific towns and areas. Farey estimates that there were 112 steam engines in London in 1805 with a total of 1,355 horsepower. By 1825 there were 290 steam engines for waterworks, small manufactures and steamboats with 5,460 horsepower. Manchester had 32 engines with 430 horse-power by 1800, and by 1825 the town claimed 240 engines and 4,760 horsepower, or nearly one fifth the steam horsepower of the county. Baines estimated that Bolton and the vicinity had 83 engines and 1,604 horsepower by 1825, and Ashworth counted 308 steam engines in the whole district of Bolton in 1836–7, but the factory returns for the parish of Bolton itself gave only 39 engines and 1,082 horsepower in July 1835. Leeds had 20 engines with a force of 270 horsepower in 1800, and by 1825 Farey was able to count 120 engines with 2,330 horse-power. R. J. Forbes claimed 60 engines for Birmingham with 1,000 horsepower in 1820, and only fifteen years later the Birmingham Philosophical Society estimated 160 engines and 2,700 horsepower. Glasgow had also made its mark by the early nineteenth century when Cleland counted 45 steam engines with 720 horsepower in 1817, and found a jump to 242 engines with 4,480 horsepower by 1825, but von Tunzelman also cites the figure for the 1831 census – 250 engines with 4,400 horsepower – and finds Cleland's estimate for 1817 to be very unlikely. Nor was this steam power concentrated in selected urban centres, for country areas, particularly mining districts, had their fair share of stationary engines. Even in 1800 the total horsepower in

Cornwall was three times as large as that of London, and six times as large as that of Manchester.[4]

If the rapid diffusion of the steam engine meant that there was justification for regarding it as the great symbol of the mechanical age, the remarkable mechanisation of the cotton industry did the same for the factory and the mill. After the innovation of the steam engine, the series of mechanical improvements which transformed the cotton textile industry certainly ranks as the most rapid and productive technical changes across the early nineteenth-century economy. The cotton industry underwent a rapid and extraordinary expansion – the number of spindles in cotton mills rose from 1.7 million in the 1780s to between 4 and 5 million in 1812 – and by the first decade of the nineteenth century it was the most important British manufacturing industry. Mills reached their peak sizes in the last decades of the eighteenth century and during the Napoleonic Wars, and by 1811 there were over 100,000 operatives in factories. But the growth of the industry was even more rapid in the decades after the Napoleonic Wars. The number of spindles doubled in the fifteen years spanning the 1830s and 1840s. There was even more striking change in the weaving branch: while in 1812 there were 2,400 powerlooms, but 200,000 handloom weavers, by the late 1830s and early 1840s the number of handloom weavers had fallen to about 50,000. By the 1820s, 1830s and 1840s the net output of the industry was over five per cent that of total national output.[5] In a town like Oldham the whole scale of the cotton industry was completely transformed between the 1820s and 1830s. While handloom weaving had been the largest employer until this time, the weaving process became almost entirely mechanised by the 1840s. Oldham mills now employed the majority of the labour force and three-quarters of cotton workers were in mills of over one hundred workers.[6] By 1838 over four-fifths of English cotton mills were steam powered.[7]

In the textile industries as a whole large parts of the country had been affected by the spread of the power loom by the mid 1830s. A survey made of the number of power looms in 1836 indicates their widespread presence in the North of England and Scotland. According to Leonard Horner's survey Glasgow had 13,253 power looms and

---

[4] These two paragraphs draw on von Tunzelman, *Steam Power and British Industrialization to 1860*, pp. 27–36.

[5] Deane and Cole, *British Economic Growth*, pp. 191–2.

[6] John Foster, *Class Struggle and the Industrial Revolution*, London, 1974.

[7] Peter Mathias, *The First Industrial Nation*, London, 1969, p. 133.

even Rothesay in Bute had 94. In areas of Lancashire superintended by J. Heathcote, James Bates, and Charles Trimmer there were 295 mills containing 62,663 power looms. In Cheshire there were 80 mills with 22,915 looms, and in Yorkshire there were 96 mills with 7,809 looms in the areas surveyed. Other parts of Britain had also witnessed the spread of the power loom, though to a much smaller degree. Factory inspectors found 2,403 power looms in Derbyshire. In Devon, Essex, Kent, Norfolk and Somerset there were 725 power looms dispersed widely through silk, flax and woollen mills. In Warwickshire, Worcestershire and Gloucestershire there were only 36 power looms in districts canvassed by the inspectors.[8] In textiles, at least, large parts of the country had countenanced the machine.

There was also very significant change taking place in processes of other branches of industry, though less drastic than the change from hand domestic work to the mechanised factory in cotton. The iron industry rose to prominence and became highly mechanised at the end of the eighteenth century and in the early years of the nineteenth century. The major process innovation in iron-puddling had largely superseded all other processes by the end of the Napoleonic Wars. The mechanised iron works of the early nineteenth century contrasted sharply with the old charcoal furnace. It employed steam engines as a source of power for increasing the blast of air needed in coke furnaces, and to drive the increasingly complex blowing mechanisms that began to replace simple bellows in the 1760s and 1770s. In addition, the industry boasted pressure regulators, mechanised feeding operations, vertical and inclined hoists powered by steam, and mechanical aids for transporting coal and ore from the mines. The refining process had undergone an even more striking change by the early nineteenth century. By this time a forge included two or three small 'refining' furnaces, a dozen puddling furnaces, and several large shingling and stamping hammers driven by a steam engine. Steam also powered the rolling and slitting mills preparing iron for the market.[9] The industry grew very slowly during the later part of the Napoleonic Wars and experienced a heavy slump in the immediate postwar period, but by the 1820s it was making new gains, and there were further substantial

[8] A Return of the Number of Powerlooms used in Factories in the
     Manufacture of Woollen, Cotton, Silk, and Linen in each County of
     the U.K. respectively, so far as they can be collected from the Returns
     of the Factory Commissioners, 15 February 1836, *Parliamentary Papers*,
     1836 (24), XLV, 145.
[9] C. K. Hyde, *Technological Change and the British Iron Industry
     1700 to 1870*, Princeton, 1977, pp. 119–20.

advances after the introduction of the Neilson hot blast process between 1829 and 1833. This bolstered the Scottish iron industry and led to a sharp increase in investment and output.[10] Other innovations of the early nineteenth century were mainly of scale. The enlargement of blast furnaces to raise the productivity of labour led to an increase in the number of puddling furnaces. The production of large pieces of metal led to innovations for lifting and transporting, including elevated platforms, rails, overhead chain pulleys and cranes. Much later in the period the innovation and diffusion of Nasmyth's steam hammer and large boring machines gave both great strength and precise control.[11]

There is little way of measuring the changes of technique taking place in the engineering industry. The last years of the eighteenth century and first years of the nineteenth century saw the first emergence of large-scale engineering works. The Soho, Maudslay, and Murray works were renowned manifestations of the industrialisation process. The major changes later took place in the range of hand tools which became characterised by greater speed, accuracy, and conformity.[12] Tools became heavier and more rigid, like Maudslay's all-metal lathe. They became adaptable to a wider range of tasks with the addition of the planing and shaping machines, and more powerful automatic and yet precise with the introduction of Nasmyth's steam hammer.[13] Certainly the industry had grown up rapidly, primarily to service the cotton industry. McCulloch commented on the excellence of the machines and steam engines made in Manchester and Glasgow, 'the preparation and repair of which employs a great number of hands and a large amount of capital'.[14]

The advances of the iron and engineering industries left their legacy in the railroad, one of the greatest symbols of the 'Mechanical Age'. Great fanfare accompanied the opening of the Manchester and Liverpool Railway in 1831, although there were then but 139.7 miles of rail open. It was only in 1838 that the railway extended for more than 600 miles.[15]

10 *Ibid.* p. 153.
11 David Landes, *The Unbound Prometheus*, Cambridge, 1969, p. 92.
12 J. B. Jefferys, *The Story of the Engineers 1800–1945*, London, 1945, p. 13.
13 Landes, *The Unbound Prometheus*, p. 106.
14 J. R. McCulloch, *A Statistical Account of the British Empire*, vol. II, London, 1837, p. 115.
15 B. R. Mitchell, *Abstract of British Historical Statistics*, Cambridge, 1962, p. 225, and B. R. Mitchell, 'Statistical Appendix 1700–1914', *Fontana Economic History of Europe*, vol. IV, London, 1971, p. 58.

The mechanical advances of these great industries were complemented in turn by technical feats in lesser-known industries and on the
land. The remarkable advances of the papermaking and printing
trades astounded all who noticed them. Manchester was the principal
seat of the papermaking industry where, 'By the agency of a great deal
of complicated machinery so admirably contrived as to produce the
intended effect with unerring precision, and in the very best manner,
a process, which in the old system of papermaking occupied about
three weeks, is performed in as many minutes.'[16] In the printing trade
the editor of *The Times* informed readers on 28 November 1814 that
they were reading for the first time a newspaper printed by steam-
impelled machinery. After this, innovations proceeded apace to increase the production of copies per hour.[17]

Even the land saw the face of the machine. Though hand technologies continued to be far more significant than mechanical ones, landed
society also tasted the bitter-sweet fruits of mechanisation in the form
of the threshing machine. In 1800 these were confined to the North
of England. The southern counties were slower to adopt them, but
by 1819 there is evidence of their widespread use in East Kent, Wiltshire, Huntingdonshire and Berkshire.[18] It was of course this machine
which was one of Swing's major victims in some of the most extensive
machine-breaking episodes of the period.

If, however, mechanisation was rapid and widely diffused in the
cases of the steam engine, cotton spinning and weaving, iron making,
printing, and threshing, there were also many processes which remained
traditional both within these industries and in other sectors. For
example, though techniques in the cotton industry appeared to be
transformed suddenly and radically, parts of the industry's visage
seemed unchanging. Although during the last years of the eighteenth
century and the first years of the nineteenth century there had been
such important innovations as fireproof buildings, gas lighting, and
steam and warm-air heating, these had only been adopted by the same
few giant firms, which were uncharacteristic of the industry as a whole.[19]
The average primary process firm in Manchester as late as 1841
employed only 260 hands, and one quarter of all firms employed less

[16] McCulloch, *A Statistical Account of the British Empire*, p. 128.
[17] Andrew Ure, *A Dictionary of Arts, Manufactures and Mines*, ed.
Robert Hunt, 5th edition, London, 1863, vol. III, pp. 533, 538.
[18] E. J. Hobsbawm and George Rudé, *Captain Swing* (1968), New York,
1975, pp. 359–63.
[19] Jennifer Tann, *The Development of the Factory*, London, 1970, p. 2.

than 100.[20] Even by 1851, in Great Britain as a whole, although three-fifths of the 500,000 member workforce were in mills, more than two-thirds of those mills employed less than 50. The average mill in the country employed less than 200, and there were tens of thousands of handloom weavers at work in rural cottages.[21]

The continuation of older methods of production was even more marked in other branches of the textile trades, though by the mid nineteenth century 2,750,000 (or 10 per cent of the total population) and 21.4 per cent of the occupied population were in textiles and clothing.[22] This indicates little about the impact of industrialisation on the trades, for most of them remained traditional. The most advanced of other textile groups before 1850 was the worsted industry. Whereas in both cotton and worsted manufacture 71 per cent of spinning engines were mechanised by 1839, only 36 per cent of those in the woollen industry were. While there were 109,626 power looms in the cotton industry in 1835, there were only 5,127 in woollen and worsted factories.[23] Even as late as 1850 more than one third of the power available to woollen manufacture came from water.[24] The silk and linen industries remained largely unmechanised throughout the period. The silk industry expanded in the second decade of the nineteenth century due to technical improvements in the throwing section, but did not lend itself easily to mechanisation. At its peak in the 1860s only one third of its employees worked in factories, and there were seven people employed for every unit of steam horsepower available.[25]

This continuing juxtaposition of large and small firms, of mechanised and hand processes, was repeated in other industries. In the engineering industry, the division and subdivision of processes and the great changes in tools did not alter the personal nature of the work. The millwright still stood at the pinnacle of the hierarchy of industrial labour by virtue of his flexibility and his role as a jack-of-all-trades.[26]

Fairbairn commented that despite all the advances of the division of

20 V. A. C. Gattrell, 'Labour, Power and the Size of Firms in Lancashire Cotton', *Economic History Review*, xxx, February 1977, p. 125.
21 Landes, *The Unbound Prometheus*, p. 120 and V. A. C. Gattrell, 'Labour, Power, and Size of Firms', p. 125.
22 Deane and Cole, *British Economic Growth*, p. 212.
23 *Ibid*. pp. 191, 200.
24 There was 12,600 horsepower of steam and 6,800 horsepower of water. See Landes, *The Unbound Prometheus*, p. 104.
25 Deane and Cole, *British Economic Growth*, pp. 206, 208, 210.
26 Jennifer Tann, 'The Textile Millwright in the Early Industrial Revolution', *Textile History*, v, October 1974.

labour it was still impossible to tell where a millwright ended and an engineer and machinist began : 'it is a curious fact that the industrial mechanical progress of the last half century has not from that period marked any reliable principle of organisation by which one mechanical operation is distinguished from another. They seem to run into one another without any definite outline of distinction.'[27]

The metal trades were much less mechanised than the engineering industry by the early nineteenth century, and change was more gradual. The nail trade was still largely a hand process, though some not wholly effective nail-making machinery had been introduced by the 1830s.[28] The Sheffield metal trades continued as hand trades into the 1860s.[29] Porter reports that most small wares were still made by individual workmen undertaking orders from merchants and agents, though there had been some change in the organisation of production by the 1830s and 1840s. The need for cheap sources of power had led to the concentration of workmen in large premises, yet these still continued to work as individuals.

> A building containing a great number of rooms of various sizes
> is furnished with a steam engine, working shafts from which
> are placed in each apartment or workshop, which is likewise
> furnished with a lathe, benches and such other conveniences
> as are suited to the various branches of manufacture for which
> the rooms are likely to be needed. When a workman has
> received an order for the supply of such a quantity of goods as
> will occupy him a week, or a month, or any other given time
> for their completion, he hires one or more of these rooms, of
> sizes and with conveniences suited to his particular wants,
> stipulating for the use of a certain amount of steam power.
> He thus realizes all the advantages that would accompany the
> possession of a steam engine; and as the buildings there fitted
> up are numerous, competition on the part of their owners has
> brought down the charge for the accommodation they offer
> to the lowest rates that will ensure to them the ordinary rate of
> profit on the capital employed.[30]

[27] William Fairbairn, *Treatise on Mills and Millwork*, 2 vols., London, 1861, p. 219.
[28] McCulloch, *A Statistical Account of the British Empire*, p. 111.
[29] G. R. Porter, *The Progress of the Nation*, London, 1851, p. 271.
[30] *Ibid.*

Hand techniques continued to dominate many other industries for most of the nineteenth century. Leather manufacture, shoemaking, glove- and hatmaking, and rein making were among the many industries which in mid-Victorian times still depended on skill and labour. The boot and shoe trade was changed not by mechanisation, but by the sub-division of labour. People were measured for boots made by hand. The few 'factories' which existed in Staffordshire and Northamptonshire were really shops, where the leather was cut up by hand and given out to bootmakers working in their own houses.[31] In pinmaking, although Wright's pinworking machine was introduced in 1824, there were so many technical difficulties that forty years later the 'nobbing' or head-ing of the pin was still often done by hand.[32] Mining, quarrying, market gardening and the food industries, building and construction, glass, pottery, woodworking, and aspects of metallurgy were expanded and transformed through the use of more labour and more skill, and not through mechanisation.[33]

In sum, mechanisation in early nineteenth-century Britain was a complex and uneven process; large parts of the country and many sectors of the economy were changing very slowly, and even in the most rapidly transforming areas there were many surviving legacies. The amount of craft and small-scale industry was high and expanding rapidly. Yet in many ways this was merely another aspect of industrial-isation. As David Landes has emphasised, the whole tendency of industrialisation and urbanisation was to specialise labour even fur-ther and to break down the versatility of the household. This in itself led to the expansion of a whole range of occupations and a general rise in consumption, and the greater portion of consumption devoted to manufacturing and services had the impact of stimulating tradition-ally organised trades as well as newly mechanised ones. Furthermore, certain kinds of technological advance created craft and domestic industry where these had not existed before, or at least extended them beyond their traditional boundaries. A type of symbiotic relationship developed between the mechanised and hand sectors in many branches of industry. The impact of the railway, for instance, was quite unex-pected. For, where the advances of the railway had generated pre-

---

[31] *Ibid.* p. 377.
[32] Raphael Samuel, 'The Workshop of the World', *History Workshop*, No. 3, 1977, p. 51.
[33] Samuel, 'The Workshop of the World', gives a survey of the skills and labour required in a number of these industries.

dictions that the use of 1,000,000 horses would be superseded allowing for the subsistence of 8,000,000 human beings, the railway instead had the effect of increasing the demand on the horse.[34] However, as Landes also says, factory industry was the trend. From 1834 to 1850 the number of cotton-mill operatives rose from 220,825 to 330,924 despite gains in productivity.[35] Factory employment rose rapidly in the paper, leather and metal industries, and the main industries in metals and engineering were gaining in size, precision and regularity. The steam engine had come to stay, and the public recognised this. Phenomena such as the public inquiry in 1819 and 1820 into the impact of steam engines and furnaces on public health, and the government promotion of investigation into designs for reducing the amount of smoke created by furnaces, indicated a recognition of the machine,[36] and simply an attempt to deal with some of its more obviously harmful effects. The machine and the factory marked out the future of the age. As Landes has put it :

> The census returns and other numbers to be found between the covers of the dusty parliamentary papers are the economic historians' butterfly under glass or frog in formaldehyde – without the virtue of wholeness to compensate for their lifelessness. As described by occupational data, the British economy of 1851 may not seem very different from that of 1800. But these numbers merely describe the surface of the society – and even then in terms that define away change by using categories of unchanging nomenclature. Beneath this surface, the vital organs were transformed; and though they weighed but a fraction of the total – whether measured by people or wealth – it was they that determined the metabolism of the entire system.[37]

In the fragile and uncertain society of the 1820s and 1830s the machine had thus implanted itself on the landscape as well as on the imagination. The question to raise was, therefore, not whether it would

---

[34] F. M. L. Thompson, 'Nineteenth Century Horse Sense', *Economic History Review*, XXIX, 1976, pp. 64–6.

[35] Landes, *The Unbound Prometheus*, p. 120.

[36] Report from the Select Committee Appointed to Inquire How Far it May Be Practicable to Compel Persons Using Steam Engines and Furnaces to Erect Them in a Manner less Prejudicial to Public Comfort, *Parliamentary Papers*, 1819 (574), VII, 271; 1820 (244), II, 235.

[37] Landes, *The Unbound Prometheus*, p. 122.

come or go, but what type of impact it would have. For some it still seemed possible to stop the 'unnatural' progress of the machine, but this was only in order to start afresh – to direct from a new beginning the speed and form of its advance. Rather than considering simply the existence of the machine, the debate on the machinery question in the early nineteenth century involved assessing the impact it would have on economy and society, and the possibility of modifying and re-directing this impact.

3

The advent of political economy

As industrialisation began several decades before 1800, so the Machinery Question had antecedents in eighteenth-century economic debate. I will now turn to these antecedents, and will then go on to examine the parallel emergence of the machinery question and the discipline of political economy in the early nineteenth century. This chapter will suggest that it was not just the economic context of rapid mechanisation, but also the intellectual context of the early years of political economy, which helped to bring the machinery question to the fore. Conversely, I shall argue that it was the problem presented to writers on economic affairs of explaining and justifying the rapid technological transformation which was formative in the development of political economy as a discipline in the early nineteenth century.

Even in the early stages of industrialisation in the eighteenth century, observers recognised the social implications of the machine. The early literary and philosophical societies in the late eighteenth century extolled the 'improvement' made manifest in the machine. They began to explore the connections between scientific discovery and the remarkable advances in technology they were beginning to witness. There was also a pamphlet literature on machinery riots. Fairly typical pamphlets were Thomas Barnes's *Thoughts on the Use of Machines in the Cotton Manufacture Addressed to the Working People in that Manufacture by a Friend of the Poor*, Manchester, 1780,[1] and the anonymous *Letters*

[1] Thomas Barnes was a Unitarian preacher and lecturer at the Warrington Academy where some of the first Lancashire cotton manufacturers were educated. He was also one of the founders of the Manchester Literary and Philosophical Society.

on the Utility of Employing Machines to Shorten Labour, 1780.[2]

At a more theoretical level, Adam Smith and Lord Lauderdale discussed central issues in the development of technology and its relationship to the dynamic transformation of the economy. Smith's theory of the division of labour was basic to his analysis of rising labour productivity, and formed the cornerstone of his theory of economic growth. Lauderdale was more interested in capital formation, and came by this route to examine the economic impact of the machine.

Smith connected the division of labour with several factors contributing to greater productivity of labour. These factors were greater dexterity, economy of time, and the introduction of machinery. Perhaps the most far-reaching step Smith took in establishing these connections was to show that the division of labour was self-reinforcing. It gave rise to vital dynamic links between an expanding market, the regeneration of skills and the emergence of a class of machine makers.[3] The definition of such connections between the market and the differentiation of technique brought with it a change in the meaning of the word skill. Skill, once identified with an 'art' or craft, became in Smith's hands a 'peculiar dexterity' which resulted from the *breakdown* of a craft.[4] The division of labour now became the material basis for a separation between mental and manual labour. The leisure it allowed the members of some classes gave them the time and cultural scope necessary to scientific discovery. This division between the labourer and the natural philosopher justified further social hierarchies, and Smith was, therefore, able to account for the separation between the machine maker and the machine minder.[5]

Smith established the equally important dynamic interaction of the accumulation of capital and technical progress: 'As the division of labour advances, therefore, in order to give constant employment to an equal number of workmen, an equal stock of provisions, and a greater stock of materials and tools than what would have been necessary in a ruder state of things, must be accumulated beforehand.'[6] The connection Smith established between capital accumulation and technical change allowed him to ignore labour displacement: 'But the

---

[2] This pamphlet is noted by Lord Lauderdale in his *An Inquiry into the Nature and Origin of Public Wealth*, Edinburgh, 1804, p. 298.

[3] Adam Smith, *An Inquiry into the Nature and Causes of the Wealth of Nations*, (1776), Oxford, 1976, vol. 1, chaps, 2, 3, 10.

[4] *Ibid.* pp. 17–18, 139–40.

[5] *Ibid.* pp. 20–1.

[6] *Ibid.* p. 277.

number of workmen in every branch of business generally increases with the division of labour in that branch; or rather it is the increase of their number which enables them to class and subdivide themselves in this manner.'[7] Machinery did not displace labour. Rather, it differentiated this labour by dismembering the old craft.

Lauderdale presented the process of technical change somewhat differently. Where Smith envisaged the expansion of employment in the process of capital formation and the division of labour, Lauderdale argued that the introduction of machinery was purely a labour-saving device. He referred to the stocking knitters and the new machine looms : 'The profit of stock employed in machinery is paid out of a fund that would otherwise be destined to pay the wages of the labour it supplants.'[8] Furthermore, Lauderdale related the impact of labour-saving machinery to the social conflict of his own time : 'It derives ample testimony of its truth from the conduct of the unlettered manufacturers themselves, as is sufficiently evinced by the riots that have taken place on the introduction of various pieces of machinery, and particularly at the time when the ingenious machines for carding and spinning were first set a-going.'[9] Smith did not refer to such social conflict, but he did show concern for the mental and cultural degeneration produced among the lower classes by the division of labour.

Moreover, both Smith and Lauderdale were worried about the connections between this degeneration and the inventive capacity of a nation. Both argued that the division of labour could have a stultifying effect on ingenuity. Smith identified barbarous societies with varied occupation : 'Invention is kept alive, and the mind is not suffered to fall into that drowsy stupidity, which, in civilized society, seems to benumb the understanding of almost all the inferior ranks of people.'[10] Lauderdale, too, believed that there was a logical gap between the division of labour and the type of conceptualisation necessary to the invention of machinery. The principle behind the invention of machinery was to combine and embrace within one machine the execution of the greatest possible variety of operations in the formation of a commodity. But the division of labour was destructive of the chain of reasoning necessary to the perfection of machinery.[11]

Smith and Lauderdale thus demonstrated an awareness of the social

[7] *Ibid.* p. 277.
[8] Lauderdale, *An Inquiry*, p. 167.
[9] *Ibid.* p. 171.
[10] Adam Smith, *Wealth of Nations*, vol. II. p. 783.
[11] Lauderdale, *An Inquiry*, pp. 294–5.

and economic dimensions of the new techniques of production. But, although we find in their writing both an impressive depth of analysis of technology and an ambivalence towards this technology which provided many nineteenth-century economic writers with their starting-points, the context was not one to make the machinery question a vital issue. In the first place the economic context was different. In part, the significance of the machinery question was defined by the economic and technological transformation which is described in the last chapter. The early nineteenth-century British economy was one where mechanisation was strikingly evident, but where large sectors of the economy still remained untouched by it. This technological setting was complemented by an economy recovering from war. Crisis, depression, and unemployment appeared to contemporaries to owe their causes as much to the new technology as to post-war economic adjustment. A second and equally important context for the emergence of the machinery question as a national issue was an intellectual one. Machinery became an issue at virtually the same time as the formation of a new intellectual discipline : political economy. It was no mere coincidence that political economy established itself as an academic discipline and popular doctrine at the same time as the industrial revolution in cotton and iron.

For it was only from the 1790s that political economy broke free from the place allotted to it by previous writers, including Adam Smith, as a branch of legislation or statesmanship. The theories and opinions to be found in earlier economic writings were not systematically set out, as were those in nineteenth-century political economy, as an accepted set of concepts and problems whose central purpose was to analyse the present position and future prospects of the economy. Significantly, Adam Smith's first intellectual biographer and re-interpreter, Dugald Stewart, was one of those who led the way in the 1790s in assigning the theory of government and political economy to two separate branches of political science. Political economy he defined as 'that which is most immediately connected with human happiness and improvement' : it could be 'studied without reference to constitutional forms – not only because the tendency of laws may be investigated abstractly from all considerations of their origin but because there are many principles of political economy which may be sanctioned by governments very different in their constitutions.'[12]

[12] Dugald Stewart, *Lectures on Political Economy*, from the *Collected Works of Dugald Stewart* ed. by Sir William Hamilton, Edinburgh, 1855, vol. VIII, p. 24.

This appointment of political economy to a separate branch of inquiry was followed some years later by J. R. McCulloch's attempt to explain its emergence on materialist grounds. The science could only arise, he argued, in a commercial capitalist society. Slave societies had no knowledge of the categories political economy dealt in, for they had no experience of relations between landlords and tenants, and between masters and servants. They could therefore take 'no interest in questions rising out of the rise and fall of rents and wages'. A further reason for the science emerging as late as it did was social climate 'prejudicial' in ancient and medieval economies to the accumulation of wealth and to commerce and manufacture.[13] The writer who reviewed McCulloch's tract for the *Edinburgh Review* tied the discipline more explicitly to recent improvements in industry. He claimed that political economy was the science which could teach us how to make industry more productive, and was therefore 'the science to which we are indebted for all the higher refinements'. It was in countries 'where circumstances were favourable or where political economy was well understood' that an intelligent artisan could 'enjoy a multiplicity of comforts and luxuries' which were 'utterly unattainable in a rude state of society'.[14] Halévy, a subsequent observer, also made some connection between economic change and the emergence of political economy. Singling out the period between Smith and Ricardo as one in which not one single complete treatise on political economy had appeared in England, Halévy argued that, without the assistance or knowledge of the legislature, or even of the intellectuals, a new industrial world had arisen. This transformation brought with it, he argued, a whole series of problems leading on the one hand to the great series of parliamentary inquiries, and on the other, in the theoretical sphere, to the theory of rent.[15]

Developing the implications of this remark, I would argue that Dugald Stewart's definition of the economy as an object of inquiry separate from the state or polity was in fact the first stage in the formation of the discipline of political economy as a response to the need to understand the economy. He not only defined political economy

[13] J. R. McCulloch, *A Discourse on the Rise, Progress, Peculiar Objects and Importance of Political Economy*, Edinburgh, 1824, pp. 8–9.
[14] 'Review of A Discourse on the Rise, Peculiar Objects and Importance of Political Economy, by J. R. McCulloch, 2nd edition', *Edinburgh Review*, November 1825, pp. 2–3.
[15] Elie Halévy, *The Growth of Philosophical Radicalism* (1928), 2nd edition, London, 1934, pp. 265, 277.

as a separate discipline; he regarded it as the most important discipline to the happiness of mankind. He argued that 'mistaken notions concerning political liberty so widely disseminated in Europe by the writings of Locke have contributed greatly to divert the studies of speculative politicians from the proper objects of their attention'.[16] Happiness was the only object of legislation which was of intrinsic value, and 'of the two branches of political science – the theory of government and political economy – the latter is that which is most immediately connected with human happiness and improvement'.[17] Such statements account in intellectual terms for the beginnings of a separate existence for political economy and of claims for its significance in providing fundamental directions and principles for government policy. But behind such reasons were to be found other deeper motivations, as hinted at by McCulloch, to understand the economy and a specific desire, perceived by Halévy, to understand an economy cast in the turbulence of rapid technological change.

Few historians, however, have given much attention to possible connections between the parallel development of industry and political economy, and there are clear historiographical reasons for this. Orthodox historians, fearing that they lacked expertise, have only paid lip-service to the significance of political economy, and have deferred to the judgements of economists who specialise in the history of economic thought. But these have not filled the gap, for they have their own concerns and orientations. Since the foundations of their discipline economists have been interested in the antecedents of their own theories. But the uncovering of antecedents is rarely a problem for the historian. However much we may know of the 'precursors' of a wide range of concepts and theories currently in vogue among economists, we actually know very little about the more fundamental problem of the origin of the discipline. This is because the question has just not been asked. It is, nevertheless, the most important historical question in any study of political economy or economic policy which requires an answer. In contrast with the economist, the historian wants to know what happened and why, and to explain change and development. The historian's history of economic thought should seek to explain what economists were doing in the past and the reasons for their work. Furthermore, it should seek to inscribe in the history of ideas the the personal and social contexts of the theorists.

16 Dugald Stewart, *Lectures on Political Economy*, p. 23.
17 *Ibid.*

The historian thus aspiring to understand the nature of the connection between industrialisation and political economy must obviously inquire into the intellectual developments which gave rise to a new discipline. But he must also understand the political dimensions of economic debate at the time, and the social nexus and institutional organisation of political economy during the years of its formation.

Dugald Stewart's long and influential tenure in the Chair of Moral Philosophy in the University of Edinburgh spanned the period of transition between the end of the Scottish Enlightenment and the emergence of the philosophic radicalism and whig liberalism which was to set the intellectual tone for the first part of the nineteenth century. The radical intellectual attitudes and innovative social theories which had characterised the Enlightenment in the eighteenth century were displaced in the aftermath of the French Revolution and the onset of the political reaction of the 1790s. The French Revolution which marked the culmination of the European Enlightenment led in Britain to political retrenchment, and to the exile, both voluntary and enforced, of intellectuals from cultural centres in Scotland and the North of England.

Political economy was to emerge in a new intellectual and political setting. Tied neither to a wider social theory nor to a political vision, it was to become a discipline apart – a set of principles to guide economic policy. This is not to say that the new discipline was apolitical. Rather, it developed against the background of the Whig and Tory struggles over how to solve the immediate problems of economic crisis and depression and the longer-term problems of how to adjust to rapid industrialisation.

At a general level, it is probably correct to depict the struggle in economics in the period between Adam Smith and the ascendancy of Ricardo as representative of that between land and industry. Ricardo, in fact, formulated his ideas in confrontation with the legacy of physiocracy and agricultural expansion. His own perspectives transmitted an older ideology which had selected passages out of Smithian economics and interpreted them as justifying the new industrial capitalism. And the ideologues of landed society continued to uphold the under-consumptionist theories of a gentry economics averse to industrialisation.[18]

---

[18] It is doubtful whether Smith himself would have supported such a purpose. For information on the reception and reinterpretation of Adam Smith's economics in early nineteenth-century political economy

This bold demarcation between the economics of land and industry must, however, be subject to many qualifications. Among those ranked on either side of this theoretical divide there were great differences in assumptions and allegiances. Furthermore, broad political divisions between types of economic theory in ascendancy were complemented by more specific divisions over policy, and these policy stands can be identified over the series of crises which punctuated the period between 1815 and the 1840s. For such crises commentators could offer a wide choice of diagnoses, between blaming trade restrictions or over-production, taxation or the paper currency, over-population or machinery. But each economic diagnosis was also a political choice, as differing schools of economic thought in these years also reflected differences in politics. G. S. L. Tucker has aptly formulated the connections of nineteenth-century theories of profit with practical questions of economic policy. The intellectual interest in explaining a secular decline in the earnings of capital was a feeble incentive beside the desire to account for the facts of contemporary experience and to give some guidance to economic policy in wartime and post-war Britain. The Corn Laws, the national debt, taxation, foreign investment and colonial development, the introduction of machinery, financial crises and trade fluctuations, were all problems requiring some analysis of the direction of profits.[19]

Thus theoretical controversy often involved political controversy, particularly between the Whigs and the Tories. The period 1815 to 1832 was dominated by the Tory ministries, all of which took on the policy prescriptions of the classical economists. As A. J. B. Hilton has put it, these governments 'broke with physiocracy, autarchy and agricultural expansion'.[20] They dismissed the benefit of public works and denied the permanent effects of a post-war glut. The alliance of Toryism and classical economics was, however, countered by a definite political economy of opposition. The Whigs were left to maintain a radical under-consumptionist theory. Policy prescriptions involved public

---

see R. D. C. Black, 'Smith's Contribution in Historical Perspective', and Donald Winch's 'Comment' in Thomas Wilson and A. S. Skinner, eds., *The Market and the State*, Oxford, 1976.

19 G. S. L. Tucker, *Progress and Profits in British Economic Thought 1650–1850*, Cambridge, 1960, p. 158.

20 A. J. B. Hilton, 'The Economic Policies of the Tory Governments 1815–1830', D.Phil. Thesis, Oxford, 1973, Abstract. Also see Bernard Semmel, ed., *Occasional Papers of T. R. Malthus*, New York, 1963, pp. 20–9.

spending and tax reduction. This was an activist policy founded on the basic fear of Malthus that demand might not keep up with production.

The machinery question arose on the basis of these two overlapping problems of economic policy – the long-term problem of adjustment to an industrialising economy and the short-term problem of explaining and solving a long series of economic crises. Machinery was considered to be a major component of both these issues of economic policy. The solutions put forward for these problems, though politically motivated, required the emergence of recognisable sets of economic principles. For a set of principles which could account for long-term and short-term economic phenomena would provide the basis for more effective and politically convincing economic policy. The intellectual interest which writers on economic issues may have had in the machinery question was thus complemented by a political interest in explanation and policy. Together, these brought political economy to the fore as the rising academic discipline in vogue in the early nineteenth century, both intellectually and politically.

The popularity of the discipline was not just founded on intellectual and political events. It also had a social base. In the last part of the eighteenth century and very early nineteenth century the economic writings of Adam Smith were taken up in radical intellectual circles and adopted by those interested in political reform. It was the progressive social philosophy that attracted the luminaries of the eighteenth-century literary and philosophical societies and the Jacobin activists. The economy stimulated the imaginations of those such as Thomas Barnes and Thomas Henry who lectured the Manchester Literary and Philosophical Society in the 1780s on the connections between the sciences, the arts, and manufacture.[21] The formulation of economic principles also attracted the interest of the Jacobin sons of the first generation of Lancashire cotton masters. Thomas Walker, Thomas Cooper, James Watt Jr. and Samuel Jackson introduced other young industrialists in Manchester to principles of liberal economic and political reform through reading Adam Smith, Priestley and Bentham in such societies as the Junior Literary and Philosophical Society, the Sciolous Society, and the Weekly Literary and Scientific Society.[22]

This young radical liberal following gave to the origins of political

[21] *Memoirs of the Manchester Literary and Philosophical Society*, vol. I, pp. 77–80 and vol. IX, p. 164.
[22] Donald Read, *Peterloo, the Massacre and its Background*, London, 1958, p. 60.

economy a social base that was liberal, middle-class, provincial and industrial. Though this base changed after the first years of the century to encompass the followers of a much more establishment form of liberalism and even of progressive Toryism, political economy never lost its cultural stamp throughout the first half of the nineteenth century. The first social following of this new discipline was one involved even to the grassroots levels in those economic and technological transformations which made the machinery question an issue of such social relevance.

Another slightly later social basis for political economy was provided by the metropolitan radicalism of the Benthamite cause, but this was never to be as extensive as the philosophic radicals hoped. A narrow sectarian group, they aspired to attach Ricardian political economy to their own political doctrines. They attempted this unsuccessfully in the Political Economy Club, and nurtured liberal debating teams for the London Debating Society and the London Co-operative Society. In addition, James Mill took on the role of shaping Ricardo into a parliamentary spokesman for the Benthamite cause.

Ricardo's rise to popularity was helped by an institutional framework. Just as significantly, however, his great prestige changed the character of these institutions. Political economy had many voices during this period, and its institutions – the clubs, journals, and newspapers which helped give definition to the discipline – were not simply avenues for dogma. The Political Economy Club was the most prestigious of these forums. Mallet's diary of the Club's proceedings during this period bears eloquent testimony to the great diversity of interests within the Club.[23] Founded by Tooke and the originators of the Merchant's Petition of 1820, the Club had a practical and not a sectarian character.

A plethora of literary reviews also encompassed political economy in their subject matter. Political economy was popular in both the *Edinburgh Review* and the *Westminster Review*. Both, however, practised exclusion of heretical views on political economy at some time.[24] Wide ranging criticism of Ricardian views was kept up by the *Quarterly Review*, the *British Critic*, *Blackwood's Edinburgh Magazine*

---

23 See *Political Economy Club, Centenary Volume*, VI, 1921, pp. XI–XIII, 2–3, 212.

24 For more discussion of these Journals see John Clive, *The Scotch Reviewers: The Edinburgh Review, 1802–1815*, London, 1957; and G. L. Nesbitt, *Benthamite Reviewing: The First Twelve Years of the Westminster Review 1824–1836*, New York, 1934.

and the *Monthly Review*. Theoretical debate was even conducted in the newspapers – particularly in the *Morning Chronicle*, and Torrens's papers, the *Globe and Traveller* and *The Champion*.[25]

Beyond this institutional framework, the popular and political impact of Ricardo's work was to extend the identity between political economy and capitalism. But such an identity was by no means easily accepted. Alternative principles and methods were constantly put forward even during the time when Ricardo's views had their greatest influence. Spokesmen for the landed and the working classes both subjected Ricardian political economy to intensive criticism, and attempted to formulate a substitute set of doctrines more in tune with their own political perspectives. The result was a great deal of controversy, both methodological and theoretical, in the emerging discipline. J. R. McCulloch, Ricardo's vociferous populariser, was very worried about 'recent great differences among its most eminent professors'.[26] And even Malthus, Ricardo's eminent critic and leading advocate of the under-consumptionist theories which appealed to landed society, felt, 'An agreement among the principal writers in Political Economy is very desirable with a view to the authority of the science in its practical application.'[27] During these very early stages of the shaping of political economy as a discipline, controversy among its advocates was rife and ranged from political principles and policy to the smallest details of economic theory. The occasion for such extensive controversy was not just capitalism, but industrial capitalism. Ricardo's own intervention was impelled by the vital issues of the contemporary economy, but his unconventional concepts and assumptions did not dissipate debate: they intensified it. It was, however, to be Ricardo's contribution which would be decisive, for all other economists of the day would answer to his work.

[25] B. J. Gordon, 'Criticism of the Ricardian Views on Value and Distribution in the British Periodicals, 1820 to 1850', *History of Political Economy*, I, Fall 1969; and his 'Says Law, Effective Demand, and the British Periodicals, 1820 to 1850', *Economica*, XXXII, November 1965. Also see Frank W. Fetter, 'Robert Torrens: Colonel of Marines and Political Economist', *Economica*, XXIX, May 1962. On the *Champion* see Ricardo, *Works and Correspondence of David Ricardo*, ed. Piero Sraffa, vol. IX, Cambridge, 1951, p. 114n.

[26] McCulloch, *A Discourse on the Rise . . . of Political Economy*, p. 8.

[27] T. R. Malthus, *Principles of Political Economy*, in *Works and Correspondence of David Ricardo*, ed. Piero Sraffa, vol. II, Cambridge, 1951, p. 5.

Ricardo's chapter

Ricardo created a new conception of political economy. Against a background of institutional and theoretical diversity in the discipline he moulded an original and unified body of theory. To contemporaries this appeared as a consolidated set of principles so systematic in nature as to be called a science. But it also appeared as a corpus of doctrine so strictly applied and so closely connected to politics and personalities that it became a creed termed Ricardianism.

Ricardo's originality lay partly in his methodology, for his systematic approach to political economy involved the explicit use of models as a basis for explanation. But it also lay in the combination of problems, judgements and conclusions he so effectively combined to provide the authority needed by contemporaries seeking a policy in a very confused economic setting. Ricardo's intervention both in politics and theory provided the connection between appraisal and policy required at the time for the strains of an unprecedented and complicated economic transformation.

The received view of classical political economy in this period emphasises its pessimism. Adam Smith's sanguine affirmation of the implications of the division of labour is contrasted with 'Malthusian' fears of overpopulation, 'Ricardian' predictions of the advent of the stationary state, and the classicals' apparent indifference to the impact of technological change. Schumpeter's criticism and explanation of the 'pessimistic' perspective supposedly to be found in the works of Ricardo, Malthus and Mill are exemplary of many.

Those writers lived at the threshold of the most spectacular economic development ever witnessed. Vast possibilities matured into realities under their very eyes. Nevertheless they saw nothing but cramped economies, struggling with ever decreasing success for their daily bread. They were convinced that technological progress and the increase in capital would in the end fail to counteract the fateful law of decreasing returns.[1]

In this chapter I shall seek to refute the standard view of Ricardo's pessimism by a close textual analysis of his writing on technical change, interpreted in the context of his works as a whole. Such an analysis will involve not only the reconstitution of his basic theory, but also the examination of his commentary on contemporary developments. In doing this I follow the essential structure of his *Principles*, where theoretical chapters on political economy were followed first by those on taxation and policy and then by those making a polemical intervention in contemporary debates. I shall give close attention to Ricardo's specific remarks on the impact of technical change, and also on its sources and mechanisms. At the same time, reference to the context provided by Ricardo's work as a whole should make it possible to identify the place of such remarks in his general theory. The task of this chapter will thus be to identify these remarks, to locate their theoretical context, and to assess their significance therein. The result will show just how extreme are interpretations, such as Schumpeter's, which criticise Ricardo for 'pessimism' and for ignoring technological change.

This approach to Ricardo's work as a whole should then allow an understanding and interpretation of the chapter on machinery which Ricardo added to the third edition of his *Principles* in 1821. In this very short but provocative piece Ricardo found some reason to support workers who resisted the introduction of new technology. His chapter created a furore of debate among contemporary political economists, and historians of economic thought have equally always found it puzzling. But if it is examined in the context of Ricardo's work as a whole and in the wider context of the debate on machinery, neither the issues it raises nor its analysis and conclusions would appear to contradict the rest of Ricardo's work as much as some historians have argued.

Formally, my analysis of Ricardian economics will be divided into

---

[1] Schumpeter, *History of Economic Analysis*, p. 571.

separate sections discussing Ricardo's ideas on the distribution of income and technical change, his view of the process of mechanisation, and his opinions and predictions on the condition and future of machinery and labour.

The distribution of income and technical change

The distribution of income was central to Ricardo's theories of economic growth. Since Ricardo assumed that all accumulation was derived from profits, the rate of accumulation was determined by the distribution of income between profits and other relative income shares. Technical change was relevant to the distribution of income in so far as Ricardo believed it would offset the effects of diminishing returns, raise profit shares, and thus increase the rate of accumulation.

Some commentators, such as G. S. L. Tucker and Luigi Pasinetti,[2] have interpreted Ricardo's theory of income distribution to mean that he did not consider technical change to be an important factor in his economic system. Tucker maintains that Ricardo assumed an economy with no capital-saving innovations and no improvements in technical knowledge. In his view Ricardo only admitted the effects of improvements as modifications at the end of his analysis.[3] Pasinetti has gone even further to argue that the law of diminishing returns (that is, the view that, with all other things equal, after a certain point there would be diminishing marginal returns for every increment of investment) was unnecessary. Unnecessary both to the theory of population and to Ricardian rent theory it functions only, he argues, as an analytical tool, making Malthus's principle of population and Ricardo's gloomy view of capitalist development impregnable to criticism.[4]

I will argue in this section that such interpretations are not adequate, since they do not explain what purposes and explanatory uses Ricardo envisaged for his model of income distribution. The case I will present can be outlined as follows: Ricardo formulated a strict model of income distribution – a model of what he called 'natural tendencies'. He then took up the greater part of his *Principles* specifying the conditions under which such 'natural tendencies' came into play and the factors which would limit and prevent such prospects. Ricardo's model was constructed for particular analytical purposes. These purposes were not,

---

2 G. S. L. Tucker, 'The Origin of Ricardo's Theory of Profits', *Economica*, XXI, 1954; L. Pasinetti, 'From Classical to Keynesian Dynamics', in L. Pasinetti, ed., *Growth and Income Distribution*, Cambridge, 1974.
3 Tucker, 'The Origin of Ricardo's Theory of Profits', pp. 96–7.
4 Pasinetti, 'From Classical to Keynesian Dynamics'.

however, the straightforward ones of proving predictive accuracy and explanatory powers.

The Ricardian economic model assumed that land was limited, that there was no technological improvement, and no international trade. In this closed economy model he made rates of capital accumulation and population growth comparable, so that with the expansion of this 'natural economy' real wages would remain the same. The point of Ricardo's exercise in constructing such a model was to allow him to separate the effects respectively of the growth of capital, the rise of population, and the extension of this population to less fertile lands.[5] He wished to analyse just what effect each of these would have in an economy which could expand neither through technological improvement nor international trade.

Under Ricardo's model of the natural economy, the increase of capital and population would have to involve resort to the cultivation of less fertile land. This would lead to a decline in the rate of profit, determined as it was by costs of production on marginal land. Thus economic growth in a closed economy with no opportunities for technological progress would lead to successive reductions in the rate of profit until the point was reached at which there would be no further incentive for investment : in other words, the stationary state. These were, indeed, gloomy prospects. But the question is, how real were Ricardo's fears?

It is interesting to note that throughout his explication of this model, Ricardo wrote of all its components and movements in terms of what was 'natural'. He refers to the 'nature of man' and the 'natural limits to population growth'.[6] There was a 'natural price of labour' and a 'natural price of commodities'.[7] The 'natural operation of the proportion of supply and demand' went with the 'natural advance of society' and the 'natural tendency of profits to fall'.[8] The dynamic of the economy would gravitate to the operations of the 'laws of nature'.[9]

---

[5] David Ricardo, *An Essay on the Influence of a Low Price of Corn on the Profits of Stock*, in *Works and Correspondence of David Ricardo*, ed. Piero Sraffa, vol. IV, Cambridge, 1951, p. 12.

[6] *Ibid.* p. 15.

[7] David Ricardo, *Principles of Political Economy and Taxation*, 3rd edition, 1821, in *Works and Correspondence of David Ricardo*, ed. Piero Sraffa, vol. I, Cambridge, 1951, pp. 93–4. All subsequent reference to Ricardo's *Principles* refer to the 3rd edition except where specifically stated otherwise.

[8] *Ibid.* pp. 101, 120.

[9] *Ibid.* p. 126.

I will argue that Ricardo, in fact, drew a sharp distinction between this 'natural world' and the socio-economic world he was attempting to analyse. This model of 'natural tendencies' had a negative purpose. It was a counterfactual, set up precisely in order to emphasise the significance of the factors from which Ricardo abstracted – free trade and technological improvement. The model thus drew attention to these two vital means of escaping the restraints imposed on the rate of capital accumulation by limited land and excessive population growth. Trade and technical progress both produced social and economic changes which considerably modified the 'natural state' of limited land.

Ricardo made his views on the role of both factors quite clear even in his first outline of the strict model in his *Essay on Profits* of 1815. For he concluded this *Essay* with the comment : 'I shall greatly regret that considerations for any particular class, are allowed to check the progress of the wealth and population of the country.' If the interests of the landlord against the free importation of corn were to be allowed, 'let us by the same act arrest improvement, and prohibit importation'.[10] The model of 'natural tendencies' made the effects of carrying out such acts crystal clear.

Ricardo's purpose in using such a model to demonstrate certain practical and empirical points must, however, be distinguished from his longer run vision of economic growth. For Ricardo did believe that the expansion of an economy faced ultimate limits in the effects of two tendencies : excessive population growth and diminishing returns. He did not, however, attach very much empirical significance to these tendencies, and regarded the limits they imposed on economic expansion in purely analytical terms. In using these tendency statements and seeking the limits of his analysis Ricardo was simply stating some basic axioms on which to base a contingency prediction : this was a method familiar to strict logical argument. He also maintained these assumptions in order to bring them into play to explain the inducements to technological change and the drive to expand markets. I will discuss this in more detail in the third section of this chapter, 'Technical change : mechanisms and progresses.'

A number of historians have begun to emphasise the particular purpose of Ricardo's model of distribution in relation to contemporary policy concern with international trade. Both Mark Blaug and Maurice Dobb have argued that its significance is only to be understood in the

---

[10] Ricardo, *Essay on Profits*, p. 41.

context of the Corn Laws. Blaug has pointed out that hindrances to foreign trade were major conditions prompting a tendency for the rate of profit to fall. The stationary state was therefore, he argues, Ricardo's 'methodological fiction' : 'The alleged "pessimism" of Ricardo was entirely contingent upon the maintenance of the tariff on raw produce . . . the notion of an impending stationary state was at most a useful devise for frightening the friends of protection.'[11] Dobb gives additional emphasis to the importance Ricardo attached to foreign trade. He cites Ricardo's argument in his article in the *Encyclopædia Britannica* that, if food and raw materials were supplied from abroad in exchange for manufactured goods, 'it is difficult to see where the limit is at which you cease to accumulate wealth and to derive profit from its employment'.[12] He uses an even more forceful statement in a letter by Ricardo to Trower in 1820 : 'I contend for free trade in corn on the ground that while trade is free, and corn cheap, profits will not fall however great be the accumulation of capital.'[13] Such evidence vindicated Edwin Cannan's judgement that 'as a basis for an argument against the Corn Laws it would have been difficult to find anything more effective than the Ricardian theory of distribution'.[14]

In fact these were not only Ricardo's programmatic and personal opinions, they were equally to be found in the argument of the *Principles*. In the chapter on profits he distinguished the future of an 'extensive country with land of poor quality and where the import of food is prohibited', from that of 'small fertile countries' with free import of food. In the first, even a very small accumulation of capital would result in a fall in the rate of profit and a greater rise in rents.[15]

More recently, Samuel Hollander has sought to restrict the significance of Ricardo's distribution model still further by arguing that even in the absence of Corn Law repeal Ricardo was optimistic about Britain's growth prospects. He was sufficiently confident of the dynamic growth of the economy and continued capital formation to play down the adverse effects of the Corn Laws and the Poor Law. Hollander draws attention to the dispute between McCulloch and Ricardo over

11 Mark Blaug, *Ricardian Economics, A Historical Study*, New Haven, Conn. 1958, pp. 31–2.
12 Contribution to the *Encyclopædia Britannica*, Ricardo, *Works*, vol. IV, p. 179, cited in Dobb, *Theories of Value*, p. 90.
13 Ricardo, *Letters 1819–1821, Works*, vol. VIII, p. 208 Letter to Trower, 21 July 1820; cited in Maurice Dobb, *Theories of Value*, p. 91.
14 Edwin Cannan, cited in Dobb, *Theories of Value*, p. 90.
15 Ricardo, *Principles*, p. 126.

the latter's speech to the House of Commons in March 1821. Ricardo's speech minimised the negative effects of agricultural protection upon the rate of domestic accumulation. McCulloch, by contrast, regarding himself as a carrier of Ricardian orthodoxy, insisted that the great source of Britain's difficulty lay in a low rate of return due mainly to the Corn Laws. Hollander notes the significance Ricardo attached to the allocation of capital and influences on accumulation, and argues that part of the explanation for his optimism is to be found in his recognition of agricultural innovation and the effects of technological progress in manufacturing.[16] Hollander points out that technical change may have mattered to him as much as did foreign trade. I will now make the case that Ricardo did indeed attach a significance to technical change at least equal to that he gave to foreign trade.

The interpretations of Blaug, Dobb, and Hollander of the contextual framework of Ricardo's theory significantly modify the import of the Ricardian models of distribution and accumulation. If, as I have argued above, the theoretical implications of Ricardo's restrictive models were meant to be negative, precisely in order to emphasise the practical significance of those factors from which he abstracted, then technical change as well as free trade would be prominent features in his dynamic forecasts.

In several places Ricardo clearly emphasised that the effect of machinery was similar to that of foreign trade. If the introduction of cheap foreign goods reduced costs of production and therefore lowered value, then technical change had an analogous effect. If cheap foreign goods lowered the costs of labourers' subsistence, thus reducing the wage share and bringing about a rise in profits, then so also did the extension of machinery.[17] Blaug and Dobb have shown that Ricardo's well-known intervention in the debates on the Corn Laws may reasonably influence the interpretation of his model of distribution because of the intimate connection between this policy context and his theoretical analysis of foreign trade. Hollander, though sceptical of the importance Ricardo attached to the repeal of the Corn Laws, likewise argues that Ricardo did not draw conclusions pessimistic of Britain's growth prospects from his theoretical growth model, and that he was well aware of the real 'dynamism of the British economy', despite protection. I would now add to these studies the suggestion that there was an

16 Samuel Hollander, 'Ricardo and the Corn Laws: A Revision', *History of Political Economy*, IX, 1977, p. 24.
17 Ricardo, *Principles*, pp. 131–2.

equally important connection between Ricardian theory and its public context in the case of technical change and the machinery debates.

We must first consider the explicit examination made by Ricardo of the impact of technical change, both in agriculture and industry, on distributive shares.

Even in his earliest writings Ricardo drew attention to improvement: 'If by foreign commerce, or the discovery of machinery, the commodities consumed by the labourer should become much cheaper, wages would fall; and this, as we have before observed, would raise the profits of the farmer, and therefore, all other profits.'[18] In addition, such improvements would 'lower for a time rents'.[19] Wage and rent shares would also fall and the profit share would rise if capitalists simply reduced their levels of investment. For in the economy with no technological improvements, high levels of investment placed strains on the market for land and labour, forcing the extension of cultivation to less productive land and raising the costs of workers' subsistence. The remaining profit share would therefore be correspondingly reduced. In such circumstances the only means of maintaining a share of profits sufficient to prevent the onset of the stationery state was to introduce measures preventing high rates of accumulation. Retrogression of this kind was not, however, necessary to maintain the rate of profit, and Ricardo emphasised this in the first edition of the *Principles*: 'The same effects may, however, be produced, when the wealth and population of a country are increased, if that increase is accompanied by such marked improvements in agriculture, as shall have the same effects of diminishing the necessity of cultivating the poorer lands, or of expanding the same amount of capital on the cultivation of the more fertile portions.'[20]

Ricardo thus envisaged two types of capital accumulation. The first took place in a situation of no technical change. When capital was accumulated without technical change, its labour cost of production, that is, its value, also rose. Such accumulation demanded a widening of the margins of cultivation and with it a rise in costs of production overall, since costs were determined at the margin. Relative wage shares thus rose and profit shares fell. Ricardo's second type of capital accumulation can be described as capital-embodied technical change. In this situation a capital stock could rise, while its value could simul-

[18] Ricardo, *Essay on Profits*, p. 26.
[19] *Ibid.* p. 19.
[20] Ricardo, *Principles*, p. 79.

taneously fall. Additions to capital need not entail the extension of the margin of cultivation, for they could be made by the aid of machinery. This would prevent any rise in necessary proportions of labour, and the wage share could stay the same or fall.[21] In order to understand more precisely the complexities of the impact of technical change on distributive shares, it will be necessary to examine in turn wages, profits, and rent.

The critical variable in the whole process of accumulation was the share of wages. What did Ricardo mean by the share of wages, and why did a high share of wages seem to be an indication of regression in the economy? The wage share was an aggregate of what Ricardo termed the natural wage, as distinct from the 'market wage'. The natural wage was the cost of workers' subsistence. Ricardo's definition of subsistence was not simply literal. It had a 'social' element, being dependent on the 'habits and customs of the people'.[22] Nevertheless, whatever the level of 'social' subsistence, the natural wage still had to be considered first in relation to the cost of food. For it tended to rise with diminishing returns in agriculture, and the consequent increase in food prices. If capital accumulation should occur unaccompanied by technical change, and hence without offsetting diminishing returns in agriculture, then the natural wage share would rise. But, in fact, most capital accumulation was accompanied by some improvements in technique which would prevent that eventuality.

> The natural price of all commodities, excepting raw produce
> and labour, has a tendency to fall, in the progress of wealth
> and population; for though, on the one hand, they are enhanced
> in real value, from the rise in the natural price of the raw
> material of which they are made, this is more than counter-
> balanced by the improvements in machinery, by the better
> division and distribution of labour, and by the increasing skill,
> both in science and art, of the producers.[23]

The wage share, of course, was also important to the condition of the working classes. However, their actual condition was dependent, not on the natural wage, but on the differential between this and the market wage. In the process of capital accumulation and economic

[21] Ricardo, *Principles*, p. 95.
[22] *Ibid.* p. 97.
[23] *Ibid.* pp. 93–4.

growth the latter would rise relative to the former, but the permanence of any increased differential between them was of course also dependent upon the movements of the natural wage. Where capital accumulation took place without technical change, marginal costs of production would ultimately rise. Any such rise in costs would also increase the share of national income required by natural wages. And high wage shares caused by a rise in the cost of subsistence would nullify the earlier gains made by increasing the differential between natural and market wages through gains in the latter. Ricardo could therefore derive from his model the conclusion that technical change could improve the condition of the working classes, by preventing a rise in the share of natural wages.

However, Ricardo still held strong doubts about the permanence of any gains to the wage-earning classes. Though technical change could prevent a rise in the costs of the subsistence wage, high market wages and a wide differential between market and natural wages would provide an incentive for population growth. Ricardo endorsed Malthusian population assumptions, and accordingly believed that any differentials that arose between market and natural wages would soon be liable to elimination by the effects of population growth.

On the other hand, Ricardo recognised that higher natural wages need not carry a negative connotation. For such gains in the natural wage could arise, not only from a higher population or higher cost of production, but from gains in the levels of social subsistence.

> The friends of humanity cannot but wish that in all countries the labouring classes should have a taste for comforts and enjoyments, and that they should be stimulated by all legal means in their exertions to procure them. There cannot be a better security against a superabundant population. In those countries, where the labouring classes have the fewest wants, and are contented with the cheapest food, the people are exposed to the greatest vicissitudes and miseries.[24]

Ricardo not only believed that a high natural wage could have this positive implication, but he thought that there was no practical necessity for a convergence between market and natural wages. In an 'improving society' market wages could stay indefinitely above natural wages, 'for no sooner may the impulse, which an increased capital gives to a new

[24] *Ibid.* pp. 100–1.

demand for labour be obeyed, than another increase of capital may produce the same effect'.[25]

If this differential between market and natural wages could be maintained for any length of time, either through the effects of an increase in capital acting on the market wage, or through the effects of technical progress on the natural wage, then it would create incentives for a change in the levels of necessary social subsistence. Goods which were formerly luxuries could become new needs, and, by this means, social subsistence wage levels could rise. A rise in the social subsistence or natural wage need not, therefore, reflect an increase in population. It could in fact, by reducing the differential between market and natural wages, have the effect of reducing population growth. This type of increase in natural wages brought great gains to the condition of the working classes. It was therefore in sharp contrast to the increase in the natural wage share brought about by rising population and rising marginal costs.

Ricardo noticed, moreover, that technical change not only affected the level of social subsistence, but also affected the composition of that subsistence. The extent to which technical change brought about a substitution of manufactured for agricultural goods in the wage basket had very real significance for the impact of the law of diminishing returns. Ricardo explicitly dissociated himself from the view he attributed to both Smith and Malthus, that the wage basket consisted entirely of corn, so that population and profits could be tied entirely to the provision of food.[26] That the wage basket might tend increasingly to consist of more than food followed from the very logic of Ricardo's model of accumulation: 'From manufactured commodities always falling, and raw produce always rising, with the progress of society, such a disproportion in their relative value is at length created, that in rich countries a labourer, by the sacrifice of a very small quantity only of his food, is able to provide liberally for all his other wants.'[27] The fact that workers could and did buy manufactured goods limited the impact

---

[25] *Ibid.* p. 95.

[26] *Ibid.* pp. 293 and 406–7; *Notes on Malthus's Principles of Political Economy*, in Ricardo, *Works*, vol. II, p. 115. Ricardo is perhaps commenting on this in his reaction to the possibility of a glut of necessaries. He replies, 'could such a state of things exist? Would only such a limited number of commodities be produced? Impossible, because the labourers would be glad to consume conveniences and luxuries if they could get them,' *Notes on Malthus*, p. 312.

[27] Ricardo, *Principles*, p. 97.

over the whole economy of diminishing returns in the agricultural sector. Ricardo, as Samuel Hollander has shown, recognised this even before his *Essay on Profits*.[28] Ultimately the wage was the crucial variable, not the price of corn. It is this attention which Ricardo gave to the composition of the wage basket that led him to a very ambivalent position on the Malthusian population theory. Ricardo's *Notes on Malthus* show that he found the Malthusian principle too crude theoretically,[29] but he endorsed the general dogma.[30] His ambivalence shows even more clearly in the *Principles* where he argued that high wages need not necessarily lead to population increase.

> The amended condition of the labourer, in consequence of the increased value which is paid him, does not necessarily oblige him to marry and take upon himself the charge of a family – he will, in all probability, employ a portion of his increased wages in furnishing himself abundantly with food and necessaries, – but with the remainder he may, if it please him, purchase any commodities that may contribute to his enjoyments – chairs, tables, and hardware; or better clothes, sugar, and tobacco.[31]

Ricardo, however, stopped at this point and conceded the argument to Malthus. In the same paragraph he concluded :

> But although this might be the consequence of high wages, yet so great are the delights of domestic society, that in practice it is invariably found that an increase of population follows the amended condition of the labourer; and it is only because it does so, that, with the trifling exception already mentioned, a new and increased demand arises for food. This demand then is the effect of an increase of capital and population, but not the cause – it is only because the expenditure of the people takes this direction, that the market price of necessaries exceeds the natural price, and that the quantity of food required is produced.[32]

[28] Samuel Hollander, 'Ricardo's Analysis of the Profit Rate 1813 to 1815', *Economica*, XL, August 1973, p. 282.
[29] Ricardo, *Notes on Malthus*, p. 115.
[30] *Ibid*. p. 262
[31] Ricardo, *Principles*, p. 406.
[32] *Ibid*. p. 407. The first edition did not refer to this as a 'trifling exception'.

Still, though Ricardo endorsed Malthusian assumptions on the inducements to population growth, it is doubtful if he was as apprehensive of
overpopulation as were many of his contemporaries. Hollander goes so
far as to argue that Ricardo regarded the rapid contemporary growth
rate of population as necessary to meet the even greater rate of increase
of capital. Hollander cites Ricardo's comment that the pernicious effects
of the Poor Laws had, for this reason, not been felt in the context of
a rapidly expanding capital and growing economy. He argued, 'Happily
these laws have been in operation during a period of progressive prosperity, when the funds for the maintenance of labour have regularly
increased, and when an increase of population would be naturally
called for.'[33] The 'pernicious nature of these laws' would only become
clear with the approach of the stationary state.

Ricardo's discussion of profits and technological improvement was
based almost entirely on what he had to say about wages. Technical
change did not have a direct impact on the rate of profit. Indeed,
profits changed, in any circumstances, only in response to developments
in the sector producing goods for the consumption of wage earners.
Technical change could thus be said to raise the rate of profit only to
the extent that it reduced the costs of 'wage goods'. Any change in
techniques which affected only luxury goods consumed by capitalists
and landlords could induce no change at all in the rate of profit. In an
extreme situation, where wage earners consumed only corn, technical
change in the industrial sector could affect prices, but not the rate of
profit.

> The rate of profit is never increased by a better distribution of
> labour, by the invention of machinery, by the establishment
> of roads and canals, or by any means of abridging labour either
> in the manufacture or in the conveyance of goods. These are
> causes which operate on price and never fail to be beneficial
> to the consumers, . . . but they have no effect whatever on
> profit. On the other hand, every diminution in the wages of
> labour raises profits, but produces no effect on the prices of
> commodities.[34]

Perhaps one of the most longstanding and polemical concerns of the
issues arising from Ricardo's work on technology and distribution was

[33] *Ibid.* pp. 108–9, cited in Hollander, 'Ricardo and the Corn Laws',
p. 12.
[34] Ricardo, *Principles*, p. 33.

that of the impact of improvements on rents. From his early corn model through to the propositions of his *Principles*, Ricardo argued that the necessary effect of both improvements and free trade in corn was the reduction of rents. The proof took on the political form that the interest of the landlord was opposed to that of every other class of the community.[35]

The level of rent on any one piece of land was established by the differential productivities of successive capital inputs. Because Ricardo assumed diminishing returns, there was a point beyond which each successive capital input generated a lower return than the previous one. Rent was determined by the difference between the return on the most recent and least productive capital input and the previous and marginally more productive capital input. Rent was therefore established at the margin of cultivation, and was high or low according to the levels of capital accumulation required. When some event occurred which had the effect of reducing the level of required capital accumulation, this would allow for a retreat in the margin of cultivation, and therefore in a reduction in the differentials or inequalities in the products obtained from each successive capital input on the land. Because the margin of cultivation had moved inwards and the capital costs of cultivation had fallen, rents too would fall.[36] Agricultural improvements and free trade in corn were major rent-reducing factors. Both allowed for either the cultivation of more land and the production of a greater output with the same capital, or for an actual reduction of land in cultivation and therefore capital accumulation in order to produce the same output. The logical conclusion of any association between agricultural improvements or freer trade and lower rents was that landlords would be against all such changes. The polemical implications Ricardo drew from this finding were, however, unacceptable to many of his contemporaries. Malthus, in particular, continually disputed Ricardo's enmity to landlords. However, Ricardo never looked on the inverse relation between rents and agricultural improvements as anything but a short-term interim effect. Sraffa has argued that Ricardo merely added a footnote in the third edition of his *Principles* conceding some ultimate benefit to the landlord.[37] But even in his polemical chapters against Malthus and the Corn Laws Ricardo had conceded that the landlord did have a long-term interest in agricultural improvements : 'The machine which

[35] Ricardo, *Essay on Profits*, p. 21.
[36] Ricardo, *Principles*, p. 83.
[37] Piero Sraffa, 'Introduction', Ricardo, *Works*, vol. 1, p. lv.

produced the most important article of consumption would be improved, and would be well paid for according as its services were demanded. All the advantages would, in the first instance, be enjoyed by labourers, capitalists, and consumers; but with the progress of population, they would be gradually transferred to the proprietors of the soil.'[38]

Ricardo most emphatically denied the charge of dissociating land-lords from the gains of economic growth in his *Notes on Malthus* :

> Perhaps in no part of his book has Mr. Malthus so much mistaken me as on this subject – he represents me as supporting the doctrine that the interests of landlords are constantly opposed to those of every other class of the community, and one would suppose from his language that I considered them as enemies to the State. . . . All I meant to say of the landlord's interest, was, that it would be for his advantage that the machine which he had for producing corn should be in demand – that in fact his rent depended on it; – that on the contrary it was the interest of the consumer to use the foreign machine, if that would do the work cheaper. It is only in this case, that the interests of the landlord and consumer really, if well under-stood, come in contact. . . . I have indeed observed that improvements in agriculture were in their immediate effects injurious to the landlord, . . . Great improvements in any branch of production are in their first effects injurious to the class who are engaged in that branch, but this is the statement of a fact or an opinion, and cannot be supposed to cast any injurious reflections.[39]

Ricardo, therefore, associated rising rents with the general tendency of capital accumulation, but with the proviso that this abstracted from technical change. The initial impact of technical change in agriculture, ceteris paribus, was to reduce rents. However, Ricardo went on to suggest that in a prosperous improving economy the advantages of technical progress might be enjoyed first by labourers, capitalists, and consumers, but they would soon also be enjoyed by landlords. Here he brought the population principle to bear, for an economy would only continue to improve because of constantly increasing demands created either by an expanding population or by new needs. Where cultivation was extended in spite of improvements, which was a likely situation in

38 Ricardo, *Principles*, p. 335; also see p. 412.
39 Ricardo, *Notes on Malthus*, pp. 117–19.

a growing economy, then rents too might rise.[40] Ricardo drew a distinction in this, as in other cases, between the results of his restrictive model, and his conception of the overall growth process.

Technical change: mechanisms and processes

I have shown that Ricardo's model of distribution gave remarkable illumination to the significance he attached to technical change. His model, which demonstrated the eventuality of the stationary state but for the social and economic effects of technical improvement and free trade, was by no means a pessimistic one. On the contrary, it was a highly systematic and very optimistic presentation of the extent of the gains to be had through technological improvement and freer trade. In addition to this, Ricardo also had a number of ideas about the processes of technical change. Not formally integrated with a model of economic growth, these have often been missed by commentators sceptical of Ricardo's recognition of the importance of technical improvement to the economy of his day.

The sceptics have generally pointed to several gaps in Ricardo's perceptions of technical change. They claim that Ricardo did not take up Smith's discussion of the division of labour, and that he did not make clear the distinction between capital-saving and labour-saving techniques. They further believe that his model did not have built into it a concept of self-generating technical change as did Smith's, where the division of labour was embodied in new techniques, or Marx's, where the drive to technical change was incorporated in the tendency to the rising organic composition of capital. However, these and other factors were discussed by Ricardo, though not in any strictly systematic fashion. He adapted the concept of the division of labour to his own purposes. He drew attention to the structure of capital, and understood the implications of the capital or labour intensities of various technologies. He investigated the ways in which the introduction of machinery saved on capital, and explored the extent of choice available in the introduction of new techniques. He examined the progressive potentials in the agricultural and manufacturing sectors, and assessed the types and relative merits of technological improvement in both. Finally, he looked at inducements to gains in labour productivity and also gave a place to the role of good government in promoting improvements.

Ricardo did not attempt to develop in more detail Smith's concept

[40] *Ibid.* p. 159.

of the technical division of labour and it is likely that he simply took it for granted. What he did do, however, was to adapt the concept to his own purposes, to help to explain the gains from international specialisation in production. He gave much more detailed attention to the structure of capital and extended this to the relative capital- and labour-intensities of various techniques. He defined quite early on in his work his notion of capital, and the criteria for its separation into its fixed and circulating elements. Capital was generally defined as time and was fixed or circulating according to its durability or the time it took to consume. But, as Ricardo noted, the division was one 'not essential, and in which the line of demarcation cannot be accurately drawn'.[41] As he was to point out later, however, the division was actually very important. The employment impact of capital accumulation was a function of the proportions embodied in fixed and circulating elements. I will discuss this in greater detail in the final section of this chapter on machinery and labour.

Ricardo went on from this analysis of the structure of capital to argue that the introduction of machinery could in part be explained by the existing composition of capital. To explain this he deployed his limiting assumptions of rising rates of population growth and diminishing returns to explain a tendency towards rising proportions of machinery to labour over time. Rising rates of population growth and diminishing returns, even if seen as limits on economic expansion in only the last analysis, might still seem to threaten the unimpeded course of future economic growth. As threats they made the drive to overcome economic necessity one of the major inducements to technical change. Technical change was thus seen as a response to the pressure of a distant tendency to rising rates of wages in old and wealthy nations. Using these assumptions, Ricardo first analysed the inducements to and effects of capital saving techniques. The introduction of machinery or the increase in fixed capital could save on total capital, for he regarded machinery as the product of less labour than that which it displaced. A rise in wages would also have a greater effect on the value of commodities produced by circulating capital than on those produced by fixed capital: 'Through their [machines'] influence an increase in the price of provisions which raises wages, will affect fewer persons . . . and the saving which is the consequence shows itself in the reduced price of the commodities manufactured.' The introduction of this fixed capital saved on total capital. Thus, 'neither machines, nor the com-

---

[41] Ricardo, *Principles,* p. 52.

modities made by them rise in real value, but all commodities made by machines fall, and fall in proportion to their durability'.[42]

Second, this peculiar effect of the introduction of machinery, as well as the influence of differing comparative capital structures, were issues which led Ricardo to take up discussion of the choice of techniques. He pointed out the impact of factor prices such as the rates of wages and interest on the introduction of new technologies.[43] Ricardo connected the tendency of wages to rise relative to interest rates to a tendency to rising capital intensity in industry. Thus he argued :

> In the distribution of employments amongst all countries, the capital of poorer nations will be naturally employed in those pursuits, wherein a great quantity of labour is supported at home, because in such countries the food and necessaries for an increasing population can be most easily procured. In rich countries, on the contrary, where food is dear, capital will naturally flow, when trade is free, into those occupations wherein the least quantity of labour is required to be maintained at home.[44]

Moreover, in the process of economic growth without substantial innovation there was an increasing tendency for wage shares to rise and 'with every rise in the price of labour, new temptations are offered to the use of machines'.[45] It was with this in mind that Ricardo came to find acceptable John Barton's argument that 'as arts are cultivated, and civilization is extended, fixed capital bears a larger and larger proportion to circulating capital'.[46] Ricardian theory contained the embryonic prediction of the fully mechanised economy.

Yet, factor prices were also the major determinants of the *slow* diffusion of technical innovation. Ricardo explained the slow diffusion of new techniques by low relative wages. It is thus that we understand his image of the American economy as a relatively labour-intensive economy. The choice of techniques was, in Ricardo's words, 'the

[42] *Ibid.* p. 42.
[43] This has previously been referred to as the Ricardo effect. I prefer to separate this term, which was Hayek's conception from Ricardo's view of the problem. The two have been distinguished by C. E. Ferguson, 'The Specialization Gap : Barton, Ricardo and Hollander', *History of Political Economy*, v, Spring 1973, pp. 6–11.
[44] Ricardo, *Principles*, p. 349.
[45] *Ibid.* p. 41.
[46] *Ibid.* p. 396.

constant competition' of 'machinery and labour'.[47] 'We here see why it is that old countries are constantly impelled to employ machinery, and new countries to employ labour. With every difficulty of providing for the maintenance of men, labour necessarily rises, and with every rise in the price of labour, new temptations are offered to the use of machinery.'[48] In such old countries, among which he included Britain, Ricardo recognised that technical change rather than simple capital accumulation was the faster and more painless road to economic growth.[49]

Ricardo's analysis of the choice of techniques became more refined as he pushed on to examine the differing potentials for technological improvement in agriculture and manufacturing. He generalised that in the course of economic growth manufacturing would come to assume larger proportions of the national economy. In a speech in 1822 he declared :

> The hon. gentleman might, perhaps, think that a manufacturing country could not be so happy as an agricultural country. But he might as well complain of a man's growing old as of such a change in our national condition. Nations grow old as well as individuals; and in proportion as they grow old, populous and wealthy must they become manufacturers. If things were allowed to take their own course, we should undoubtedly become a great manufacturing country, but we should remain a great agricultural country also.[50]

He was also sensitive to the fine divisions and types of change in techniques which were particular to each sector. He did not regard agricultural improvements as just another variation on improvements in the manufacturing sector, for he identified two types of improvement in the agricultural sector each of which had very different implications. One type of improvement added to soil fertility by better crop rotation or the use of fertilisers; this land-saving innovation reduced real rents. The second type of improvement raised capital and labour productivity, but the effectiveness of this capital-saving improvement was limited by physical diminishing returns.

The analysis of improvement in the agricultural sector clarified

[47] *Ibid.* p. 395.
[48] *Ibid.* p. 41.
[49] *Ibid.* p. 279.
[50] Ricardo, Speech of 9 May 1822, *Speeches and Evidence, Works*, vol. v, p. 180, cited in Hollander, 'Ricardo and the Corn Laws', p. 37.

Ricardo's choice of the key dynamic factors in growth. It was, further-more, the style of improvement in this key sector which was funda-mental to the rate of capital accumulation. This rate depended in the first instance on labour productivity and the fertility of the soil. Ricardo agreed with Smith that in new settlements 'where the arts and knowledge of countries far advanced in refinements are introduced', the rate of capital accumulation exceeded the rate of population growth.[51] Labour productivity, however, was equally dependent on capital formation, and Ricardo therefore reproved Malthus for com-paring the labour productivity of various nations on the basis of the inclination to work. Such criteria completely neglected relative levels of capital formation.[52]

Labour productivity, as I noted earlier, was central to Smith's conception of the growth process. It is popularly believed that, in contrast with Smith, Ricardo was so entrenched in a model based on the accumulation of capital that he ignored the significance of labour productivity. Here one can see, however, that Ricardo carried over the spirit of Smith's ideas by seeing labour productivity along with the fertility of the soil as factors affecting the rate of capital accumulation. Ricardo not only sought to explain national differences in labour productivity, but also to dissect this productivity by inquiring into skill. Labour productivity depended on comparative levels of skill, which in turn were related to comparative levels of capital formation. Ricardo, unlike Smith, did not regard skill as an attribute given by the division of labour. Skill was instead a capital good, provided by the labourer. Skill was 'dependent on the interests fathers may feel to give their children this dexterity and ingenuity', and the supply of such labour depended on the costs of conferring this dexterity.[53] The subsistence of labour now was regarded as providing not only for the continuity of the day-to-day labour of a worker and his descendants, but for the production of more and more complex and skilled labour.

Finally, Ricardo also conceived a definite role for good government in the direction of capital accumulation and growth. Again, like Smith, he distinguished badly governed from well-governed nations.

> In those countries where there is abundance of fertile land,
> but where, from the ignorance, indolence, and barbarism of
> the inhabitants, they are exposed to all the evils of want and

[51] Ricardo, *Principles*, p. 98.
[52] Ricardo, *Notes on Malthus*, p. 87.
[53] *Ibid*. p. 226.

famine, and where it has been said that population presses
against the means of subsistence, a very different remedy should
be applied from that which is necessary in long settled countries,
where, from the diminishing rate of the supply of raw produce,
all the evils of a crowded population are experienced. In the
one case, the evil proceeds from bad government, from the
insecurity of property, and from a want of education in all
ranks of the people. To be made happier they require only to
be better governed and instructed, as the augmentation of
capital, beyond the augmentation of people, would be the
inevitable result. No increase in the population can be too great,
as the powers of production are still greater.[54]

The transfer to good government in such a country would involve
higher rates of capital accumulation benefiting all.[55]

Ricardo's comments on the government of nations did not stop with
this judgement on the problems of young nations. For he also believed
that government had a great deal to do with the difficulties of old
nations, notably England. In arguing that older nations would tend
to become manufacturing nations, he had taken care to add, 'If things
were allowed to take their course, we should undoubtedly become a
great manufacturing country, but we should remain a great agricultural
country too.' In this speech Ricardo was not only making the point that
the rising dominance of the manufacturing sector was inevitable for
the British economy – he was arguing that it was desirable. The implication was that things were not being 'allowed to take their course'
because they were being held back by government. Ricardo was issuing
his warning to policy makers that a nation which expanded its capital
and its population without the benefit of international trade and technical improvement would soon find itself on the road to falling rates of
profit and an imminent stationary state.

Furthermore, Ricardo was not just preaching to a society still dominated by the landed interests; he was preaching to a government which
was equivocal if not hostile to the current rapid progress of industrialisation. I would argue that Ricardo was deploying his economic analysis
not to represent the manufacturing as opposed to the landed classes but
to replace a dominant ideology of economic policy. His analysis of a
progressive continuously transforming economy was in stark contrast

[54] Ricardo, *Principles*, p. 99.
[55] *Ibid.* pp. 99–100 and 100n.

to the assumptions of a static self-regulating economy then underlying government policy.

Boyd Hilton in *Corn, Cash, Commerce* has demonstrated that the so-called liberal Tory governments of 1815 to 1830 dominated by Lord Liverpool and Huskisson were not particularly concerned for the expansion of industry and commerce. They sought to feed and to employ a rapidly expanding population, but saw themslves doing so within a finite international economy currently under the strain not of industrialisation but of the consequences of war and monetary depreciation.

Industrialisation could not be accommodated within the terms of debate known by these policy makers. When they decided on the return to the gold standard in 1819 it was interpreted as a restoration of the currency to its pre-war or 'natural' state. The policies of the liberal Tories were inspired, as Boyd Hilton has expressed it, not by a belief in utilitarianism but in 'naturalness'. Though they recognised that the economy must not be allowed to retrogress, they also maintained that growth must be confined to 'legitimate bounds'. For 'overstepping the natural level of economic activity would cause overproduction and gluts'.[56]

Ricardo's model of 'natural tendencies' which so incisively traced out the connections between natural prices, laws of nature and natural tendencies of rates of profit to fall, seemed eminently suited to analysing an economic policy which assumed legitimate levels of economic activity and natural states for the economy. Ricardo's strict model of income distribution was a negative model in the sense that its purpose was to demonstrate the importance of trade and technical progress by analysing an economy which lacked these. However, it was also a model which can be seen as effectively encapsulating the basic assumptions of the current economic policy, and proceeding to analyse the dire and gloomy prospects of continuing on the basis of a belief in legitimate and natural paths to stability.

These governments did introduce a number of free trade reforms and often justified these by referring to political economy. But such justifications were in the main opportunistic. Boyd Hilton shows how in agricultural trade policy their main interest was in the best guarantee of subsistence, and they endorsed protection, then free trade accordingly. I will outline in Chapter 9, 'The Export of Machinery', the extent to

[56] Boyd Hilton, *Corn, Cash, Commerce*, pp. vii–ix, 3–30, 303–15. The above two paragraphs are a summary of Hilton's argument.

which their industrial trade policy was also based on expediency and not theory. Ricardo cannot be neatly summed up as one who provided a theory which was obviously influential to a willing government carrying forward the interests of the rising manufacturing classes. Ricardo's *Principles* put forward a new ideology of economic and technological improvement – if not of limitless growth, then of growth to which an empirical limit could not yet be set. But he was a missionary in a land of pagan naturalists.

Machinery and labour

Ricardo's interest in the connections between a country's capital structure and its technology did not at first go any further than a few remarks on inter-country comparisons of economic development and explanations for existing techniques and trade patterns. However, he soon came to realise that the composition of capital in a country, and through this its choice of a suitable technology, could have important implications for employment. His chapter on machinery, the only significant change in the third edition of his *Principles*, detailed his recognition of the employment impact of a change in techniques. Ricardo's change of view did not have purely theoretical implications, for the problem could not be separated from the contemporary debate on machinery and labour.

This chapter represented a fascinating and provocative development in Ricardo's economic theory, and the findings he described there seemed to be at variance with the optimistic perspectives he offered on technology throughout the rest of the book. Furthermore, its claims appeared to be so directly addressed to a central issue of public debate, that theory and politics must have been closely entwined. In this one small section of the *Principles* Ricardo presented his readers with the political economy of radicalism, reaction, and liberalism of his own time. It is a chapter which can only be understood through a historical interpretation, for it touched on a contemporary issue which was far-reaching in its social significance.

When Ricardo publicly announced the change he had made in his opinions on machinery he said that though he had not published anything on the subject, 'yet I have in other ways given my support to doctrines which I now think erroneous'.[57] This probably referred to the part he took in the anti-Owenite campaign about which I will say more below. However, Ricardo had also referred to labour-saving machinery

[57] *Ibid.* p. 386.

explicity in his *Essay on Profits* where he argued that the impact of
a low price of corn on the working classes 'would be nearly the same as
the effects of improved machinery, which it is now no longer questioned,
has a decided tendency to raise the real wages of labour'.[58] In the first
edition of the *Principles* Ricardo had taken this for granted, and only
recognised capital transfer costs. It is also true that even when something
other than an Owenite argument for technological unemployment was
put to him, Ricardo was similarly unimpressed. Ricardo's early reaction
to John Barton, whose work he came later to endorse, bears this out. In
answer to Barton, Ricardo simply asserted that the accumulation of
fixed capital would not have any adverse impact on employment. The
quantity produced over and above necessary consumption would be
the same in both cases. Moreover, he regarded the possibility of technological unemployment as highly unlikely: 'The case is evidently put
for the sake of argument, and could not really take place, for there is no
new creation of machinery which entirely supersedes the use of the
labour of man. A steam engine requires the constant labour of man –
he must regulate its motion and velocity – he must procure coals for the
fire necessary to work it – he must attend to its annual repairs.'[59]
Ricardo repeated his general reaction when he commented on
McCulloch's partial endorsement of Barton's theory of technical
change.[60]

Ricardo's change of mind, as embodied in the third edition of his
Principles, took place when he came to consider not simply the effect
of technical change in a situation of gradual and balanced growth but
also the case where a change in techniques involved a strong switch to
fixed capital. He discovered that where the introduction of such new
technology took place in a situation of capital scarcity there would
probably have to be a change in the composition of a country's capital
stock. A country's stock of circulating capital would have to be reduced
in order to raise a stock of fixed capital sufficient to introduce the new
technique. But its level of employment was dependent upon its circulating capital, that is its wage goods and materials. If capital was shifted
from the production of wage goods to the construction of machinery,
then employment over the whole economy would have to fall. There
were several implications of such a change in the composition of capital
during the construction period of new machinery. The first was that

[58] Ricardo, *Essay on Profits*, p. 35.
[59] *Letters 1816–1818, Works*, vii, Ricardo to Barton, 29 May 1817,
   pp. 158–9.
[60] *Letters 1819–1821*, Ricardo to McCulloch, 29 March 1820, p. 171.

final output could actually fall during this period, as wage goods were definitely a part of the final output. The second was that the whole stock of capital could actually rise at the same time that circulating capital and final output were falling. For, though circulating capital was being transferred to the construction of fixed capital, the new machines could add to the capital stock by more than the reduction in circulating capital. Finally, inventions could be labour saving, not for any one industry or sector, but for the economy as a whole. During a construction phase total employment could actually fall because of the decline of circulating capital and final output both of which would reduce the demand for labour. However, as Ricardo emphasised just as strongly, these eventualities were only possible during a time of construction and rapid accumulation of fixed capital. As soon as the new machine came into operation such high costs of accumulation would be compensated by the lower labour or 'circulating capital' input required in running the new machines. This would seem at first sight only to add to the level of unemployment. But it was not so. For the fact that labour was displaced from the sector using the new machines would lead to lower costs of production, and therefore create a surplus which would in turn create the means for re-employing labour in other sectors.

Ricardo did not believe that technological unemployment must be the necessary result of any change in techniques in a particular industry. It did not occur because a machine replaced a labourer, but rather, because investment in machinery had to claim priority over the production of final output. Technological unemployment would therefore only take place in those extreme situations where a country's capital was very scarce and where the construction of the new machines demanded a strong switch to fixed capital. Ricardo's analysis was an original one, distinct from the case made by many of his contemporaries. Where others maintained merely that machines displaced labour in any industry where they were introduced, Ricardo claimed that the replacement of men by machines in particular industries need not extend any further. In fact, the displacement of labour in one industry, by increasing productivity, might compensate for a form of technological unemployment which arose from the quite different causes of capital scarcity and sudden changes in the composition of capital. The lower labour or circulating capital input required in the operation of the new machines in any one sector would generate a surplus to re-employ labour in other sectors. The new machines or fixed capital stock, once accumulated, would generate gains in productivity and therefore increase the surplus. Rising rates of growth would release the strains on saving in the original capital scarce economy, and would ultimately result in higher levels of capital and a rising demand for labour. Ricardo confined the time of difficulty to the period of accumulation prior to the full operation of the new machines. The crucial problem lay in the possibilities of labour-saving effect which extended over the economy as a whole – that is, an interim period when capitalists expected to invest in machinery, and to gain themselves the same return, yet to produce for a time a smaller final output. After this interim period there ought to be no further restriction of this nature on the demand for labour.[61]

Ricardo himself emphasised that he was analysing a relatively restricted case, and warned his readers not to make the inference that machinery should be discouraged. These results applied only to the situation where machinery was suddenly discovered and extensively introduced. Generally, discoveries were more gradual, and, rather than diverting capital from another sector, they encouraged a higher rate of saving.[62]

Ricardo's discovery that technical change could result simultaneously in a rise in net income or total surplus, and in a decline in gross income or total output, did not, however, disturb his general theory of capital accumulation. Prior to this discovery he had analysed the sources of capital accumulation in terms of the distinction between gross and net revenue. He had disputed Smith's view that the power of any country was to be assessed in proportion to the value of its annual product, because this was the fund from which taxes were ultimately paid. Ricardo separated himself from this view and argued that taxes and savings could only be derived from rent and profits, that is, from net revenue and not from gross revenue. He saw no reason for supporting Smith's preference for agricultural investment. This preference was

[61] Ricardo, *Principles*, pp. 389–91. See also J. R. Hicks, *A Theory of Economic History*, Oxford, 1969, p. 153; and Hicks, *Capital and Time*, Oxford, 1973; also Hicks, 'A Reply to Professor Beach', *Economic Journal*, LXXXI, December 1971, p. 925. Ricardo himself clearly explained the dynamic process. 'I have before observed, too, that the increase of net incomes, estimated in commodities, which is always the consequence of improved machinery, will lead to new savings and accumulations. These savings it must be remembered are annual, and must soon create a fund, much greater than the gross revenue, originally lost by the discovery of the machine'. *Principles*, p. 396.

[62] Ricardo, *Principles*, p. 395.

based on what Ricardo regarded as the misguided view that agricultural investment created the greatest annual product because it gave motion to the greatest amount of 'industry', that is, productive labour. Ricardo added a footnote in the third edition of his *Principles* denying Say's charge that he 'considered as nothing, the happiness of so many human beings',[63] in other words, that he ignored the employment-generating characteristics of particular industries.

Ricardo's discovery was completely compatible with his previous analysis of the mechanisms of accumulation. The rate of accumulation was dependent on net revenue. The capitalist only had an interest in maintaining his rate of profit, and therefore this net revenue. His total product had no bearing on this. However, as Ricardo pointed out, the 'power of supporting a population' and the 'situation of the labouring classes' depended on total product and not on the surplus,[64] and he showed that the condition of the working classes was also dependent on unproductive employment.

> Independently of the consideration of the discovery and use of machinery, to which our attention has been just directed, the labouring classes have no small interest in the manner in which the net income of the country is expended ... As the labourers, then, are interested in the demand for labour, they must naturally desire that as much of the revenue as possible should be diverted from expenditure on luxuries, to be expended in the support of menial servants.[65]

The chapter on machinery has created major difficulties for historians of economic thought who have wondered about Ricardo's own assessment of its significance. They have been even more puzzled by its apparent contradiction with the rest of Ricardo's model. Most historians of thought have seen it as something of a quirk. Pasinetti has argued that the introduction of machinery violated the assumptions of Ricardo's model: the chapter may perhaps not have been a contradiction but was 'an honest acknowledgement' by Ricardo 'of the limits of his own theory'.[66] Blaug argues that Ricardo had hidden motives for not carrying through with the analysis of labour-saving technical change, 'to have done so would have vitiated the simple model which he had con-

[63] *Ibid.* p. 349.
[64] *Ibid.* p. 390.
[65] *Ibid.* pp. 392–3.
[66] Pasinetti, 'A Mathematical Formulation of the Ricardian System', p. 92.

structed to convey the undesirable consequences of the corn laws'.[67] Finally Hollander argues that Ricardo's failure to examine his model in the light of his new chapter simply reflected his adherence to the methodological position that the realism of the assumptions was of less significance than the predictions derived from them.[68] Hollander has argued more recently that Ricardo's change of position was not really as significant as he had imagined – that the raw materials for the new theory were implicit in the first edition of his work.[69]

All these views of Ricardo simply deny his own perception of the chapter. An analysis of ideas which dismisses the very point a thinker insists he is making is very unsatisfactory history. We can learn more about the significance and implications which Ricardo attached to this chapter if we look at contemporary reactions and his own defences.

The chapter was of obvious importance to the current machinery debates, the debates on technical change and unemployment which pervaded most of this period of the Industrial Revolution. Ricardo himself participated in discussions of Owenism, spade husbandry and the plight of the handloom weavers. I will say more about this below, as the whole issue became very important to subsequent debate. Ricardo's early attitude both to Owen and schemes for the re-employment of the weavers was quite disparaging. He regarded Owen as a visionary as little deserving of attention as Tory fanatics such as Southey.[70] He was scornful of Owen's hopes that community feeling would overcome self-interest.

Ricardo's mind on this issue was not closed, however. He did become involved in a committee of Owenite sympathisers to examine Owen's plans, but Ricardo explicitly separated himself from any commitment to the cause.[71] The most he would concede was what he stated in the House of Commons : 'In a limited degree he thought the scheme likely to succeed, and to produce, where it did succeed, considerable happiness, comfort, and morality, by giving employment and instruction to the lower classes . . . He could not, however, go along with him [Owen]

[67] Blaug, *Ricardian Economics*, p. 71.

[68] Samuel Hollander, 'Some Technological Relationships in the *Wealth of Nations* and Ricardo's *Principles*', *Canadian Journal of Economics and Political Science*, xxxii, May 1966, 187.

[69] Samuel Hollander, 'The Development of Ricardo's Position on Machinery', *History of Political Economy*, iii, Spring 1971, pp. 116, 118.

[70] Ricardo to Trower, 26 January 1818, *Letters 1816–1818*, p. 247.

[71] See the correspondence between Trower and Ricardo : *Letters 1819–1821*, Trower to Ricardo, 4 July 1819, p. 42, and Ricardo to Trower, 8 July 1819, p. 46.

in the hope of ameliorating the condition of the lower classes to such a degree as he seemed to expect.'[72] He saw himself purely as an economic consultant on the committee. The committee, however, concluded in generally favourable terms to Owen's views, and several critics soon accused Ricardo of complicity in the heresy of Owenism. Trower reported his own amazement at Ricardo's action.[73] Ricardo attempted to exonerate himself by claiming he was not bound to approve the plans, only to question them : 'Can any reasonable person believe, with Owen, that a society, such as he projects, will flourish and produce more than has ever yet been produced by an equal number of men, if they are to be stimulated to exertion by a regard to the community, instead of by a regard to their private interests? Is not the experience of ages against him?'[74]

Similarly, Ricardo was not at all convinced by the early strategy of the handloom weavers' lobby. John Maxwell presented the motion, which was to recur throughout the 1820s and 1830s, that there be a tax on the power loom to compensate for the tax on workers' consumption goods. Ricardo regarded this as yet another restriction on trade, and argued that it was, rather, the duty of government to provide incentives for the development and not the restriction of industry.[75]

However, Ricardo seems to have expressed less opposition to the Owenite schemes for spade husbandry. He consistently disclaimed any knowledge of agricultural techniques, but saw no reason why the scheme would not work. As he stated in the House of Commons, 'For what did the country want at the present moment? A demand for labour. If the facts stated of spade husbandry were true, it was a beneficial course, as affording that demand.' He separated this scheme from other aspects of Owenism: 'a division of the country into parallelograms, or an establishment of a community of goods, and similar visionary schemes'. Ricardo went so far as to urge that the government circulate 'useful information', and supported the appointment of a committee to look into the matter.[76]

---

72 'Meeting on Mr. Owen's Plan', 26 June 1819, *Speeches and Evidence*, pp. 467–8.
73 *Letters 1819–1821*, Trower to Ricardo, 8 July 1819, p. 42.
74 *Ibid*. Ricardo to Trower, 8 July 1819, p. 46.
75 Ricardo, 'Cotton Weavers', *Speeches and Evidence*, 29 June 1820, 68–9.
76 'Sir W. de Crespigny's Motion Respecting Mr. Owen's Plan', 16 December 1819, *Speeches and Evidence*, pp. 31, 35. Also Ricardo's reaction to Malthus's sarcasm towards spade husbandry, *Notes on Malthus*, p. 239.

Just as Ricardo, prior to his rethinking of the machinery and labour question, played an active part in contemporary discussions, so he continued to do so after publication of his chapter, and even there he recognised the political implications of his logic and wrote, 'That the opinion entertained by the labouring class, that the employment of machinery is frequently detrimental to their interests, is not founded on prejudice and error, but is conformable to the correct principles of political economy.'[77] Ricardo, moreover, reaffirmed these views in a speech in the House of Commons by criticising a potentially 'useful' popular pamphlet against machine breaking by Cobbett. Here and in his correspondence, Ricardo now dissociated himself from the popular middle-class dogma on machinery. He stood up to McCulloch's wrath that he had given authority to 'all those who raise a yell against the extension of machinery', and that by his word, 'the laws against the Luddites are a disgrace to the Statute Book'.[78] Malthus also objected to the implications of what Ricardo had to say – that his views were 'Liable to be taken fast hold of by the labouring classes'.[79] Ricardo, undaunted, pressed consideration of the question through the Political Economy Club. After two delays it was finally discussed in February 1822. But Ricardo was left disappointed in the reception of his views, 'I could hardly satisfy myself of the general opinion on that disputed point.'[80] Ricardo also continued to stress the importance of his new

[77] Ricardo, *Principles,* p. 392.

[78] *Letters 1819–1821*, McCulloch to Ricardo, 5 June 1821, p. 385. McCulloch's anger was justified since Ricardo had only recently criticised him for his view that an increase in the proportion of fixed capital reduced the demand for labour. See *Letters 1819–1821,* McCulloch to Ricardo, 21 June 1821, p. 393, and Ricardo to McCulloch, 30 June 1821, p. 400. This reason for McCulloch's anger was also mentioned by Malthus in his letter to Ricardo, *Letters 1821–1823, Works,* IX, 7 July 1821, p. 9.

[79] *Letters 1821–1823*, Malthus to Ricardo, 16 July 1821, p. 18. Malthus was the first to find out about Ricardo's new views. He at first saw them as supporting his own views on machinery and over-production; see Malthus to Sismondi, *Letters 1819–1821,* 12 March 1821, p. 377. Ricardo, however quickly dissociated himself from Malthus's views; see *Letters 1819–1821*, Ricardo to Malthus, 18 June 1821, p. 387.

[80] The question 'Whether machinery has a tendency to diminish the demand for labour' was proposed by Ricardo for discussion on 25 June 1821. This was deferred until the next meeting, then deferred again at this meeting on 3 December 1821. It was finally discussed on 4 February 1822. *Political Economy Club Minutes of Proceedings 1821–1882*, vol. IV, London, 1882, pp. 43–6; and Ricardo's report on the discussion in his letter to McCulloch, *Letters 1821–1823,* 18 February 1822, p. 159.

position, particularly by criticising the popular political economy of his supporters. He drew repeated attention to this in his notes on McCulloch's lecture. At three different points in his criticisms he objected to McCulloch's persistently stated views that the demand for labour was a function of the accumulation of capital and that the interests of masters and workmen were always harmonious.[81] Ricardo placed similar weight on the point in his criticism of James Mill's popular work, *Elements of Political Economy.*

Ricardo's unequivocal faith in his stand did not, however, encourage him to change his practice and to recommend any change in policy towards machinery. He concluded his chapter by arguing that nothing should be done to discourage technical innovation for fear of capital export. If the use of machinery led to higher returns, capital would flow to the country which encouraged technical change : 'By investing part of a capital in improved machinery, there will be a diminution in the progressive demand for labour; by exporting it to another country, the demand will be wholly annihilated.'[82]

The critical reaction to Ricardo's chapter was primarily a doctrinal and empirical one. Most complained that the case he had set up was a very peculiar one. Few inquired into the analytical implications of the chapter. Malthus was one of these few who complained that he had not 'considered all the bearings of your concession on the other parts of your work'.[83] Ricardo did not take up this challenge. The reasons for this were most likely not those given by Hollander, Blaug and Pasinetti. Rather, it would simply not have worried Ricardo that the assumptions of the new chapter did not fit his model, for, as I have shown, this was a highly specific tool set up to show the consequences of hindrances to technical change and foreign trade. The difficulty posed by his new discovery was that it tempered only the positive force of his policy proposals on technical change.

Ricardo's faith in the gains from trade, science, and technology was not left completely unassailed. His chapter on machinery was testimony to that. But few historians have drawn attention to his general optimism otherwise. Even the threat of the stationary state was an unreal one. Not only did the stationary state have no bearing on the immediate future, but the tendency of profits to fall in Ricardo's counterfactual model would be constantly checked in the real world by improvements in

---

[81] *Letters 1821–1823*, Ricardo to McCulloch, 7 May 1822, p. 194, one of the MS. lectures sent by McCulloch to Ricardo, 17 April 1822.

[82] Ricardo, *Principles*, p. 397.

[83] *Letters 1821–1823*, Malthus to Ricardo, 16 July 1821, p. 19.

science and technology. 'Man from youth grows to manhood, then decays and dies; but this is not the progress of nations', for they could 'continue for ages, to sustain undiminished their wealth, and their population'.[84]

The historian need no longer contrast the rapid technical change of the Industrial Revolution with the pessimism and gloom of classical economics. Ricardo's model of distribution and accumulation was an analytical tool moulded to clarify the primary importance of technical change and foreign trade. This purpose becomes obvious once we go beyond the confines of Ricardo's analytical model to what he actually said about the processes and impact of technical change. His purpose was misunderstood by most of his contemporary critics and supporters. But Ricardo none the less dominated early nineteenth-century discussion of the machinery question. His critics based their own contributions on an analysis of technology. They began from a criticism of Ricardo's strict model, yet in so far as they had neglected his wider discussion, they often returned in the end to Ricardo.

[84] Ricardo, *Principles*, p. 265.

5

Political economy and the division of labour

Ricardo's novel analysis of the machinery issue provoked not only his critics but his closest followers. The latter were often more interested in the practical implications of the conclusion of his chapter on machinery than they were in the novelty of the theoretical analysis. The chapter on machinery obviously opened deep social concerns among Ricardo's contemporaries. His new ideas rankled, for they sharpened a source of contention already apparent in working-class dissent from industrialisation. Owenism and anti-machinery riots had by now become very real bogies for the optimists of early nineteenth-century industrial capitalism. In the years following Ricardo's death much of the new work in political economy which addressed itself to the future economic prospects of Britain projected a certain polemical tone. It was a polemic incorporated in a purposive inquiry into the universal benefits of industrialisation. Political economists conducted their inquiries into the benefits of industrialisation against the background of both the theoretical heritage of Smith and Ricardo and the practical issues of crisis and depression, Owenite radicalism, and resistance to machinery that flared up in the anti-machinery riots of 1826. It was the response to Ricardo's legacy plus such pressing issues of economic policy which made political economy a discordant though exploratory discipline in the 1820s.

Economists after Ricardo faced many difficulties in coming to terms with his *Principles* which even in his own time was an intellectual tour de force. Not least among these difficulties was the problem of understanding the status of and the relationship between his twin interests in the analysis of the falling rate of profit and the optimistic growth prospects of Western economies. Equally, problems of crises, gluts and machinery were constantly in the air on the level both of practical politics and of general theory. The recovery from the post-Napoleonic depression, the confrontation with Owenite socialism, and the 1826 anti-machinery riots only pinpointed more general phenomena, pressed political economy into local and political life, and redirected and influenced future developments in theory.

This was a period when class connotations were not the clear ones of master versus workman. Radical and reactionary visions were often similar, and 'honourable' masters often joined forces with insurrection-ary artisans. The optimism behind the advance of the Industrial Revolution was not complacent. It was established in struggle against both those who looked to some alternative pattern of development and those who sought control over the directions of technology. The heroic dream of technological inevitability met with a formidable opposition which deployed Malthus and some gentry followers with Sismondi, Owen, the radical weavers, and the small masters. This was, further-more, only the most articulate form of dissent. Technological innova-tion was challenged in everyday struggle in the workplaces of most industries throughout this period. Workers and their trade unions were not ashamed to denounce the type of progress which brought redundancy and few aids to mobility, and which enforced higher labour productivity with inadequate compensation. Such central difficulties of policy and social conflict moulded political economy in the 1820s into a practical science in as important a sense as Ricardo's legacy had stamped it as a theoretical discipline. Both the institutional context of the discipline of political economy and these practical and theoretical issues characterised this period as one of a wealth of dissident literature. This was not, as has often been believed, a period of the unequivocal ascendance of classical or Ricardian economics. Pressing practical problems and a real intellectual struggle with Ricardo's ideas prevented this.

Several of the economists of the period were genuinely involved in the development and diffusion of Ricardo's ideas, in particular McCulloch, Ellis, and James and John Stuart Mill. Ricardo's allies gave great publicity to the significance of the Ricardian achievement. James Mill and J. R. McCulloch both dwelt on the scientific character of Ricardian economics, and attempted to turn political economy into a fixed body of doctrine. McCulloch's *Principles* combined outright plagiarism of his master with an evangelism on the behalf of industry.[1] James Mill's *Elements of Political Economy* presented economics as a dogma – a theory with no qualifications.[2] The early writings of John Stuart Mill in these years were also notably polemical, and he later referred to them as 'mere reproductions'.[3] Another of the Ricardians, William Ellis, was also a man of practical and doctrinal concerns. He was a member of Mill's Utilitarian Society, and, though described as 'an original thinker in the field of political economy',[4] he himself recognised his real interests :

> In those discussions which we used to hold, the difference
> between John Mill and me was brought out very often. He was
> for enquiring into everything, and going to the bottom of
> everybody's theories and ideas; I cared only for the practical
> value of political economy and did not want to think deeply on
> points which could have no bearing on social affairs and human
> conduct.[5]

Ellis expressed these practical concerns in the main pieces he wrote for the *Westminster Review*: 'Charitable Institutions' (1824), 'Exportation of Machinery' (1825) and 'Effect of the Employment of Machinery on the Happiness of the Working Classes' (1826).

These followers of Ricardo were challenged by a series of critics. Dissent, with intent to develop new theories, characterised the work of Robert Torrens on value and technical progress, of Thomas Hopkins on rent, and of a range of anonymous writers on the impact of increases in labour productivity.[6] These critics were complemented by the under-

---

1 McCulloch's earlier and later writings were, however, much more Smithian. See D. P. O'Brien, *J. R. McCulloch*, London, 1970.
2 James Mill, *Selected Economic Writings*, ed. Donald Winch, London, 1966, p. 188.
3 J. S. Mill, *Autobiography*, London, 1873, p. 119.
4 *Ibid.* p. 81. Ellis's role in popular political economy and in the Birkbeck Schools has been recounted by R. Gilmour, 'The Gradgrind School : Political Economy in the Classroom', *Victorian Studies*, xi, December 1967, pp. 213–18.
5 Cited in E. K. Blyth, *Life of William Ellis*, London, 1892, p. 40.
6 Robert Torrens, *An Essay on the Production of Wealth*, London, 1821; Samuel Bailey, *A Critical Dissertation on the Nature, Measures, and Causes of Value*, London, 1825; John Barton, *Observations on the Circumstances which Influence the Condition of the Labouring Classes of Society*, London, 1817; Thomas Hopkins, *On Rent of Land and its Influence on Subsistence and Population*, London, 1828; [Anon.], *An Essay on the Political Economy of Nations*, London, 1821.

consumptionists Thomas Chalmers, T. R. Malthus, and Simon Gray.[7] British economists of the period also paid significant attention to the work of two foreign critics : J. C. L. Simonde de Sismondi and J. B. Say. Sismondi and Malthus were frequent correspondents, and Ricardo, though not impressed with Sismondi's political economy, did hold him in generally high regard.[8] J. B. Say was an honorary member of the Political Economy Club, and was also known for his notes on the French translation of Ricardo. He corresponded frequently with Ricardo and was one of his most consistent critics on value. Say had also worked in England for a time as the manager of an insurance firm, followed by a period as one of Napoleon's industrial informants, reporting on English factories and techniques.[9]

The political economy of the 1820s, in confronting the economic and social issues of rapid industrialisation, took on a form distinct from that of later decades. As far as generalisation is possible, it does seem that certain assumptions and concepts influenced the way in which particular

---

[7] Simon Gray, *The Happiness of States or an Inquiry Concerning Population*, London, 1815, and, under pseud. George Purves, *All Classes Productive of National Wealth*, London, 1817; Thomas Chalmers, *An Enquiry into the Extent and Stability of National Revenue,* Edinburgh, 1808, *On Political Economy in Connexion with the Moral State and Moral Prospects of Society*, Glasgow, 1832, and *The Christian and Civic Economy of our Large Towns*, 3 vols., Glasgow, 1821–6. Chalmers was a prolific writer who saw his life's work as the unification of religious doctrine and laissez faire economic theory. See R. M. Young, 'Malthus and the Evolutionists', *Past and Present*, no. 43, May 1969, pp. 120–1.

[8] J. C. L. Simonde de Sismondi, *De La Richesse Commerciale*, Geneva, 1803, and *Nouveaux Principes d'Economie Politique*, 2nd edn, Paris 1827. Ricardo's opinions on Sismondi can be found in letters to McCulloch, 7 April 1819, *Letters 1819–1821*, p. 22; to Mill, 6 September 1819, *ibid*. p. 57; to Mill, 17 September 1822, *Letters 1821–1823*, p. 218; to Trower, 14 December 1822, *ibid*. p. 244.

[9] Say sent questions to the Political Economy Club as noted in *Political Economy Club, Centenary Volume*, vi, London, 1921, pp. 11, 16. Ricardo was unimpressed similarly both with Say's *Notes* on Ricardo's own *Principles, Des Principes de l'Economie Politique et de l'Impôt, par M. David Ricardo, avec Notes par M. Jean Baptiste Say*, 2 vols., Paris, 1819 and with Say's 'Letters to Mr. Malthus on Various Subjects of Political Economy Particularly on the Causes of the General Stagnation of Commerce, *The Pamphleteer*, vol. xii, No. 34, London, 1821. See Ricardo to Mill, 28 December 1818, *Works*, vii, 378; Ricardo to Mill, 9 October 1820, *Letters 1819–1821*, p. 276. At any rate the idea of the *Notes* prompted his own *Notes on Malthus*. See P. Sraffa, 'Introduction', *Notes on Malthus*. Say's business life is detailed by G. Koolman, 'Say's Conception of the Role of the Entrepreneur', *Economica*, xxxviii, August 1971.

problems such as the machinery issue were discussed. Investigation of ideas on technology among the political economists of the 1820s seems to indicate a frame of reference dominated by the division of labour. But economists of the time were also coming to give greater consideration to the predominance of the machine and the form taken on by capital.

These followers and critics of Ricardo, however great may have been their differences on theories of value, economic fluctuations and distribution,[10] maintained an underlying consensus on the role of labour and its technical attributes. This interest formed the background for debate on productive and unproductive labour, and on the determinants and effects of population growth. Most economists of the 1820s subscribed to the broad categories of productive labour described in Patrick Colquhoun's *Wealth, Power and Resources of the British Empire* (1814). Colquhoun described as productive all labourers in trade, manufacturing and agriculture who in some way added to wealth. Unproductive labourers added to the value of nothing, though many of them might be useful.[11] Economists assumed that growth was generated by shifting resources from unproductive to productive sectors. Growth was founded not just on the optimal allocation of capital, however, but on the level of productivity within the 'productive' sectors. It was here that economists concentrated their interests in the technical attributes of labour. They argued that higher productivity was related to the incentives of high wages and the intensification of labour. The pace, discipline and skill with which work was done were the keys to higher productivity and a nationally superior technology. The evidence for these ideas grew out of the sensitive work done by several political economists of the time on the determination of wages and labour supply, in other words, the population question.

The following section of this chapter will set out the manner in which labour, the division of labour, and wages and population were discussed

10 For discussion of differing theories of value and distribution in the 1820s and 1830s see N. B. de Marchi, 'The Success of Mill's Principles', *History of Political Economy*, VI, 1974; and Samuel Hollander, 'The Reception of Ricardian Economics', *Oxford Economic Papers*, XXIX, July 1977, No. 2.

11 P. Colquhoun, *A Treatise on the Wealth, Power, and Resources of the British Empire*, London, 1814. The broadening of the categories had indeed been attempted before by both James Mill, in *Commerce Defended* and Robert Torrens, *The Economists Refuted,* in their critiques of Spence's physiocratic views that agriculture was the only productive enterprise.

Over-population. Source : (The Comic Almanack for 1851),
*Cruikshank Reflections; The Past and Present in Merry Tales and
Humorous Verse Illustrated by George Cruikshank*, London,
1912.

in order to set out the theoretical framework into which the analysis of machinery was integrated. The final two sections of the chapter will then analyse the role given to industry, machinery and economic crises in a set of theories in which the division of labour was chosen as the primary dynamic factor of industrialisation.

Wages and population
The attention given to the role of labour and the possibilities of increasing productivity through the better organisation and intensification of work, and through the incentives of higher wages, made it natural for economists to dissent from the Malthusian population doctrine. There was a wave of revulsion against the doctrine, not only among radical and tory romantic critics, but among established political economists. Malthus's own adamant defence of his doctrine was probably reinforced by his fears of the urban horde : 'Late events must make us contemplate with no small alarm a great increase in the *proportion* of our manufacturing population, both with reference to the happiness, and to the liberty of our country.'[12]

But although such fears were certainly widespread, they were not considered acceptable as reasons for a blind faith in Malthusianism. Writers of the period showed more interest in the actual material constitution of labour as distinct from its purely abstract conception as a perfectly mobile factor of production. Thus Sismondi, a constant critic of 'crude Malthusian tendencies', hailed the empirical work of John Barton on population movements. Barton's close statistical work showed that there was no clear evidence that wage rates had any direct influence on birth and death rates or labour supply. Those who refused to promote higher wages on the grounds of fears of population increase and excess labour supplies argued on false premises. For, as Barton had argued, the motivation of the labourer was determined by 'custom' rather than by abstract reasoning about quantitative estimates of wage movements. If any factor was important to the timing of marriage aside from custom, it was not wage levels but employment prospects. Barton, moreover, accounted for the recent rise in population, not by factors influencing the birth rate, but by reductions in the death rate brought about by the completely exogenous factor of better health and medicine. The idea that lower death rates and not higher birth rates were at the basis of the contemporary population boom complemented Barton's views on the supply of labour. For he had shattered the accepted identity

12 Malthus, *Principles*, p. 205.

between population and labour supply. He made the obvious point, but one that needed to be made in criticism of Malthus, that an increase in the birth rate did not automatically mean an increase in labour supply. An increase in wages would have no immediate impact on labour supply because the creation of an adult labourer was a long-term process. Between an increase in population and an increase in the active labour force lay long years of maturing, socialising, skill acquirement, and apprenticeship.[13]

Several main-line theorists such as Ricardo, Torrens and Senior were already sensitive to the role of custom and the social determinants of subsistence levels.[14] Soon even McCulloch, after reading Barton, was moved to reject Malthusianism, and went so far as to argue that population pressure was necessary to growth.[15]

Though Malthus believed there would be a tendency to low real wages because of population growth, his attitudes to policies for low wages were, however, quite different. Both Ricardo and Malthus, along with most contemporary writers on political economy, condemned the cry of manufacturers and merchants for low wages.[16] Most agreed that high wages were conducive to high productivity. McCulloch in his earlier writing, before he had come to accept Barton's criticisms, depicted very well the character of this dual belief in high wages and in the Malthusian population theory:

> No country can flourish, if the *necessary* rate of wages be low;
> nor can it long be depressed, if the rate of wages be high.
> Labourers are the sinews of agriculture, of manufactures, of
> commerce; it is by their labour that our machines are
> constructed and set in motion; it is by their ingenuity, frugality,
> and perseverance, that we have become what we are . . . so
> long as the standard of REAL WAGES is high, and it is in
> their power to keep it so, so long will the social fabric be stable.

[13] Barton, *Observations*, pp. 41–3. Also see his *An Inquiry into the Causes of the Progressive Depreciation of Agricultural Labour in Modern Times*, London, 1820, pp. 22–9.

[14] See Ricardo, *Principles*, chap. v, 'On Wages'; Robert Torrens, *An Essay on the External Corn Trade*, London, 1815, p. 62. Senior drew attention to the connection between the progress of wealth and the consumption patterns of workers. As workers came to consume more manufactured goods, the cost of employing them fell. See [N. Senior], 'Report on the State of Agriculture', *Quarterly Review*, xxv, July, 1821, pp. 469–70.

[15] O'Brien, *J. R. McCulloch*, p. 318.

[16] Malthus, *Principles*, p. 220. Also see Ricardo's note on this page.

But if the standard of REAL WAGES be permanently reduced, and it must be their own fault if it be reduced, if by an improvident increase of their number they be once brought to place their dependence on . . . the mere necessaries of life, . . . The spirit of industry by which they are so eminently distinguished will be destroyed, and with it the morals, the prosperity and the tranquillity of Britain.[17]

The apparently religious enthusiasm for high wages, and the crucial role of labour depicted in the first part of this passage, were typical of the style of mystical exultation of the role of labour in growth and technological transformation : 'The world is the theatre of labour, and labour is the origin of wealth, and the most certain and salutary preventive of poverty, wretchedness and disaffection.'[18] High wages could produce a capital-intensive bias, or, as McCulloch put it, a country with high wages and low profits would produce machine-made goods much cheaper.[19] Such an analysis was indeed topical. It 'sets the impolicy of the restrictions on the exportation of machinery used in cotton-mills in a very striking point of view'.[20]

The productivity of labour was increased by technical skill, 'the useful arts', 'the faculty of labour'.[21] Indeed, wage levels reflected skill requirements. Theorists made the connection between the dilution of skill and the new employment possibilities for women and children. One of these, Thomas Hopkins, devised a scale of wage differentials ranging from weaver to machine maker. Wages in weaving were low because of a widening labour market. The trade demanded little skill as apprenticeship regulations broke down, and it offered remunerative employment

[17] [F. Place], *Notes of Mr. McCulloch's Lecture on the Wages of Labour and the Condition of the Labouring People*, London, 1825, p. 15.

[18] See W. R. A. Pettman, *An Essay on Political Economy*, Part I, London, 1828, p. 72. For similar views see *An Essay on the Political Economy of Nations*, p. 30. Pettman was a captain in the British Navy in the 1820s; see R. D. C. Black, 'Parson Malthus, the General and the Captain', *Economic Journal*, LXXVII, March 1967, for discussion of some of his underconsumptionist views.

[19] [J. R. McCulloch], 'On the Rise, Progress, Present State and Prospects of the British Cotton Manufacture', *Edinburgh Review*, XLVI, June 1827, pp. 30–1. A similar point was made by the anonymous author of *A Few Observations on Some Topics of Political Economy*, London, 1825.

[20] J. R. McCulloch, *Principles of Political Economy*, London, 1825, p. 323. See below chapter 9 on the export of machinery.

[21] These are the words of the anonymous author of *An Essay on the Political Economy of Nations*, p. 35.

to women and children. Highest wages went to the fully-qualified machine maker, because the trade restricted its labour market by offering little for the labour of learners during the long years of apprenticeship. Few could afford to put their children in such occupations with only the expectation of eventual high returns.[22]

The division of labour

Associated with this search for the sources of higher labour productivity went an interest in wider aspects of the division of labour. Smith provided the point of reference. Torrens, first in *The Economists Refuted* and again in his later work, reminded his readers of the dialectic worked out by Smith between technique and market. The '*expectation* of exchanging gives rise to the division of labour'.[23] McCulloch expressed the same ideas in term of the 'facility of exchange' which acted as the 'vivifying principle of industry'. 'Like the different parts of a well constructed machine, the inhabitants of a civilized country are all mutually dependent on and connected with each other.'[24] Free trade was a source of invention. It extended business, and it would 'diffuse a greater, a more extensive, a more emulous, and a more successful spirit of active industry'.[25]

Again, Smith's remarkable theories of the relationship between town and country in Book III of the *Wealth of Nations* found their way into Torrens's theories of inter-dependent growth in agriculture and industry.[26] The novel feature which Torrens did add was a distinction between the mechanical and the territorial divisions of labour. To the original mechanical division corresponded a vast regional and global differentiation. The real measure of the gains from trade was the degree to which territorial specialisation increased productivity.

McCulloch's national perspectives complemented Torrens's international ones, for he believed that Britain's future lay with the division of labour, the invention of machinery and the development of manufacturing industry. Agriculture and industry might complement each

22 Thomas Hopkins, *Economical Enquiries Relative to the Laws which Regulate Rent, Profit, Wages and the Value of Money*, London, 1822, pp. 58–60.
23 Torrens, *The Economists Refuted*, p. 17.
24 McCulloch, *Principles*, p. 90.
25 Pettman, *An Essay on Political Economy*, Part I, p. 71.
26 Torrens, *An Essay on the External Corn Trade*, 3rd edition, London, 1826, pp. 44, 45.

other in the international sphere, but in the national context he believed it was only industrial progress which mattered. He dismissed all compromises between industry and agriculture, and freely expressed how much he detested the domestic system of industry: 'I consider the combination of manufacturing and agricultural pursuits, to be proof of the barbarism of every country in which it exists; and so far from its being advantageous to the country, I think it decidedly the reverse.'[27] He was completely derisive of schemes to introduce a 'cottage economy'. The great cause of the improvement of society was the division of labour and this could not be properly introduced in such systems because few surplus goods were produced for exchange. In such systems it would be impossible to 'realize capital'.[28] McCulloch looked to the machine-making sector as well as the manufacturing sector as fundamental, even to the development of agriculture. He emphasised the labour of the ploughwright, millwright, smith, and other artisans preparing the tools of the farmer as manufacturing labour which was crucial to agriculture.[29] The indefinite extension and improvement of machinery were the companions of the continued and indefinite improvement of the skill and industry of labour.[30]

Despite the great enthusiasm of theorists in this period for the Mechanics Institutes, McCulloch was one of the few who explicitly connected education with his theory of invention. He proposed that there be a cordial reception for foreigners who brought technical improvements or skills with them,[31] and he saw the acquisition of talent and skill as an actual capital investment. The entire success of the cotton industry was to be attributed to the discoveries and inventions of Hargreaves, Arkwright and Watt. McCulloch, however, added another meaning to skill, and defined it as Smith had, as 'expertness in manipulation and in the details of various processes [which] can only be attained by slow degrees'. Skill was also defined, however, as 'industrious habits'.[32] This very significant addition to its meaning, as the latter part of this book will demonstrate, also pervaded the

27 Quoted in O'Brien, *J. R. McCulloch*, p. 283.
28 [J. R. McCulloch], 'On Cottage and Agrarian Systems', *The Scotsman*, 1 March 1817, p. 41.
29 McCulloch, *Principles*, p. 147.
30 [J. R. McCulloch], 'Effects of Machinery and Accumulation', *Edinburgh Review*, xxxv, March 1821, p. 104.
31 See O'Brien, *J. R. McCulloch*, p. 280.
32 J. R. McCulloch, 'Cotton', *Dictionary of Commerce and Commercial Navigation*, London, 1832, p. 419.

Mechanics Institutes Movement, for which McCulloch had great hopes.[33]

Political economists drew immediate practical conclusions from their ideas on the role of labour. Their assessments of the prospects of the agricultural and manufacturing sectors were grounded on the optimistic implications they drew from the division of labour.

Land and agricultural improvement

Britain's economic transformation did not raise questions simply about industry and the towns. It created great concern over the prospects of agriculture and the future of rural society. The landed classes sought to protect themselves and to maintain a place for the country against the encroachment of the city and the industrial middle class. They did this by creating artificial barriers to the untrammelled aggrandisement of industry – the Corn Laws – and Ricardo's persistent attack on these laws led many to identify in his theories negative attitudes to the land. In their attempts to discredit these theories, most of them, as I have shown, simply misunderstood the logical framework of Ricardo's theory of diminishing returns, and adopted an extreme interpretation of his attitude to landlords.

Malthus and Chalmers may have had a gloomy vision of the tendency to overpopulation and the general glut, but it was they, significantly, who gave the greatest coverage to technical progress in agriculture. Chalmers argued that agricultural labour became more efficient with the intervention of tools of husbandry. It was 'not a matter of hunger and necessity enforcing the cultivation of new regions, but of the triumph of new energies and acquisitions seeking to subdue new territory and get equal subsistence from it'.[34] Malthus believed that rising rents required agricultural improvement, and conversely that improvements would bring advantages to landlords on the renewal of leases. 'To the honour of the Scotch cultivators it should be observed, that they have applied their capitals so very skillfully and economically, that at the

---

[33] McCulloch, *Principles*, pp. 117, 118. Cf. Torrens, *An Essay on the External Corn Trade*, 3rd edition, p. 201, who described skill as a form of 'moral capital'. See a similar argument in *An Essay on the Political Economy of Nations*: if a 'considerable industry' was 'superseded', the 'faculty of labour remains to the workpeople, but their skill is eclipsed', p. 133.

[34] Chalmers, *On Political Economy*, p. 7. Though written in 1832, this text brought together Chalmers's views of the 1820s on political economy.

same time that they have prodigiously increased the produce, they have increased the landlord's proportion of it.'[35] Malthus also impressed Ricardo with a perceptive comparison between the land and machinery. He clearly distinguished the mechanisms of technical progress in agriculture from those of industry : 'The great inequality in the powers of the machinery employed in producing raw produce, forms one of the most remarkable features which distinguishes the machinery of the land from the machinery employed in manufactures . . . Every extensive country may thus be considered as possessing a gradation of machines for the production of corn and raw materials.'[36]

Malthus and Chalmers defended the prospect of a protected agriculture. Torrens did not. His optimism was based on the prospects of agriculture in an open economy. Throughout the whole period he defended the most forward-looking ideas on agricultural change. In the second edition of his *Essay on the External Corn Trade*, he conceded that agricultural protection would increase rents, but only temporarily. Any cutback on profits caused by rising food prices would lead to the export of capital and therefore limit expansion of the manufacturing sector. This would stop local accumulation and progress, and would ultimately have adverse repercussions on landowning interests. Torrens also made the very 'adventurous' proposal that the import of foreign corn, by making marginal corn production unprofitable, would raise the profitability of producing luxury food products. Thus free trade and economic progress could not but raise the landlord's income.[37]

At a surprisingly early period, Torrens also introduced the conception of high farming. In disputing with Owen he argued :

> If our improved machinery did not tend to reduce the expense
> of producing manufactured goods, we could neither sell our
> fabrics in the foreign market, nor keep our inferior lands under
> cultivation . . . A reduction in the value of manufactured goods,
> which allows lands of an inferior quality to be taken in, also

35 Malthus, *Principles*, p. 159. Malthus's authority here was John Sinclair's *An Account of the Systems of Husbandry Adopted in the More Improved Districts of Scotland*, 3rd edition in 2 vols., Edinburgh, 1814.

36 Malthus, *Principles*, p. 168. See Ricardo's note on this, p. 169. Hopkins, too, made use of the analogy to argue the development towards peak productivity on a piece of land, and diminishing returns after that point. See Hopkins, *Economical Enquiries*, pp. 31–3.

37 See Lionel Robbins, *Robert Torrens, and the Evolution of Classical Economics*, London, 1958, p. 46.

admits of the additional application of capital to our better
soil, and promotes that *system of high farming* for which
England is so conspicuous. Were it not for the application of
that scientific power and improved machinery, to which Mr.
Owen erroneously attributes our distress, the whole of our
foreign trade would be annihilated, and our tillage reduced one
half.[38] [my italics]

A few years later, Torrens spoke of high farming as synonymous with
heavy capital investment in the soil. If such farming was undertaken,
the cultivator had to be left with a reasonable return, so that during the
period of such investment the landlord would have to be satisfied with
lower rents.[39] Torrens also went as far as identifying farm size as a
possible source of technical innovation. Larger farms allowed for the
use of better agricultural machinery, such as threshing machines, and
for a larger marketed surplus, and could therefore pay a proportionately
higher rent. Landlords would be prompted to let their whole estate to
fewer farmers, which meant smaller farmers would sink to being
agricultural labourers : 'the employment of more efficacious machinery,
and the more economical application of labour, which are found ad-
missable into large concerns, and which enable the great farmer to tempt
the proprietor with the offer of a higher rent, would also enable him,
. . . to raise a greater produce than before.' Small farmers, though
reduced to farm labourers, would probably gain a greater subsistence
than previously.[40]

This fascination with the potentiality of technical progress in agriculture did not, however, convince the theorist who was later to become
the most influential. John Stuart Mill continued to believe, as an
empirical fact, that agricultural improvements could have no permanent
impact :

The improvements which have been introduced into agriculture
are so extremely limited, when compared with those of which
some branches of manufactures have been found susceptible;
and they are, besides, so very slow in making their way against
those old habits and prejudices, which are perhaps more deeply
rooted among the farmers than among any other class of

---

[38] [Robert Torrens], 'Mr. Owen's Plans for Relieving the National Distress',
  Edinburgh Review, XXXII, October 1819, p. 469.
[39] Torrens, *An Essay on the Production of Wealth*, p. 116.
[40] *Ibid.* p. 140.

producers, that the progress of population seems in most
instances to have kept pace with the improvement of cultivation
... It has not, hitherto, indeed been at any time the effect of
an improvement to drive capital from the land, nor consequently
to lower rent.[41]

Industry, entrepreneurs, and science

If agriculture was believed by most political economists to respond so
readily to technological innovation, the prospects for industry seemed
even more inspiring. Political economists chose from the industrial
sector their endless examples of the extension of the division of labour,
the origins of capital and machinery, and the contribution of entrepreneurial skill and scientific knowledge. Skill and the division of
labour were widely celebrated as causes of industrial growth, but so
also were capital accumulation and the introduction of machinery. A
novel perception making its first appearance in writing on the industrial
sector was an idea of the importance of capital and machinery. Political
economists wondered at the possible connections between capital
accumulation, the progress of civilisation, and the division of labour. It
was argued that industrial growth brought greater security, and created
the stable foundations for the emergence of a capital market.[42] It was
widely assumed, though only occasionally made explicit, that private
property, especially in human industry and capital, was sacred to the
creation of wealth.[43]

When political economists such as Say or McCulloch referred to
capital formation, they included the development of labour productivity.
They regarded education and other institutions for the training and
socialisation of labour as aspects of capital formation. The sums spent
on rearing a worker were consumed in a reproductive way, and education yielded an interest payment independent of the ordinary profits of

---

[41] J. S. Mill, 'The Nature, Origin, and Progress of Rent' (1828), *Essay
on Economics and Society, Collected Works*, iv, Toronto, 1967, p. 177.

[42] J. B. Say, *A Treatise on Political Economy*, trans. of 4th edition by
C. R. Prinsep, London, 1821, vol. i, pp. 128–9. Few theorists in this
period distinguished decisions to save from decisions to invest. One who
did, William Ellis, rejected the fixed fund analysis of many classical
economists and argued that fresh savings were induced by the
expectation of greater profits. See [Willam Ellis], 'Effects of the
Employment of Machinery upon the Happiness of the Working Classes',
Westminster Review, v, January 1826, p. 116.

[43] Say, *A Treatise*, vol. ii, 22, cf. T. Hopkins, *Economical Enquiries*, p. 67.

industry.[44] Though great attention was given to such factors which tended to increase the productivity of labour, it was also recognised that capital formation included the introduction of machinery. The introduction of machinery into industry seemed to constitute a sharp break from the general division of labour. McCulloch in fact chastised Smith for giving all his attention to the division of labour and neglecting the breakthrough constituted by machinery.[45] Mechanisation was not simply another stage of or implication of the division of labour, for there were many structural limitations on any easy transition from the latter to the former. Mechanisation, he argued, had to meet with the limitations imposed by high capital investment requirements, by immobile labour, and by patents or other forms of restriction.[46] It was, therefore, seldom sudden, particularly because entrepreneurs were themselves slow to move from industries where they had gained their habits, experience and talent.[47]

The manufacturing sector was endowed, it was argued, with special attributes for the extension of capital and machinery. Torrens argued that the existence of manufacturing capital could be traced back to the very earliest of times. He did not believe that the existence of manufacturing was based on surpluses generated in agriculture, as in the pattern of the stages theory of economic development popular in eighteenth-century social analysis. This theory, simply put, concluded that economic development ought to occur via an advance from hunting and gathering stages to an agricultural stage, and thence from agriculture to manufacturing and commerce. Torrens, disregarding such an idea, claimed that manufacturing industry actually succeeded the phase of appropriative industry (or hunting and gathering). The power of manufacturing would be unlimited so long as capital continued to accumulate and population to increase.[48] The employment of machinery, if only in manufacturing industry, would also have great repercussions on the agricultural sector by lowering the costs of the farmer's outlays on industrial goods. Torrens's farseeing technological imagination was also manifest in his later work where he envisaged steam replacing horses on 'all the great lines of traffic', and thought it

[44] Say, *A Treatise*, vol. II, 102–6, 92. McCulloch, *Principles*, pp. 112–19.
[45] J. R. McCulloch, 'On the Effects of the Employment of Machinery in Manufacturing', *The Scotsman*, 19 April 1817, p. 99.
[46] J. R. McCulloch, 'On Cottage and Agrarian Systems', *The Scotsman*, 1 March 1817, p. 41.
[47] Say, *Des Principes de l'Economie Politique*, vol. I, p. 269, vol. II, p. 3.
[48] Torrens, *An Essay on the Production of Wealth*, p. 90.

not improbable that 'plough and harrow would be moved by steam as well as carriage and wagon'.[49]

This perception of technological advance within and from the industrial sector was embellished by the attention given by political economists to entrepreneurial skill and scientific knowledge. There was actually little overt discussion among British political economists of the 'labour' or skill of the capitalist. It was, rather, the French theorist J. B. Say who claimed the entrepreneur as his own concept. Say defined the entrepreneur as someone who was master of all that was known in a particular branch of industry, and who had collected the requisite capital and labourers. And he attributed commercial success in Great Britain to the 'wonderful practical skill of her adventurers' in the application of knowledge.[50]

Prinsep, the translator of Say's *Traité*, in fact found it difficult to translate the word entrepreneur. He decided on the word 'adventurer' to describe the person who took on himself the immediate responsibility, risk and conduct of a concern.[51] Say argued that the technical skill necessary to the entrepreneur could only be gained in the practical pursuit of the occupation concerned. In most industries there was a need for repeated experiment attended by more or less risk. This risk had to be borne by the entrepreneur.[52] He justified entrepreneurial income as a return for the moral qualities required, for the necessity of ensuring an enterprise had capital, and for undertaking the risks and hazards associated with enterprise. The entrepreneur was, therefore, drawing in three incomes: a wage payment, interest on capital, and a premium for risk.[53] Say criticised Smith for neglecting the difference between gains of superintendence and the return on capital. The profits of the labour of superintendence were dependent on skill, activity and judgement, while those on capital were dependent on scarcity of capital and security of investments. Since the manager of a firm rarely borrowed all his capital, he was entitled to one portion of his revenue as manager and to another as capitalist.[54] Most of the English writers took the entrepreneurial function for granted as an initial condition for the accumulation of fixed and circulating capital. A few commented on the

49 Robert Torrens, *On Wages and Combinations*, London, 1834, p. 43.
50 Koolman, 'Say's Conception of the Role of the Entrepreneur', p. 272.
51 Say, *A Treatise*, vol. I, 41.
52 *Ibid.* pp. 55–6.
53 Koolman, 'Say's Conception of the Role of the Entrepreneur', pp. 277, 278.
54 Say, *A Treatise*, vol. II, pp. 102–6.

role of 'supervision' and were only keen on patent regulations to ensure that sufficient time and energy be devoted to the discovery of new techniques.[55]

Say's attention to the entrepreneur probably also influenced his singular interest in the practical uses of scientific advance. Though English economists showed interest in the inducements to invention, and recommended patent regulation to promote advances in technology, none of them showed any interest in advances in scientific knowledge. Say had enlightened ideas of the direct and indirect influences of science. He perceived the direct impact of the utility of many sciences which, until recently, had only been seen as 'objects of curiosity and speculation'. What most impressed him, however, was the powerful indirect influence of science. Science dispelled prejudice. It taught man to rely on his own exertions rather than on supernatural powers. 'Ignorance' was the 'inseparable concomitant of practical habits' and of 'that slavery of custom'.[56] If workmen understood the nature of the things they worked with, they would be more productive. Furthermore, science could 'increase social happiness' by acting as an antidote to alienation.[57]

This is not to suggest, however, that Say regarded science as the key to industrial advance. Scientific knowledge was indispensable, but it was not a major bottleneck. Men of science were interested in the diffusion of their ideas, so that scientific knowledge circulated rapidly and the nation without scientists need be at no disadvantage. Say identified the crucial bottlenecks as the 'application of knowledge' and the 'skill of execution'. These attributes were extremely difficult to transmit to others.[58]

Say, however, kept his analysis of the role of entrepreneurship and science within the confines of the division of labour, for he associated both with the social division of labour. Sismondi, his contemporary, made the connection explicit by arguing that the specialisation gave rise to a group in society that abandoned manual labour to study the means of controlling the forces of nature.[59] Say gave practical effect to such ideas by suggesting the employment of surpluses via government expenditure on the promotion of science. Science could only be applied to practical purposes if it was discovered and preserved by the theorist.

[55] For instance, [Ellis], 'Employment of Machinery', p. 126.
[56] Say, *A Treatise*, vol. I, p. 49.
[57] *Ibid.* vol. II, pp. 311–14.
[58] *Ibid.* and vol. I, p. 53.
[59] Simonde de Sismondi, *Nouveaux Principes,* 2nd edition, vol. I, p. 87.

Thus, the government should find some means of paying theoretical scientists : 'A government that knows and practises its duties and has large resources at its disposal should not abandon to individuals the whole glory and merit of invention.'[60] Government support for scientific research was not to be deducted from national capital, but from national revenue. If the burden was paid by all, then all would benefit.[61] Further, government support by honours and rewards to 'artists' and mechanics was also to be encouraged : 'They excite emulation and enlarge the general stock of knowledge without diverting industry and capital from its own most profitable channels.'[62] Finally, Say argued that another form of encouragement, patents, acted as a premium from the government chargeable on the consumers of the new article. They were harmless, since they offered no interference with other branches of industry.[63]

The great enthusiasm for the extension of science, capital and machinery felt by many of the economists of the time even found its way into political thought. The growth of capital was the fulfilment of the public interest.[64] The rise of the middle classes derived from the expansion of fixed capital. As W. A. MacKinnon put it, the middle class was created on the basis of the social mobility brought about by the extension of machinery :

> in all establishments where machinery is used, a great expansion takes place amongst the leading men of every branch of the department, amongst the engine makers, etc., men who by their industry, knowledge and attention to business have attained such situations; or by others who, from their probity, good conduct and fair dealing, have the loan of some capital, which enables them in time, to create some for themselves. All these descriptions of persons originating in the lower class, rise by degrees into the middle.[65]

---

60 Say, *A Treatise*, vol. I, pp. 57–8.
61 *Ibid.* p. 58.
62 *Ibid.* p. 252.
63 *Ibid.* pp. 268–70.
64 *An Inquiry into those Principles Respecting the Nature of Demand and the Necessity of Consumption Lately Advocated by Mr. Malthus,* London, 1821, p. 28. This pamphlet was sent to Ricardo by Tooke. Ricardo to Malthus, 21 July 1821, ed. Sraffa, *Works,* IX, pp. 26–7.
65 W. A. MacKinnon, M.P., *On the Rise, Progress and Present state of Public Opinion in Great Britain,* London, 1828, p. 161.

The social division of labour also accounted for the distinctive positions of capitalist and worker, for these were related to the emergence of particular divisions of income. Sismondi distinguished the revenue of capitalists from fixed and circulating capital. It was only the capitalist who possessed consumer goods, primary materials, and machinery. He put these out to work for him and as compensation received the greater part of the fruits of labour – the profits of capital. The poor had only their labour and were dependent on a superior class to make that labour effective.[66] This social division of labour was further reinforced, argued Say, by the technical one. The worker's incapacity for anything but one occupation rendered him less powerful to enforce his right to an equitable portion of the gross value of production.

> The workman, that carries about with him the whole imple-
> ments of his trade, can change his locality at pleasure, and even
> his subsistence wherever he pleases : in the other case he is a
> mere adjective, without individual capacity, independence or
> substantive importance, when separated from his fellow
> labourers; and obliged to accept whatever terms his employer
> thinks fit to impose.[67]

Smith's analysis of the division of labour was in effect revitalised during these years and extended to its limits in the consideration of machinery.

Though the framework of analysis adopted by political economists in the 1820s centred on the division of labour, the way the concept was used thus underwent many changes. A recognition of the significance of labour to the new industrial processes, as well as a perception of the characteristics of the many varieties and levels of skill, gave political economists a critical approach to theories of wages and population. Debate over the future of the agricultural sector also generated new theories of agricultural improvement. But in turning to the analysis of industry it was also apparent that political economists had come to use the concept of the division of labour in a sense increasingly associated with labour discipline, industrial concentration, and the subordination of the labourer to the subjective framework of the entrepreneur and the capitalist. This orientation became even clearer when political economists were presented with practical problems of economic crisis and technological unemployment.

---

[66] Simonde de Sismondi, *Nouveaux Principes*, vol. I, p. 87.
[67] Say, *A Treatise*, vol. I, p. 88.

Crisis, machinery and politics

The theoretical interests economists of the period had in analysing and explaining industrialisation were compounded by practical concerns. Economists in the decade of the 1820s were capable of showing great interest in the processes of scientific and technical change, and indeed great enthusiasm for it. However, this was not a blind optimism, for the outcome of all the great advances in technology over the period extending back to the late eighteenth century was still too uncertain to predict. Alongside the hopefulness for economic growth, there was an atmosphere of ambivalence in many economic tracts of the period, and even some attempts to look critically at the costs and benefits of the industrialising process. The age of mid-Victorian self-satisfaction was yet to come. Major areas where some estimate of gains and losses became an issue were the fears of overproduction, gluts and underconsumption left by the post-Napoleonic depression, the challenge of Owenite and other radical alternative production arrangements, and the confrontation between the advocates of machinery and labour.

In many ways the debate on public works and other social schemes was part of the wider debate on the crisis. Most politicians recognised the existence of an economic depression from 1816 to the mid 1820s, but they differed on policy proposals to bring the crisis to an end. Boyd Hilton has recently defined a bold demarcation between Tory and Whig policies as a contrast between passive and active philosophies. Tory policies could be justified by Ricardian theories which condoned inaction, and Whig policies were backed by Malthusian underconsumptionist demands for radical intervention.[68] Those hoping for novel policies to revive the economy felt great frustration with the current policy or rather 'non-policy' of allowing the crisis to work its own way out. As one malcontent put it :

> Nothing can be more annoying than the levity with which
> some persons . . . treat the present state of the country, fancying
> that its distress will correct the mischief, and that things will
> find their proper level. Perhaps some of these wise people might
> as well talk of the advantage of re-organizing by returning to
> a state of nature. But we are in a very artificial state.[69]

[68] See A. J. B. Hilton, *Corn, Cash, Commerce; The Economic Policies of the Tory Governments 1815–1830*, Oxford, 1977, chap. 3 'Depression and Discontent'.

[69] Sheffield to Sidmouth, 19 January 1816, Sidmouth Mss. 152 M. (1816 C–M), cited in Hilton, *Corn, Cash, Commerce*, p. 69.

The machinery question added to the complexities of the debate on the crisis. A letter from Lord Kenyon to Liverpool in December 1819 highlights the predicament. Kenyon accepted that there should be no government interference. He acknowledged, however, that such non-intervention would not mitigate the crisis, since he believed that there was little prospect of any return to affluence. This was because rising rates of mechanisation had 'rendered the present crisis much more serious and less self correcting than previous depressions'. 'I should concur with you in thinking that any interference on the part of Government was altogether undesirable (except in a trifling degree on acct. of local distress) but I much fear we cannot hope for any return of such sort of prosperity on account of the extensive use of machinery and the contemplated increased use of it.'[70]

The promotion of employment schemes did, however, continue throughout this period. But now it was increasingly identified with underconsumptionist economics. Malthus's interest in public works derived from his underconsumptionist ideas. Thus he argued that any transfer of funds from productive to unproductive expenditure increased the level of effective demand and the profit rate.[71] Malthus's under-consumptionist fears were refuelled by the prospect of machinery leading to general overproduction. Such fears rested on his assumption that a leisured unproductive class was necessary to soak up the surplus. For he believed that neither capitalists nor workers had very expansive consumption patterns.[72] In contrast, Sismondi, who also believed that the widespread use of machinery would lead to overproduction, explained this by the unequal distribution of income. He believed that the working classes had a very high elasticity of demand, and a shift in the distribution of income from the rich to the poor would open an infinitely extendible market. Hence there would be no need to worry about the prospects of a general glut.[73]

The underconsumptionist idea also informed much of the basis of Robert Owen's schemes. Owenite utopian schemes found their roots in

[70] Kenyon to Liverpool, 20 December 1819, Liverpool Papers 38281ff. 363–6 cited in Hilton, *Corn, Cash, Commerce*, p. 75.

[71] S. Hollander, 'Malthus and the Post Napoleonic Depression', *History of Political Economy*, 1, Fall 1969, p. 332.

[72] Malthus, *Principles*, pp. 120–3, 312–13.

[73] Simonde de Sismondi, *Nouveaux Principes*, vol. 1, pp. 120–3, 327 and 352–3. Note that Ricardo, too, had pointed out that there was no reason why labourers should not take over the consumption of conveniences and luxuries. *Notes on Malthus*, pp. 312–13.

the disputes over gluts and crises, in the schemes for the employment of the poor, and in the public works projects which had been in great vogue in the period just prior to the 1820s.[74] The government, in 1817, had granted funds for public works schemes, and in fact Owen had been put on the committee of the Association for the Relief of the Manufacturing Poor in the same year. His plans were very much in the tradition of the comprehensive blueprints drawn up to solve a whole range of social evils, and usually involved varying themes on resettlement and cottage industry for the poor.[75] However, by the time of Liverpool's ministry and the adoption by the government of its economic policy of inaction, schemes such as Owen's were no longer regarded seriously by those in power. Liverpool claimed that short-term aid to workers in redundant occupations would only impede beneficial redeployment.

Owen was not perturbed by such dismissive attitudes on the part of the state, and like Malthus continued to develop his own approach to economics, an approach which absorbed underconsumptionist assumptions but gave these a radical twist. He argued, for instance, that it was the lack of a profitable market that alone checked the beneficial industry of the working classes.[76] Owen's underconsumptionist economics justified his negative attitudes to industrialisation. But he argued that the consequent social dislocations could be prevented by positive action in favour of education and new forms of social organisation. Owen relates carrying on extensive discussions with political economists. He was 'desirous to convince them that national education and employment could alone create a permanent national, intelligent, wealthy, and superior population, and that these results could be attained only by a scientific arrangement of the people, united in properly constructed villages of unity and co-operation'.[77]

Whatever the views of the government on the Owenite projects, Robert Owen did not lack followers. Certainly Owenism was what caught the imagination of those who conceived either of some alternative direction or of more equitable distribution of the benefits of the

---

[74] J. R. Poynter, *Society and Pauperism, 1795–1834*, London, 1969.

[75] R. G. Garnett, *Co-operation and the Owenite Socialist Communities in Britain 1825–1845*, Manchester, 1972, p. 4.

[76] Robert Owen, *A New View of Society and Report to the County of Lanark*, ed. V. A. C. Gattrell, London, 1969, p. 210.

[77] *The Life of Robert Owen Written by Himself*, ed. John Butt, London, 1971.

industrial transformation of Britain. The movement was eclectic enough to gather :

> artisans with their dreams of short circuiting the market economy; skilled workers with their thrust towards general unionism; the philanthropic gentry, with their desire for a rational planned society; the poor with their dreams of land or Zion; the weavers with their hopes of self employment; and all of these with their image of an equitable brotherly community, in which mutual aid would replace aggression and competition.[78]

The impact of machinery was a key element of Owenite economics. Owen argued that the huge productivity increase consequent on technical change entailed the exploitation, misery, and moral degradation of labour. He argued in his *Report to the County of Lanark* for an intensive agriculture based on spade husbandry which would enable food supply both to keep pace with population growth and to provide for greater employment.[79] He maintained, in addition, that commercial competition had stimulated invention, but had made men selfish.

Machinery used in the context of the wage bond had degraded labour into a dispensable commodity. It had encouraged competition for wealth and divided men when they should have been united.[80] Owen wished to extract technical progress from the social arrangements in which it had been developed, and to redirect it in an attempt to avoid the minute division of labour.[81] In his community he envisaged all taking part in one or more of the occupations in a department, 'ordered by every improvement that science can afford', and that this employment would alternate with work in agriculture and gardening.

Needless to say, there was almost an over-reaction to Owen in middle-class circles. Torrens referred to him as belonging 'to the order of political alchemists'.[82] 'Mr. Owen shows himself profoundly ignorant of all the laws which regulate the production and distribution of wealth. He tells us, that the distress to which the people of this country are

---

[78] E. P. Thompson, cited in Garnett, *Co-operation*, p. 11.
[79] Owen, *A New View of Society*, pp. 211–15.
[80] V. A. C. Gattrell, 'Introduction', *A New View of Society*, pp. 12–13.
[81] Owen, *A New View of Society*, p. 251.
[82] Robert Torrens, *A Paper on the Means of Reducing the Poor Rates and of Affording Effectual and Permanent Relief to the Labouring Classes*, London, 1817, p. 514.

exposed arises from scientific and mechanical power producing more than the existing regulations of society permit to be consumed.'[83] McCulloch was no less scathing of the political economy of Owenism. He reported Owen's speech on the crisis in the *Scotsman* in 1819, but it was not until 1821 that he came to vent his full wrath. He pointed out that Owen's theories on spade husbandry, the division of the population into parallelograms, and the discarding of the minute division of labour were all wrong. The greatest drawback of such ideas was that they led to indolence. No individual could 'raise himself above the common herd'. The commercial arrangements of his textile communities were defective, and they had no mechanism for adjusting the quantity of yarn produced to effective demand.

However, incredulity on the part of most political economists did not perturb Owen from seeking the ear of the Political Economy Club. He attended as a guest of Grote in 1822 and presented the particulars of his plan for 'ameliorating the condition of mankind', and some of the principles of his system.[84]

The conflict between the political economists and the Owenite 'visionaries' was dramatised in the public debating sessions of the philosophic radicals and members of an Owenite co-operative society.[85] The sectarian spirit of the philosophic radicals here found a platform, though not a particularly acrimonious one. J. S. Mill reports one such debate on population which went on through five or six meetings. Another on the general merits of Owen's system lasted for three months.

> It was a little corp à corps between Owenites and political economists, whom the Owenites regarded as their most inveterate opponents; but it was a perfectly friendly dispute. We who represented political economy had the same objects in view as they had and took pains to show it; and the principal champion on their side was a very estimable man, with whom

83 Torrens, 'Mr. Owen's Plans for Relieving the National Distress', p. 468.
84 Minutes, 6 May 1822, *Political Economy Club, Centenary Volume*, VI, p. 14.
85 Joseph Hamburger, *Intellectuals in Politics. John Stuart Mill and the Philosophical Radicals,* Yale, 1965, p. 26. The latter was probably the London Co-operative and Economical Society, a working-class organisation set up in 1821 by a group of printers. They also set up a co-operative housing experiment at Spa Fields and a co-operative store. See J. F. C. Harrison, 'The Steam Engine of the New Moral World: Owenism and Education 1817–1829', *Journal of British Studies*, VI, 1967.

I was well acquainted, Mr. William Thompson of Cork, author of a book on the Distribution of Wealth and of an 'Appeal' on behalf of Women against the passage in my father's Essay on Government.[86]

This is not to say, however, that Mill took a particularly favourable view of Owenism. Rather, he hoped that middle-class fears of the extremes of Owenism would encourage reform, working-class education, and more democratic institutions.[87]

Certainly it was not only the entrenched members of the Political Economy Club who took exception to Owen's schemes. Several dissidents too were not very convinced. John Barton, though he had taken great pains to stress the many limitations on the demand for labour in an industrialising society, did not promote projects for employing the poor. He argued that neither the manufacturing corporations of Josiah Child nor the village co-operatives of Owen could increase the demand for labour: they only drew labour from other employments.[88] Simon Gray questioned only what he regarded as the anti-technology bias in Owen; he found Owen's views curious for one who was a manufacturer employing a large capital in machinery.[89]

Machinery and labour

The disputes on machinery were, however, much more far-reaching than the hopes and threats of Owenism. An immediate concern to political economists was Ricardo's remarkable intervention in the issue as well as actual events of machine breaking. This made machinery both a real practical concern and an analytical puzzle to the economists of the 1820s. The machinery question became one of the most important incidents of the interrelation of theory and a political issue. It became a discussion question in the Political Economy Club,[90] and was debated at the most concrete levels among manufacturers during the 1826 riots.

The destruction of machinery was a definite part of working-class struggle in early industrial England. The critique of machinery was to remain an important part of working-class ideology until well after

[86] J. S. Mill, *Autobiography*, p. 125.
[87] *Ibid.* p. 172.
[88] Barton, *An Inquiry*, p. 77.
[89] Gray (pseud.) Purves, *All Classes Productive of National Wealth*, p. 301.
[90] This question was raised by Ricardo at the second meeting of the Club, but was not discussed until 4 February 1822. See *Political Economy Club, Centenary Volume*, VI, 7.

Chartism and indeed, even until the end of the nineteenth century.[91] The pre-industrial riot was characteristically the food riot, and was directed against the corn middleman.[92] But it was mechanisation which took the centre stage from the late eighteenth century onwards. Machinery became the most immediate basis for the relationship between capitalist and worker. It was the machine which defined the organisation of work and which held the balance of power in the determination of the distribution of returns from labour. More fundamentally, machinery threatened displacement of labour in a period of low labour mobility, no industrial retraining schemes, and no redundancy payment. The machinery issue also provoked significant divisions among the radicals. William Cobbett, for example, took a stand against many of his fellow radicals on the Luddite question. In his 'Letter to the Luddites', published in the *Political Register* in 1816 and reprinted in 1823, he had argued that there could be no solid objection to machinery in general. He accused writers 'on the side of corruption' of 'inculcating notions hostile to machinery as well as notions hostile to butchers and bakers', and went on to argue that the wages saved by the employment of machinery in one sector could be used to employ labour in a different sector. He concluded his pamphlet with a threat of a loss of foreign trade if technical change was held back, and blaming the burden of taxation for the distress.[93]

This pamphlet provoked a public reply from Ricardo, who, in debate in the House of Commons, said he was not satisfied with its reasoning. It was 'evident, that extensive use of machinery, by throwing a large portion of labour into the market, while, on the other hand, there might not be a corresponding increase of demand for it, must, in some degree, operate prejudicially to the working classes'. But he stressed he would not tolerate any law to prevent the use of machinery. If the country 'gave up the system that enabled [it] to undersell in the foreign market,

---

91 See E. J. Hobsbawm, The Machine Breakers', *Labouring Men* (1964), New York, 1967; Joy McAskill, 'The Chartist Land Plan', in Asa Briggs, ed., *Chartist Studies* (1959), London, 1965; and Raphael Samuel, 'Introduction', Raphael Samuel, ed., *Village Life and Labour*, London, 1975. For a full discussion of working-class attitudes to machinery see below chapter 11.

92 See E. P. Thompson, 'The Moral Economy of the English Crowd in the Eighteenth Century', *Past and Present*, no. 50, 1971, 78–9, and George Rudé, *The Crowd in History*, New York, London, Sydney, 1964, chap. 2.

93 William Cobbett, 'A Letter to the Luddites', *Cobbett's Weekly Political Register*, London, 30 November 1816.

would other nations refrain from pursuing it? Certainly not.' They were bound by their own interest to continue it.[94]

The Tory ministers saw the anti-machinery aspect of the reaction to distress as a political affair. Liverpool had admitted in 1819 that industrialisation brought social problems, however, he believed the French Revolution was responsible for the democratic ideas which led to the resistance to its effects:

> Tho' it cannot be denied that the great increase of our manu-
> facturing population, the dependence of a great part of that
> population on Foreign Demand, and the refinements in
> Machinery (which enable manufacturers to perform that work
> in weeks which formerly occupied months and which leads
> consequently to extravagant wages at one time and to low and
> inadequate ones at another), have recently subjected this
> country to evils with which in the same degree we were formerly
> unacquainted, yet all these circumstances would not have
> accounted for the present state of the Public Mind in certain
> parts of the Country if the events of the French Revolution
> had not directed the attention of the lower Orders of the
> Community and those immediately above them to Political
> Considerations, had not shaken all respect for established
> authority and ancient Institutions and had not familiarized
> mankind with a system of organization which has been justly
> represented to be as ingenious and appropriate to its purpose
> as any Invention of Mechanics.[95]

The 1826 riots in Lancashire posed the issue squarely. These riots took place in a year of crisis which had opened with financial disruption; amid signs of increasing wealth in 1825 the capital market had collapsed. There had been a flurry of joint stock ventures and speculation, and the final crash in December 1825 brought down forty-three country banks. Hilton has given a very compelling picture of the impact of the 1825–6 crisis on public consciousness. He argues that the crisis left its mark on economic thought and literature by creating a gloomy preoccupation with business failures.[96]

[94] 'Wages of Manufacturers – Use of Machinery', *Hansard*, ix, 30 May 1823, col. 601.

[95] Liverpool to Grenville 14 November 1819 cited in Hilton, *Corn, Cash, Commerce*, p. 51.

[96] Hilton, *Corn, Cash, Commerce*, p. 228. The course of these riots has been described by Archibald Prentice, *Historical Sketches . . . of Manchester*, Manchester, 1851, pp. 274–6.

One effect of this crash was a series of riots in the manufacturing districts in the early spring of 1826.[97] The reaction to the riots was sharp. Local newspaper editors who endorsed classical political economy wrote tracts on machinery to be distributed among the workpeople. The most well known of these were Archibald Prentice's 'On the Causes and Cure of the Present Distress' and Edward Baines's *Letter to the Unemployed Workmen of Lancashire and Yorkshire*. Prentice's pamphlet blamed the depression on the currency, the Corn Laws, and excessive government spending.[98] Baines stressed the advance of continental industry, especially cotton manufacturing in Rouen, and predicted that the machine breaking at Blackburn would encourage manufacturers to leave the country and set up in France.

Baines's pamphlet was widely distributed and praised in government and industry. Lord Lansdowne wrote: 'It is seldom indeed that the subjects connected with the most important principles of political economy are discussed in a manner so calculated to make them acceptable to the understanding of the many.'[99] Bannister Eccles, one of those Blackburn manufacturers whose mills had been attacked, thought Baines's pamphlet had done much good in the area by removing the prejudice against the power loom.[100]

The *Letter to the Unemployed Workmen* was also the subject of a significant correspondence between Baines and Simonde de Sismondi. The correspondence is an interesting study of the confrontation of theory with the practical issues of the day, and depicts the interaction between a provincial industrial ideologue and an internationally known intellectual. Baines sent Sismondi a copy of the *Letter*, which he regarded

---

97 See Hume's speech on the riots, *Hansard*, xv, 5 May 1826, col. 910.
98 Liverpool again asserted his view that government aid to workers in redundant occupations would be useless: 'There is no prospect of the Hand-Looms ever being able to compete again with the Power-Looms. This must throw an immense part of population out of employment, and be the cause of appalling distress till the individuals interested shall have been dispersed and engaged in other pursuits.' Liverpool to Herries, 24 January 1827, Herries MSS, cited in Hilton, *Corn, Cash, Commerce*, p. 84. Archibald Prentice, 'On the Causes and Cure of the Present Distress', *Manchester Gazette*, 15 July 1826 and 22 July 1826. Edward Baines, jun., *Letter to the Unemployed Workmen of Lancashire and Yorkshire*, London, 1826.
99 Lord Landsdowne to E. Baines, sen., 22 May 1826, Baines Papers (Leeds Public Library). Also see letter from Byng, Commander of the Northern District to Baines, sen., 15 May 1826, Baines Papers.
100 Bannister Eccles to Edward Baines jun., 22 June 1826, Baines Papers.

as a refutation of the latter's doctrines.[101] Sismondi took the opportunity of reply to reassert his underconsumptionist beliefs. He regarded 1826 as 'giving a fatal direction' to the efforts of a people to become the manufacturers of the world.[102] He objected, not to machinery, but to the unjust division of its products, and counselled Baines to look at the 1826 crisis in terms of the glut and the social organisation of industry :

> This permanent and universal glut is absolutely inexplicable
> on the system of your economists Messrs. Ricardo, McCulloch
> etc., but it is in my opinion a necessary consequence of the
> direction industry has taken ... I have never dreamt of
> preventing by any law the improvement of machinery, nor
> even of discouraging ingenious men from the invention of new
> machines; all that I should wish is to render it impossible for
> the master manufacturers to extort from their workmen what
> they cannot obtain from the consumer.[103]

McCulloch and Place took predictable stands on the riots. Both confronted the machinery issue of 1826 in the context of previous working-class revolt. McCulloch thought popular ignorance of political economy was one reason for the opposition to technical progress.[104] He argued that the Lancashire riots would discourage investment and lead to further reductions in the demand for labour.[105]

The struggle of the working classes against the encroachment of machinery was an unending preoccupation of Francis Place. Over the years he had corresponded on the issue with trade associations, unions, and political groups. Not only the recent weaving riots, but the problems of the operative sawyers, the Frome woollen committee, newspaper printers, and paper makers gave him ample evidence for a series of letters on machinery to the *Bolton Chronicle* in 1826.[106] Place simply repeated

101 Information on Baines and local politics can be found in Derek Fraser, 'Edward Baines', *Pressure from Without*, ed. Patricia Hollis, London, 1974.
102 J. C. L. Simonde de Sismondi to Edward Baines, jun., 19 July 1826, Baines Papers.
103 J. C. L. Simonde de Sismondi to Edward Baines, jun., 27 July 1826, Baines Papers. I am editing this Sismondi–Baines correspondence for publication.
104 McCulloch, *A Discourse on the Rise ... of Political Economy*, p. 84.
105 [J. R. McCulloch], 'On Economic Distress and Pauperism', *The Scotsman*, 22 July 1826.
106 See Place Collection of Newspaper Cuttings (British Library), vol. LVII, pp. 1–60.

his old views that distress was not due to machinery, but to population increase.[107] William Ellis's apt piece, the 'Employment of Machinery', raised the level of debate by pointing out the significance of the timing of technical change. He argued that most new processes were introduced in times of prosperity, not in times of crisis.[108]

The analysis of the phenomenon of resistance to machinery was continued at a more sophisticated level by political economists who tried to respond to Ricardo's difficult and provocative chapter on machinery. The ideas developed by John Barton and Ricardo on the relationship between fixed capital investment and the demand for labour provoked severe reaction. Unlike the underconsumptionists, they both started from the assumption of fully-employed factor markets. Barton was the first to distinguish fixed and circulating capitals according to their impact on the labour market. In his *Observations*, 1817, he took issue with the view that every increase of capital set in motion an additional quantity of labour :

> The demand for labour depends, then, on the increase of
> circulating and not of fixed capital. Were it true that the
> proportion between these two sorts of capital is the same at all
> times and in all countries, then indeed it follows that the number
> of labourers employed is in proportion to the wealth of the
> state. But such a position has not the semblance of probability.
> As arts are cultivated and civilization extended, fixed capital
> bears a larger and larger proportion to circulating capital . . .
> It is easy to conceive that under certain circumstances the whole
> of the annual produce of an industrious people might be added
> to fixed capital, in which case they would have no effect in
> raising the demand for labour.[109]

Barton argued that there was a long-run tendency to rising capital intensity. As capital became more plentiful it was invested in the construction of machinery, in making roads, digging canals, and other improvements which brought about some saving in labour. Barton tempered the force of his conclusions, however, by pointing out that as long as capital accumulation, development, and technical change

---

[107] Relevant copies of the *Bolton Chronicle* no longer exist. Place
collected most of the letters in his Collection of Newspaper Cuttings,
vol. XVI, pp. 171–236.

[108] [Ellis], 'Employment of Machinery'.

[109] Barton, *Observations*, p. 16.

continued to take place, there need never be great fears over the demand for labour. The actual process of fixed capital formation was a great employer of labour.[110]

Ricardo's reformed views on machinery and labour, incorporated into the third edition of his *Principles* were, as I have shown, a development of Barton's possible case. Given a fixed supply of capital, labour was transferred from the production of necessaries, or consumer goods, to the production of machinery. This decline in the funds for the employment of labour would lead to a decline in the demand for labour over the economy as a whole.[111] There would be an increase in net revenue or surplus, and a decline in gross revenue or total final product while the machinery was under construction. Demand for labour would always be dependent on the expansion of gross revenue.

The reaction provoked by this analysis was not only the immediate one I have described in Chapter 4 above, but a long-term interest in the issue. Torrens and Ellis both made more serious attempts to come to terms with Ricardo's chapter on machinery, mainly by investigating alternative sources of investment. Torrens, for instance, argued that the capitalist would have no motive for constructing a machine unless it led to a higher rate of profit. But, as profits increased, capital would accumulate more rapidly, and this more rapid accumulation would restore the original demand for labour.[112] Torrens also saw fit to include an entire chapter refuting Ricardo's views in his popular work *Wages and Combinations* in 1834. Ellis went yet a step further to argue that the original investment for the machine-making sector need not be taken from a 'wage fund' but could be drawn from increased savings induced by the expectation of higher profits after the machinery was built, and that this process would be self-perpetuating: 'When that additional capital is introduced, motives in abundance are presented for a still further accumulation, since profits will have risen in as much as the same number of labourers, aided by more powerful instruments, will be able to produce a larger quantity of commodities.'[113]

[110] John Barton, 'Effects of Rising Wealth on Luxury and Prices', Manuscript Notebooks (British Library of Political and Economic Science), written between 1814 and 1817, p. 159.
[111] Ricardo made it quite clear in his speech on Cobbett's pamphlet in Parliament on 30 May 1823 that he was referring to a decline in the demand for labour, not in any one sector, but over the economy as a whole. 'Wages of Manufacturers', *Hansard*, IX, col. 602.
[112] Torrens, *An Essay on the Production of Wealth*, p. xi.
[113] [Ellis], 'Employment of Machinery', p. 116.

The impact of higher saving and profit rates was a very important counteracting factor, but even more so was the relative time period in which new machinery would be introduced. Simon Gray was the one who pointed out that the major periods for the introduction of new machinery were advancing ones, when both prices and wages were high. The wages of both the makers and users of the new machinery had historically been higher than those of former employees. Furthermore, the construction of machinery was a new and thriving branch of industry which could only be regarded as an important spin-off of mechanisation.[114] Arguments along the lines of these criticisms of Ricardo's chapter were echoed frequently through the pamphlet literature of the period in what were often long and turgid justifications of the introduction of machinery.[115]

Even Malthus held no real objections to the extension of machinery *per se*. His real worry was the extension of demand in proportion to the increase in productivity. He was, however, never very impressed with Owen's proposals for spade husbandry, and his reason for this can be found in his dispute with John Barton.[116] Malthus at first disagreed with Barton's view that the demand for labour was tied to the increase of circulating, not fixed capital. This disagreement rested on Malthus's belief that any increase in fixed capital was generally favourable to circulating capital. If the advance in fixed capital was gradual, it would lead to increased productivity and cultivation of waste land. A higher proportion of population would be released to manufacturing, the value of general production would rise, and with it the demand for labour.[117] The natural tendency of machinery was to cheapen a commodity and thus to extend the market. In practice, however, there was often a substantial loss involved in transferring capital from one employment to another: 'The power of the whole capital to command the same quantity of labour would depend on the contingency of vacant capitals being withdrawn undiminished from old occupations and finding equivalent employment in others.'[118] Malthus's obsession with the market led him to enthuse over the reciprocal action of the extension of foreign markets and the invention of machinery.

This reaction to the doubts of Ricardo and Barton was soon to become

114 Gray, *The Happiness of States*, p. 106.
115 See, for example, Pettman, *An Essay on Political Economy*, Part II, pp. 40–61.
116 Malthus, *Principles*, p. 237.
117 *Ibid.* p. 239.
118 *Ibid.* p. 350.

the characteristic one. Theorists admitted the conceptual possibility of technological unemployment, but mitigated the force of Ricardo's case by seeking counteracting factors. The pessimism of Barton and Ricardo on the question of the impact of machinery on the working classes was thus successfully relegated to the realm of analytical puzzles. The theorists who followed Ricardo were uncertain enough of economic prospects to comment extensively on the Ricardo case or the problem in general. However, the end of their investigation was to submerge these doubts by drawing practical and policy attention to the over-powering counteracting factor of the growth potential in the total British economy.

Stationary states

Finally, therefore, after a wide-ranging and remarkably intensive discussion on the prospects of British industry, economists seem to have concluded on a fairly sanguine plane. Even if population or capital should grow more quickly than was desirable, or even if capital was scarce or wages high, there was always a self-generating form of technical progress which could ultimately overcome all these problems. But there is still to be found in this period the shadow of those depressing concepts of the declining rate of profit and the imminence of the stationary state. Did economists in this period give any serious thought to these apparently ambiguous concepts of Ricardian economics?

Many historians of economic thought have given rather excessive concern to the role of the stationary state in classical economic theory. They have accepted the classicals too easily as prophets of doom, and have seldom stopped to question the status of the falling rate of profit and the stationary state. They have too often confused the conceptual systems of the classical economists with their individual attitudes to reality.[119]

I have shown the attitudes of Ricardo and his contemporaries could hardly be called ones of despair. And certainly the condition of the first industrial workers had little to do with their ideas on the prospects of British growth. If anything, it was the economist above all others who was either optimistic or blind, and possibly both, to the conditions of the working classes in northern towns or southern villages during the period. It is certainly true that Ricardo's analytical system was set up to

[119] See, for example, Michel Lutfalla, *L'Etat Stationnaire*, Paris, 1964, p. 153. Lutfalla argues that it is paradoxical that in the period of the Industrial Revolution there should be this tradition of despair in economic theory.

explain the *tendency* towards a declining rate of profit, and it is also true that he spoke of a future stationary state. But the practical eventuality of either of these phenomena was almost inconceivable. It is important to remember that Ricardo's system was also built up to recommend ways of avoiding the falling rate of profit. Even Malthus regarded the falling rate of profit as extremely remote. He argued that the decline in the rate of profit that came from the progressive cultivation of poorer land could be extremely slow or more than balanced by continual agricultural improvement, including improved implements and machinery as well as better systems of cropping and managing.[120] McCulloch, in the 1820s, still believed in the final eventuality of the stationary state. But again such a possibility was very remote. He argued that the productive energies of the earth were constantly rising due to discoveries and inventions: 'improvements in the skill and industry of the labourer and in machinery may counterbalance the disadvantages of an inferior soil and an unfavourable climate'.[121] But still from the operation of 'fixed and permanent causes', the 'rise in the sterility of the soil must in the long run overmatch the increasing powers of machinery'.[122] McCulloch, however, eventually gave up his earlier predictions of diminishing returns and the stationary state altogether.[123]

This optimism was continued by both James and John Stuart Mill who conceived of an *ideal* stationary state. The fame of the latter's stationary state has often obscured that of the former. Winch, however, has pointed out that James Mill introduced a series of social arguments explaining why capital accumulated more slowly than population increased: men reached a certain plateau of wealth where they had not further motivation to accumulate, but many inducements to enjoy their leisure.[124] John Stuart Mill did not give up the final stationary state, though he left it a benevolent one. As Neil de Marchi puts it: 'Mill's belief in the "habitual antagonism" of the "progress of civilization" did not in any way undermine his opinion that diminishing returns tended to outweigh cost-reducing improvements as such.'[125]

---

120 Malthus, *Principles*, p. 127.
121 [J. R. McCulloch], 'The Opinions of Messrs. Say, Sismondi, Malthus on the Effects of Machinery and Accumulation', *Edinburgh Review*, xxxv, March 1821, p. 117.
122 McCulloch, *Principles*, p. 383.
123 See O'Brien, *J. R. McCulloch*, p. 298.
124 See *James Mill*, ed. Donald Winch, p. 195.
125 N. de Marchi, 'John Stuart Mill and the Development of English Economic Thought', (ANU.Ph.D. Thesis, 1970), p. 160.

The political economists of the 1820s attached little practical significance to the imminence of the stationary state. The power of technical
progress had gripped the imagination of most. The economists who
followed Ricardo criticised the conclusions of his model, but found in
it a source of inspiration. The model provoked many to investigate ways
of avoiding falling rates of profit and stationary states. One key was for
them to reveal the gains from technical change. The economists and
their substantially middle-class public showed great zeal in observing
and promoting the mechanisms of technological transformation in the
industrialising British economy. Their zeal was prompted partly by intellectual debate and partly by pressing economic and political concerns.
After Ricardo no economist of the period, at least until the 1840s, could
ignore the influence and impact of his theories. His provocative formulation of the economic problems of his time was vital to the direction of
development of economic ideas. I have already shown the degree to
which Ricardo's work was stimulated by contemporary issues and events;
and this chapter has indicated the extent to which this interaction of
theory and politics also continued throughout the 1820s. The response
to machinery had even greater political consequence in the wake of
economic crisis, Owenite radicalism, and the machine-breaking events
of 1826. The economists of the 1820s responded to Ricardo and to these
economic and political events by describing and endorsing the process
of industrialisation. With Adam Smith's perspectives on improvements
as their model, they developed a framework for economic development
which they believed to be an alternative to Ricardo's. Their theories
centred on the concept of the division of labour, but they used the
concept in new ways in order to integrate the machine and capitalist
accumulation into their visions of economic progress. The pattern of
their observations, defined by the idea of the division of labour, was
perhaps suggestive of the outline of the stage of economic development
defined by Marx as the 'phase of manufactures'. However, the
continuity of this pattern of ideas from the time of Smith into the 1820s
definitely underwent a change of emphasis in the 1830s. Political
economists moved on to describe, or at least to predict, a structural
shift in the economy to one based on fixed capital. Using Marx's terms
once again, this change in analysis could be described as belonging to
the new period of 'modern industry' in contrast with the period of
'manufactures' which still underlay the 1820s.

6

Political economy and capital

The determination of political economists in the 1820s to repudiate what they understood to be the pessimistic conclusions of Ricardo's theory was continued by the next generation of economists in the following decade. Their ideas, however, were placed in fundamentally new perspectives, for the organising principle of their discussions of technological improvement shifted from the division of labour to capital formation. This shift was not a sharp intellectual break, but rather a change in emphasis. As has been shown, both Torrens and McCulloch placed a certain significance on capital formation and machinery, while later writers including Senior and John Rae, continued to develop the analysis of labour productivity, examining in detail skill and the organisation of labour. It is, however, evident that 'technology' was reformulated in the 1830s in terms of fixed capital and machinery.

This theoretical shift occurred within a definite intellectual and social context. Intellectually, the economists of this decade were self-conscious of their critical view of Ricardo and thought seriously about the implications of this for the public image of their discipline. They also responded to political and social disturbance at the time, and attached importance to the ideas and opinions they expressed on such matters and to their authority as political economists. Both these intellectual and social contexts were directly related to the theoretical analysis made of the origins, prospects and form of technological improvement.

There has been a good deal of debate on the relationship of the political economists of the 1830s to Ricardo. It has become almost traditional to refer to economists such as Senior, Whately, Lloyd, and Longfield

as the critics of Ricardo. It was Schumpeter's view that by the early
1830s Ricardian economics was 'no longer a living force'.[1] Previously,
Marx had made the same point in his own way, regarding the 1830s as
the years when scientific economics gave way to apologetics.[2] Many
historians of economic thought have argued to a varying extent with
these two assessments.[3] It is only very recently that Samuel Hollander
and Neil de Marchi have questioned this breach. They have argued the
case that many of the points made by the critics were based on mis-
understanding of Ricardo, and that their critical economics was
actually much more compatible with Ricardo's than we have been led
to believe.[4] If the critics were indeed offering genuine alternatives to
Ricardo, then this also was not new, for diverse and critical inquiry
was just as much a characteristic of the previous decade as it was of
this one. It is true that mention is often made of a meeting of the
Political Economy Club on 13 January 1831 to discuss the progress
which had been made since Ricardo, and the extent to which Ricardian
economics had been undermined. But the conclusion reached by the
meeting indicated no major criticism. Mallet reports that :

> McCulloch stood up vigorously for Value as well as Rent and
> paid very high compliments to Ricardo whom he still considered
> as right in most points, and at all events as having done the
> greatest service to the science, his methodical and scientific
> way of treating it, so that even where he was mistaken, his
> errors could be detected by a subsequent and more correct
> analysis.

The Political Economy Club, in fact, finally agreed that Ricardo's
Principles were 'in the main right'.[5]

Open dissension with Ricardo's views was feared for the effect it

---

[1] Schumpeter, *History of Economic Analysis*, p. 478.
[2] Karl Marx, *Capital*, vol. I, trans. Samuel Moore and Edward Aveling,
New York, 1967, pp. 14, 16.
[3] R. L. Meek, 'Economics and Ideology', in *Economics and Ideology and
Other Essays*, ed. R. Meek, London, 1967, p. 208; Dobb, *Theories of
Value*, p. 98; Marian Bowley, *Studies in the History of Economic Theory
before 1870*, London, 1973, pp. 154–6, 211–15; F. W. Fetter, 'The Rise
and Decline of Ricardian Economics', *History of Political Economy*,
Spring 1969.
[4] Hollander, 'The Reception of Ricardian Economics'; de Marchi, 'The
Success of Mill's Principles', *History of Political Economy*, VI, 1974.
[5] Mallet's Diaries, 13 January 1831, *Political Economy Club, Centenary
Volume*, VI, p. 223.

might have on the public authority of the discipline. As Samuel Read put it :

> By all who are acquainted with the most recent and most noted works on Political Economy, it will be readily admitted that the science is at present in a very unsettled and unsatisfactory state. There is indeed scarcely a single doctrine – if we except that of *commercial freedom*, as expressed long since by the French economists – upon which there is perfect and uniform, or even general agreement, among the numerous sects and schools into which the science is now divided.[6]

But such fears of differences of opinion in political economy were endemic also to the years before and after the 1830s,[7] and concerns over the public image of the discipline were only meaningful in a specific social context – the practical political problem of Swing riots and socialism. For these constituted a fundamental challenge both to the success of the Industrial Revolution and to political economy's optimistic predictions of its benefits.

Most economists of the time felt the need to respond to the social conflict generated by the agricultural riots of 1830 and by trade unionism, and their concerns were soon increased by the emergence of organised, doctrinal socialism. The agricultural riots had an immediate and extensive influence on the political economists.[8] Mallet found the Political Economy Club meeting of 3 December 1830 abuzz with news of the disturbance : 'We were rather too full of politics, the destruction of machinery, and so forth : the general opinion seems to be that if these disorders lasted there must be either an increase of military force or some sort of National Guard.'[9] The situation led to a special debating session on 13 January 1831 on the subject of the causes of discontent and distress in the agricultural districts. The members seem to have agreed that there was no particularly pressing distress among the agricultural labourers, and that the disturbances had 'originated in political

6 Samuel Read, *An Inquiry into the Natural Grounds of Right to Vendible Property or Wealth*, Edinburgh, 1829, p. v.

7 McCulloch voiced such fears in the 1820s, and Torrens in the 1850s. J. R. McCulloch to D. Ricardo, 5 June 1821, *Letters 1819–1821*, pp. 382, 385; and A. W. Coats, 'The Role of Authority in the Development of British Economists', *Journal of Law and Economics*, VII, October 1964, p. 194.

8 For a comprehensive history of the agricultural riots of these years and their outcome see Hobsbawm and Rudé, *Captain Swing*.

9 Mallet's Diaries, 3 December 1830, *Political Economy Club*, XI, p. 281.

excitation' : 'The concurrence I have mentioned as to the great exaggerations which prevail and are industriously disseminated on the subject of agricultural distress is the more remarkable as there are all shades of political opinion among the Members of the Club, several of whom are radical reformers.'[10]

Senior opened his *Three Lectures on the Rate of Wages* by explaining that they were written in a period of tranquillity, but that the country was now 'in a state which may require the exertions of every individual among the educated classes, and many may have to assist in executing, or even in originating measures for the relief of the labouring population, who are not yet sufficiently familiar with the principles according to which that relief is to be afforded'.[11] The agricultural riots, too, were the motivation for his long discussion in these lectures on machinery and labour. His major fears were that 'The consequences of the present system' had not been explained to labourers, hence the declaration of their right to good wages. The greatest danger came from those who 'assumed the fund out of which the labourer is fed was unlimited'.

> Have not even magistrates and landlords recommended the destruction, or, what is the same, both in principle and effect, the disuse of every machine of which the object is to render labour more efficient in the production of the articles consumed by the labourer in the production of that very fund on the extent of which, compared with the number to be maintained, the amount of wages depends? . . . Threshing machines are the present objects of hostility, ploughs will be the next.[12]

A reviewer of the second edition of McCulloch's *Principles* saw utility in poiltical economy at a time 'when the south of England is spread with the smoking ruins of farm houses and the ashes of cornstacks and barns'. He, too, claimed a lack of 'politico-economical knowledge' as the major culprit : 'The outrages which the enemies of political economy deplore in common with its friends, arise in the greatest part, and immediately, from the vulgar errors concerning machinery and wages, which a knowledge of the natural laws that regulate the production and

---

[10] Mallet's Diaries, 3 December 1830, *Political Economy Club*, VI, p. 222.

[11] N. W. Senior, *Three Lectures on the Rate of Wages* (before the University of Oxford, 1830), London, 1831, p. iii.

[12] *Ibid*. p. xiii. For a discussion of the actual extent of feeling among farmers and magistrates against the threshing machine, see E. J. Hobsbawm and George Rudé, *Captain Swing*, chap. 2.

distribution of the wealth of nations can alone dissipate.'[13] Another *Edinburgh* reviewer returned to the issue two years later to point out the educative role of recent works of popular political economy in aiding the introduction of agricultural machinery.[14] Neither did the readers of the *Westminster Review* escape the topical lessons of political economy. T. Perronet Thompson reviewed *The Life and History of Swing the Kent Rick-burner* to warn readers of the outcome of an ignorance of political economy.[15]

If rioting in the countryside provoked such a reaction, there was probably equal concern over the issue of trade unions and mechanisa-tion. In 1832 Senior, along with Thomas Thomlinson, drew up a 'Report on Combinations'. The Report showed great concern with trade union interference in technical progress, and even included interviews with anonymous textile manufacturers. These interviews, conducted with an elaborate questionnaire, helped Senior to 'prove' that certain combinations had indeed interfered with the introduction of new techniques.[16] The message was also clear in E. C. Tuffnell's *Objects and Effects of Trades Unions* of 1834.

This very specific context of immediate class struggle is to be distin-guished from another bogey of the political economists. They also voiced strong objections to the socialist vision. James Mill wrote to Brougham in 1832 on the idea of the rights of the labourer to the whole produce of his labour. He described this as 'the mad nonsense of our friend Hodgkin which he has published as a system . . . These opinions, if they were to spread, would be the subversion of civilized society.'[17]

13 [E. Coulson], 'McCulloch's Principles of Political Economy', *Edinburgh Review*, LII, January 1831, 33–8.
14 [William Empson], 'Mrs. Marcet, Miss Martineau', *Edinburgh Review*, LVII, January 1833, pp. 17, 18.
15 T. Perronet Thompson, 'Machine Breaking: A Review of *The Life and History of Swing the Kent Rick-burner Written by Himself*, 1830', *Westminster Review*, XIV, January 1831, pp. 191–210. Reviewing this pamphlet gave Perronet Thompson the chance to encapsulate his temperate views on economic development in a pithy saying: 'Machinery then, like the rain of heaven, is a great blessing to all concerned, providing it comes down by drops and not by tons together.' (p. 194).
16 Report on Combinations by N. W. Senior and Thomas Thomlinson. Presented to Rt. Hon. Lord Viscount Melbourne, Secretary of State, 21 August 1832. Senior Papers, National Library of Wales, Aberystwyth.
17 Cited in Anton Menger, *The Right to the Whole Produce of Labour*, London, 1899, 'Introduction by H. S. Foxwell', p. lxxvi. 'Hodgkin' was actually Thomas Hodgskin, the radical political economist.

Longfield warned that opinions were no longer inactive. The question was no longer whether the working class would generate opinion, but how 'a true sense of their own interests' was to be made clear to them. Political economy was a 'defensive science' which attempts to 'prevent the injudicious interference of speculative legislation'.[18] Scrope drew attention to a general feeling throughout society that the 'physical and mental happiness of man' were socially determined. Thus 'social arrangements' could be infinitely improved. For Scrope, however, political economy was not defensive; welfare was the primary object of policy.[19] Finally, Senior saw himself grappling in his *Outline of Political Economy* with a new race of visionaries. One of his reviewers, in setting out Senior's dilemma, described the situation of many of the theorists of the 1830s.

> There is at work a wide-spread dissatisfaction with the present state of society; and a disposition to trace all evils which afflict it to the competition of capitalists and labourers amongst themselves, and their supposed competition with each other. It is as if the philosophical world, never long contented with a simple adherence to the same system, had tried the *laissez faire* theories of Smith and Turgot to the uttermost, and thrown them aside in mere weariness, and through a desire for new excitements.[20]

The work of individual socialist economists was usually mentioned with respect to the discussion of attacks on profit and capital. Apart from James Mill's allusions, Hodgskin was sketched by a writer in the *Quarterly Review* as an influence more 'pernicious than the Owenites'.[21] Scrope objected to the Owenites and the Saint-Simonians : 'Its designers forget that the industry of which in the present advanced state of society they witness the fruits, has been brought into being, and has hitherto grown and thriven, only under the shelter of the institution of private property and the stimulus of competition.'[22] But again it was Hodgskin

---

[18] Mountfort Longfield, *Lectures on Political Economy*, Dublin, 1834, pp. 6–10, 17–18.

[19] G. P. Scrope, *Principles of Political Economy, Deduced from the Natural Laws of Social Welfare*, London, 1833, pp. viii–ix.

[20] [Herman Merivale], 'Definitions and Systems of Political Economy', *Edinburgh Review*, LXVI, October 1837, p. 80.

[21] [G. P. Scrope], 'Rights of Industry and the Banking System', *Quarterly Review*, XLVII, July 1832, pp. 411–12.

[22] Scrope, *Principles*, p. 63.

who came under his wrath when capital was the subject of discussion. Hodgskin was identified with declamations 'against capital as the poison of society, and the taking of interest on capital by its owners, as an abuse, an injustice, a robbery of the class of labourers'.[23] Hodgskin was not mentioned by Longfield, but he, too, identified as the source of socialist doctrine one of those men who were 'conscious of their invalidity', whose object was 'to create disturbance, by stimulating the passions of the poor and ignorant, and persuading them that their poverty is caused by oppression'.[24] Much of this polemic was situated within discussions of the role of capital and the determination of the rate of profits. It is indeed quite obvious that much of this new theory was defensive and apologetic.

However, these same economists were simultaneously seeking an escape from the political connotations of political economy. They addressed themselves to those who dismissed political economy because it was 'political'. One answer was that of Richard Whately who preferred to describe political economy as 'catallactics', the science of exchanges. He used his credentials as a theologian in the Drummond chair to fight the prejudice against political economy 'among those who represent it as unfavourable to religion'.[25] Scrope argued that this attitude to political economy was prevalent only because of the mistakes of the economists themselves. Political economy had been discredited by the 'dogmatism of the hyper economists'. He blamed empiricism and practical men for the most pernicious errors. He also disclaimed the tendency to see political economy as a physical science and was not enthusiastic over any fashionable 'political mathematics'.[26]

This rhetoric, directed at those ignorant of the new discipline, was increasingly put in terms neutral to politics. A debate on methodology obscured more fundamental political differences. By professing to go beyond politics, political economists hoped to open the discipline to a wider audience. With this aim in mind Nassau Senior left behind the political overtones to be found, for example, in his *Introductory Lecture on Political Economy*, in favour of greater methodological sophistication. In 1826 he had complained of the 'many crude and mischievous theories about, which are dignified with the name political economy',

23 *Ibid.* p. 150.
24 Longfield, *Lectures on Political Economy*, p. 158.
25 Richard Whately, *Introductory Lectures on Political Economy*, London, 1831, p. vi.
26 Scrope, *Principles*, pp. 36, 41.

and he feared that the subject would be 'left by the advocates of religion and social order to those hostile to both'.[27] In 1831 he argued

> Hitherto, it has been common to defend every existing practice as agreeable to common sense, in opposition to the visionary scheme of political theorists . . . To what has common prejudice, reigning under the title of common sense, brought me? Have the practical men who have hitherto administered our system of poor laws, saved us from being brought to the very brink of ruin?[28]

These political and methodological concerns added fuel to the efforts of political economists in the 1830s to provide a theory of economic development alternative to those of Malthus and Ricardo. For they blamed the unfavourable light in which political economy was held by much of the common public on the pessimistic predictions which followed from Malthus's law of population and Ricardo's theory of rent. They continued the critique of Ricardo which had occupied economists of the 1820s. But great political and social tensions now made a defence of the achievements of the Industrial Revolution all the more pressing. To the critique of Ricardo, therefore, they appended a detailed description and analysis of the technological improvements and tendency to increasing returns evident in the past few decades. Their defence of existing patterns of economic development and of the credibility of the political economist's explanation of these became in the political setting of the 1830s a strident polemic in favour of capital and machinery. Economists argued on the basis of the economic and technological advance of the past few decades that Malthus's law of population and Ricardo's theory of rent appeared to be theoretical irrelevancies. Herman Merivale pithily summed up the situation when he said of the one 'The doctrine of population is, in Political Economy, what that of original sin is in theology, – offensive to philosophical pride, and irksome to sanguine temperaments.' People preferred to be told 'There are extrinsic causes at work, which promise to render the ancient law of our nature a mere philosophical curiosity – a theorem without application, – that machinery and science, and facilities of communication, are outstripping . . . numbers.'[29]

27 Quoted by [Richard Whately], 'Oxford Lectures on Political Economy', *Edinburgh Review*, XLVIII, 1828, pp. 170, 173.
28 Senior, *Three Lectures on the Rate of Wages*, p. xii.
29 [H. Merivale], 'Definitions and Systems of Political Economy', *Edinburgh Review*, LXVI, October 1837, p. 95.

The other, Ricardian rent theory, he described as 'a *Pupsis offencionis*, startling and offending many'.[30] Senior and Scrope pointed out the effects of technological improvements: increasing returns to labour due to economies of large-scale production, and advances in agricultural techniques.[31] Richard Jones marshalled a barrage of empirical and historical data to refute the Ricardian theory of rent. The history of crop rotations, field combinations, fertilisers and artificial grasses was evidence enough that the 'powers of the earth had come to be kept in more constant and vigorous action'. 'The produce of the earth, so far from experiencing a gradual diminution, is capable of being indefinitely augmented, in proportion to the increase of skill, and assistance it receives from capital.'[32] Scrope continued the reproof, attaching such importance to technological improvement that he made one of the primary objects of his *Principles* the refutation of the 'gloomy predictions of the Malthusians'. He condemned Chalmers for his obsession with the rate of population growth and the limits to agriculture, 'a most portentous and abominable doctrine', which kept him 'bound within the necromantic circle which Malthus has forbidden him to dream of overstepping'.[33]

The attitudes of many of these critics can be summed up in the words of George Ramsay's praise for recent progress:

> The products of manufacturing and commercial industry as steadily increase in quantity as they improve in quality. The rise in the raw material, which they derive from agriculture, retards them, no doubt, a little in their course, but the vast discoveries in machinery, and the prodigious facilities for intercourse afforded by numerous canals and rail-roads far outstrip this obstacle to their progress, and leave us lost in amazement as well at their present state as at the prospect of their future advancement. Now these improvements must

[30] Cited in Gordon, 'Criticism of Ricardian Views on Value and Distribution', p. 378.
[31] N. W. Senior, *Two Lectures on Population*, London, 1829; [G. P. Scrope], 'The Political Economists', *Quarterly Review*, XLIV, January 1831, 49; [G. P. Scrope], 'Jones on the Doctrine of Rent', pp. 112–14.
[32] Richard Jones, *Literary Remains*, ed. William Whewell, London, 1859, p. 258.
[33] [G. P. Scrope], 'Dr. Chalmers on Political Economy', *Quarterly Review*, XLVIII, October 1832, pp. 69, 51.

greatly tend not only to increase the mass of commodities, and diminish their price, but also to raise the rate of profit.[34]

The efforts made by these economists to discount Ricardo's views were redoubled in their many projects to provide an alternative form of analysis. There were many similarities in these individual contributions. There was in the first place a common set of themes to which economists of the day addressed themselves, among which were a number dealing explicitly with economic development and the advance of technology. The concept of abstinence was the first and most central theme to their alternative perspectives on technology. They then went on to examine entrepreneurial activity. On the basis of their endorsement of the attributes of abstinence and entrepreneurial ability they made a critical reassessment of the division of labour, placing it squarely under capitalist subordination. After charting the paths to progress on the basis of ideas of abstinence, entrepreneurship and division of labour, economists went on to analyse capital and skill, the introduction of machinery, and the emergence and choice of alternative technologies. Finally, one other theme they explored to illustrate further their views on the progress of technology was the contrast between the economic structure of civilised and savage societies.

Abstinence

The firm belief in the gains from technical change was, as we have seen, challenged by anti-machinery rioters, trade unionists and socialists, but the challenge of the two latter groups went deeper, and questioned the distribution of these gains. The gains of workers were small or non-existent, they claimed, beside the colossal windfalls made by capitalists. Economists, in answer, applied themselves to the defence of the capitalist's share. This share of income was justified as a return for a certain activity – abstinence. Senior made abstinence a factor of production in the same sense as labour, 'by the word Abstinence, we wish to express that agent distinct from labour and the agency of nature, the concurrence of which is necessary to the existence of Capital and which stands in the same relation to Profits as Labour does to Wages'.[35] If abstinence was a recurring activity fundamental to the creation of

---

[34] George Ramsay, *An Essay on the Distribution of Wealth,* London, 1830, pp. 189–90.
[35] N. W. Senior, *An Outline of the Science of Political Economy*, London, 1836, p. 59.

capital, then so too, argued Senior, were other attributes of the capitalist class, namely knowledge and skill. Wages and profits were a human creation, and both depended on the sacrifice of ease or present enjoyments. Profits should therefore include the 'wages' of the 'labour' of the capitalist.[36] Senior considered the source of capital to be abstinence, but the use of capital required two necessary corollaries : the use of 'implements' and the 'division of labour'. In the discussion of 'implements' he sets out his ideas on the special place of fixed capital and machinery, which he distinguished from capital in general. These were categorised into those that produced power such as machines worked by wind, water, or steam, and those that transmitted power such as hand-impelled tools. Implements could not be brought into use without some exercise in abstinence. Carrying his theory of abstinence to an extreme, he argued furthermore that it was a fiction for economists to speak of landlord, capitalist and labourer as sharing in production. All that was produced was, in the first instance, the property of the capitalist. It was the capitalist who paid rent and wages prior to the production process; it was the capitalist who abstained to make production possible.[37]

Senior's hypothetical history of the origin and development of capital was indicatively static. He failed to consider the possibility of one production process growing out of another, or that the relations between social groups or classes involved in the production process might have differed over time. However, his hypothetical history suited his purposes, as was admirably borne out by the conclusions of those critics who used a similar historical model. Longfield, too, made a case for the application of capital 'in the support of labour' as the prior condition of the introduction of machinery. This was the basis of wage payments. The capitalist paid the labourer as much as he could earn without the aid of machinery. Any productivity differentials after the introduction of this fixed capital were defined as the property of the capitalist.[38]

Neither Senior nor Longfield found it convenient to say anything of the differences in the character or structure of a production process after the introduction of the fixed capital they so hypothetically out-

[36] N. W. Senior, 'Ambiguous Terms in Political Economy', Appendix to Richard Whately, *Elements of Logic* (1826), 2nd edition, London, 1827, p. 320.
[37] Senior, *An Outline*, p. 69.
[38] Longfield, *Lectures on Political Economy*, p. 190.

lined. W. F. Lloyd, however, was more explicit : 'Employers, the owners of much fixed capital, have a strong and direct interest in over-working their labourers, and the smallness of their number, joined to the superiority of their intelligence and other circumstances, gives to them a power which throws the workmen entirely at their feet.'[39]

The payment of wages and the form in which those wages were paid very closely mirrored these attitudes. Hobsbawm has evidence to show that employers in the nineteenth century acquired their skilled labour at less than market price because the workers' wage calculation was for a long time determined by a customary pre-industrial wage hierarchy.[40] The form of wages, however, became a major preoccupation to employers after the first third of the nineteenth century. Economists in the 1830s turned from an interest in wage levels to the systematic treatment of the form of wage payments. They gave greater favour to piece rates, and recognised this as a method of uniting the interests of the worker to the output of machinery, a combination encouraging greater efficiency.[41]

These political economists praised investment in fixed capital, but, because they did not attempt its description or analysis they could only assume a benign role for it. John Rae, the one economist who did start such a classification scheme for capital, indeed developed the means for explaining the very different types of impact any increase in fixed capital might have. Furthermore, his system of classification provided a quantitative measure of the impact of fixed capital. He argued that capital was made up of what he termed 'instruments'. These included all durable capital and other physical transformations designed to affect future events, and each 'instrument' had a particular capacity to produce desired events. He measured this capacity by a standardised daily wage because the cost of production of the instruments themselves was measured by labour inputs. Each instrument not only had a capacity to affect the future, but was subject to a process of 'exhaustion'. An instrument was exhausted either when it was transformed into new materials or when simply dissipated. It was exhausted more or less slowly; food and fuel were quickly used up and machinery slowly. Instruments could be placed in some quantitative order on the basis

[39] W. F. Lloyd, *Two Lectures on the Justice of the Poor Laws and One Lecture on Rent*, London, 1837, p. 105.
[40] Hobsbawm, 'Custom, Wages and Workload', p. 409.
[41] L. Bernhard, *Die Akkordarbeit in Deutschland*, Leipzig, 1903, cited Hobsbawm, 'Customs, Wages and Workload', p. 420.

of their relative costs of production, their 'capacities', and their 'exhaustion' times. If they had a great capacity and a low cost of production, capital would receive a fast return, rapidly reproducing itself. The rate of return on capital could be raised by altering the capacity, the cost of production or the exhaustion of an instrument. The capacity of an instrument could be raised by adding either to its durability or to its efficiency. However, without at the same time changing the techniques of production, 'neither of these could be indefinitely increased without carrying instruments to orders of slower and slower return'. If the capacity of an instrument was increased and the order of an instrument either did not change or became one of faster return, this was evidence of technical change. Furthermore, the impact of any change in technique could be measured by comparing the change in capacities with the change in the orders of the instrument in question.[42]

Entrepreneurship

Abstinence formed only one of the justifications for the capitalist's share. Others were his 'labour', skill, and enterprise. J. B. Say's pronouncements on the importance of entrepreneurship were extended by these economists to justify high capitalist profits.[43] 'Productive service' and the 'wages of superintendence' were moulded into the conception of industrial progress. Read asked : 'How much should be allowed as the wage of the "owner of capital" superintending the industrious undertaking?'[44] John Rae answered that the profit of stock must include a return for the mental exertion and anxiety of the owner of stock.[45] J. S. Mill argued that such a wage was not determined in the same way as other wages, but was a commission on capital employed.[46] And Ramsay went yet further, by distinguishing the functions of supervisor and entrepreneur from that of the capitalist. The entrepreneur did not do manual labour, and his profits could not be said to be proportional to his 'mental qualities' as these could not be quantified.

42 John Rae, *New Principles of Political Economy*, Boston, 1834, pp. 109–17.
43 Koolman, in 'Say's Conception of the Role of Entrepreneur', argues that it was not until this period in Britain that some recognition was given to the role of entrepreneurship, and that G. P. Scrope, Samuel Read, and George Ramsay took the concept from Say.
44 Read, *An Inquiry*, p. 247.
45 Rae, *New Principles*, p. 195.
46 J. S. Mill, 'Of the Influence of Production on Consumption' and 'On Profits and Interest', in J. S. Mill, ed., *Essays on Some Unsettled Questions*, London, 1844, pp. 59 and 107.

> On the one hand there are masters, on the other labourers,
> capitalists and landlords, combined. The interests of these two
> grand classes are diametrically opposed to each other. It is the
> master who *hires* labour, capital and land, and of course tries
> to get the use of them on as low terms as possible; while the
> owners of these sources of wealth do their best to *let* them as
> high as they can.[47]

It was not just trouble and skill, however, which should be compensated by the wage of superintendence, but, as was maintained by Scrope,
the risks of obsolescence. 'The risks of these kinds attached to manufacturing operations are . . . much greater than in agriculture; and
hence the compensation or insurance against such risks must be
proportionately large.'[48] The level of payment for these qualities of
entrepreneurship and abstinence was expected to be determined by
social criteria. Returns, argued Scrope, were to be sufficient to pay the
ordinary rate of profit on total capital, 'as well as remunerate him for
his skill and trouble, according to the *standard of remunerations generally expected by his class*'.[49]

Paths to progress

Political economists who looked to capital, and especially fixed capital,
to understand the sources of increasing returns went on from here to
describe the origins of existing techniques and to explain why certain
techniques had become predominant over others. They looked at the
different paths to progress in old and new countries, demonstrating the
different ways in which the division of labour was related to the origins
of capital accumulation and invention. To do this they discarded
Ricardo, and returned to the study of Smith. Like their predecessors
in the 1820s they sought ways of adapting the Smithian concept of the
division of labour to their understanding of contemporary patterns of
economic development. From the standpoint of their perspectives on
the central position of capital, therefore, they turned Smith's concept
of the division of labour on its head. It became the combination of
labour and concentration of capital, generated not just skill but 'mental

---

[47] Ramsay, *An Essay on Distribution*, pp. 209–11, 219.
[48] Scrope, *Principles*, p. 209. Scrope's source for this was Babbage who
claimed machinery seldom wore out before it became technically
obsolescent. He calculated that any piece should have paid for itself
in five years, p. 210.
[49] *Ibid.* p. 211.

capital', and created the conditions for the emergence of the principles behind invention.

Many of the ideas for the adaptation of the division of labour to the context of capital were formulated in policy debates over colonisation. The 'colonisers' combined their discussion of 'fields for the employment of capital' with a political economy of new countries. They stressed, not just technological improvement and capital formation in the British economy, but the imperative of efficient production in new countries. Malthus, Scrope, and Torrens all agreed that unless productivity in agricultural countries kept pace with that of British industry, the net barter terms of trade would turn against Great Britain. Colonising would raise the rate of economic development in new countries,[50] but only under certain conditions. As Wakefield argued, this development was dependent upon what he termed the 'complex combination of labour'. This principle included the creation of markets, the division of labour, and capital accumulation. It was a principle natural enough to old countries, but not to new colonies: 'without co-operation and the division of employment, capital and labour are so weak and so unproductive that surplus produce, either for foreign exchange or for accumulation at home, cannot be raised. This is a primitive or barbarous state of things.'[51]

He argued that the prosperity of old countries was based on slavery which had prevented the initial dispersal of industry, and referred to his own recommendation of complex combination as one of 'natural slavery'.[52]

McCulloch's continued interest in the division of labour and the limitless prospects of invention gathered momentum as he traced the interaction between concentration and the division of labour, and accumulated evidence in favour of his prejudices for growth biased to the manufacturing sector.[53] But he met his match in his enthusiasm for the division of labour in Senior, who harnessed the principle to his analysis of the British economy, but subordinated it to capital. Senior

---

[50] See Bernard Semmel, *The Rise of Free Trade Imperialism*, Cambridge, 1970, pp. 186–93.

[51] E. G. Wakefield, Report of the Select Committee on South Australia, Appendix, quoted in Robbins, *Robert Torrens*, pp. 158–9.

[52] A detailed discussion of Wakefield's system can be found in Robbins, *Robert Torrens*, and Winch, *Classical Political Economy and Colonies*, pp. 90–8.

[53] See O'Brien, *J. R. McCulloch*, pp. 275–80, and McCulloch, *A Statistical Account of the British Empire*, p. 37.

not only made capital a prior condition of the division of labour, but, by association, of the possession of tools and the creation of private property as well. He described as a 'rude state' one where everyone owned all the implements. Technological progress itself confirmed this. When expensive machinery and a great variety of tools had superseded the few simple implements, 'those only who can profitably employ themselves in any branch of manufacture' are those 'who can acquire machinery or are trained to work it'.[54] The division of labour would react in turn by helping to generate a transfer of labour from unproductive sectors to those under capitalist control.

> The division of labour has banished from our halls to our manufactures the distaff and the loom : and if the language to which we have been adverting were correct, the division of labour must be said to have turned spinners and weavers from unproductive into productive labourers and from producers of immaterial services into producers of material objects.[55]

Richard Jones provided a yet more effective integration of the division of labour and capitalist control. The division of labour was implemented in agriculture and in manufacturing by the knowledge and superintendence of the capitalist :

> observe the skill, knowledge, and thoughtfulness by which the whole complex business of cultivation is conducted; ... well devised continuous industry aided by animal power, by manures, by implements and machines, supplies to the task of tillage a power far beyond what the more manual labourer can command ... The scattered artizans of other realms collected, here, into workshops and manufactories, the eye of a superior enforcing everywhere steady and continuous labour; knowledge and science importing to human industry a sovereign power over the material world.[56]

Jones stressed that the division of labour was 'only one, and a subordinate, though important effect of the accumulation of capital in production'.[57]

[54] Senior, *An Outline*, p. 74.
[55] *Ibid.* p. 53.
[56] Richard Jones, *Literary Remains*, p. 12.
[57] *Ibid.* p. 33.

The formation of the human agency, by which the continuity of labour is secured; the maintenance of the intellect which enlightens its application; the employment of power which resides either in a higher order of moving forces or in mechanical contrivance, . . . are contributions of capital . . . it is the same capital which makes the division of labour possible by maintaining the workmen in the progress of their task till markets are found for their commodities.[58]

Private property and capitalist control were seen by Senior, Jones, and their contemporaries to be the natural foundations for the division of labour. Scrope made a political point of the necessity of the principle of private property. Objecting to the Owenites, he quoted various historical examples to show that those societies which had existed under communal property arrangements had been 'rarely . . . observed to make any advance in the arts of production or the accumulation of wealth'.[59] On the advantages of the division of labour, Scrope, greatly influenced by Babbage, stressed the economy of time and power 'due to a well regulated division of labour' and he drew attention to McCulloch's extension of the concept of the division of labour to include the division of labour of the mind, as, for instance, when chemistry became separated from natural philosophy. Scrope was also one of the few to mention the property of the labourer. Generally, the only property of the labourer was a little acquired skill. The land, tools and machinery indispensable to labour and the food that formed the labourer's subsistence were all appropriated by other classes. This placed the people 'in a precarious position', and it was in an area like this that the paternalist Scrope saw a need for government intervention to give protection to the working class.[60]

Capital and skill

The domination of capital even extended to the analysis of skill. In Senior's *Outline of Political Economy* knowledge and education were defined as 'mental capital', the most adaptable form of capital. But the action of the division of labour in further processing and refining skills also made them a less fluid form of capital, less able to be transferred easily between industries and branches of production. 'The skill which

[58] *Ibid.* p. 32.
[59] G. P. Scrope, *Principles*, p. 61.
[60] *Ibid.* pp. 299–308.

the division of labour gives to each class of artificers prevents the peculiar dexterity an individual may have from being of any value in a business to which he has not been brought up.'[61] Senior applies his analysis of capital wholesale to the concept of skill. 'Acquired abilities' were 'fixed and realized in the person of the possessor . . . The greater part of the remuneration for skilled labour is the reward for the abstinence implied by a considerable expenditure on the labourer's education.'[62] The accumulation of skills was, as Scrope noticed, similar to the accumulation of capital. Skills were taught by actual exhibition and repeated experiment, and when these skills were passed on from master to pupil they accumulated the improvements of their various users on the way. Many progressive innovations had also been developed from 'useful knowledge', the 'accumulated ability stored in books'.[63]

The acquisition and application of skill in some circles also required the creation of a separate class of workmen or supervisory capitalists. As Jones saw it, skill implied creative organisation and required the creation of a class 'freed from the necessity of mere manual labour', and 'at liberty to employ their intellect, to facilitate the application of labour to its task'.[64] In agriculture, capitalist farming would form the basis for such gains in skill. For the skill of the cultivating class increased as they were 'freed from the toilsome and absorbing occupations of the mere labourer, and not distracted by loftier pursuits and more enticing occupations'. Ultimately, skills would accumulate and there would be 'an increase in the efficiency of capital employed in cultivation'.[65]

The predominance of capital found its way not only into the analysis of the division of labour and skill, but even into explanations of invention. Political economists investigated the social and psychological motivations behind discovery, and came up with the banal assertion that inequality was necessary to create an atmosphere of emulation. The belief in this inequality did not demand adhesion to the classical class divisions, for the conception of a gradation of ranks suited just as well. It was argued by some that the major motivation behind industry was the wish to preserve rank in society. The gradual advance

[61] Senior, *An Outline*, p. 217.
[62] *Ibid.*
[63] [Scrope], 'The Political Economists', p. 13 and *Principles*, chap. 5; Babbage was the direct source for Scrope's examples if not for many of his ideas in this chapter of his book.
[64] Jones, *Literary Remains*, pp. 21, 29.
[65] Richard Jones, *An Essay on the Distribution of Wealth, I, Rent*, London, 1831, p. 236.

of the few produced a feeling of emulation.[66] 'Indolence' was the product either of a 'want of neighbourhood' where no extensive gradation could be established, or the lack of a supply of luxuries: 'if the acquisition within his reach be lower, he may give way to indolence. Every improvement in art and skill which renders labour more productive, adds to the quantity of labour performed by offering a higher reward for it.'[67] But inequality would create not only envy but the necessary 'share of leisure' for the 'cultivation of genius'.[68]

Man and machine

The central role given to fixed capital in the 1830s was buttressed by the analysis of machinery and the accumulation of capital. The occasion for this analysis was the continued preoccupation with the machinery and labour question both at the level of practical politics and at the theoretical level of responding to Ricardo. Senior felt it necessary to carry out a complete critique of Ricardo's chapter on machinery. Longfield and Scrope also dealt with the issue in some detail.

Senior, after examining the hypothetical case put forward by Ricardo, agreed like earlier critics that it was true in principle that the rate of wages could be reduced by the introduction of machinery. Where capital was scarce and technical change sudden, the costs of constructing machinery could create a real setback for labour. Lower wages or reduced employment would result if labour generally employed in the consumer goods sector was transferred to the production of capital goods, and if the latter absorbed commodities otherwise consumed by labour. But Senior saw little prospect of Ricardo's hypothetical case ever coming to pass, for the reality was, he argued, that the expense of machine building was paid out of profits and rent.[69] Longfield, similarly, gave little credence to Ricardo's example, and simply retorted that in all practical cases a machine was never introduced unless it led to lower costs of production.[70]

There were, in the wake of all these attempts to discredit the theoretical position of the critics of machinery, two political economists who recognised the existence of technological unemployment. Scrope, because of his paternalist concern for the poor, conceded that any

66 [George Robertson], *Essays on Political Economy*, London, 1830, pp. 35–6.
67 Robert Hamilton, *The Progress of Society*, London, 1830, p. 32.
68 *Ibid.* p. 179.
69 Senior, *Three Lectures on the Rate of Wages*, pp. 39–62.
70 Longfield, *Lectures on Political Economy*, p. 219.

sudden change of techniques might lead to problems of occupational and geographical mobility. A change in the mode of production in particular industries did lead to the unemployment of those who had worked with an older method. Labour was not perfectly mobile between techniques or branches of industry. 'The prejudice against machinery, still prevalent among the poor and ignorant' was understandable, and ways had to be found of increasing the mobility of labour.[71] But it was Jones who went so far as to declare employment to be a limit on the accumulation of fixed capital. The wages of labour, he pronounced, had to be kept proportionate to the prosperity of capitalists. Capitalists could only have momentary advantage in the deprivation of labourers. The ultimate effect would be a drop in productivity, and a decline in the security of property : 'The accumulation of large masses of auxiliary capital cannot go on undisturbed in the midst of a degraded and turbulent population.'[72]

The discussion of capital and machinery in the 1830s and the place given to them in generalisations about economic development disclosed a break in ideas about technology between the 1820s and the 1830s. Where earlier political economists had focussed on the division of labour they now gave pride of place to fixed capital. The machine came to the fore in economic thought in the 1830s, but its authority was to be short lived. For in the late 1840s political economists found a new centre of attraction in discovering the implications of self-regulating power. After 1848 the issue with machinery died away, as political economists and their public submitted to the all-powerful discipline of the physical forces apparent in steam and other forms of power. The views of Nassau Senior and Richard Jones were two of the best examples of this shift in the interests of political economists.

Senior showed interest during the 1830s in the attributes of inanimate power, but directed his attention mainly to the 'improvement' entailed by power machinery. He was fascinated by Marsland's Stockport factory which he reports seeing in 1825. He enthused : 'if the power of directing inanimate substances, at the same time to exert the most tremendous energy, and to perform the most delicate operations, be the test, that dominion and power are nowhere so strikingly shown as in a large cotton manufactory'.[73] Senior went into some detail describing the water-power system and the connection of all the shafts in Marsland's

---

71 Scrope, *Principles*, p. 192.
72 Jones, *Essay on . . . Rent*, p. 291.
73 Senior, *An Outline*, p. 70.

factory. He conceived of power in the same terms in which he thought of machinery: 'In the operation of machinery, power, like matter, seems susceptible of indefinite aggregation and of indefinite sub-division. In the performance of some of its duties the machinery moved at a rate almost formidable, in others at one scarcely perceptible.'[74] One of Senior's major sources in this discussion was the Report of the Select Committee on Combination Laws, Artisans and Machinery of 1824, which I will discuss in greater detail in Chapter 9. The Report gave Senior ample evidence of one essential quality of machinery – its 'susceptibility of infinite improvement'. And it was to cotton machinery combined with the steam engine that he attributed the major economic transformation he was living through.

> Sixty years form a short period in the history of a nation; yet what changes in the state of England and the Southern parts of Scotland have the steam engine and cotton machinery effected within the last sixty years. They have almost doubled the population, more than doubled the wages of labour, and nearly trebled the rent of land.[75]

The position of fixed capital was treated more systematically by Richard Jones who analysed the development of what he termed 'auxiliary' capital within the general history of capital formation. He argued that the 'enormous development' of 'aids to human power' had 'created a new era in the history of human industry'.[76] There was, he pointed out, a constant tendency to the accumulation of auxiliary capital, that is, continuously improving fixed capital.

> Where capital abounds, owners of it are always impelled by self interest to use the various additions which they employ as much as possible in the shape of auxiliary capital, and as little as they can help in the shape of the wages of labour ... The gradual increase of the relative quantity of auxiliary capital is, therefore, the ordinary effect of the progressive increase of the whole mass of capital employed in agriculture.[77]

Contrasted to a world view, in which fixed capital was defined as a material substance which was more durable and efficient than labour

[74] *Ibid.* p. 71.
[75] *Ibid.* p. 72.
[76] Jones, *Literary Remains*, p. 10.
[77] Jones, *Essay on ... Rent*, p. 241.

and therefore displaced it, came a new perception expressed in the 1840s. Senior, in his lectures of 1847 gauged that the real triumph was not with machinery but with inanimate power, particularly that which began with steam. What distinguished it from all other forms of power was its 'manageableness' and regularity: 'The engine does all that requires force. The workman has only to supply it with materials and to perform the services which being irregular and unforeseen cannot be obtained from an irrational agent.'[78] The regularity of this force allowed for greater precision in verifying the quantity of quality of goods so produced.[79]

Senior now saw that the essential qualities of modern machinery were force, dexterity, uniformity, and safety.[80] Gone was the interest in giving material description to fixed capital as machinery. Gone was the interest in describing the production process as a structure where labour co-operated with fixed capital, albeit dominated by the 'more superior' capital. Now, attributes of both machinery and labour were derived from the domination of moving power. This conception of the new industrial dimension offered by the use of power also prompted Senior to look into the sophisticated combination of the types of force generated by hand tools and those based on moving power. Not just steam power, but tools, had been integral to England's industrial transformation. 'Few things in England are so striking to a foreigner as the abundance and variety of our tools.'[81] Such tools, combined with power, produced ever new innovations, such as the adaptation of the simple hammer to the steam hammer. Moreover, steam, according to Senior, created the conditions for the introduction of electricity: the railway provided the long level lines along which wire could be conveniently extended.[82]

This new attention to power and force was also evident in Richard Jones's later observations. In an essay, probably written in the late 1840s though it was not published until after his death in 1852, he set out the influence and growth of mechanical power. Jones made a very important distinction between force and the mode of applying force, that is machinery: 'Whatever the moving force, . . . we can have no measure of the power with which it is employed in production, unless we are

[78] Senior Papers, N. Senior, 'Lectures', Course II, Lecture 7, 1848, pp. 23–4.
[79] *Ibid.* p. 33.
[80] *Ibid.* p. 42.
[81] *Ibid.* Lecture 7, p. 31.
[82] *Ibid.* Lecture 8, p. 42.

familiar with the greater or less degree of perfection of the machinery and implements.'[83] Motive force and machinery affected countries differently according to their stages of development and endowments. In England and France he judged that there had been recourse to 'the higher orders of moving force' to such an extent that differences of mechanical advantage did not have any great impact. In poorer countries, however, it was not 'moving force' but basic implements, tools and machinery, which made a much greater contribution to efficiency.[84] Jones even went so far as to analyse the differences in the frequency and style in invention in the newly significant power technologies.

> The discoveries of new moving forces are made rarely and at
> considerable intervals; the discovery of new modes of applying
> forces already known, by improved machinery and tools, is of
> daily occurrence, and facilitates the application of increasing
> masses of capital on a much more extensive scale, though in a
> less striking manner, . . . than when such inventions as wind
> and water mills, or even steam were in the first instance
> applied.[85]

These remarkable visions of the economic future were later to inspire Marx to write of the automatic mechanical system which dominated the place of economic development which he formulated as 'modern industry'.

Alternative technologies

The social and historical view of the origin of fixed capital that interested political economists in the 1830s also prompted them to look at alternative technologies, and to assess the conditions which influenced the advance or development of a particular set of techniques. Scrope investigated the impact of wage changes under various technical conditions. In the case of a technique using high proportions of fixed capital and small amounts of labour, a wage rise was likely to have a minimal effect on profits. In the other case where the proportion of labour was high, the impact of any change in wages on profits would be substantial. Scrope also pointed out that capital could be transferred from a sector dominated by one set of techniques to that dominated by another. The effect of an influx of capital into the sector dominated

---

83 Jones, *Literary Remains*, p. 25.
84 *Ibid.* p. 28.
85 *Ibid.* p. 73.

by capital intensive methods would be to reduce the price of its products. But such a transfer of capital away from labour-intensive production, in order to escape the impact of high wage claims, would raise the price of goods produced by labour-intensive techniques. Scrope did not, however, think that high wage demands would ever actually result in a large-scale transfer from labour-intensive to capital-intensive production. For the rise in wages would also affect the cost of acquiring machinery. The high costs of switching techniques from labour-intensive to capital-intensive ones would substantially reduce the level of expected profits, and thus the motives to change processes and patterns of production. Scrope did not, however, make clear the final implication of this analysis. A disequilibrium in the rate of profit between sectors could be indefinite.[86]

The comparative and historical approach to economics gave John Rae a sense of the social determinants of techniques of production : he came to see that alternative technologies could be developed to suit different environments. Rae went further and suggested that the efficiency of techniques was not technically but socially defined. It was thus he came to distinguish the production conditions of intensive agriculture from those of extensive cultivation.

> An English farmer . . . who comes to North America to pursue his art, almost always commences on the system which he followed in Britain. His agricultural implements, his harness, his carts and waggons, etc. are all of the most durable and complete, and therefore, of the most expensive construction, and his fields are tilled as laboriously and carefully as were those he cultivated in his native land. Some time usually elapses, before he discovers that he might do better by being content with more simple, and less highly finished implements, and that it will be for his advantage to cultivate . . . less laboriously, though not less systematically. His neighbours tell him indeed from the first, that if he expects the same profits as they have, he must have less dead stock on his hands, and must give more activity to his capital; but he is slow of believing them.[87]

It is true, however, that any notice taken of the choice of techniques was only to add evidence to the belief that the most capital-intensive techniques in a society dominated by the accumulation of capital indicated

[86] Scrope, *Principles*, chaps. 5 and 7.
[87] Rae, *New Principles*, p. 207.

the highest stage of development. George Robertson affirmed the pervasive fusion of the accumulation of capital and best practice techniques : 'By means of an abundant capital, the makers of machinery likewise are enabled to provide the most suitable materials and the most expert workmen, for constructing what their employers consider best calculated for the proper performance of the work in contemplation.'[88] John Rae, too, connected the social conditions conducive to the accumulation of capital with those conducive to the invention and introduction of machinery. Accumulation was helped by these factors : a concern for the future welfare of society which allowed for programmes of investment in social overhead capital; intellectual awareness of and reflection on future needs; and social stability. The motivations for the introduction and invention of machinery were similar. But Rae did notice a key exception. As discussed above, few of the political economists made any distinction between inventors and innovators. Rae, however, did observe that the distinction mattered. Capital accumulation and the innovation of techniques suffered from any disturbance in the social order, but it was precisely this disturbance that stimulated scientific advance :

> Men are so much given to learning, that they do not readily become discoverers. They have received so much, that they do not easily perceive the need of making additions to it, or readily turn the vigour of their thoughts in that direction . . . Whatever, therefore, breaks the wonted order of events, and exposes the necessity or the possibility of connecting them by some other means, strongly stimulates invention.[89]

Machinery was connected to the accumulation of capital in another way. John Rae laid bare the social relations generated by their dual development. It was in the nature of progress to convert the original simple tools into more complex machinery. 'And so it is with all our implements, they are passing on to great machines. This process can be averted by no conceivable process that would not have the effect of fettering all the active powers of humanity.'[90] This raised the question *cui bono*. With the accumulation of capital it was obvious that the 'former artisans, in giving up their tools have never become the owners

88 Robertson, *Essays on Political Economy*, p. 353.
89 Rae, *New Principles*, p. 223.
90 John Rae, 'Essay on Education' (1843), in C. W. Mixter, ed., *The Sociological Theory of Capital*, London, 1905, p. 235.

of the machines that have succeeded them'. Rae concluded that machinery and factories came to be owned by a particular class – 'the operative . . . owns nothing but his hands and the art of using them fitly'. The artisan was forced to sell his labour to the owner of the machine and was degraded in social status. 'Formerly he was a small capitalist, now it is the characteristic of his condition to be a mere operative, destitute of capital.'[91] Rae compared the 'industrious apprentice' to the 'present factory boy' and predicted the fate of handicraft manufacture after the current 'revolution' in industry.[92]

The savage mind and civil society

The political economy of the 1830s and early 1840s also had a distinctive social framework. A remarkable theme running through the writings of the political economists of the period was the idea of a contrast between their own economy and that of primitive cultures. The analysis of technical change and the accumulation of capital was coloured by images of progress and primitivism, and backed up by the hypothetical history and anthropological findings of the period. Economists of the period had a great deal to say about primitive economies, but their emphasis was on the contrast with industrialised societies and not on the development of those cultures in themselves.

The role that savages played in early nineteenth-century thought was perceptively uncovered by one of the colonial reformers, Herman Merivale. Merivale made telling comment on the uses of savages for political economists and political philosophers: their culture was 'a sort of zero in the thermometer of civilization', and thus appeared to give some scientific status to a theory of the gradual rise towards perfection. He did not doubt that the model was of value in hypothetical reasoning, but argued that historically it was false. His own diffusionist approach reflected the assumption of a great divide between primitive and modern cultures, or what Levi-Strauss calls 'a level plain between two ascents'.[93] 'We do not know a single instance of a savage tribe raising itself by unassisted efforts to a state of civilization. This has always been effected by foreign emigration from a more civilized state.'[94]

Almost all the theorists discussed in this chapter had implicit social

---

[91] Rae, 'Essay on Education', p. 235.
[92] *Ibid.* p. 236.
[93] Quoted in E. Gellner, *The Legitimation of Belief*, Cambridge, 1974, p. 153.
[94] [Merivale], 'Definitions and Systems of Political Economy', p. 90.

theories and models of underdevelopment. Senior distinguished savage man by his lack of abstinence. The savage exercised labour and providence. But the pre-requisite for a rise from hunting or fishing to a pastoral, then arable, phase was abstinence.[95] Similarly, Rae produced the example of the American Indian whose concern for future welfare was seen in terms of the tribe. In this situation 'prudence and foresight' could have little effect on the future welfare of the individual. In any case, the direction of events was obviously beyond the control of the hunter in the woods.[96] If economists could define modern man on the basis of his capacity for abstinence, then it is not surprising that they also defined 'the modern economy' in terms of its fixed capital and machinery. In a savage state labour could acquire only minimal productivity because of lack of fixed capital. Scrope argued that 'by practice, and the exercise of his native ingenuity, in . . . fabricating instruments, a clever savage may increase the productiveness and reward of his labour far beyond that of his companions'. But this allowance for some form of advancement was set up by Scrope only as a contrast to the much better conditions of even the lowest level labourer in a civilised society. Modern society was distinguished by its accumulation of fixed capital.[97] Scrope also defended the diffusionist view of civilisation. He found it quite easy to dispose of Whately's platonic conception that man was created with innate knowledge, and was unconvinced by his idea that present-day savage tribes were formerly civilised nations now in a state of deterioration.[98]

The use of the image of the savage to illustrate a social theory of the accumulation of capital reached its limits in John Stuart Mill's *Principles*. Like the political economists before him he argued that the egalitarian structure of savage societies was based on an equality of poverty and a non-existent rate of capital accumulation. Such peoples lived exclusively on wild animals; their habitations were made of logs or the boughs of trees and abandoned at an hour's notice; the food they used could not be stored. The great advance, he claimed, came with the domestication of useful animals and the emergence of inequality. Mill regarded the origin of such inequality as natural : 'large flocks and herds are in time possessed by active and thrifty individuals through their own exertion and by the heads of families and tribes,

95 Senior, *An Outline*, p. 69.
96 Rae, *New Principles*, pp. 131–2.
97 Scrope, *Principles*, p. 88.
98 *Ibid*. pp. 259, 260.

through the exertions of those connected with them by allegiance'.[99] The tilling of the ground, which was stimulated by population pressure, created a greater surplus which was taken from the producers by those who had established themselves as lords of the soil.[100] He cited Charleroix on the natives of Paraguay and John Rae on the North American Indians to back up his claims for the inadequacy of fore-thought, and thus accumulation, among primitive peoples. He also echoed the old prejudice against the Chinese for the inferior durability of their 'instruments'.[101] However, unlike his predecessors, Mill went on to criticise the excessive spirit of accumulation among the European middle classes. These saved without purpose or forethought for anything but the process of saving itself.[102]

The savage was also a tool both for those who espoused a social theory of ranks and those who pretended to a theory of social classes. Whately drew on the work of the physical anthropologist James Cowles Prichard and Dr Taylor, and used as his examples the Indians of New Guinea, the natives of the Pellew Islands and the American Indian. He postulated a series of gradations between the highest and the lowest state of human society. He compared the conditions of those on the bottom rungs of this ladder to 'as low a state as some tribes with which we are acquainted'. Both were incapable of any improvement by their own unassisted efforts.[103] As pointed out (p. 129), Hamilton's definition of primitive culture was expressed as a state lacking distinctions of rank and fortune, and the force of emulation. Lloyd contrasted the societies of the Otaheiti and the Hayti to prove that the inequality of property encouraged the production of luxuries and conveniences.[104] But he revealed the essential class nature of the production process in a way no other economist of the period did. He made very little of the difference between free labour and slavery : 'Whether the system of free labour or of slavery be established, we may equally find a class of society enjoying,

[99] J. S. Mill, *Principles of Political Economy with Some of the Applications to Social Philosophy*, vol. ii, *Collected Works*, University of Toronto Press, 1965, p. 11.
[100] *Ibid.* p. 11.
[101] *Ibid.* pp. 166–7.
[102] *Ibid.* pp. 167–8.
[103] R. Whately, *Introductory Lectures*, p. 127 and Lecture v.
[104] As far back as the 1750s, Turgot had made similar arguments. He believed that inequality was the necessary precondition for the extension of the division of labour, exchange, commerce and the accumulation of capital. See Ronald Meek, *Social Science and the Ignoble Savage*, Cambridge, 1975, p. 71.

without personal labour, the necessaries, conveniences, and luxuries of life, and another class performing the labour requisite for purchasing these necessaries, conveniences, and luxuries at the hands of nature.'[105] This analogy between the exploitation of capitalist and slave societies was tempered by the attempt to discover which form of exploitation was most favourable to growth. The case that slave labour was more inefficient than free was a part of the armoury of the humanitarian cause in the anti-slavery debates. Scrope developed this form of argument using Richard Jones's work on types of agricultural labour. It was his characterisation of the cottier that

> Poverty, the constant fatigues of laborious exertion, and the grasping blindness of his landlord, put both science and the means of assisting his industry by the accumulation of capital out of reach of the peasant. And from the landowners themselves it is vain to hope for either much steady superintendence of cultivation, or the accumulation of capital. They are not a saving class.[106]

Scrope later went on to trace the different patterns of development between the East and the West. The pattern of land occupation constituted the basic difference, and from this he traced the slow shift from serfdom to free tenancy, the object of which was to 'encourage the industry' of the cultivator by guaranteeing 'some return for his efforts'.[107] This transition from servitude to free labour was achieved by force, but liberty and pauperism grew up together. Scrope blamed the contradiction on the management of the Poor Laws, which was left to the magistracy and landed groups, precisely those elements which had an interest in keeping wages low and rents high. He accused them of 'forcibly metamorphosing the whole labouring population into paupers'.[108]

Political economy in the early 1830s gathered together the strands of thought defining civil society. This was the most advanced form of society developing over time, and acted as the cocoon for the protection and nourishment of fixed capital. It was the assumption of political economy that the historically unprecedented role of fixed capital was socially determined by a class structure and ideologically extended by the state. Read, Hamilton and Rae all limited the role of the state to

[105] Lloyd, *Two Lectures on the Justice of Poor Laws*, p. 17.
[106] [Scrope], 'Jones on the Doctrine of Rent', p. 91.
[107] Scrope, *Principles*, pp. 117–23.
[108] *Ibid.* p. 312.

paving the way to new inventions and new ways of acquiring fixed capital.

The sources for these images of past and primitive societies are not difficult to locate. J. W. Burrow blamed the contemporary lack of understanding of the alien and the primitive on the narrowness of utilitarianism and political economy, which produced an atmosphere of dogmatism. But the situation was more complicated than this. For, increasingly throughout this period, there was direct contact with the problems of alien cultures, and greater interest in collecting data to reinterpret concepts of society and social change.[109] Political economists were taking their examples, not only from history and the contemporary accounts of other European economies, but also from the data of the slavery debates and from early anthropological writings.

The more historical approach of political economists in this period recalls the social theories of Adam Smith and other writers of the Scottish Enlightenment. Many of these writers ascribed to a theory of progress in which the economy advanced through a series of stages, with savagery and barbarism as the lowest. They believed in the positive development of humanity and ascribed the superiority of contemporary European society to the existence of certain important socio-economic institutions and phenomena such as property rights, inequality, and the accumulation of capital.[110]

The stages theory was developed and adapted by the nineteenth-century inheritors of the Scottish tradition. James Mill made overt use of these philosophical principles to write his *History of India*. Mill ranked cultures by their achievements, and had great contempt for 'degenerate' Hindu society.[111] He also believed that Africa illustrated the earlier stages through which India had passed.[112] The comparative and historical analysis of many of the economic theorists of the 1830s also owed much to the Scottish tradition. Many of these theorists, like James Mill, had been educated in the Scottish universities, and had attended the lectures of Dugald Stewart.[113]

[109] J. W. Burrow, *Evolution and Society*, Cambridge, 1970, pp. 77–8.
[110] Meek, *Social Science and the Ignoble Savage*, pp. 117, 153.
[111] William Barber, *British Economic Thought and India*, Oxford, 1975, p. 129. For a discussion of the bearing of James Mill's intellectual formation on his *History of India* see Duncan Forbes, 'James Mill and India', *The Cambridge Journal*, v, October 1951.
[112] Philip Curtin, *The Image of Africa*, London, 1965, p. 250.
[113] Among others from the Scottish universities were John Rae, Samuel Read, and Robert Hamilton, Professor of Mathematics at Marischal College, Aberdeen.

This apparent continuity between eighteenth- and nineteenth-century ideas would seem to contradict Burrow's case for the death of conjectural history and the Scottish mode of thought at the end of the eighteenth century. But, in fact, for a host of reasons not mentioned by Burrow, intellectual conditions from the 1790s radically altered the Scottish legacy.

Another source for the developmental social framework of political economists of this period was the emerging discipline of anthropology.[114] From the 1830s onwards anthropology was feeling the impact of a re-orientation in the life sciences and geology, which, in turn, were becoming infused with a historical perspective. This was completed in the latter half of the nineteenth century with the entry of the theory of evolution.[115] It is striking, however, that the critique of Ricardo in the 1830s was developing in its method and approach along very similar lines to developments in anthropology and the life sciences. Scrope was only an ideal example of the connection between the disciplines. His geological work has been credited with laying the basis for Lyell's *Principles*. Scrope generalised a new idea of time and evolutionary change, and his demonstration of the progressive stages in the development of the earth's surface were compatible with his views on the historical development of capitalist society:

> Just as the causation of geological events, however unusual,
> was referable to the ordinary laws of nature, so Scrope
> believed that the most effective political economy would be
> one based on the 'natural laws' of social welfare . . . Just as
> the general 'invariability' of the laws of nature was in no way
> contravened by demonstrating that the earth had 'passed
> through several progressive stages of existence in the past',
> so the detection of laws of social behaviour was compatible

114 Little of the writing about Africa in the early years of the nineteenth century was politically neutral. It was dominated by debates between slavers and anti-slavers. Anthropology, at its barest beginnings, was still divided between biology and moral philosophy. The first anthropological societies came from a merger of J. C. Prichard's biological orientation with the political concerns of the humanitarians. Dr Thomas Hodgkin, a Quaker humanitarian, Professor of Anatomy at Guy's Hospital and a friend of Prichard's, began to supply the 1837 Parliamentary Committee on Aborigines with ethnographic data. Out of this he formed a permanent organisation, the Aboriginees Protection Society, to study the Aboriginees. See Curtin, *The Image of Africa*, pp. 217, 329-33.

115 Young, 'Malthus and the Evolutionists'.

with an optimistic outlook for the future progress of mankind. And at the deepest level, just as Scrope wished his geology to demonstrate the overall providential design behind the law bound progressiveness of the earth's history, so also he wished his political economy to vindicate the providential character of the world of human affairs by refuting the gloomy predictions of the Malthusians.[116]

Ideas of the development of primitive economies were culled from the prevailing attitudes in ethnography and travel literature. As Gellner puts it, what dominated was a theory of primitive mentality as steeped in intellectual error.[117] Nineteenth-century thinkers had an evolutionist vision of continuous growth, and used the contemporary primitive culture as a fossil of their own society.

The correspondence between the historical perspectives of political economists and those of the life scientists and anthropologists indicates a wider intellectual context for the economists' models of progress and capital accumulation. It does not, however, tell us about the social and political issues in which political economists intervened so vigorously. The appeal to anthropology was a way of writing political economy which, along with other factors, gave it a more scientific posture. The volume of scholarly work on the savage gave scientific status to a theory of the gradual rise towards the perfection of industrial capitalism. Earlier sections of this chapter have indicated the extent to which the economists' emphasis on the capacity for abstinence and the role of fixed capital was predicated on their desire to defend industrialisation against socialist critics and prejudices against the machine. But the image of the savage in the work of these and other social theorists had a definite ideological setting in contemporary attitudes towards the poor and labour.

There was, for instance, a definite analogy, current in the work of social reformers, between the savage and the poor and unemployed.[118]

---

[116] M. J. S. Rudwick, 'Poulett Scrope on the Volcanoes of Auvergne', *British Journal for the History of Science*, VII, March 1974, p. 238.

[117] Gellner, *The Legitimation of Belief*, pp. 149–52.

[118] See Lynn Lees, 'The Irish in London', in S. Thernstrom and R. Sennet, *Nineteenth Century Cities*, New York, 1969. Also see Gay Weber, 'Science and Society in Nineteenth Century Anthropology', *History of Science*, XII, 1974.

Kay Shuttleworth, then Chadwick, developed themes of social disease and urban degeneracy endemic to industrialism. Neither of these, however, challenged the industrial system; they, too, echoed support for the introduction of machinery.[119] Certainly, as well, the social reformer found his kinfolk among the missionaries to Africa and Asia, and among the scientists who encouraged them.

This social analogy between savages and the outcasts of advanced industrial society was, however, only the surface of much deeper concerns within political economy. I have shown how, for many of these economists, the savage represented a type of 'fossil' to nineteenth-century British culture. These economists had distinguished the savage by his lack both of abstinence and of the institutions of private property. But the idea of the savage also went alongside a definite change in ideas about labour in an industrial system. Just as the savage was regarded as a relic, so now was the ingenious artisan. John Rae traced with regret the transformation of the artisan into a 'mere operative'. These theorists saw the first transition, in their own time, of vital aspects of the work process. The new face of technical change was fixed capital and machinery. The labour that went with this was not that of the craftsman, but that of the factory hand. Some, indeed, feared explosive consequences from this process. Hamilton noted that the complex division of labour entailed by technical change had made workers increasingly inflexible and had gathered them together in large factories, full of sophisticated machinery. This labour was now simply the appendage of machinery, but its concentration allowed a basis for political organisation. The result, he predicted, was that in such a setting any sudden introduction of new fixed capital which substituted for human labour would create struggle in the factory and lead to the 'destruction of machinery'.[120]

This change in the idea of labour was also reflected in middle-class attitudes to workers' education. I will say much more of this in Chapter 7 on the Mechanics Institute Movement. Suffice it to say that these early campaigns for an appropriate vocational education had their counterpart in plans for the training of 'savages'. Policy makers and reviewers in the late 1830s and 1840s were demanding instruction in

[119] See James P. Kay, *The Moral Condition of the Manufacturing Population*, London, 1834, p. 87. Cf. Chadwick's question to the Political Economy Club on Smith's views of the excessive division of labour, 2 December 1839, *Political Economy Club, Centenary Volume*, VI, 280.

[120] Hamilton, *The Progress of Society*, p. 359.

agriculture and the mechanical arts for the African natives. But this was to be only an adequate education for an inferior people : it was proposed that industrial training be limited to such an extent that Africans should be taught to repair, but not to manufacture, the industrial products of England. Education was to consist of religious instruction along with agriculture for boys, and domestic science for girls. Its object was to provide a docile workforce. The children were to be 'taught habits of self control and moral discipline'. They were to be instructed in 'the mutual interests of the mother-country and her dependencies; the rational basis of their connection, and the domestic and social duties of the coloured races'. Their education in economics and politics was to include 'the relation of wages, capital and labour, and the influence of local and general government on personal security, independence, and order'.[121]

On the British scene, the mere operative and the factory hand were concepts proceeding out of a political economy which gave an unprecedented role to the abstaining capitalist and predicted gains from greater capitalist control of the production process. A more detailed examination of the role of the 'mere operative' took place in the context of the scientific movement. The promotion of Mechanics Institutes to provide a practical education for workers developed a rhetoric from the early 1820s to the early 1840s in a way which paralleled the shifts of emphasis in political economy over the same period. The changing attitudes to labour reflected in this rhetoric were complemented by new concerns at a grass-roots level with industrial management and labour discipline. The scientific movement carried the debate on the definition and significance of skills in the context of the machine age to broader audiences. The writers of management manuals and technological histories on the margins of this movement gained an enormous popularity for their attempts to deal with the practical problems of workshop and factory. It is to them and not to the political economists, therefore, that we must now look for ideas on the implementation of capitalist control of the production process through the organisation and pace of work, and the redefinition and breakdown of skills.

[121] Curtin, *The Image of Africa*, p. 427.

7

The scientific movement

Economists of the 1820s and 1830s welded their perceptions of the advance of technology to their concepts of economic development. But what they accomplished did not have implications for only the theoretical sphere of political economy. It reached beyond political economy to a far-reaching cultural sphere which took up the machinery question in political economy's terms and made a doctrine of technological progress. This cultural sphere was the scientific movement. The early nineteenth-century scientific movement was also to link the perception of technology to the promotion of economic improvement. The scientific movement formed the meeting point between the popular discipline of political economy and an extensive underworld of popular science.[1] This movement became an important avenue for the dissemination of vulgarised forms of political economy to the middle and working classes, for in it was assumed an ideology of economic growth in the technological vision which characterised the scientific culture of the time. The study of the economy met the study of science.

This chapter will move on from the analysis of political economy's perception of the machine to the analysis of the images of technological

[1] *The Mechanics Gallery of Science and Art, The Mechanics Weekly Journal and Artizans Miscellany, The Mechanics Oracle and Artizans Laboratory and Workshop, The Repertory of Arts, The London Mechanics Magazine* and *The Glasgow Mechanics Magazine*. There were also many journals which were either very short lived or non-starters. Fairbairn's project for a working-class quarterly called 'The Workshop' was one such journal which never came into being : see W. Pole, ed., *Life of Sir William Fairbairn*, London, 1877, p. 156.

advance conjured up in the scientific movement. It will do this by examining in detail the tracts and societies of the Mechanics Institute Movement, and by demonstrating complementary concerns in the British Association for the Advancement of Science. Furthermore, this chapter will establish the material basis of this social context by linking the rhetoric and purpose of the Mechanics Institute Movement directly to concerns about the structure of the labour market.

The Mechanics Institute Movement reflected the desires among middle-class ideologues to improve the understanding of the connections between the advances of technology and the doctrines of political economy. A literature which brought together ideologies of economic and technological advance had obvious social connotations for its middle- and working-class audience. Popularisers found support for their doctrines of social harmony in rising productivity and advances in technology. The machine and the practical implementation of the division of labour were to bring the capitalist and the worker together, to the ultimate benefit of all. The ascription of utilitarian and commercial value to scientific and technological endeavour goes back to much earlier times, finding its immediate ancestor in the eighteenth-century literary and scientific society. The assignment of 'usefulness' by contemporaries to science and technology need not of itself imply any specific connection with the economy. This connection, however, was apparent in the Mechanics Institute Movement. The Machinery Question created the basis for a connection between the economy and technology; the Mechanics Institute Movement had specific aims which linked the advance of science and technology with the structure of the labour market.

The Mechanics Institute Movement was initially built up on the basis of a passionate concern among middle-class reformers for providing a scientific education for the artisan, but these goals changed as the movement evolved. It has already been demonstrated that political economy between the 1830s and 1840s had become increasingly concerned with charting a programme for the progress of wealth, which was contingent not on the genius but on the discipline of the labour force. Political economists drew attention, as the period progressed, to the precision, regularity and standardisation constantly pressing on industry. However, these demands for both an ingenious artisan and a disciplined labour force were not contradictory. For the ingenious artisan which the Mechanics Institute Movement aspired to create was in fact functionally identified with demands for a newly adaptable labour force and with the hardening of social hierarchies within the work process.

The founding programmes and the organisation of the Mechanics Institutes in their early years were very different from those of later stages in the movement's development. The movement was composed of a myriad of local societies whose structures and constitutions varied widely. Most of the institutes, however, contained within themselves a tension between middle-class patrons and the desired working-class subscribers. This tension was in turn related like the rhetoric to the concern with developing a labour market suitable to an industrialising society.

In the London Mechanics Institute the early ascendancy of Place, Brougham and Birkbeck established patronage and control by middle-class subscribers.[2] But the story of the London Mechanics Institute was not that of all the provincial institutes, for these took shape under their own local social circumstances.[3] Members of provincial élites took an active role in the formation of many, ceding more or less than the two-thirds control to ordinary members as recommended by Brougham. The Manchester, Leeds, Liverpool, Ashton-under-Lyne, and Nottingham Institutes were started up and controlled by whig-liberal élites.[4] The Manchester Institute was one of solid middle-class control, and Benjamin Heywood, the banker, made no bones about this when rebuking Brougham for his criticism of the system of management. He stressed that the Mechanics Institute had not been formed in obedience to any call on the part of the mechanics, but had originated with the employers. It was a philanthropic effort on the part of the employers to place within the reach of their workmen 'the means of improvement'.[5]

2 See J. F. C. Harrison, *Learning and Living, 1790–1960*, London, 1961; Thomas Kelly, *George Birkbeck, Pioneer of Adult Education*, Liverpool, 1957; J. L. Dobson, 'The Contribution of Francis Place and the Radicals to the Growth of Popular Education 1800–1840', Ph.D. Thesis, Newcastle upon Tyne, 1959; Mabel Tylecote, *The Mechanics Institutes of Lancashire and Yorkshire*, Manchester, 1957.

3 Kelly, *George Birkbeck*, and Place Papers, B.L. Add. Ms. 27823, fol. 269.

4 See Tylecote, *Mechanics Institutes*; R. J. Morris, 'Organization and Aims of the Principle Secular Voluntary Organizations of the Leeds Middle Class 1830–1851', D.Phil. Thesis, Oxford, 1970; Thomas Kelly, *A History of Adult Education*, Liverpool, 1970; and S. D. Chapman, 'William Felkin', M.A. Thesis, University of Nottingham, 1962. These indicate the diversity of the origins of some of the provincial institutes.

5 Benjamin Heywood to Lord Brougham, 17 February 1825, Brougham Papers (University College, London).

Birmingham's institute was more problematic. It is true that a leading part was taken by Joseph Parkes, a well known philosophic radical,[6] but, equally, Parkes could report in 1826 that the institute was not supported by the more educated classes. The fact that the constitution was in the hands of the members had 'given great offence to the higher classes'.[7] The Institute was also strongly influenced by the Birmingham co-operator, W. Hawkes Smith.

Birmingham's case was not unique, and it is important not to forget both the tradition of 'mutual improvement' in working-class culture and the strong scientific tradition in nineteenth-century radicalism. Those who set up the Glasgow Gasworkmen's Library in 1823 stressed equality and culture. The pre-eminence of the few could only be broken down by measures to alleviate the ignorance and poverty of the many. The value of science was cultural : 'Even in our workshops and manufactures will we find many who are little better than parts of the machines around them'.[8] Hawkes Smith claimed the rights of the 'ingenious population' to be instructed in the sciences in general, and not simply in those related to their occupations. He also pointed to the possibilities for the equalisation of education.

> When the *steam engine* was perfected, half the *external* distinctions of rank vanished ; – the new power rendering manufactured articles more accessible. But the effects of scientific advancement will not be branded by the cheapening of silks, calicoes and hardwares. There is an *intellectual* machinery, a *mental steam power* at work, and still rising in its action which renders *education* proportionately as cheap and as attainable to the man of small means as his clothing and his domestic appointments.[9]

This pattern was typical of institutes founded by artisans themselves. They sought personal and educational advantages in the context of co-operation in the pursuit of knowledge. The institutes at Keighley, Halifax and Bradford, Stalybridge, Bolton and Hyde, and Kendal,

6 G. B. Finlayson, 'Joseph Parkes of Birmingham, 1786–1865, A Study in Philosophic Radicalism', *Bulletin of the Institute of Historical Research*, XLVI, November 1973, 186.
7 Joseph Parkes to Lord Brougham, 18 November 1826, Brougham Papers.
8 'Introductory Address Delivered to the Glasgow Gasworkmen's Library', *Glasgow Mechanics Magazine*, IV, 29 October 1825, 171.
9 W. Hawkes Smith, 'On the Tendency and Prospects of Mechanics' Institutions', *The Analyst*, II, 1835.

Morpeth and Birmingham were all founded by artisans and in some way carried the banner of 'mutual instruction'.[10]

Just as organisation and management differed according to local circumstances, so the justifications, programmes and ideas proposed in the movement all expressed local pecularities. However, from the plethora of introductory addresses to a wide range of institutes, the statements of various mechanics' journals, and a number of reports on the progress of the movement, it is possible to delineate the outline of a composite picture of themes and images.

The declared aims and principles of most of the institutes invoked some combination of three assumptions. The first was that the programme offered by the institutes would foster egalitarianism and social mobility, the second that skill and science both in some way contributed to industry, and the third that technical change occurred in a piecemeal and empirical fashion. The combination of these assumptions fostered the views that the industrial transformation the country was experiencing was conducive to harmony and stability, and that science was merely an appendage of technological knowledge. Harmonious expansion and technological knowledge embedded in the empirical skills of the artisan appeared to project a vision of a labour market stamped by hierarchical divisions and social mobility. The entrepreneurs of the movement viewed science as a type of superior technical knowledge which, when added to the empirical skills of certain highly placed groups of workers, would generate all kinds of technological and economic improvements. Most of the founders of the movement hoped for some optimal combination of 'science' and skill. The implication they had in mind for such a combination was the creation of a higher form of skilled labour, one freed from the degradation of the division of labour and imbued with creative and innovative instincts. James Hole's view, though stated much later, did sum up the outlook of the earlier period : 'The nation which possesses the largest number of skilled artisans, capable of availing themselves of the aids which science lends to industry, will, . . . be the richest nation.'[11]

But the founders were anxious to stress that science did have some direct connection with technology. At its most extreme, this was voiced in the view that the origins of the steam engine were to be traced to Black's research into the nature and properties of latent heat, with

[10] Tylecote, *Mechanics Institutes*, pp. 53–66, 124, 229, 241.
[11] James Hole, *An Essay on the History and Management of Literary, Scientific, and Mechanics Institutions*, London, 1853, p. 49.

Watt's discoveries as but a logical extension of this.[12] Brougham's views at the outset were also somewhat extreme and untypical. He stressed that few great discoveries were made by chance and by ignorant persons – that Watt's discoveries were based on a learned investigation of mathematics, mechanics and chemistry, and that even Arkwright had devoted five years to the invention of the 'spinning jenny' and was conversant with everything that related to the construction of machinery.[13] Most of the provincial institutes simply drew a loose connection between science and the artisan. According to the Darlington Institute, the knowledge of science would 'acquaint them [the working classes] with more certain rules than the mere imitation of what they have seen done by another', and there was 'no trade which does not depend more or less, upon scientific principles'.[14]

James Hole's statement of the relations between science and industry was much the more common one. Such an attitude often involved a mystical view of the artisan. The imitation and instinct of a machine or 'Indian weaver' were often contrasted to the innovative spirit of the educated artisan. The institutes by 'adding knowledge to your industry and skill', would lead to 'rich veins of practical talent' being 'brought to light'.[15] The imitative behaviour of the Indian weaver whose process had remained the same for centuries was contrasted with the observant mind of a Hargreaves. Changes were brought about by observation followed by inquiry involving the principles of science.[16] Aside from this Baconian view of the advance of science on the basis of the number of educated artisans, there was also the view of science as a cultural antidote to the division of labour. James Hole quoted Lyon Playfair to support his view that the division of labour had been carried to extremes. He saw science as a '*synthesis* of labour', or 'the bringing together the knowledge required in each department of industry'.[17] Science was to

12 *First Report of the Directors of the School of Arts of Edinburgh for the Education of Mechanics in such Branches of Physical Science as are of Practical Application in their Several Trades*, May 1822, p. 12.

13 [H. Brougham], *A Discourse on the Objects, Advantages, and Pleasures of Science*, London, 1827, printed in The Library of Useful Knowledge, London, 1829, pp. 39–44. The leaders of the movement were often careless with their history of technology.

14 *First Report of the Mechanics Institute of Darlington*, Darlington, 1826, p. 7.

15 Benjamin Heywood, 'An Address Delivered at the Opening of the Manchester Mechanics Institution', 30 March 1825, in Heywood, *Addresses*, London, 1843.

16 Tylecote, *Mechanics Institutes*, p. 131.

17 Hole, *History . . . of Mechanics Institutions*, p. 49.

be 'injected' into the workshops, and men daily employed in handling tools and working amongst the elements of mechanical science would be the best suited to making discoveries and inventing improvements. Brougham singled out Watt as the model to the members of the institutes. He saw it as 'their own fault' if they did not 'rise out of their level' and 'take the chances of making discoveries which would secure them affluence and the fame of extending the boundaries of science and art'.[18]

Brougham used his opportunities to point out that ingenious models and apparatus were frequently brought forward 'by persons from whom little beyond ordinary handicrafts would have been expected'.[19] The *Glasgow Mechanics Magazine* advised workmen to keep a pencil and notebook while at their work to record observations and ideas. There was also no lack of schemes for patent protection of artisan inventors. The Wakefield Mechanics Institute included assistance, when funds would permit, to members for the patenting of any useful inventions they might make.[20] The *Mechanics Magazine* in 1825 announced steps towards the formation of a joint stock company, 'The British Invention and Discovery Company for the Assistance, Encouragement and Protection of Native Genius, and the Profitable Investment of Capital in the Prosecution of Original Inventions and Discoveries by British Subjects'.[21]

This combination of science and industry was a mythical one. There was rarely any attempt to specify the connections or to test the models and folk heroes put forward. The combination was, however, closely connected with the social ideals of the movement. In one sense the 'artisan inventor' was a direct challenge to the aristocracy of theory. Discovery was to become an everyday employment, and not an 'exclusive philosopher's right'. As late as 1837, the President of the Bradford Mechanics Institute could exclaim : 'Who can tell but that some happy thought, suggesting itself to the mind of an hitherto obscure member of a Mechanics Institute, may pave the way to results, far surpassing in splendour and usefulness those which the genius of a Watt, a Boulton, or an Arkwright has achieved.'[22] There may, indeed, have been a sense

18 *Address of Henry, Lord Brougham to the Members of the Manchester Mechanics Institution*, 21 July 1835, p. 172.
19 [H. Brougham], *Practical Observations upon the Education of the People Addressed to the Working Classes and their Employers*, London, 1825, pp. 26–32.
20 Harrison, *Learning and Living*, p. 64.
21 *London Mechanics Magazine*, IV, 23 April 1825, p. 43.
22 Harrison, *Learning and Living*, p. 64.

in which the empiricist approach of the movement was political. The inductivist movement during this period was a challenge to the theoretical enclaves of metropolitan science and classical political economy. However, it is important to note that the challenge to the exclusiveness of intellect was a very measured one. Much of the verbiage was aimed at a particular type of workman : the practical man was to hold the key place in the development of industry, but the 'mechanic' the institutes envisaged was a new type of workman evolved by the methods of industry itself. The heroes of the movement were not typical London artisans. The 'new race of philosophers' was a particular corps within the working class which was made up of the new technical workers of the Industrial Revolution. When reference was made to 'the ingenious artisan' what was envisaged was the new engineering worker. The Mechanics Institute Movement was organised not around equality but around hierarchical divisions within the labour market. The engineering industry itself, from which the movement took much of its rhetoric and example, well illustrated these divisions. The many differentiated skills which had recently arisen within the engineering industry were the result of a successful subdivision of the work. In the eighteenth-century, engineering skills had been integrated in the person of an all-round skilled craftsman, the old corn millwright and early millwright engineer. Though his craft was highly exclusive – one had to be 'born and bred a millwright' in order to gain entry to the trade – it was also the wide-ranging one of the jack-of-all-trades.[23] With the emergence of new factory millwork and the early steam engine came a new demand for millwrights, and with it a two-edged process of levelling of craft skill and professionalisation. When Smeaton established the Society of Civil Engineers in 1771, he complained, 'Not only are all the inferior departments ambitious to become practical engineers, but even members of the committee have a propensity that way too – by which means all becoming masters and he who ought to be so being deprived of authority, it is easy to see the confusion that must follow.'[24] Professionalisation of some members of the trade was established through membership in the Smeatonian Society, and education in the Dissenting Academies.[25]

The introduction of the Boulton and Watt steam engine brought the

[23] Tann, 'The Textile Millwright', p. 81.
[24] Sidney Pollard, *The Genesis of Modern Management*, Harmondsworth, 1965, p. 157.
[25] Tann, 'The Textile Millwright'.

emergence of the 'trouble shooting' Boulton and Watt engine erector in the late eighteenth century to early nineteenth century. The introduction of the steam engine brought new demands for millwork, but it 'nevertheless lowered the profession of the millwright and levelled it in a great degree with that of the ordinary mechanic'.[26] Fairbairn described the history of the training up of workmen in the early engineering industry, then the gradual removal of their skills. Accurate fittings could not be secured as long as manufacture was conducted by hand. The introduction of new tools brought greater precision, but in addition, 'the facilities these afforded led to a constant progressive improvement in the character of the work done, at the same time constantly reducing the dependence on mere manual skill'.[27]

By the 1820s and 1830s there was a broadly based skilled hierarchy of engineering workers in the engineering plants of the Midlands and the North. The high degree of specialisation is depicted by the work force of Peel, Williams & Co., which by the early 1820s included at the least a principal engineer, draughtsmen, head clerks, engineers, millwrights, patternmakers, fitters, turners, moulders in brass and iron, and boilermakers.[28] With the breakdown of the craft and job specialisation there emerged new closely knit and separate trade societies. One finds in 1824 the establishment of the Steam Engine Makers' Society, in 1826 the Society of Journeymen Steam Engine Machine Makers and Millwrights, and in 1830 the Associated Fraternity of Iron Forgers.

The division of labour and hierarchy of skills in the engineering industry was created in the context of new large-scale capitalist enterprises. By the 1820s and 1830s James Nasmyth, James Fox, Matthew Murray, Sharp, Roberts & Co., Hicks, Hargreaves & Co., Fairbairn and Lillie, and Joseph Whitworth were directing large-scale machine shops,

---

26 Fairbairn, *Treatise on Mills*, p. vii. Tann also found that the dimensions of early factories were nearly constant. Even though the basic plan of the factory was decided by the millwright or engineer in consultation with the manufacturer, the process was standardised enough for there to be a number of builders' manuals with details of acceptable forms for doors, windows and even cupolas. *The Development of the Factory*, pp. 103, 149.

27 Pole, ed., *Life of Sir William Fairbairn*, p. 39. This process was taking place rather later in the 1820s and 1830s in Cornish engineering. The foundry came to usurp the position of the independent engineer and produced engines to standard designs. See D. B. Barton, *The Cornish Beam Engine*, Truro, 1966.

28 A. E. Musson, 'An Early Engineering Firm: Peel, Williams, and Company of Manchester', *Business History*, III, 1960, p. 14.

foundries and engine factories in the Midlands and the North.[29] With the appearance of this corps of industrial magnates at the pinnacle of the industry came professionalisation. The professional and proletarian created parallel organisations as the mental and manual distinctions of the trade became formalised. But, like the trade societies, the professional bodies were exclusive and hierarchically organised according to age. The exclusive Smeatonian Society was first challenged in 1818 with the emergence of a new Institute for Civil Engineers which included those engaged in public works and transport. New reasons for professionalisation were devised. The society was to provide a forum for reading practical papers and for assigning professional status. H. R. Palmer, in opening it, argued : 'An engineer is a mediator between the philosopher and the working mechanic, and, like an interpreter between two foreigners, must understand the language of both . . . Hence the absolute necessity of possessing both practical and theoretical knowledge.'[30] Similarly, such professional status was given to railway engineers with the emergence in 1846 of the Institute of Mechanical Engineers, so that 'by a mutual exchange of ideas regarding improvements in the various branches of Mechanical Science', they might 'increase their knowledge and give impulse to mechanical Inventions likely to be useful to the World'.[31]

The history of the engineering industry was used as a paradigm to substantiate the arguments of the Mechanics Institute Movement for a division of labour, specialisation, and gradations of skill within the labour market. The movement reinforced these developments by widening the gap between skilled workers and common labourers, and it focussed on the highly skilled sector of the working class, giving formal recognition to the emerging gradations and hierarchies in the labour force. One of the aims of the movement appeared to be to promote the role of the skilled labourer, and to increase the supply of this labour. But in so doing it ignored the historical breakdown of skills even within these 'privileged' groups. The 'skilled labourer' in this period acquired new class connotations not just in terms of the technical characteristics of the various skills but in social terms. As against the type of social mobility inherent in the old craftsmanship tradition, the new paradigm was a separation between the skilled and the unskilled in the working

[29] L. T. C. Rolt, *Victorian Engineering* (1970), Harmondsworth, 1974. pp. 131–5.
[30] W. H. G. Armytage, *Social History of Engineering*, London, 1961, p. 131.
[31] *Ibid.* p. 131.

classes, and a split between both and the middle classes. This consciousness of separate classes is aptly characterised by one of Benjamin Heywood's remarks in 1837, when he described the workmen of Sharp, Roberts & Co. as 'of the first class as regards skill and rather high wages'. One learns more of his perception of the social status of these workmen, however, from his complaint which follows, 'it would be well if their habits corresponded with their skill'.[32] The founders of the Mechanics Institute Movement made constant appeals to social mobility, but these appeals were in contradiction to the role it was simultaneously playing, of creating new social barriers between groups within the working class, and of limiting the mobility of labour into the middle classes.

This process was inadvertently borne out by some of the rhetoric of the movement. The first provisional committee of the London Mechanics Institute defined as mechanics all who earned their living by the work of their hands, but included the proviso that if the institute became overcrowded, preference would be given to those in the trades who worked for daily, weekly or quarterly wages.[33] The successful Mechanics Institute in effect as well as idea was seen to act as a labour exchange for superior workmen. Heywood claimed that many members of the Manchester Mechanics Institute had been 'raised in the conditions of life'. 'Masters wanting superior workmen, foremen or overlookers, are beginning to come here to inquire.'[34] Brougham, also, stressed the pecuniary benefits of scientific instruction, and was at no loss for examples of the great engine makers 'taking men of humble rank for important posts because of their knowledge of science'.[35] Apostles spoke of the 'getting up of a new aristocracy – an aristocracy of science, composed exclusively of the working orders, which is to be the enemy and ruler of the old'.[36] The Mechanics Institutes were seen as a way of

[32] Brougham Papers, Benjamin Heywood to Lord Brougham, 28 September 1837.
[33] Kelly, *George Birkbeck,* p. 86. Kelly takes pains to point out that this was not a deliberate preference for a superior type of artisan, but a preference for those who, because of the nature of their work, were most likely to benefit. But this argument is circular: the type of workforce aimed at was the basis of the type of instruction.
[34] Heywood, 'Sixth Address', 26 February 1835, in Heywood, *Addresses,* p. 84.
[35] [Brougham], *Practical Observations upon the Education of the People,* pp. 12, 15.
[36] Richard Burnet, *A Word to the Members of Mechanics Institutes,* Devonport, 1826, p. 67.

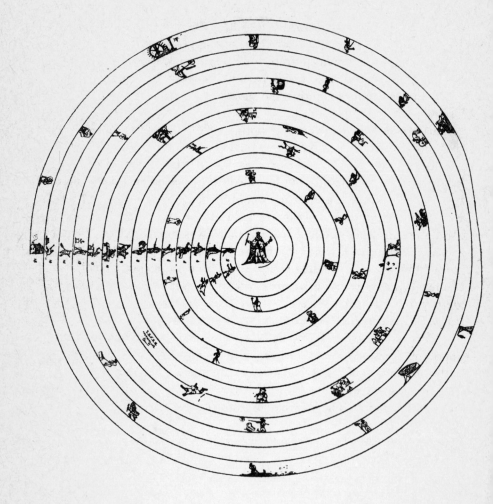

THE SPIRAL OF SUCCESS

Let us, therefore, place the universal good – the object of every man's ambition – the grand desideratum of all, as a centre, around which a spiral, in the form of a volute, or pyrotechnical wheel, of fifteen revolutions, should be drawn. At the extreme point the work house should be fixed. The radius from it should be described by the figure of a man, at the bisection of each revolution, to represent the head of every class in society. The internal orbicular lines should be filled up with the different classes, shaded downwards in proportion to their relative situations or stations in life.

We will, therefore, place the king on the inner circle.
The ministers of state on the second.
The members of the House of Peers on the third.
The members of the House of Commons on the fourth.
The heads of professions, professors of the universities, judges, first rate merchants, generals, Braham, Talma, Keen on the fifth.
First class barristers, aspiring to be judges; colonels, looking for the rank of general, etc. on the sixth.
The seventh should contain middle class barristers, captains etc.
The eighth lieutenants etc.
The ninth, mechanics, and others, earning more than forty shillings a week.
The tenth, mechanics and others earning between twenty shillings and forty shillings.
The eleventh, those who earn less than twenty shillings.
The twelfth, labourers who earn more than twelve shillings.
The thirteenth, labourers who earn less than twelve shillings.
The fourteenth, paupers, having casual relief only.
The fifteenth, paupers in the work house. . . .
The best informed and the most industrious will always, in their exertion to get forward, thrust out the more ignorant in the rear. . . .
If diagrams of the kind described were suspended in Mechanics Institutions, and every member were furnished with them, they would stir up a spirit of emulation, and have a marked effect on society.

[See p. 158 for discussion of the spiral of success.]
Source : Richard Burnet, *A Word to the Members of Mechanics Institutes*, Devonport, 1826, pp. 17–21.

meeting the social change following from scientific advancement. It was recognised that the effect of the introduction of new technology would be the displacement of labour. But though machinery might reduce the role of unskilled labour in the production process, it might also generate a greater significance and technical expertise. Economic expansion would now depend on a labour force which was more polarised and more hierarchic in its social organisation. It was with this in mind that James Martineau, an engineer who therefore represented such technical expertise, spoke to the Liverpool Mechanics Institute of machinery 'rapidly supplanting human labour and rendering mere muscular force ... worthless ... That natural machine, the human body, is depreciated in the market. But if the *body* have lost its value, the *mind* must get into business without delay.'[37] His was a new world where 'Mechanical invention, and not mere labour, is the great source of national wealth'.[38]

The hierarchy of labour found vivid expression in Richard Burnet's spiral of success (see pp. 156–7). The spiral of success traced out the position of all in society, and was kept moving by the social assumption that the best informed and most industrious always moved forward by thrusting out the more ignorant. The spiral was based on the concept of society as a system of ranks, 'Rank keeps the labouring classes from combining into a whole',[39] but rank too implied the idea of duty in order to relate ranks divided by huge inequalities of wealth and privilege in a framework of mutual obligation.[40] Burnet suggested his spiral be displayed in all Mechanics Institutes in order to stir up a spirit of emulation.[41] But even the unprecedented position of this new class of scientific and technical workers was to be limited. The assumption of a strict distinction between employer and employed was seldom challenged by middle-class founders. Leonard Horner stressed that his School of Arts was to 'give some *select* instruction to the mechanics in those branches of science which will be of use to them in the *exercise of their trade* . . . to give them education suited to their circumstances'. He maintained that there must be '*master mechanics* in the direction of the institutes to prevent anything being done contrary to the habits

37 Hawkes Smith, 'On the Tendency and Prospects of Mechanics Institutions', p. 336.
38 *London Mechanics Magazine*, quoted in Tylecote, *Mechanics Institutes*, p. 33.
39 Burnet, *A Word*, p. 66.
40 Morris, 'Organization and Aims of the . . . Voluntary Organizations of the Leeds Middle Class', D.Phil. Thesis, pp. 113–14.
41 Burnet, *A Word*, p. 21.

and feelings of the workmen'.[42] This reality of the appeal to a hierarchy of skilled labourers was directly at variance with much of the mythology of the movement. The founders generally held fast to the image of the humble inventor and made much of the spectacular success story.

But there was one at least who challenged the conception of innate workshop genius.

> The mechanics of Great Britain can claim no merit as mere workmen, which every machine in the country may not claim just as well . . . Not a class of men can be mentioned, whose avocations place them more in the way of those discoveries by which the arts and sciences are improved, and the resources of a country augmented; it is their constant business, in fact, to be making those changes in material substances by which their capabilities are best developed; and yet where are the great discoveries in art or science, that can be fairly traced to the observations of the *workshop?* . . . by far the greatest number of those discoveries . . . by which even the arts themselves have been improved . . . have been made *out of the workshop*.[43]

There was some attempt to tone down the success stories in a later period. It was said of the mechanical drawing and chemistry classes that 'if from such classes does not spring a James Watt, or a Christopher Wren, a Simpson or a Davey, yet from them come supervisors of railway works, foremen of foundries and machine makers' establishments, and "clerks of the works" at the erection of great public buildings'.[44] And a witness to the Select Committee on Arts and Manufactures argued that ten years of experience of the institutes had produced some social mobility, as well as 'more skilful constructors, more ready contrivers, more expert workmen, and more tasteful designers'.[45] Commentators also touched a constant source of anxiety – the difficulties of diffusing new techniques. It was claimed that the operative had a conservative outlook on the work process because he mechanically

42 Brougham Papers, Leonard Horner to Lord Brougham, June 1824.
43 'Tom Telltruth', *London Mechanics Magazine*, I, 22 November 1823, 196.
44 Quoted in Tylecote, *Mechanics Institutes*, p. 262.
45 Select Committee on Arts and Manufactures, *P.P.* 1835, v, Q 1554, p. 114, *P.P.* 1835. There are similar comments in the Select Committee on Education in England and Wales, Appendix No. 2, *P.P.* 1835, VII, pp. 105, 110.

followed rules laid down for him and became attached to a certain way of working. This was part of the explanation of 'why improvements are so ill received among the working class of society'.[46] The artisans with a scientific education would be creative, innovative and perceptive to the introduction of new techniques. The more realistic claims that the Mechanics Institute Movement produced greater numbers of skilled and adaptable workmen were in keeping with the actual role it played in creating new social and economic hierarchies. These hierarchical aims were reinforced by the other purpose of the Mechanics Institute Movement, to act as an instrument of social discipline.

Moral virtue was an intrinsic part of the ideology of science for the working man. Industry and temperance were the virtues of the good mechanic. Benjamin Heywood expressed the middle-class fears of anarchy in the heart of the metropolis.

> Living as they do in the midst of a dense and teeming
> population, I'm thoroughly persuaded that the best and easiest
> method which they can adopt for obviating the risks necessarily
> incidental to such a state of society, is by diffusing . . . sound
> and useful knowledge . . . which imparts those principles in
> which are ever to be found the safest guides for individual
> conduct, and the surest guarantee of public order.[47]

These concerns led to emphasis on the moral advantages of knowledge. Education was 'to rouse the mental activity', to 'teach them [the poorer classes] the acute discernment of their best interests'. The Mechanics Institutes were, to 'fit men more wisely to direct their own conduct in whatever situation they may be placed in society'.[48] They would direct the habits of the working class to 'respect for the laws' and 'that due

---

46 'On Founding an Institute for the Cultivation of Mechanical Science', letter to the Editor of the *London Journal of Arts*, July 1822 in Place Papers, B.L. Add. Ms. 27824, fol. 31.

47 Heywood, 'Address', 14 January 1834, *Addresses*, p. 72. See S. Shapin and B. Barnes, 'Science and Nature : Interpreting Mechanics Institutes, *Social Studies of Science*, VII, 1977.

48 W. P. Gaskell, *An Address to the Operative Classes, being the Substance of a Lecture Explanatory and in Defence of the Nature and Objects of the Cheltenham Mechanics Institute*, 8 May 1835, pp. 4–7. Also see [William Rathbone], *Suggestions Regarding the Object and Management of Mechanics Institutes*, Manchester, 1830, pp. 8–9. *A Lecture Delivered on the Opening of the Sheffield Mechanics Institution on the 14th of January, 1833 by the Reverend Thomas Allin*, Sheffield, 1833, p. 16.

subordination of rank on which the well being of every gradation in society depends'.[49]

This concentration on morality was another point of entry for political economy. Political economy was an important influence on the movement from its inception, and this influence grew stronger over the years, particularly after the first decline of the movement in the late 1820s.

Political economy for mechanics

It was, in fact, always taken for granted that a certain type of political economy should be taught in the Mechanics Institutes. Political economy had become the peculiar creed of the middle classes; it justified claims to middle-class superiority and offered a millennial picture. The great work of popularisation began in the 1820s: political economy was presented as a science which would explain the triumph of British industry and British economic supremacy. Popularisations displayed the natural laws by which the economy and society operated, explained all social problems in terms of the violation of these laws, and encouraged the view that submission to the laws led to infinite progress. The supreme concern of this popular political economy was with the problems of production, and, as a corollary of this, the absolute benefit of machinery.[50] The Mechanics Institutes were thus a natural place for the interests of political economy.

The Mechanics Institutes were generally left in the hands of the popularisers. They did, however, attract the patronage of certain key figures in the establishment of economic theory. McCulloch discussed the place of the Mechanics Institutes in his *Principles of Political Economy*. He claimed that they gave the working classes an opportunity to perfect themselves by learning the principles on which their arts depended.

> The lustre which now attaches to the names of Arkwright and Watt may be dimmed, though it can never be wholly effaced, by the more numerous, and, it may be, more important discoveries that will, at no distant period, be made by those who would have passed . . . in the same obscure and beaten track

49 *Observations Addressed to all Classes of the Community on the Establishment of Mechanics Institutes,* Derby, 1825, p. 9.
50 R. K. Webb, *The British Working Class Reader, 1790–1848,* London, 1955, p. 99. For further work on the popularisers see W. F. Kennedy, 'Lord Brougham, Charles Knight and the Rights of Industry', *Economica,* xxix, February 1962; and R. Gilmour, 'The Gradgrind School of Political Economy'.

as by their unambitious ancestors, had not the education now so generally diffused, served to elicit and ripen the seeds of genius.[51]

The reviewer of his *Discourse on the Rise . . . of Political Economy* suggested the pamphlet for use in the Mechanics Institutes where the artisans 'learned things far more difficult and less interesting every day', and he did not doubt that 'when the doctrine of wages and population is clearly explained at these institutes, they will be eagerly listened to'.[52] By 1829, a mutual instruction class at the London Institute was using McCulloch's *Principles*.[53] McCulloch also gave the introductory address to the London Literary and Scientific Institute, formed for lower-middle-class clerks. The committee included businessmen and political economists, among them John Smith M.P., James Mill, C. P. Thomson, William Ellis, Alexander Baring and S. Jones Loyd. Here the study of political economy was justified as the path to social mobility. The hero now was Ricardo who 'entered on that great arena which you have entered with prospects probably inferior to those of the majority amongst you'.[54]

Aside from McCulloch, both Torrens and Senior took an active part in the early life of the movement. Torrens was among the first subscribers, and also took part in the speeches of the first anniversary of the London Institute.[55] Senior frequently adjudicated competitions for essays on topics of political economy and offered prizes. From 1831, he offered prizes for essays on emigration, the distribution of revenue, combinations, and capital and wages.[56] Babbage contributed the third edition of his *Machinery and Manufactures* along with one hundred copies of his chapter 'On a New System of Manufacturing'.[57] John

51 McCulloch, *Principles*, p. 119.
52 [Francis Jeffrey], 'Political Economy by J. R. McCulloch', *Edinburgh Review*, XLIII, November 1825, 14.
53 Birkbeck College, London, London Mechanics Institution, Minute Books of the Committee, 3 October 1831, p. iii.
54 J. R. McCulloch, *A Discourse Delivered at the Opening of the City of London Literary and Scientific Institution, 30 May, 1825*, London, 1825, p. 27.
55 See 'London Mechanics Institution', 23 April 1824, Place Papers, BL Add. Ms. 27824, fol. 43.
56 'Address to the London Mechanics Institute', 3 December 1831, Place Papers, BL Add. Ms. 27824, fol. 150. Also see London Mechanics Institution, Minute Books of the Committee, 28 January 1833, iv.
57 London Mechanics Institution, Minute Books of the Committee, 18 March 1833, iv. The chapter 'On a New System of Manufacturing' appears in the 2nd edition of Babbage's *Machinery and Manufactures*.

Parton was a member of the First General Committee of Managers of the London Mechanics Institute,[58] and T. Perronet Thompson was asked several times in 1837 to lecture at the London Institute.[59]

The systematic teaching of popular political economy was regarded as central to the artisan's education in much the same way as was practical science. The institutes became a centre for a burgeoning industry in popular political economy. Most of this work was middle-class propaganda of the crudest kind. Francis Place was a keen advocate of this political economy, and Brougham produced a series of lectures for use in provincial institutes. Thomas Chalmers believed that the Mechanics Institutes worked the 'greatest of economic improvements' by giving a 'higher tone to the character' and leading to later ages of marriages,[60] and that political economy had a definite role in the Institutes as he 'was not aware of a likelier instrument than a judicious course of economical doctrine for tranquilizing the popular mind and removing from it all those delusions which are the main cause of popular disaffection'.

Political economy was a 'sedative to all sorts of turbulence and disorder'.[61] Further, the attention drawn by Chalmers to the affinity between 'the taste for science' and the 'taste for sacredness'[62] became the principle behind the co-operation of the church and the mechanics institutes at a much later date. Political economy within the institutes taught moral virtue, and the church was quick to follow in this role.[63]

The promotion of the teaching of political economy was accompanied by the emergence of popular lecturers. The best known of these at the London Institute were William Ellis and Wilmot Horton. Ellis's teaching was constantly urged on the London Institute by Francis Place.

---

58 See G. Sotiroff, ed., *John Barton, Economic Writings*, i, Regina, Sask., 1962, xi.
59 London Mechanics Institution, Minute Books of the Committee, 17 April, 20 August, 13 November 1837.
60 Thomas Chalmers, 'On Mechanics Schools and on Political Economy as a Branch of Popular Education', *Glasgow Mechanics Magazine*, v, 3 June 1826, pp. 217–21.
61 *Ibid.* 24 June 1826, pp. 262–3 and 1 July 1826, pp. 285–8.
62 *Ibid.* 3 June 1826, p. 218.
63 See [Thomas Coates], *Report on the State of Literary, Scientific and Mechanics Institutes in England*, London, 1841, p. 15 for evidence of the religious affiliations of newly formed institutes.

Ellis sat on the Committee and adjudicated essay competitions.[64] He held a discussion group at the Institute on social issues, the results of which were published in 1829 as *Conversations upon Knowledge, Happiness, and Education.*[65] His lectures to the London Literary Society were probably used by Brougham as the core of the famous Brougham lectures on political economy,[66] and he ran a session of lectures at the London Mechanics Institute in December 1832.[67]

Meanwhile Wilmot Horton had given his lectures 'Statistics and Political Economy especially with reference to the Condition of the Operative and Labouring Classes' in December 1830. In 1830 Horton also had the idea of discussing his emigration schemes with a group of working men, and Birkbeck arranged a group for him at the London Mechanics Institute.[68] The discussions were followed by a series of ten lectures, reported to have been very bad.[69] Horton's lectures are also reported to have raised some turmoil; he complained to the Committee of the London Institute 'I understand that many members threatened to take their names out of the Institution and to induce their friends to do so, if ever I lectured again – that there was no general wish to hear discussions on political economy – and that I had better go elsewhere etc. etc.'[70] Horton published both the discussions and the lectures in 1831, so one can see just what tedious content there was to some of the political economy taught in the Mechanics Institutes. He presented his purpose to the discussion groups as 'impressing on your minds certain important and vital truths affecting the labouring classes and operating

---

[64] London Mechanics Institution, Minute Books of the Committee, 31 October 1831, iii.

[65] E. E. Ellis, *Memoir of William Ellis*, London, 1888, pp. 18–20.

[66] See [B. F. Duppa], *A Manual for Mechanics Institutions*, London, 1839. pp. 196–229, for the content of Brougham's course. Brougham stated in an address of 1835 that his lectures on political economy were written by a friend 'whose name I am not at liberty to mention'. See address of Henry Lord Brougham to the Members of the Manchester Mechanics Institute, 21 July 1835, pp. 184–5.

[67] London Mechanics Institution, Minute Books of the Committee, 1832. Also see R. Gilmour, 'The Gradgrind School of Political Economy', for Ellis's later career in popular political economy.

[68] Dobson, 'The Contribution of Francis Place', Ph.D. Thesis, p. 363.

[69] See, however, Greville's comments. He attended the lectures at the Mechanics Institute with several other personages, and described them as well done and eloquent. *The Greville Memoirs, a Journal of the Reigns of King George IV and King William IV*, ed. H. Reeve, 3 vols., London, 1875, vol. II, p. 95, 23 December 1830.

[70] London Mechanics Institution, Minute Books of the Committee, 5 March 1831, iii.

in all countries', and his opinions were not to relate 'to the policy of changing institutions, but to mere matters of fact'.[71] Horton lectured on the determinants of wages, emigration, distribution of income, taxation, skill and machinery. In a way suitable to his view of the Mechanics Institutes he stressed the superiority of the skilled labourer who had claim to two types of wage – that of manual labour and that of skill. The skilled labourer had a qualified monopoly in the area of the second type, and was more immune than the unskilled to economic pressures. Horton's lecture on machinery typically called attention to the agricultural labourer and he drew heavily on Senior's view of the issue.

Many of the other speakers to the Mechanics Institutes spoke of political economy in the context of concern over machine breaking. Heywood spoke several times to the Manchester Mechanics Institute of advances in technology and the errors behind the destruction of machinery.[72] The Newcastle upon Tyne Institute heard lectures, in May 1825, and again in May 1826, 'on the utility of machinery, in promoting the comfort and happiness of the working classes of society'.[73] Baines lectured to the Leeds Mechanics Institute on machine breaking and foreign competition, and Marshall saw one of the advantages of the Mechanics Institutes as subduing popular errors in trade, wages and machinery.[74] Birkbeck lectured at the London Institute on the employment of machinery in 1831.[75] Place, as always, was very clear about the social meaning of the movement.

> The Mechanics Institute is one, if not the most important, of our institutions. The better sort of working people have received a portion of instruction and whether this can be described as either good or bad it cannot be undone ... if the people had remained in their former ignorance, the burnings now so rife among the farmers would be as rife among the manufacturers.

71 *Correspondence between the Right Hon. R. Wilmot Horton and a Select Class of the Members of the London Mechanics Institution*, London, 1830, p. 8.
72 Place Papers, B. L. Add. Ms. 27824 fol. 123 and Heywood, 'Second Address', *Addresses*, pp. 30–1.
73 *Second Annual Report of the Literary, Scientific and Mechanical Institution of Newcastle upon Tyne*, Newcastle upon Tyne, 1826; *Third Annual Report of the Literary, Scientific and Mechanical Institution of Newcastle upon Tyne*, Newcastle upon Tyne, 1827.
74 Lectures by Edward Baines, September to November 1830, Baines Papers. John Marshall to Brougham, 1826, Brougham Papers.
75 London Mechanics Institution, Minute Books of the Committee, 1831.

> The knowledge obtained by the manufacturing people in the
> North has led many to the conviction of the fact that machinery
> is not and has not been their enemy.[76]

As J. F. C. Harrison has shown, popular political economy prolifer-
ated in the provincial institutes. Many provincial patrons collected
tracts, promoted classes, or, like John Marshall, lectured and wrote the
necessary material themselves.[77]

The Mechanics Institute Movement, during its heyday of the 1820s,
fitted into the improvement ideology of political economy. As I have
shown in previous chapters, labour and the innovating artisans were
regarded as integral to the process of technical change and economic
growth. I have also shown that from within this framework of political
economy emerged new programmes for the progress of wealth which
were contingent on the discipline of the labour force. Though the concern for labour discipline had always complemented the hierarchical
aims of the movement, the aspirations to promote the role of the skilled
labourer in industrialisation had taken precedence. These aspirations,
as this chapter has thus far indicated, certainly had class connotations.
The emotive meaning behind concepts such as 'the arts', 'inventive',
'ingenious', 'experiment', and 'improvement' was meant to camouflage
a central concern with creating a separate class sphere for skilled
labourers. As the movement changed over the 1830s and 1840s the
significance attached to the role of skilled labour appeared to recede
just as it did in political economy. A greater concern with labour
discipline and with industry in its dual meaning came to dominate over
all other aims.

New programmes and social change

A slump in the movement was followed by a resurgence in the 1830s
and another in the 1840s. With this, however, came concern over
membership and programmes. Fears about middle-class infiltration into
the membership went as far back as 1826. Concern mounted that the
aspirations of middle-class founders to appeal to factory operatives and
mechanics had not been fulfilled.[78]

[76] J. L. Dobson, 'The Contribution of Francis Place', p. 389.
[77] See Harrison, *Learning and Living*, pp. 80–2.
[78] See Heywood, 'Eighth Address', 25 February 1836, *Addresses*, pp.
85–6; and Samuel Smiles's report to the Select Committee on Public
Libraries, 1849, pp. 124–8.

The concern to maintain a popular following lay behind a shift in aims from that of educating a class of inventive artisans to that of engendering an atmosphere of temperance, rational entertainment and industrious virtue. But this shift also coincided with the change in political economy's theories of technological improvement. Concerns had shifted away from the central role of labour, 'ingenious', 'industrious', or otherwise to the more important role of capital. Simultaneously, patrons of the institutes shifted their interests from encouraging and extending a small technical élite of workers to gaining more popular audiences amenable to moral suasion and social harmony. These latter aims, of course, had always been assumed by middle-class patrons, and it would be wrong to see this as a sharp shift from technology to entertainment. In the London Institute subjects from the arts such as history, French and eloquence, and clerical skills such as stenography accounted for at least one quarter of lectures over the 1820s. In the 1830s these subjects gained, accounting for half the lectures and classes given. Science and technology, however, retained a strong position in a greatly expanded lecture programme.[79]

Provincial leaders, at least, took pains to justify some change in orientation. Edward Baines justified entertainment in the Leeds Mechanics Institute as a way to greater understanding between social classes. The conditions of social peace, like science, would be conducive to industry.[80] Baines put this into practice by giving a series of lectures on his travels in Europe. He received support from John Marshall who, in 1830, complained that 'the sanguine predictions of the probable enlargement of science are . . . trite and out of date'.[81] Heywood, too, produced a programme for more entertaining lectures. He argued for more entertaining education which would give the working classes the desire for improvement. He was 'anxious for an altered system of instruction, not merely that we may give it more variety and interest, but that we may combine it with moral improvement'.[82]

The middle class was encouraged to accept the value of class contact,

79 This assessment is based on an analysis of lecture topics discussed in the Minute Books of the Committee of the London Mechanics Institution for the period 1824 to 1839.
80 Baines Papers, Edward Baines, 'On the Spirit of the Student and the Combination of Amusement with Study in Mechanics Institutions'.
81 Cited in Harrison, *Learning and Living*, p. 66.
82 Heywood, 'Third Address', 11 October 1830, *Addresses*, p. 37. He reiterated his new aims to Brougham in 1838, writing that his 'hobby now is to make Mechanics Institutes places of entertainment'. **Brougham Papers**, 1838.

conciliation and co-operation. The Leeds Institute avoided topics at issue between middle and working classes.[83] The Newcastle Institute was proud that it had 'opened its doors to every description of persons desirous of mental improvement . . . accordingly, we see in our rooms, mixed together, the modest and ingenious apprentice with the experienced and respectable tradesman. This generous mixture must produce the happiest effects, by separating youth from the insidious temptations of vice, and affording incitements to improvement and virtue.'[84] Heywood complained of the 'lack of personal contact and kindly feeling' between classes. He sought ways of breaking down this barrier, through provident or visiting societies.[85] By 1833 he envisaged close connections between the Mechanics Institute and the newly formed Statistical Society, which he would have preferred to have called a political economy club. He was well aware of problems of class conflict and saw his own role as one of mediating this conflict. He spoke of the 'benefits of his own circumstances' (as a banker) in not being in an occupation which mixed him up in 'disputes between masters and workpeople' and therefore 'less subject to the imputation of interested motives'.[86]

Like the changes in the orientation of political economy in the 1830s, these new directions in the Mechanics Institute Movement can be partially explained by the threat of working-class critiques and alternatives. Just as socialist critiques of the distribution of income elicited new justifications for capital, so new radical combinations of science and social science evoked moral and social vindications of the existing system.

An indigenous working-class and radical–scientific tradition reaching as far back at least as the earliest years of the nineteenth century, generated a confrontation both inside and outside the Mechanics Institute Movement with the aims of middle-class patrons. In the early

---

83 R. J. Morris, 'Organization and Aims of the . . . Voluntary Organizations of the Leeds Middle Class', D.Phil. Thesis, pp. 330–7. See Fraser, 'Edward Baines', for a discussion of Edward Baines's gradual move towards class conciliation. His early opposition to universal suffrage was based on what he regarded as the short-sighted commercial views of working men 'advocating restrictions in industry and exchange under the idea of protection, opposing machinery and all improvement, calling for a minimum of wages, condemning competition etc.'.

84 *Third Annual Report of the Literary, Scientific, and Mechanical Institution of Newcastle upon Tyne*, Newcastle upon Tyne, 1827.

85 Heywood, 'Fourth Address Delivered at a General Meeting of the Members of the Institutions, November 19, 1832', *Addresses*, p. 57.

86 B. Heywood to H. Brougham, 30 October 1833, Brougham Papers.

years of the London Mechanics Institute, a radical element was never lacking, with Robertson as editor of the *Mechanics Magazine*, and Hodgskin in an influential position. Many of the Institutes felt the cold draughts of Owenism when Robert Owen became an honorary member and lectured the London Mechanics Institute on 'The Employment of Machinery'. Owenite, Chartist and other radical lecturers featured at the Birmingham, Stalybridge, Sunderland, and Cheltenham Institutes. Outside the movement there were also alternative socialist scientific institutes. In Manchester, the break-away New Mechanics Institute led by Owenites was set up as a direct challenge to the economic and social assumptions of the established Institute.[87] In Coventry sixty or seventy socialists seceded from the Institute there and formed their own establishment.[88]

Radicals looked to science and invention as part of the working-man's heritage. At times they seemed to echo middle-class propaganda by claiming that most inventors had been working men like themselves, or that there were inventive faculties in the people which had been left 'smouldering unmatured'.[89] But they used these arguments not to profess any belief in social harmony but to demonstrate that capital had aggrandised improvements, most of which were first suggested by men on the job.[90] Radicals of many shades of opinion looked to the more equitable distribution of scientific knowledge and advised workmen to learn their scientific principles in preparation for the day when they would take control of production.[91] Radicals were, also, very critical of the undemocratic structures of the Mechanics Institutes and the content of the knowledge conferred there. *The New Moral World* in 1838 called the name 'mechanics institute' a misnomer 'where mechanics are excluded from participation in the management of the institution', 'where their numbers are few compared to other classes' (due to long hours of labour), and 'where they are looked on more as individuals receiving a boon from charity'.[92] When Rowland Detrosier opened the New

---

87 For further details see Edward Royle, 'Mechanics Institutes and the Working Classes, 1840–1860', *Historical Journal*, 1971, p. 318; Tylecote, *Mechanics Institutes*, p. 125; and Kelly, *George Birkbeck*, pp. 235, 252.
88 See Royle, 'Mechanics Institutes', p. 318.
89 *The New Moral World*, vol. II, 24 September 1836, p. 380.
90 *The Pioneer*, vol. I, no. 32, 12 April 1834, pp. 290–1.
91 *The Crisis*, vol II, no. 35, 31 August 1833, p. 273. Also see *The New Moral World*, vol. II, no. 22, 12 March 1836, pp. 153–5; and *The Economist*, vol. I, no. 5, 24 February 1821, p. 66.
92 *The New Moral World*, vol. XIV, no. 201, 1 September 1838, pp. 362–3.

Mechanics Institute he declared : 'Give to the mechanic that knowledge which enables him to outvie the workmanship of every other country, and of what moment is it to him, if the greatest portion of those means for which he has toiled . . . are taken from him by the operations of a vicious government.'[93] Wealth was not to 'exclude us from the temple of science', but equally the working man 'must grapple with the questions relating to capital, population, supply and demand; he must study not only the creation, but the distribution of wealth'.[94] The radical critics were not satisfied with knowledge of the physical sciences. They wanted more than such 'puny morsels of mental food'.[95] Of what consequence was it to the working man, they asked, 'to understand the theory of the winds' which it is impossible he could control 'when he needed a theory of government which would render him either happy or miserable'.[96] Radicals complained bitterly that workmen had been permitted to 'enter the portals of science' provided 'we would not appropriate to ourselves any of the benefits a knowledge of those sciences is calculated to confer'.[97]

These demands had the backing of a popular political economy, one conceived of from the standpoint of the working classes.[98] When one thousand Dumfermline working men subscribed to Dr Thomas Murray's political economy lectures in 1838 they did so because they 'expected to hear the doctrines of radicalism demonstrated'.[99] This alternative political economy, like its middle-class counterpart, analysed the connections between economic improvement and technology. Thomas Hodgskin, who had continued his association with the London

[93] Rowland Detrosier, *An Address Delivered to the New Mechanics Institution, December 30, 1829*, Manchester, 1829, p. 15.

[94] Rowland Detrosier, *The Benefits of General Knowledge, more especially the Sciences of Mineralogy, Geology, Botany, and Entomology in an Address delivered at the Opening of the Banksian Society, 5 January, 1829*, Manchester, 1829, p. 14; *An Address on the Advantages of the Intended Mechanics Hall of Science delivered at the New Mechanics Institution*, Manchester, 1831, p. 4; also see his *An Address Delivered to the Members of the New Mechanics Institution on the Necessity of an Extension of Moral and Political Instruction among the Working Classes*, Manchester, 1831.

[95] *Poor Man's Advocate*, no. 6, 23 February 1832, pp. 43–5.

[96] *Ibid.*

[97] *Chartist Circular*, vol. II, no. 109, 23 October 1841.

[98] Elie Halévy, *Thomas Hodgskin*, trans. A. J. Taylor, London, 1956. p. 89.

[99] A. Tyrrell, 'Political Economy, Whiggism and the Education of Working Class Adults in Scotland 1817 to 1840', *Scottish Historical Review*, XLVIII, 1967.

Mechanics Institute, lectured there on 'the natural science of national wealth', despite Francis Place's objections.[100] Hodgskin's conception of the movement was published in his anonymous *Labour Defended against the Claims of Capital*.

> The Mechanics Institutes will teach men the moral as well as the physical sciences. They will excite a disposition to probe all things to the bottom and to supply the means of carrying the research into every branch of knowledge. [The Labourers] may care nothing about the curious researches of the geologist or the elaborate classifications of the botanist, but they will assuredly ascertain why they of all classes of society have been involved in poverty and distress.[101]

He lectured the Institute in 1826 on Malthusian population theory and the 'progress of knowledge', claiming a contingency between population growth and technical change, or what he called 'a knowledge of the wealth creating arts'.[102] Extending Smith's discussion of the division of labour, he studied the impact of greater knowledge on productive power. The division of labour in Hodgskin's system was not the source of the degeneration of work, but of potential benefit.

> Why the *labourers* actively reap no benefit from division of labour, why their tasks seem rather to augment than lessen, with all those improvements which add to their skill and productive power, in such a degree even as to have given rise to an opinion, that the division of labour inflicts on them a serious injury ... as all the advantages from division of labour naturally centre in, and naturally belong to the labourers, if they are deprived of them, and in the progress of society those only are enriched by their improved skill who never labour, – this must arise from unjust appropriations; from usurpation and plunder in the party enriched, and from consenting submission in the party impoverished.[103]

---

100 Francis Place to George Birkbeck, Place Papers, B.L. Add. Ms. 27823, fol. 369.
101 [Thomas Hodgskin], *Labour Defended against the Claims of Capital*, London, 1825.
102 London Mechanics Institute 'Political Economy', July 1826, Place Papers, B.L. Add. Ms. 27824, fol. 11. These lectures were later published as *Popular Political Economy*, London, 1827.
103 Hodgskin, *Popular Political Economy*, pp. 108–9.

But Hodgskin also viewed fixed capital as embodied labour, so that the knowledge and skill of the labourer who both made and used the machine became fixed in the machine.

> The enlightened skill of the different classes of workmen alluded to, comes to be substituted in the natural progress of society for less skilful labour; and this enlightened skill produces an almost infinitely greater quantity of useful commodities, than the rude labour it has gradually displaced . . . the productive power of this skill is attributed to its visible products, the instruments, the mere owners of which, who neither make nor use them, imagine themselves to be very productive persons.[104]

The division of labour and the introduction of machinery were neither to be stopped nor tempered in Hodgskin's system. Rather, since skill had been transferred to the machine, the worker had a right to the ownership of the physical embodiment of his skill.

Hodgskin and other radical lecturers called into question all the ideals espoused in the rhetoric of the Mechanics Institute Movement. Rival scientific institutions challenged the conception of science and the type of knowledge imparted at the establishment institutes. This revolt soon evoked a response from the traditional societies. Thomas Coates, who made a study of the many local institutes in 1841 in order to make recommendations on future directions, urged the movement to recognise the challenge from both radical and religious circles, and to broaden its scope. He pointed out that the socialists and the chartists not only included in the plan of their societies some of the most attractive subjects of the traditional mechanics institutes, but that they had added lectures on politics and music, and that they also frequently held tea parties and dancing. These radical societies had a much wider appeal than did the Mechanics Institutes, and they were also able to attract the best scientific lecturers.[105]

The Mechanics Institute Movement responded to this challenge by making philanthropy and entertainment its keynote. Increasingly, patrons came to see the institutes as adjuncts of another movement they had just founded – the statistical movement. The purpose of the new statistical societies was to provide a suitable mix of philanthropy and political economy. Patrons, furthermore, came to recognise the per-

104 *Ibid.* p. 251.
105 Thomas Coates, *Report on the State of Literary, Scientific, and Mechanics Institutes in England*, London, 1841.

manence of classes lower than those aimed for by the Mechanics Institutes. A new pastime was the formation of Lyceums. These were to be as cheap as possible, and to offer recreation and elementary education. Manchester's was founded in 1838, and was followed by those in Salford, Ancoates, and Chorlton on Medlock.

The significance of the Mechanics Institute Movement extends, however, beyond its role in promoting social hierarchies in the work place and labour discipline. The movement gave a sense of purpose and cultural affirmation to its patrons – the provincial and industrial middle-class élites. The success of this movement in bringing this patronage together, in teaching the connection between science and industry, and in discovering the worth of provincial culture inspired other scientific movements. These patrons revived their interests in the older philosophical and scientific societies and made them relevant to the present day. The organisational experience of the Mechanics Institute Movement as a national movement based on provincial grass roots support was also to give patrons the confidence to extend their efforts to other philanthropic organisations, such as the statistical societies, and to other provincial scientific organisations, which soon found national bearings in the British Association for the Advancement of Science. This chapter has so far shown how the ascribed relationship between science and technology was exploited in the Mechanics Institute Movement to impose middle-class views of the structure and discipline of the labour force on workers. But the relationship between science and technology was also used by middle-class patrons in a more enlightened and illustrious movement in the British Association, to capture science for their own project of economic and technological improvement.

British Association

In the 1830s the old patrons of the Mechanics Institute Movement moved on to recruit new allies by pouring new life into their local literary and philosophical societies. They gave these societies the national bearings the old Mechanics Institutes had had by creating, in alliance with metropolitan scientists, the British Association for the Advancement of Science. This brought intellectuals, politicians, and businessmen together to promote applied science, with the platform that economic improvement went hand in hand with scientific progress. This connection was promoted both by scientists seeking wider markets for their research, and by industrialists seeking some higher rationale for their technological choices and expanding enterprises than individual

Science making gigantic strides. Source : George Cruikshank,
Our Own Times, London, 1846.

economic gain. The rhetoric of this movement tried to impress on its
public that technological improvement was not just a creative combination of productive labour and capital. Science, too, was integral
to technological improvement. The marriage was ideal for it gave to
scientists a part in the industrial development of the day, and to
industrialists a sense of civic value. By following their own self-interest
and simply taking up new inventions they could claim to be adding
to scientific enlightenment and the improvement of society in general.

Where science in the Mechanics Institutes had simply meant technological knowledge, to the new scientific movement of the 1830s it
meant theory – it was the 'research and development' which could place
special economic claims for government support. David Brewster
forged science, technology, and the economy in his gloomy denunciation
of the general neglect of abstract science.

> In this rivalry of skill, England alone has hesitated to take part
> . . . she seems to have looked with contempt on the less dazzling
> achievements of her philosophers, and, confiding in her past

pre-eminence in the arts, to have calculated too securely on
their permanence. Bribed by foreign gold, or flattered by foreign
courtesy, her artizans have quitted her service – her machinery
has been exported to distant markets – the inventions of her
philosophers, slighted at home, have been eagerly introduced
abroad. Her scientific institutions have been discouraged and
even abolished – the articles which she supplied to other states
have been gradually manufactured by themselves; and, one
after another, many of the best arts of England have been
transferred to other nations.[106]

A major focus of the national institution of the movement, the
British Association, was to give effect to the relationship between science
and technology at something more than a rhetorical level. Charles
Babbage attempted to take credit for any success in this. He argued
forcefully for the meetings to be held in manufacturing towns with the
object of bringing theoretical science into contact with the practical
arts. 'I was, myself, particularly anxious for this, owing as I do a debt
of gratitude for the valuable information which I have received in
many of the manufacturing districts, where I have learned to appreciate still more highly than before, the value of those speculative pursuits which we follow in our academical labours.'[107] Babbage also
claimed credit for another scheme which he saw as solving a fundamental defect in the Association. He thought the basis of the Association was
limited, that it provided little to interest landed gentry or manufacturer.
He saw the solution in the adoption in 1838 of his plan for an exhibition
of the specimens of various manufactured and commercial products of
the districts successively visited by the Association.[108]

William Whewell, in his address to the third meeting of the Association, managed to combine his plea for greater support to theoretical
science with his tribute to technology :

Still, it would little become us here to be unjust to practical
science. Practice has always been the origin and stimulus of
theory : Art has ever been the mother of science ... there are
no subjects in which we can look more hopefully to an advance

106 [David Brewster], 'Charles Babbage, Reflections on the Decline of
  Science in England', *Quarterly Review*, XLIII, October 1830, p. 305.
107 *Reports and Transactions of the British Association*, I, no. 2, 1832,
  p. 107.
108 Babbage, *Passages in the Life of a Philosopher*, p. 432.

in sound theoretical views, than those in which the demands of practice make men willing to experiment on an expansive scale.[109]

And Professor Daubeny, at the 1836 meeting, stressed the usefulness of the various abstract sciences to the chemical manufacturer, the miner and the agriculturalist.[110]

The direct connection between science and technology was established at the 1836 meeting when a special Mechanics Section was added to the Association. Nearly £500 was allocated in the first year for special research into the Cornish steam engines, into the strength of cast iron, and into railroad and steamboat research. And the first committee of the Section included an eminent cast of engineers: Babbage, Charles Donkin, John Robinson, George Stephenson, Fairbairn, Professor Willis, and George Rennie.[111] This Section G became one of the most active of the Association. Most of the papers presented in the first years were concerned with aspects of the steam engine, the railroad, and fuel saving. By 1840 there were so many papers and abstracts passed on to the Section that assessment of main interests is difficult. Fairbairn presented several papers to it, and several more on practical technical problems to the Manchester Literary and Philosophical Society. He produced one in 1837 'On the Strength and other Properties of Cast Iron obtained from Hot and Cold Blast', and one for the 1844 meeting of the British Association 'On the Consumption of Fuel and the Prevention of Smoke'.[112]

The rhetoric of the British Association appeared to further the economic interests of scientists seeking a new style of patronage. It also apparently satisfied some of the social aspirations of industrialists, but after a time they had no further need to claim a special suitability for extending scientific culture. If its purpose was just to contribute to the social status of those involved, then any other cultural activity – music, art collections, antiquarian societies – would do just as well. Where science did appear to have some ultilitarian value as, for example, the way it was used in the Mechanics Institute Movement to extend a disciplined and hierarchical labour force, then industrialists would continue to have some stake in it. For the most part, neither the British Association nor the many provincial literary and philosophical societies

[109] *Reports of the British Association*, II, 1833, p. xxv.
[110] *Ibid.* v, 1836, pp. xxxiv–xxxv.
[111] *Ibid.* VI, 1837, p. xxi.
[112] Pole, ed., *Life of Sir William Fairbairn*, Appendix.

were able to demonstrate the existence of a relationship between scientific theory and any practical technological advance. Neither did many of these societies go beyond mere rhetoric in trying to promote such a relationship. The Mechanics Section of the British Association, despite its impressive array of papers and projects, did not demonstrate any interdisciplinary activity between scientific theory and practical mechanics or technological knowledge. It existed as an island for technology among the practitioners and consumers of science. The efforts of the provincial societies varied. The Manchester Society ranked quite high with five papers on mechanics in its 1831 Memoirs.[113] Both the Newcastle Literary and Philosophical Society and the Geological Society of Cornwall had been specifically set up to encourage cooperation between men of science and men in the mining industry. But this was the early project of the Newcastle Society, founded in 1793, and by the late 1830s the Society was dying.[114] The Cornwall Society, set up in 1814 with Davies Gilbert as President,[115] achieved a successful fusion of geology and mining in its papers, and a local social identification between cultured gentry and mine adventurers.[116]

The new scientific movement which took off from the 1830s certainly owed much of its vitality to the interest in science in provincial areas. It is, however, questionable whether this science was perceived to have any special economic value. The relationship which was claimed between science and technology was rhetorical only, and the relationship between scientific and economic improvement was actually perceived to be a connection between technological knowledge and economic improvement. The scientific movement of the early nineteenth century acted as a social context for political economy's efforts to demonstrate the benefits of the contemporary industrial transformation. A series of provincial societies for the education of the working man, the Mechanics Institutes, brought together popular political economy and popular technology. The changes in the aims and rhetoric of these societies echo those of political economy. The effort to promote the

---

113 *Memoirs of the Manchester Literary and Philosophical Society*, 2nd series, IV.
114 R. S. Watson, *History of the Philosophical and Literary Society of Newcastle upon Tyne*, London, 1897.
115 A. Hume, *The Learned Societies and the Printing Clubs of the U.K.* (1847), 2nd edition with supplement, London, 1853, p. 142.
116 Roy Porter, 'The Industrial Revolution and the Rise of the Science of Geology', in M. Teich and R. M. Young, eds., *Changing Perspectives in the History of Science*, London, 1973.

role of the skilled artisans on a special level of a hierarchically structured labour market gave way to the purpose of training up a disciplined adaptable labour force amenable to factory employment and receptive to technological improvements. In earlier chapters I demonstrated the similar shifts in the orientation of political economy. Just as these shifts in political economy were prompted in part by radical working-class activity, so too in the Mechanics Institutes Movement radical approaches to scientific knowledge and alternative scientific societies provoked the Mechanics Institutes to change the focus of their educational plans. The Mechanics Institute Movement soon found another context in philanthropic societies such as the statistical societies.

The alignment between technology and the economy was continued in the middle-class scientific societies – the literary and philosophical societies and the British Association for the Advancement of Science. But in these societies there was an extension of the connection between economy and technology. Scientific theory was added to the formula, but, although both scientists and industrialists initially found either social or economic appeal in the combination of science and technology, the British Association did not make many efforts beyond the level of rhetoric to put this into effect. The efforts of provincial scientific societies varied, but there were few attempts even in this scientific movement to distinguish scientific and technical knowledge, and then to relate the two. The attraction of this scientific movement to provincial industrialists was soon divested of any substantive utilitarian value, and became the attraction of social status gained by cultural affiliation to science, music, art or antiquarianism. More immediate concern was shown both by provincial businessmen and by technological–scientific writers, not so much in the connections between technology and science, but in the connections between technology and the 'science' of the workshop and factory organisation. The study of economics and of technology was engaged in at a grass-roots level in business correspondence, management manuals and industrial histories. Responses to new technology were related at this level to practical questions of production management. Technology was not just to be understood by provincial employers and workmen in terms of the high principles of science; it was also integral to the 'domestic economy of the factory'.

8

The order of the factory

The rhetoric on the connection between technological progress and economic improvement in the Mechanics Institute Movement had an explicit economic and social meaning. It was meant to contribute to the formalisation of hierarchies in the labour movement. The skilled artisan was to be separated from unskilled common labour, and both were to be detached from the middle class. This design for creating a 'labour aristocracy' was complemented by efforts to contribute to the discipline of the labour force. The concern with labour hierarchies and discipline was also expressed at much more concrete levels in industrial histories and manuals. The writers of these manuals also addressed themselves to the question of the relationship between science and technology. They wrote of the use of science in the improvement of actual production processes, but they took an original approach to the issue by examining the connections between technology and the science of workshop organisation. By the 1830s there was already a large number of industrial histories and lives of inventors. The cotton industry was a popular subject; McCulloch's history of the rise and progress of the industry had reached readers of the *Encyclopaedia Britannica*, the *Edinburgh Review*, and *The Scotsman*.[1] John Kennedy's commentaries on the development of cotton textiles had fuelled local pride in the readers of the *Memoirs of the Manchester Literary and Philosophical Society*.[2] As early as 1835 Edward Baines produced a large and defini-

[1] McCulloch, 'On the Rise, Progress, Present State and Prospects of the British Cotton Manufacture'.
[2] John Kennedy, 'Observations on the Rise and Progress of the Cotton Trade in Great Britain', (read 1815), *Memoirs of the Manchester Literary and Philosophical Society*, 2nd series, III, 1819.

tive history of the industry.[3] Memoirs and biographies of early industrial magnates and inventors were common in the popular mechanics' journals,[4] encyclopaedias, and journals of the philosophical societies. Technology had become so popular a subject that journalists such as George Dodd could describe their factory tours and observations on industrial processes with as much alacrity as they had once reported voyages to distant lands.[5] The *Encyclopaedia Metropolitana* could describe its project as one 'derived from the peculiar circumstances of our times', where 'new discoveries in the different branches of experimental philosophy in the last twenty years are unparalleled in the history of human knowledge'. The reasoning behind the plan of the work, divided between pure and applied science, and historical and technological study, 'will be found in the manifest tendency of all the arts and sciences at present, from the most purely intellectual events to the labours of the common mechanic, to lose their former insulated character, and organize themselves into one harmonious body of knowledge.'[6] McCulloch and Ure found ready markets for their *Dictionary of Commerce* and *Dictionary of Arts Manufactures and Mines*.[7] Even highly technical accounts of the steam engine acquired an avid readership.[8] In conjunction with their history and description of technology was to be found an ample supply of manuals on production processes and on factory organisation and management. Several

[3] Edward Baines, *History of the Cotton Manufacture of Great Britain*, London, 1835.

[4] For example, The London and Glasgow *Mechanics Magazines*, the *Mechanics Weekly Journal and Artizans Miscellany*, and the *Mechanics Gallery of Science and Art*.

[5] George Dodd, *Days at the Factories, or The Manufacturing Industry of Great Britain Described*, London, 1843.

[6] *Prospectus of the Encyclopaedia Metropolitana or Universal Dictionary of Knowledge, to be published 1 January, 1818*, p. 7.

[7] McCulloch, *Dictionary of Commerce*. Ure, *A Dictionary of Arts, Manufactures and Mines*, London, 1839. Details of the life, personality, scientific efforts and manufacturing connections of Andrew Ure can be found in W. V. Farrar, 'Andrew Ure', *Notes and Records of the Royal Society of London*, xxvii, February 1973, pp. 299–324. Also see Peter Barlow, *A Treatise on the Manufactures and Machinery of Great Britain to which is Prefaced an Introductory View of the Principles of Manufactures by Charles Babbage*, London, 1836.

[8] John Farey, *A Treatise on the Steam Engine*, London, 1827; and C. F. Partington, *Account of Steam Engines and Other Models of Machinery, Illustrative of Improvements in Railroads, Steam Navigation, and the Arts and Manufactures, with an Historical and Descriptive Account of the Steam Engine*, London, 1840.

published manuals on the scientific principles of organising a workshop or factory, from James Montgomery on cotton spinning to Robert Owen on personnel management, were backed up by many unpublished essays, notes, and memoirs of industrialists themselves who made efforts to systematise and write about their own practice. It is in the context of these manuals of management and the broader underworld of industrial–technological commentary that we find two important tracts, Charles Babbage's ingenious and quirkish *On the Economy of Machinery and Manufactures*, and Andrew Ure's extraordinary and blatant panegyric in apology for the factory system, *The Philosophy of Manufactures*.[9] This chapter will concentrate on analysing these two tracts and will relate them to the context of this popular industrial–technological literature. It will focus on the attempts of these writers to relate their perception of technology to actual production practice, and will examine their attempts to systematise the organisation of work. Finally, it will examine the analogies between the relationships of technology and economic growth as perceived at their grass roots level, and those set out in the scientific movement and in political economy.

These tracts by Babbage and Ure were popular for the connections they forged between scientific and technological knowledge, and the theory and practice of the early industrialists. They clarified, in a way that neither political economists nor the popular scientific movement did, that the new machines and new skills could not be discussed in abstract, in isolation from the factory and the division of labour in the workshop. Babbage and Ure both had backgrounds in the scientific movement, being both scientists and leading propagandists of it, and their tracts on the factory were certainly influenced by this context. Ure, who had taught at the Andersonian Institute, was a scientific consultant at the time he wrote *The Philosophy of Manufactures*. Babbage's books were, in an indirect way, a result of his scientific interests, particularly his obsession with his 'calculating machine'. However, both writers stressed the non-academic basis of their studies and the significance of observation as the foundation of their ideas.

9 Charles Babbage, *On the Economy of Machinery and Manufactures*, London, 1832, 4th edition, 1835. Andrew Ure, *The Philosophy of Manufactures*, London, 1835. Other writers who have commented on Babbage, Ure, and their context in nineteenth-century manuals and observations on management are Pollard, *The Genesis of Modern Management*, R. Bendix, *Work and Authority in Industry* (1956), Berkeley, 1974, and Stephen Marglin, 'What Bosses Do', in André Gorz, ed., *The Division of Labour*, London, 1976.

Babbage regarded his book as the result of a series of observations made over several years of visiting 'workshops and factories', both in England and on the continent, 'for the purpose of endeavouring to make myself acquainted with the various resources of mechanical art'.[10] Ure, too, stressed that his studies 'derived from a summer wandering through the factory districts of Lancashire, Cheshire, and Derbyshire'.[11]

Workshop organisation

Babbage's *On the Economy of Machinery and Manufactures* first came out in 1832 with the object of presenting the reader with the mechanical principles of arts and manufactures, 'which struck me as the most important, either for understanding the actions of machines, or for enabling the memory to classify and arrange the facts connected with their employment'.[12] As stated above, Babbage collected most of his information on visits through the factory districts of Britain and the continent. In the first edition of his book, he both exempted himself from taking up specific questions of political economy, and criticised political economists generally as 'closet philosophers . . . too little acquainted with the admirable arrangements of the factory'.[13] He specified that he had not 'attempted to examine all the difficult questions of *political economy* which are intimately connected with such enquiries'.[14] His second edition of November 1832, however, was an attempt to correct this. He added three new chapters – one on 'The New System of Manufacturing', proposing a piece-rate wage system, another 'On the Effects of Machinery in Reducing the Demand for Labour', and one 'On Money as a Medium of Exchange'.[15]

In many ways, too, the book was an ingenious offshoot of Babbage's work on the calculating engine. As he pointed out himself in his first preface, the book was an application of the principles of the calculating engine, bringing to bear the mathematical precision and predictability of his machine on the factories he had toured.[16] The underlying interdependence in the engineering industry between the machine produced

---

10 Babbage, *Machinery and Manufactures*, 4th edition, p. iii.
11 Ure, *The Philosophy of Manufactures*, p. ix.
12 Babbage, *Machinery and Manufactures*, Preface to 1st edition, pp. iii–iv.
13 *Ibid.* p. 156.
14 *Ibid.* Preface to 1st edition, p. iv.
15 *Ibid.* p. viii. This may have been in response to McCulloch's criticism. 'Babbage on Machinery and Manufactures', *Edinburgh Review*, LVI, January 1833. It is possible Babbage heard these criticisms soon after his first edition appeared.
16 Babbage, *Machinery and Manufactures*, p. iii.

and the technical process was completely explicit in Babbage's work. His vivid application to the factory of 'these principles of generalization to which [his] other pursuits have naturally given rise' quite likely had an important precedent in the similar attributes of the engineering workshop or factory. The influence of the calculating engine was noticed by his readers. *Cobbett's Magazine* for instance, wrote 'The work bears the traces of the correctness of this account of its origins . . . [It] is the emanation of a mind habituated to mathematical precision and arrangement', and 'directed to a subject not previously treated with such exactness'.[17]

But the connections between the book and the situation in the engineering industry were more than mere parallels. The engineer who was trying to build Babbage's machine was John Clement, a Maudslay pupil. Furthermore, Clement's bills for building the machine were paid by a Commission of the Royal Society made up of Donkin, Rennie, Brunel and Maudslay.[18] Even if the actual influence of the work process in the engineering industry may have been a very indirect one in Babbage's mind, the implicit context was certainly plain.

Babbage's overriding concern was with what he called 'the domestic economy of the factory'. He argued that if the maker of an article wished to become a manufacturer he had to pay attention to principles other than merely mechanical ones. He had to attend to the principles of domestic economy, and arrange the whole system of his factory in such a way as to sell articles at the minimum possible price.[19] This domestic economy was to be achieved in the first instance by attention to scale. 'When the number of processes into which it is most advantageous to divide it, and the number of individuals to be employed in it, are ascertained, then all factories which do not employ a direct multiple of this latter number, will produce the article at a greater cost.'[20] Large factories, however, generally bring out problems of communication between departments. The implications of early communication innovation were recognised by Babbage. In discussing the economy of time which could be achieved through the introduction of machinery, Babbage noted the use of tin tubes for speaking through, used in London shops and trades. It was in his discussion of *The Times* as a large

17 'Mr Babbage and the Useful Arts', *Cobbett's Magazine*, ii, December 1833, no. 11, p. 383.
18 Armytage, *A Social History of Engineering*, p. 128.
19 Babbage, *Machinery and Manufactures*, p. 203.
20 *Ibid.* p. 212.

establishment applying an extensive mental and bodily division of labour that Babbage noticed the possibilities arising from a system of wires and pullies for transmitting things. He proposed the use of stretched wire for a 'species of telegraphic communication'.[21] Babbage's early perceptions of the development and uses for what would later be the telephone, the telegraph and overhead assembly track, were generated by the contemporary concern he perceived for more effective 'organization in the works'.

Babbage went on to relate the scale of the factory to the division of labour. 'We have seen that the application of the *Division of Labour* tends to produce cheaper articles; that it thus increases the demand; and gradually, by the effect of competition, or by the hope of increased gain, that it causes large capitals to be embarked in extensive factories.'[22] The implication to be drawn from this interdependence of scale and the division of labour was that throughout every stage of manufacture in such a factory the same economy of skill prevailed.[23]

Babbage's domestic economy of the factory was fundamentally based on the Smithian division of labour. He reiterated those effects of the division of labour analysed by Smith, but added to this what became known as the 'Babbage principle'.

> That the master manufacturer by dividing the work to be
> executed into different processes, each requiring different
> degrees of skill or of force, can purchase exactly that precise
> quantity of both which is necessary for each process; whereas if
> the whole work were executed by one workman, that person
> must possess sufficient skill to perform the most difficult and
> sufficient strength to execute the most laborious, of the oper-
> ations into which the art is divided.[24]

The division of labour also applied to the use of machinery. According to Babbage there were two types of machine: that which produced power, and that which transmitted force and executed work. It was here that Babbage used the very far-seeing example of the application of rollers and grease for reducing friction. 'The man who contrived rollers, invented a tool by which his power was quintupled. The workman who first suggested the employment of soap or grease, was immediately

21 *Ibid.* p. 275.
22 *Ibid.* p. 216.
23 *Ibid.* p. 217.
24 *Ibid.* p. 175

enabled to move, without exerting a greater effort, more than three times the weight he could before.'[25] Babbage was one of the few observers in his own time to recognise the significance of lubrication, and David Landes has been one of the few historians in recent times to give grease its due. As Landes put it :

> This is a subject that has been much neglected by observers and students of technology and its history. The great international expositions of the nineteenth century collected and displayed industrial activities and products of man with a comprehensiveness and taxonomic enthusiasm that never fails to astonish. They assembled all manner of tools and machines, the raw materials they worked, the finished articles they made. They did not neglect the products of the soil or the sea, even the take of the hunt. But they took grease for granted.[26]

The question of the durability of machinery was taken up by Babbage during his discussion of the speed of production. He stressed the importance not so much of velocity in the running of machinery as of regularity, that is 'the uniformity and steadiness with which machinery works'. Examples of this were the governor of a steam engine and the regularity in supplying fuel to the fires of boilers. Uniform action in both cases led to greater 'duration' by economising on coal consumption.[27]

Babbage pursued the significance of 'velocity' not in relation to machinery but in relation to labour. It was the problem behind his very sophisticated discussion of time and motion. Here he argued that fatigue was not dependent on force, but on the frequency with which that force was exerted. There were two parts to any exertion : first, the expenditure of the force necessary to drive the tool or instrument, and secondly, the effort required for the motion of some limb of animal or man producing the action. In order to economise on labour, it was necessary to adjust the weight of the part of the body that was moved, the weight of the tool it urged, and the frequency of repetition of these efforts so as to produce the greatest effect.[28] The possibility of raising the speed of production, or in other words the intensity of labour without increasing the labour input in the same proportion, depended on the order, precision, and discipline with which this labour was exerted. Babbage recognised that it was often impossible to extort such discipline

[25] *Ibid.* p. 8.
[26] Landes, *The Unbound Prometheus*, p. 298.
[27] Babbage, *Machinery and Manufactures*, p. 28.
[28] *Ibid.* p. 31.

from labour. He looked, therefore, to the extension of machinery to replace labour, and thereby to allow for the more accurate determination of the force and frequency necessary to production. Babbage regarded the machine as a great corrective of the indiscipline of labour: it could function as a check against the inattention, idleness, and dishonesty of human labour. The regularity allowed by machinery contributed to the precision and predictability. Such machinery introduced the possibility of precise measurement, and Babbage indulged himself in proposing instruments for counting the number of steps made, the distance travelled, and the number of strokes made by a steam engine.

As a follow up to this interest in measurement, Babbage devised a questionnaire to aid those investigating factories in the same manner as he had done. The questionnaire, a form of time and motion study, included questions on the possible processes for producing an article, possible defects, waste allowed, weight of the product compared to its raw material, provision and repair of tools by masters or men, cost and wear and tear of all machinery, and the number of processes together with the exact number employed in each process.[29] A separate questionnaire was to be provided for each process, and was to include information on the type of machine used, the number of operatives attending it together with their age and sex and the pay and hours of each, the provision of tools, skill required, the number of times each operation was repeated, and the system of payment.[30] He even included warnings on the verification of all statements made, and experimental methods of observing work.

Babbage's account of the impact of the division of labour on skill levels and labour displacement was conventional. That is to say, he did not add a great deal to the analysis of technology and skill advanced by economists of the 1820s and early 1830s. But he did recognise transitional problems due to labour immobility, and was suitably ambivalent on the question of skill. The power loom, for example, required less strength and skill than the handloom, but this was not to say the industry as a whole showed a tendency to degrading skill. New skills were called into action in building factories, making steam engines and machinery, in devising improvements in the structure of looms, and finally in regulating the whole economy of the factory. Such work, 'calls in labour of a higher order than that superseded'.[31]

[29] *Ibid.* pp. 115–16.
[30] *Ibid.* p. 117.
[31] *Ibid.* p. 339.

Babbage did, however, propose what he called his 'new system of manufacture' as a way of overcoming workers' opposition to technological improvements. He argued that machinery was often prevented from advancing as fast as it might, particularly in smaller establishments, because workers feared a loss of jobs and wages. He therefore contrived a system of profit sharing and co-operative production, and argued that if workers had some financial stake in an enterprise, if they were able to gain from any increases in productivity, then they would welcome all technological improvements. Babbage recommended that all workers be paid a basic wage and that the rest of their earnings be made up of a percentage of the profits of the enterprise, finding examples of their type of organisation in the tin mines of Cornwall and on whaling vessels. However, he also carried these plans further, to include collective decision making on hiring and dismissal, and productivity by goals and the introduction of all manner of devices and new forms of organisation which would economise on labour. There would, however, be an extensive division of labour in such works, not in order to control and subordinate labour, but rather as a co-operative decision of workers themselves in their efforts to introduce the most efficient methods of production. Babbage conceded that there would be little hope for introducing his new system of manufacture in large established firms, for it would most certainly involve a reduction in the capitalist's share of profits. Few industrialists could be expected to sacrifice, even for a time, their own personal gains to the higher productivity potential of their enterprises. He had higher hopes that his plan might be implemented in small firms, particularly those where the owners had formerly been foremen themselves, or that groups of higher paid workmen would pool their savings and found a co-operative along the lines he proposed.[32] His scheme was a far-reaching one for a man of establishment circles. Though many entrepreneurs were aware of and made use of incentive schemes to increase workers' productivity, the lengths to which his suggestions went were probably surpassed by only radical and Owenite co-operative ventures.[33]

Though it had little that was new to add to the discussion of technological unemployment and skill, *On the Economy of Machinery and*

[32] *Ibid.* chap. 26, pp. 250–9, 295.
[33] *The New Moral World*, Robert Owen's journal, reviewed Babbage's book favourably. Though clearly interested in his plans for profit sharing and co-operation, it foresaw little advantage to the workers in the scheme while employment was determined by a 'fluctuating commercial rivalry', *The New Moral World*, 8 April 1836.

Manufactures also contained some strikingly novel ideas on the implications of a growing interdependence of science and technology. Babbage applied his concept of the division of labour not just to material but to mental production.

> The efforts for the improvement of its manufactures which any
> country can make with the greatest probability of success, must
> arise from the combined exertions of all those most skilled in the
> theory, as well as in the practice of the arts; each labouring in
> that department for which his natural capacity and acquired
> habits have rendered him most fit.[34]

But Babbage left only hints of his views on the role of science in his small concluding chapter 'On the Future Prospects of Manufacture, as connected with Science'. Much of the chapter was taken up with expressions of Babbage's discontent with the Royal Society and with the lack of state support for scientific enterprise. He also used the chapter to advertise the recently formed British Association for the Advancement of Science. Babbage looked to the industrial bourgeoisie for the fountainhead of the new class of scientists which he hoped would be spawned by the social division of labour.

> It is highly possible that in the next generation, the race of
> scientific men in England will spring from a class of persons
> altogether different from that which has hitherto scantily
> supplied them. Requiring for the success of their pursuits,
> previous education, leisure and fortune, few are so likely to
> unite these essentials as the sons of our wealthy manufacturers,
> who, having been enriched by their own exertions, in a field
> connected with science, will be ambitious of having their
> children distinguished in its ranks.[35]

Babbage went on to list several of the chemical sciences which had a direct impact on industry. But his application of his theory of the mental division of labour was used to greatest effect not in his discussion of science and technology but in his analysis of the development of the sciences themselves.

Babbage discovered that the division of labour was evident too within the world of science itself. The cultivation of botany, for example, came to require greater specialisation than could be provided by the comprehensive Royal Society. The Linnaean Society was the result, and this

[34] Babbage, *Machinery and Manufactures*, p. 379.
[35] *Ibid.*

was soon followed by the Geological Society and the Astronomical Society.[36] These more specialised societies led to greater knowledge of the chemical and physical properties of bodies, and promoted interest in less tangible areas like light, electricity and heat. But the ultimate result of the mental division of labour was an even higher science – Babbage's 'science of calculation'. Even more than others this science would be intimately connected with technology. It 'becomes continually more necessary at each step of our progress and which must ultimately govern the whole of the applications of science to the arts of life.'[37]

The science of calculation developed to the degree where machinery would take over all numerical calculation. It was, furthermore, based on the division of labour within the sciences, and would therefore eventually emerge as the science of all sciences. But calculation was also based, as stated, on the 'division of mental labour', the title of Chapter 20 of Babbage's tract. Applying his principle that each process of any task should have only the precise quantity of skill and knowledge required for it, he separated arithmetical exercise from higher mathematical reasoning. The arithmetical exercise on the lowest rung of the science of calculation could be formalised into mathematical tables and eventually mechanised by means of his wonderful calculating engine. Babbage's calculator 'based on the method of differences' brought a vision of a computer-run technology. The description Nassau Senior came to make over ten years later of a modern industry comprised of physical force was matched by these remarkable 'ground level' predictions of automation and computer-based technology.

Babbage and the industrial context

Babbage's study of workshop organisation and the practical implications of the division of labour was not unique for its content. For, seen against a background of contemporary accounts of industry, it reflected many of the interests of its genre. His book did offer, however, what no other study of the time did – an integrated analysis of the economic and technical implications of the division of labour based on a synthesis of his observations on workshop and factory practice. Its originality was in the breadth of its conception and the fact that it was not a mere series of observations, but an *analysis* of the workshop and factory systems of production.

[36] Charles Babbage, *Reflections on the Decline of Science in England*, London, 1830, pp. 40–3.
[37] Babbage, *Machinery and Manufactures*, p. 388.

The early attention Babbage gave to problems of the size of work-shops and factories and economies of scale was also of concern to industrialists. William Fairbairn connected scale with techniques: 'The improvements in tools changed the mode of doing mechanical work, by rendering necessary large and carefully laid out manufactories.' Watt's steam engine had created such stringent requirements in tools and organisation that the large factory came to replace the small mill-wright's shop.[38] Furthermore, Watt's patent, it was believed, had brought internal economies of scale with its prolonged period of monopoly.

> for by concentrating the business in their hands, they always had orders for a sufficient number of engines of the same kind, to enable them to arrange their manufactory upon system, with a great division of labour, whereby all their workmen acquired dexterity from continual repetition of the same work, and the work was better executed, at a less expense than if they had made fewer engines.[39]

Where Babbage had pointed out the relationship between economies of scale and the development of innovations in communication, some years later the journalist George Dodd noticed how such innovations had been integrated into the production process of the factories he visited. In his *Days at the Factories* he found in a copper and lead factory an ingenious rail fixed near the ceiling or roof, whereby boilers, coppers, stills, and engines etc. were suspended from a wheeled car-riage.[40] And in a bookbinder's he noted 'one of those simple but valuable expedients for saving time, now so much employed in large factories, – we mean a series of "speaking tubes" ' which passes to 'the office of all the foremen above and below stairs'.[41]

The significance Babbage accorded to grease was not to receive any notice for a long time. It was to be as late as the 1860s when William Fairnbairn wrote his *Treatise on Mills and Millwork* that the connection between durability, velocity and grease was again to be raised.

> In large cotton mills I have known as much as ten to fifteen horses' power absorbed by a change in the quality of oil used for lubrication; and in cold weather, or when the temperature of

[38] Pole, ed., *Life of Sir William Fairbairn*, p. 47.
[39] Farey, *A Treatise on the Steam Engine*, p. 647.
[40] George Dodd, *Days at the Factories*, p. 517.
[41] *Ibid.* p. 364.

the mill is much reduced (as is generally the case when standing over Sunday), the power required on a Monday morning is invariably greater than at any other time during the week.[42]

Though Babbage was to claim credit for pointing out the way the division of labour allowed for the precise quantification and allocation of tasks, skills and time, industrialists, perhaps unconsciously, had implemented policies of skill distribution. Long before Babbage outlined his famous principle, Boulton and Watt had implemented a policy of division of labour and skill distribution in their Soho foundry. They left behind two papers describing the details of this policy. The first paper, 'Specifications of the Fittings of the Engine Materials and the Shops where it is to be Done', gave a complete list of the constituent parts of the steam engine with all its subdivisions. It set out in detail all the operations to be performed on each article in its proper sequence. This paper was followed by 'Arrangements of Workmen and Distribution of Work at Soho', which indicated extensive division of labour and careful job specification, with detailed lists of jobs assigned to each workman throughout the factory. As Sir Eric Roll has pointed out, the papers show that at Soho the production processes for each part had 'been broken up into a long series of various minor operations, showing a very high degree of the application of division of labour to factory routine'.[43]

The good order and domestic economy of the factory were recognised to be very significant to the profitability of any enterprise, not just by Charles Babbage, but by many contemporary industrialists. These businessmen were, moreover, very articulate on the question of efficient work processes. William Brown, a Dundee flax spinner who sometimes gave consultancy service on the organisation of other mills, gave high accord to the efficient ordering of the work process. 'The first and great object to be aimed at by the Manager of East Mill is PROFIT. The chief requisites to profit are: a good quality of yarn – large quantity, little waste – moderate expenses – and a good state of the machinery.'[44] To secure this in the case of his mill, he thought it necessary that the business be laid out in twelve different departments, each of which

42 Fairbairn, *Treatise on Mills*, vol. II, p. 77; cited in Landes, *The Unbound Prometheus*, p. 298.

43 Eric Roll, *An Early Experiment in Industrial Organization*, London, 1930, pp. 178–81.

44 Dennis Chapman, 'William Brown of Dundee 1791–1864; Management in a Scottish Flax Mill', *Exploration in Entrepreneurial History*, IV, February 1952, p. 124.

required its own separate portion of attendances and consideration.[45] These priorities in management were reflected in his attitude to improvements :

> every mill manager [should] devote a portion of his time to the cultivation of improvements. Should this be neglected the consequences must be disagreeable as one must be left behind his neighbours. Improvements may be made in two ways : either by invention or adoption. If invention is to be tried, the best way of proceeding is to understand the present machinery well, to be familiar with its imperfections, and to remedy them accordingly. If adopting is to be tried, the only way is to visit improved mills, to acquaint oneself with the nature of their improvements, and to adopt accordingly . . . One thing, however, I require to keep in mind, and that is – that the success of a mill depends much more upon keeping the machinery in good order and managing well on the present plan, than on pursuing and looking after what are commonly called alterations and improvements.[46]

The successful entrepreneur had a broad knowledge of new techniques, and thought carefully of their application to his particular use, thus taking up all those questions of technical interrelatedness, layout, power sources, and costing. John Marshall, the Leeds flax spinner, was one such example. Throughout the 1820s, he visited not only flax mills but leading cotton and woollen mills to observe new techniques and inquire into adapting them to the linen industry. He kept special notebooks on processes throughout this period.[47] In a 'General Notebook' kept between 1790 and 1830, he kept the names of a number of specialised machine makers, information on sizes and types of textile machinery, calculations of the power required to work various types of machinery, and details of steam engine types including information on coal consumed, power, strokes per minute and the diameters of each. The Notebook also included the opinions of several other proprietors and engineers on the best ways of increasing the speed of machinery, as well as information on the employment of children and the hours worked at various cotton mills.[48]

---

45 *Ibid.* p. 124.
46 *Ibid.* p. 126.
47 Brotherton Library, Leeds University, Marshall Papers, Salop Notebooks on Processes, 1826–9 and 1829–35, Ms. 200, nos. 36 and 37.
48 Marshall Papers, General Notebook, 1790–1830, Ms. 200.

An interesting counterpart to the discussion of the domestic economy of the factory was provided by Owen's application of management principles to the care and order of what he called the 'living machines'. Babbage hoped the machine would do away with the inadequacies of labour. But Owen put across his philanthropic personnel policy in mechanical terms to his audience of manufacturers. He compared the up-to-date treatment of machinery with the treatment of labour. He argued that successful manufacturers knew the advantages of 'a substantial, well contrived and well executed machinery', but that they had an equal interest in the good arrangement of their labour.

> The more delicate, complex living mechanism would be equally
> improved by being trained to strength and activity; and that
> it would also prove true economy to keep it neat and clean;
> to treat it with kindness, that its mental movements might not
> experience too much irritating friction; to endeavour by every
> means to make it more perfect; to supply it regularly with a
> sufficient quantity of wholesome food and other necessaries of
> life, that the body might be preserved in good working con-
> dition, and prevented from being out of repair, or falling
> prematurely to decay.[49]

Good order in a textile mill as in an engineering plant was, in addition, connected with precision and measurement. Both Brown and Montgomery were completely uncompromising as to the role of calculation in good management. Montgomery noted that those in charge of spinning factories as well as all young carding and spinning masters were required to make calculations quickly.

> It is a most essential qualification on the part of the manager
> that he be expert in performing *all kinds* of calculations con-
> nected with the business; the advantage of which will be
> apparent in various respects. First, in regulating the *speed* of
> the different machines; second, in adjusting the draughts of
> the various machines; and third, in making changes in the
> qualities of the cotton and sizes of the yarn.[50]

[49] Robert Owen, 'Address to the Superintendents of Manufactures', in
   Owen, *A New View of Society*, p. 96.
[50] James Montgomery, *The Theory and Practice of Cotton Spinning; or
   the Carding and Spinning Master's Assistant*, 2nd edition, Glasgow,
   1833, p. 243.

He also included several model calculation problems on such questions as the cost of yarn and the size of roving.

Measurement was a part of discipline and William Brown directed his undermanager thus :

> a desk to be placed in the reeling room and a new book begun
> for keeping the accounts of the spinners and reelers work and
> waste, the weight of the yarn, the quantity spun etc. The
> overseer with your assistance will daily attend to it and it will
> be highly beneficial for you to spend a portion of time with it
> every day, examining and considering the state of the different
> hands' work and waste, comparing the one with the other,
> yesterday's with today's, and making yourself intimately
> acquainted with all their performances.[51]

Dodd, too, noticed a similar concern with precise accounting in some of the factories he visited. In a copper and lead factory he found great care and completeness in measurement 'necessary for the complicated operations of the factory . . . The mode in which every hour of every man's time has been employed is strictly ascertained, in connection with the symbols attached to the respective orders; the "time" of each workman is so ascertained and recorded that an error can hardly occur.'[52]

The major area where there was considerable overlap between the ideas of Babbage and other popular writers on the textile industry such as McCulloch, Baines and Kennedy was the same that preoccupied industrialists such as William Brown and James Montgomery – the division of labour and skill. In fact, Montgomery quoted McCulloch on the significance of the division of labour in the factory.

> Our establishments for spinning, weaving, printing, bleaching
> etc, are infinitely more complete and perfect, than any that
> exist elsewhere : the division of labour in them is carried to an
> incomparably greater extent, the workmen are trained from

---

[51] D. Chapman, 'William Brown of Dundee', pp. 128–32.

[52] George Dodd, *Days at the Factories, or The Manufacturing Industry of Great Britain Described*, p. 548. This precision seems to have been in marked contrast to the primitive accounting methods in use at the time. See S. Pollard, 'Accounting and Management', *The Genesis of Modern Management*, Harmondsworth, 1965, chapter 6, and G. A. Lee, 'The Concept of Profit in British Accounting 1760–1900', *Business History Review*, Spring 1975.

infancy to industrious habits, and have attached their peculiar
dexterity and sleight of hand in the perfection of their separate
tastes, that can only be acquired by long and unremitting
application to the same employment.[53]

Britain's international superiority depended on the division of labour.
In other countries, 'Their establishments cannot at first be sufficiently
large to enable the division of employments to be carried to any considerable extent; at the same time that expertness in manipulation and
in the details of the various processes, can only be attained by slow
degrees.'[54]

The role of the division of labour in actual technical improvement
in the cotton industry had been singled out some years before in an
influential essay by John Kennedy. He constructed a hypothetical
history of the cotton industry around the principle of the division of
labour. Kennedy argued that the division of labour led to small improvements made by workers in a series of hand implements. This
continued until their cottages filled with machinery and they were
'forced out of their dwellings by the multiplication of their implements'.
It was at this point that the factory system started, as well as the division
of one branch of the trade into two distinct parts – carding and spinning.
There were subsequent improvements in carding and in the spinning
jenny. It was in following up these important improvements that manufacturers found rotary motion could be applied to all the new
machines.[55]

As in the engineering industry, so in the textile industry, skill and
control were the logical corollaries of the division of labour. Kennedy
found the source of skill in his factory system. The use of water power,
on his telling, had forced the removal of manufacturers from urban
centres. This resulted in difficulty in procuring or repairing machinery,
which led to a new demand for a 'higher class of mechanics . . . watch
and clockmakers, white-smiths, and mathematical instrument-makers'.[56]
But the skill required to produce the machines also brought the displacement of skills of the supposedly lower class of labourers who worked
on the machines. However, Baines saw this in a more positive light. It
was the steam engine, not the workman, which had become the drudge:

[53] Montgomery, *Theory and Practice of Cotton Spinning*, p. 287.
[54] *Ibid*. p. 288.
[55] Kennedy, 'Observations on . . . the Cotton Trade', pp. 118, 121.
[56] *Ibid*. p. 124.

as to their motions 'rivalling the mathematical precision, the incessant motion, and the exhaustless power of the machine', nothing can be more mistaken. It is the very reverse of the fact. All the precision, power and incessant motion belong to the machines alone; and the work-people have merely to supply them with work, to oil their joints, adjust their slight inaccuracies, and piece the threads broken by the mechanical spinner.[57]

As Baines saw clearly, all of this brought greater control to the master manufacturer. He recognised that carrying out a number of operations in the same building allowed the master spinner to superintend every stage of manufacture. It gave him greater security, saved time, prevented the inconvenience of having one class of manufacture fail to complete its part, and allowed mechanics to be employed on the spot over a large number of machines.[58] It was machinery itself that brought even greater control. 'This country excels every other in the making of machines and in the means of working them advantageously, and besides this for the reason just mentioned, our manufacturers are interested in having their goods produced as much as possible by machinery.' This reason was control. The machine, Baines argued, caused the price of goods to be regulated more according to the profits of capital than to the wages of labour.[59] This principle applied just as forcefully to the machine making industry. Fairbairn admitted that with the advent of the new large engineering factories

the designing and direction of the work passed away from the hands of the workman into those of the master and his office assistants. This led also to a division of labour; men of general knowledge were only exceptionally required as foremen or outdoor superintendents : and the artificers became, in process of time, little more than attendants on the machines.[60]

Control was also the concern in labour discipline. William Brown made this a particular concern, and attached great importance to a 'set of good hands'. He advised liberal wages for the spinners, and moderate wages consistent with the state of trade for other workers. Disciplined attention to their duty and good habits were absolutely necessary attri-

[57] Baines, *History of the Cotton Manufacture of Great Britain*, p. 460.
[58] *Ibid.* p. 185.
[59] *Ibid.* p. 507.
[60] Pole, ed., *Life of Sir William Fairbairn*, p. 47.

butes of his employees.[61] Marshall's mill evoked his praise for the iron discipline among employees in the works.[62] In his passages on the exercise of authority he stressed incentive. 'Masters reap great benefit from having the art of making their servants interested in their work.'[63]

The commonest incentive over the period was the piece rate. Brown followed conventions on this. The application of the piece rate system had, however, been developed to a high sophistication in the engineering industry in the last years of the eighteenth century. Boulton and Watt devised very complicated combinations of time and piece rates with bonus payments years earlier than Brown gave his advice. Another incentive was the delegation of authority. Sub-contracting various jobs within the works had long been practised.

The automatic factory

Early industrialists and their commentators were aware that the success of any new technology they introduced was dependent on the extent to which they were able to control the productive process. This control was to be achieved through order, measurement, precision, economies of scale, division of labour and above all the control of skill. I have already shown the interest the Mechanics Institute Movement and political economy had in the division of labour and skill. But Babbage indicated how the machine could bring even greater control of production. Baines and other commentators showed how the machine brought production under the closer control of the capitalist. The writer who was to describe the immense possibilities for capitalist power in the machine and factory production was Andrew Ure. While Babbage had a vision of a computer-run technology, Ure envisaged the fully automated factory that would bring complete control of production into the hands of the capitalist.

Ure saw his work as a definite advance on Babbage's and thought his own experience as a consultant in industry conferred greater authority on his writing. Cardwell has described Ure's *Philosophy of Manufactures* as a fairly obvious imitation of Babbage with some insight into the automatic factory.[64] But, in fact, Ure took pains to distinguish himself from Babbage. He rejected the principle of the division of labour

---

[61] D. Chapman, 'William Brown of Dundee', p. 128.
[62] *Ibid.* p. 132.
[63] *Ibid.*
[64] D. S. L. Cardwell, *The Organization of Science in England*, London, 1957, revised edition, 1972, p. 39.

as the significant feature of the factory, and referred to Babbage by implication when he argued that the 'scholastic dogma of the division of labour into degrees of skill has been exploded by our enlightened manufacturers'. They are 'better acquainted with the general economy of the arts, and better qualified to analyse them into their real principles, that the recluse academician can possibly be, who, from a few obsolete data, traces out imaginary results, or conjures up difficulties seldom encountered in practice'.[65]

Ure saw himself as eminently more qualified than Babbage on this issue. He had taught at the Andersonian Institute for many years, and, when the City of Glasgow decided to create a monument to Watt, he was asked to give the public lecture on the steam engine.[66] In 1830 he had moved to London, and set up in private practice as a consultant in science. In this guise, he visited professionally most of the new midland industrial areas and some in Belgium and France. He advised mainly on technical improvements in the cotton industry, bleaching and dyeing processes, glass manufacture, and mining.[67] This is corroborated in the Preface to his *Dictionary of Arts, Manufacture and Mines*, where Ure says he was consulted professionally by the proprietors of factories, workshops and mines here and abroad, and that the stores of information collected in the process were used in his *Dictionary*. His consultancy fees, standardised over the period, indicate a very diverse and formally constituted consultancy practice, and Copeman even found a 'scientific salon' attached to him in 1835.[68]

The purpose of his book, *The Philosophy of Manufactures*, based on this experience, was purely pedagogical. 'Were the principles of the

[65] Ure, *The Philosophy of Manufactures*, pp. 23–4.
[66] W. S. C. Copeman, 'Andrew Ure', *Proceedings of the Royal Society of Medicine*, 1951, pp. 658, 661.
[67] Ure, *A Dictionary of Arts, Manufactures and Mines*, London, 1839, pp. iv–v.
[68] W. S. C. Copeman, 'Andrew Ure', p. 661, gives the following table:
Fees or Charges for Chemical Analysis or for Business Relative to the Application of Science to the Arts and Manufactures
Consultation
Written opinion on a short case or letter of inquiry. *Fee* £2.2.0.
For a series of chemical experiments per day. *Fee* £5.5.0.
Attendance in London to view any manufactury; to examine apparatus or inspect any chemical process. *Fee* £4.4.0.
For similar attendance which shall occupy the whole or chief part of the day. *Fee* £6.6.0.
Attendance at a distance from London exclusive of travelling expenses per day. *Fee* £7.7.0.

manufactures exactly analysed, and expounded in a simple manner, they would diffuse a steady light to conduct the masters, managers, and operatives, in the straight paths of improvements, and prevent them from pursuing such dangerous phantoms as flit along in the monthly patent-lists.'[69]

Ure's factory was a much more restricted one than Babbage's. The factory was defined as the combined operation of many orders of labourers attending a system of productive machines continuously impelled by a central power. Under this definition, any mechanism that did not form a connected series of operations was excluded, such as iron works, dye works, and brass foundries. McCulloch found such a narrow definition applicable only to textile mills, and it totally ignored the all-important machine making sector.[70] However, in Andrew Ure's mind, the factory had taken on distinctly mystical qualities: 'the idea of a vast automatum, composed of various mechanical and intellectual organs, acting in uninterrupted concert for the production of a common object, all of them being subordinated to a self regulated moving force.'[71]

In Ure's factory the division of labour was a thing of the past :

> wherever a process requires peculiar dexterity and steadiness
> of hand, it is withdrawn as soon as possible from the *cunning*
> workman, who is prone to irregularities of many kinds, and
> it is placed in charge of a peculiar mechanism, so self regulating,
> that a child may superintend it ... on the automatic plan,
> skilled labour gets progressively superseded, and will eventually,
> be replaced by mere overlookers of machines.[72]

Ure was more than ordinarily paranoid about the skilled worker. In his view, the more skilled the worker, the more 'self willed and intractable' he became, 'the less fit a component of a mechanical system, in which, by occasional irregularities, he may do great damage to the whole'.[73] Ure's 'philosophy of manufactures' was an exposition of the general principles by which industry could be conducted by self-acting machines.[74] This perfection of automatic industry was to be found in

[69] Ure, *The Philosophy of Manufactures*, p. viii.
[70] [J. R. McCulloch], 'Philosophy of Manufactures', *Edinburgh Review*, LXI, July 1835, p. 454.
[71] Ure, *The Philosophy of Manufactures*, p. 13.
[72] *Ibid.* pp. 19, 20.
[73] *Ibid.* p. 22.
[74] *Ibid.* pp. 1–2.

a modern cotton mill. But Ure also drew attention to the machine factory, which displayed the division of labour in many gradations. However, the dexterous and skilled labour of filer and driller had been superseded by planing, key grove cutting and drilling machines. The self-acting slide lathe had taken the place of iron and brass turners.[75]

Ure's ideas on self-acting machinery found their greatest application in the new power machinery of the cotton industry. His *Philosophy of Manufactures* was thus logically completed in his empirical study, *The Cotton Manufacture of Great Britain*. He was most impressed with the self-acting mule and the power loom. This new mechanical union would put an end to the folly of trade unions and secure a monopoly of coarse cotton fabrics to Great Britain.[76] The power loom, in contrast to the handloom, represented the first principle of all mechanisms impelled by steam and water power, that is continuity of action. On the other hand, the characteristic of human labour was alternate effort and repose. Furthermore, the interruption in the movement of the shuttle which took place while the weaver was dressing a portion of the work served mainly to diversify his labour. Such diversity would be intolerable in the automatic factory where power and time had to be economised to the utmost.[77]

Moreover, the self-actor of Sharp, Roberts and Co. not only defused the effect of trade union action, but had actually been invented on the impulse of the 'injurious effects resulting from turnouts, and other acts of insubordination on the part of the work-people'.[78] This at least was one part of Ure's book that impressed McCulloch. It allowed him to give even greater emphasis to the 'evil effects of combinations', and to the identity of interests of workers and their employers.[79]

Just as his contemporaries had given thought to the layout and design of the factory, so Ure repeated this counsel and gave high praise to William Fairbairn. His automatic factory could be built in the age of factory architecture. In his view there was at that time little awareness of how much the different orders of machines depended for the production and precision of their performance on the right magnitudes, proportions and adjustments of the mainshafting and wheel gearing. But something like Fairbairn's factory–architect business offered a com-

[75] *Ibid.* p. 21.
[76] *Ibid.* p. 331.
[77] A. Ure, *The Cotton Manufacture of Great Britain*, London, 1836, II, p. 287.
[78] *Ibid.* p. 194.
[79] [McCulloch], 'Philosophy of Manufactures', p. 470.

plete package deal to the manufacturer. The capitalist had only to state the extent of his resources, the nature of his manufacture, and his intended site and coal or water facilities, and he would be furnished with complete 'designs and estimates on economical terms'.[80]

If Babbage's workshop found its closest image in the calculating machine, Ure's automatic factory was the image of war. Ure several times alluded to the parallel. His preface spoke of the 'bloodless but still formidable strife of trade'.[81] He described the introduction of the self-acting mule in terms of the classical battlefield and the destruction of union militancy.

> Thus the *Iron Man*, as the operatives fitly call it, sprung out
> of the hands of our modern Prometheus at the bidding of
> Minerva – a creation destined to restore order among the
> industrious classes, and to confirm to Great Britain the empire
> of art. The news of this Herculean prodigy spread dismay
> through the Union, and even long before it left its cradle, so
> to speak, it strangled the Hydra of misrule.[82]

There were also social spin-offs to these methods of organising the production process. One example of this is to be found in the work of Bentham. Samuel Bentham was a specialist in organised production techniques and he himself had devised the assembly line production of ships' biscuits at the victualling office in Deptford. He was also responsible for Maudslay's and Brunel's production layout.[83] Bentham adapted these organisation schemes to the social projects of his brother Jeremy and other Utilitarians. One such project was the Benthamite 'Panopticon' which showed the real integration of Utilitarian philosophy with technology. Most of the Utilitarian educational schemes were also structured on the basis of mass production, assembly line techniques as first devised in the factory. The factory, in turn, as Ure demonstrated, found its most sympathetic analogue in war, and the division and discipline of labour in military hierarchy and authority. Marx was later to make this explicit in his comment on the factory system : men were 'the sergeants', women and children, 'the soldiers of the line'.[84]

80 Ure, *The Philosophy of Manufactures*, p. 33.
81 *Ibid.* p. vii.
82 *Ibid.* p. 367.
83 Armytage, *A Social History of Engineering*, p. 117.
84 See Dobson, 'The Contribution of Francis Place', Ph.D. Thesis; Armytage, *A Social History of Engineering*, p. 117; H. Braverman, *Labour and Monopoly Capital*, New York, 1974; and M. Foucault,

The ingenious insights of Babbage and Ure written in the early days of the factory system very much reflected contemporary opinion and vision. The very popularity of their work attests to this conclusion. The inter-connections between technology and the organisation of production had become familiar themes in the popular work on technology throughout this period. The popular literature and societies which made up a scientific–technological movement were orientated in their objects and assumptions to the goals and interests of commerce and political economy. It was precisely the writer from within this movement – the Babbage, Ure, Baines or Kennedy – who was able to keep in close touch with the provincial élites of industry. He played the part of adapting the programmes and perspectives of the intellectual circles of political economy to the practical and local concerns of the provincial manufacturer.

Discipline and Punishment, the Birth of the Prison, trans. A Sheridan, London, 1977. Braverman notes the connection Marx makes between the division of labour and the army; see *Labour and Monopoly Capital*, p. 64.

9

The export of machinery

A network of voluntary scientific societies and a popular literature on technology and political economy brought political economists, scientists and popular or journalistic commentators into contact with the provincial and industrial middle classes. A platform which brought these groups even closer was that of political debate. Where technology became a matter of economic policy, industrialist, worker and political economist debated with each other directly. A debate on commercial and economic policy would challenge a theorist both to apply and to develop his ideas. Equally, it would open an avenue for political action on the part of particular commercial and industrial interest groups. Above all, the policy debate highlighted the key role of ideas in social practice. For ideas acted to translate the crude opinions of particular interest groups into a generalisation of some theoretical conviction. Theory and systems of ideas played a definite part in the acceptability of argument, and in this way functioned as limits on the legitimacy of action. Moreover, the types of argument used in a policy debate reflected the position not only of their proponents but of those whom they sought to persuade. On the one hand, the group which stood to benefit from the acceptance of certain policies naturally phrased its arguments to advance these. But their arguments had equally to extend to the antagonistic group which had to be convinced. Politicians, there-fore, often used the terms and concepts of their foes in order to gain their ear, and their arguments appealed to the general interest rather than to self-interest.

The first such debate I have chosen for examination is that on the export of machinery and emigration of artisans. This was a debate which, though it was certainly of less political and economic significance than the great Corn Law debates of the same period, occupied the interests of many political economists both at the time and for years after. The complexities of the issues involved were a challenge, and the subject demanded direct discussion of technology at an empirical and not just an abstract level.

The policy debate on the export of machinery and emigration of artisans which occurred between 1824 and 1841 was at first sight a debate on trade policy. But discussion focussed on the sources of technological innovations, and branched into a wide-ranging commentary on the distinguishing characteristics of British industrialisation. The debates were of enduring interest to political economists over the period. They used them as a quarry and as an example in their many-sided analyses of the characteristics and role of technological change in British economic growth.

This chapter will present the narrative of these debates in the wider context of economic policy making in the period. It will then analyse the terms and concepts used in the various arguments put forward, and place these in the context of the debate on technology in political economy. Subsequently it describes the economic and social interests behind the debate, and finally examines the interrelationship displayed by this debate between political economy and economic policy.

The debate on the export of machinery became a policy issue for the first time in the 1820s when it was the subject of the parliamentary select committees on Combination Laws, Artisans and Machinery, and on the Laws Relating to the Export of Tools and Machinery.[1] It was discussed briefly in the early 1830s, and was finally debated at length and resolved in the early 1840s, under the aegis of the Select Committe Appointed to Inquire into the Export of Machinery.[2] The issue was not, however, forgotten in the intervening years, and was frequently alluded to in other policy debates, and in the work of political economists. The debates were significant in these years as part of the circumstances challenging public complacency with the remarkable superiority of the British economy. The nature of this superiority now came to be defined

---

[1] Select Committee on Combination Laws, Artisans and Machinery, *Parliamentary Papers*, 1824, v. Select Committee on the Laws Relating to the Export of Tools and Machinery, *P.P.* v, 1825.

[2] Select Committee Appointed to Inquire into the Export of Machinery, *P.P.*, 1841, VII.

in relative terms, as concern grew over continental industrialisation and
its challenge to Britain's technological lead. The controversy mobilised
and divided politicians and administrators, industrialists and labourers
from many parts of the country. The issue was of concern not only to
M.P.s but to the arms of the bureaucracy in the Board of Trade, the
Home Office, and the Customs. Provincial élites were starting to form
their own Chambers of Commerce. For some time these bodies did not
have a very large impact on policy formation, since politicians continued to seek the opinions not of organisations but of individual
industrial magnates.[3] However, many manufacturers joined these bodies
and they regarded their commercial associations as a forum for the
discussion and presentation of the views of the manufacturing interests.
Political economists were also called upon to comment, and to demonstrate that the principles of free trade were operational for the machine
making industry. The debate hinged on the recognition of machine
making as the pivot of the whole system of production.[4] Previously,
free trade had always been conceived in terms of manufactured commodities. The actual process of manufacturing had not been looked on
as a market product in its own right. Now contemporaries saw that the
tools, machines, sources of power, and expertise out of which they
fashioned their exportable consumer goods were also attractive in foreign
markets. In addition, the debates reveal in a remarkable way contemporary thought on skill, machinery, tools, and the process of invention.
As we shall see, there was a clear change in the pattern of discussion
between the debates around the first committees in 1824–5 and the
second in 1841.

Most of the restrictions against machinery were enacted between
1750 and 1785. These were roundly condemned by Adam Smith in his
Wealth of Nations.[5] By 1785 the tools and machinery used in the cotton,
woollen, and silk textile industries, as well as the tools and utensils used
in the iron and steel manufacture, had been banned from export. Two
acts in 1719 and 1750 prohibited skilled artisans from leaving the
country. The result of the Select Committee on Combination Laws,
Artisans and Machinery in 1824 was the repeal of restrictions on the
movements of skilled artisans. But the prohibitions on machinery

3 Lucy Brown, *The Board of Trade and the Free Trade Movement*,
  Oxford, 1958, p. 14.
4 See Nathan Rosenberg, 'Capital Goods, Technology and Economic
  Growth', *Oxford Economic Papers*, xv, 1963, pp. 217–27.
5 Adam Smith, *Wealth of Nations* (1776), vol. II, Oxford, 1976,
  pp. 659–60.

remained intact, though discretionary powers to grant licence for export were given to the Board of Trade. For a time the laws were not strictly enforced and licences were not difficult to obtain for those who applied. But trade depressions prompted more agitation for enforcement, and vigilance was tightened. There was more agitation to enforce the laws in 1833 in response to fears of the impact of a new Customs Regulation Act. There were also over this period a number of attempts to have the laws repealed. These were led by Joseph Hume and supported by groups of machine makers and other interested parties. But all efforts failed until the final Select Committee on the Export of Machinery of 1841. By this time the forces opposing repeal had disintegrated so that the Committee succeeded in recommending it.[6] Before then, opinion over the laws remained sharply divided, even though they were almost universally recognised to be practically inoperative and impossible to enforce.

The style of policy making in these decades, along with conflicts of private interests, provide some context for such a seemingly inexplicable dilemma. There has been serious revision of the view that the 1820s was a heyday of liberal Toryism and free-trade economics.[7] The issue of the export of machinery arose within the context of an approach to economic policy which pragmatically accepted industrialisation, and also made adaptable use of classical economic theory. Thus Huskisson could invoke Ricardo on the issue and yet, a few years later, endorse a policy of countervailing duties 'which should be sufficient to place our commerce and manufactures in a state in which they could fairly compete' so as 'to excite his [the manufacturer's] emulation and his industry'.[8] This was part of a general attitude on the part of the 'liberal Tories' of recognition of possible distress from foreign competition. It was common for some form of protection to be left in place where industrial interests were strong enough to mobilise pressure for their retention.[9] For its part, the expression of northern industrial interests in key policy issues was often random and arbitrary. Although Chambers of Commerce or commercial associations began to revive in

---

6 Musson, 'The Manchester School', gives an extended account of the restrictions and some of the events as seen from Manchester's perspective which led up to repeal of the laws. See also Jeremy, 'Damming the Flood', which came to my notice after this book was in the press.

7 Hilton, *Corn, Cash, Commerce*, chaps. 1, 9, 10.

8 House of Commons Debates, *Hansard*, new series, xv, 18 April 1826, col. 349.

9 Brown, *The Board of Trade*, p. 14.

the 1820s, they were not viable organs of opinion. Trade associations such as the London West India Company and individual industrial groups such as the cotton spinners had a more important political role.[10] Debates on economic policy affecting provincial areas, moreover, revealed great social and economic divisions within the manufacturing class itself. Conflicts between large and small capitalists and between various branches of the textile industry prevented unity in the opinion of the 'manufacturing interest'.[11] It was thus difficult for a clear view on the export of machinery to emerge.

The establishment of the Select Committee on Combination Laws, Artisans and Machinery also highlighted an absence of strategic thinking and administrative capacity in the civil service. The Board of Trade had been in an obscure position and was only just beginning to emerge from this after Huskisson became president in 1823. The Board of Trade had little to do with the calling of this Committee and, indeed, participated minimally in the proceedings.[12]

The outcome of the 1824–5 Committee was, however, to make provincial pressure groups and the Board of Trade much more important. The Committee recommended repeal of the Combination Laws and the laws against emigration, but it left intact the laws against the export of machinery, allowing discretionary power on the part of the Privy Council. Decisions after the Committee had concluded were left to the Board of Trade, and, during the first period, most of these were taken by William Huskisson. Huskisson disliked this arbitrary power, primarily because he possessed no theoretical criteria for decision on licensing and prohibition. He based his discretion at various times on

---

10 *Ibid.* pp. 182–5.
11 V. A. C. Gattrell, 'The Commercial Middle Classes', Ph.D. Thesis, University of Cambridge, 1972, pp. 323–7; Arthur Redford, *Manchester Merchants and Foreign Trade 1794–1858*, Manchester, 1934, pp. 127–9; cf. William Radcliffe, *Origin of the New System of Manufacture*, Stockport, 1828.
12 The only activities of the Board during the Committee were to send a directive to Customs asking for a detailed statement of the laws on machinery and artisans and a list of prosecutions. The Board was also fed information on the continental machine industry by Charles Ross and Richard Chenevix, who were functioning as industrial spies. Public Record Office, Board of Trade Papers, B.T. 3–18, 15 April 1824 and B.T. 1–195, 31 May 1824. See also [Richard Chenevix], 'Comparative Skill and Industry of France and England', *Edinburgh Review*, XXXII, October 1819, and 'History and Prospects of English Industry', *Quarterly Review*, XXXIV, June 1826; and [Charles Ross], 'Artizans and Machinery', *Quarterly Review*, XXXI, March 1825.

the amount of skilled labour embodied in a machine, on the expressed interests of groups of manufacturers, or on the 'present state of trade'. In 1841 it was reported that the criterion was none of these, but rather a distinction between preparatory and manufacturing processes.[13]

Manufacturing associations also became very active following the conclusion of the first Committee. Commercial crisis in the north in 1826–7 prompted further debate on the issue. A flurry of memorials went to the Board of Trade, petitions were presented in Parliament, and a long exchange took place in the House of Commons. Memorials against the export of machinery arrived in the Board offices from the Manchester Chamber of Commerce, and from manufacturing associations in Leeds, York, Halifax, Bradford, Huddersfield and Birmingham. The Manchester Chamber of Commerce discussed the issue at length in November 1826 and sent a deputation to the Board of Trade to ask for stricter enforcement of the laws against the export of machinery.[14] Hume presented two petitions from Manchester machine makers on 5 May 1826 which argued that the restrictions on the export of machinery exacerbated their distress and unemployment. Contrary petitions were presented by Huskisson and Littleton in the exchange in the House that took place on 6 December 1826. This exchange involved a long debate on the matter between Hume, Huskisson, Warburton, Parnell, Bright, Peel and Colonel Torrens.[15]

The Manchester Chamber of Commerce continued its vigilance and agitation until the end of the 1830s. It kept in close touch with other provincial chambers, with the Board of Trade, with the Comptroller of Customs, with the Parliamentary representatives, and with the Chancellor of the Exchequer.[16]

There was little change in policy throughout the 1830s. Though the Board of Trade came to form a congenial framework for intellectuals of the free trade movement, initiative in lifting restrictions was not the

---

[13] Huskisson complained of his powers many times. 'Speech', 14 June 1825, *Speeches of the Rt. Hon. William Huskisson*, London, 1831, ii, 425; *Hansard*, 6 December 1826, xvi, col. 293. For changes in licensing criteria see: *Hansard*, xvi, col. 293; B.T. 5–35, Letter, 19 July 1826; B.T. 5–35, Letter 22 July, 1826; and Select Committee on the Export of Machinery, *P.P.*, 1841, vii, Testimony of J. D. Hume, 11–15.

[14] Minute Book, Manchester Chamber of Commerce, 8 and 15 November, 13 December 1826.

[15] See B.T. 5–36, 28 April, 12 May 1827; B.T. 5–35, 25 November 1826; Speeches, *Hansard*, xvi, cols. 291–8; and 5 May 1826, *Hansard*, xv, cols. 908–11.

[16] See Minute Book, Manchester Chamber of Commerce, 1826–30.

hallmark of the Cabinets of the period. However, when J. D. Hume, former Comptroller of Customs and an active member of the Political Economy Club, moved to the Board of Trade, he did try to carry on the pragmatically liberal tradition of Huskisson. Even so, the next main Select Committee on the Export of Machinery was not called until 1841, and the laws were not repealed until 1844.

The terms of debate

The fact that restrictions on the export of machinery were fervently supported by the Manchester circle of free trade manufacturers was certainly an anomaly in the general run of free trade rhetoric. But we can only see why this should have existed if we understand both the intellectual terms of the debate and the economic and social interests behind it. The issue of the export of machinery could produce such confused and divided opinion precisely because the intellectual terms by which it was analysed extended much further than conventional questions of free trade. This was not just a question of protecting one industry against international economic development, but of protecting all industries by controlling the markets of one key industry – the capital goods or machine making industry. The debate made clear the continuity in the aims of protecting and extending markets between this period and the more explicitly imperialist years of the end of the nineteenth century.[17]

Debate on the export of machinery and the emigration of artisans was not only conducted in the form of the parliamentary speech, select committee, memorial and petition, but also in the London and provincial press and in the texts of political economists. The two major select committees on the issue also reveal a definite shift in the terms of debate. Of primary concern in 1824 was the course of overall industrial progress. By 1841, analysis focussed on the balance of a specific capital-goods sector. In the debates of 1824–5, there was very close consideration of the nature of technical change and the role of artisan skills. Techniques were conceived of as embodied in these skills, and machines, in turn, were regarded as adjuncts and embodiments of the 'artisan'. A major problem area was the extent to which development was possible both at home and abroad, given the free availability of patent specifications, plans and models. Attention thus focussed not only on

17 See J. Gallagher and R. Robinson, 'The Imperialism of Free Trade', *Economic History Review*, VI, 1953.

the generalisation of skill and the division of labour but also on the technical heritage and the cultural and economic milieu for the generation of innovation. By 1841, emphasis had changed to the problems of a capital-goods sector. Commentators stressed the advance of the Belgian machine making industry, the significance of the tool manufacture, and the integrated nature of innovation between the textile and engineering industries. It is striking to note the very significant parallels between the shift in the terms of discourse in this particular policy debate, and the shifts in theoretical political economy from an emphasis on labour productivity and skills to machine technology and capital. Even within this schematic division, however, there were many differences and ambiguities in the style of debate. These reveal the complex interplay of theory and policy. An attempt to follow the many twists and turns in the major themes of the debates will help to clarify and explain some of these interactions.

The following themes of debate will now be discussed in some detail : justice and property rights, the role of skills, the diffusion of new techniques, the division of labour among machine makers, the growth of the capital goods sector, and the structure of the labour force.

The first theme of discussion was justice and property rights. Justice was the subject of the debate over the emigration of artisans, and thus we find the debates on emigration fitting naturally into the discussion of the Combination Laws which were considered by the same select committee. The laws were subversive of the rights of individual property.[18] 'Liberal and not restrictive laws . . . were the source of England's prosperity.'[19] The laws were also oppressive since they were actually operative only on the poorer tradesman. Earlier in 1821, this was the reaction to the indictment of several artisans attempting to leave the country.

> If a labourer or artisan is thrown out of employment in his
> own immediate neighbourhood, he is to be deprived of parish
> support; if, to avoid starvation, he seeks work in any other
> district, he is to be seized as a vagabond and flogged, – and if
> he attempts to escape to other countries he is arrested by
> indictments and beggared by fines.[20]

Some saw this not just as personal or social oppression but as an econ-

18 J. R. McCulloch, Editorial in the *Scotsman*, 16 August 1823.
19 *Leeds Mercury*, 29 May 1824, and *Liverpool Mercury*, 11 June 1824.
20 'Attempts of Artificers to Leave England', *The Traveller*, 20 April
1821, Place Collection of Newspaper Cuttings, xix, p. 76.

omic liability. The real loss was the middle-class manufacturer or skilled mechanic who could and would leave.[21] The theme of justice and individual rights was clear in a representative correspondence in the *Birmingham Chronicle* which upheld the liberal principles of 'a mechanic' and the actions of the 'theoretical legislator' against the national interests of 'the manufacturer'.[22] The *Morning Chronicle* even added a note of conspiracy, but not the conspiracy of the smuggler or enticer. It carried the story that Manby's prosecution for enticing artisans abroad had been led by those who were trying to increase the price of iron to the consumer.[23] There were certain elements who argued that the mechanic's skills were not his own property. John Kennedy and the Manchester Chamber of Commerce claimed that the real inventor was the manufacturer. The machine maker was only his assistant.[24] The reply to this was that Kennedy had made a false distinction between machine maker and manufacturer with respect to the ownership of machinery.[25] The question of the ownership of skill, as I have shown, was central to the radical critique of political economy made by Thomas Hodgskin. It was this issue, too, which later provoked some of the Drummond Professors to claim the entire production process including ingenuity, invention and skill for the capitalist.

Among the labourers themselves, although the justice of free mobility was urged, opinion was divided as to the effect of emigration of members of the craft. Gravenor Henson, a Nottingham bobbin net lace-maker who was almost fanatically opposed to free emigration, argued that it was a general opinion of the working classes that 'he [the emigrant craftsman] is only endeavouring to get away from misery; but doing that which will bring misery upon him and his trade, by taking the arts of his country to put bread into the mouths of foreigners . . . it is only postponing his own misery by ruining his trade, which will affect him also in a foreign country'.[26] A group of radical artisans, the Select Committee of Artisans of Great Britain, also hoped both to

---

21 Robinson, *A Treatise*, p. 17.
22 *Birmingham Chronicle*, 26 February, 4, 8 and 11 March 1824.
23 *Morning Chronicle*, 26 February 1824.
24 Kennedy, *On the Exportation of Machinery*, p. 20; Minute Book, Manchester Chamber of Commerce, 8 November 1826, pp. 457–61.
25 *Manchester Guardian*, 24 April 1824. Select Committee on Combination Laws, Artisans and Machinery, *P.P.* 1824, v, Testimony of Gravenor Henson, 279.
26 Henson's campaign against the export of machinery and emigration of artisans is described in S. D. Chapman, 'Introduction' to Henson's *The Civil, Political and Mechanical History of the Framework*

prevent the export of machinery and the emigration of artisans, and to bring forward a tax on machinery. It referred to plans for free emigration as a 'mere theoretical conceit'.[27] And Richard Needham, a Bolton cotton weaver, told the Committee of 1824 that he had been 'sent to state the opinion of a large body of weavers that if artisans were to leave the country, it would produce deplorable consequences. Since cotton twist had been exported, wages had fallen continually. If machinery were to be exported, wages would fall still further.'[28] The discussion of the emigration of artisans continually returned to the question of justice, and the inherent legitimacy of the removal of restrictions on labour. The emigration of artisans thus fell well within the terms of debate of the Combination Laws, and those who opposed emigration were of course not likely to win an argument by challenging the 'justice' of free mobility. They had to seek some other form of analysis to support their arguments.

One answer was to shift the discussion of the role of artisan skills in technical change away from the artisan himself to the machine. This led to the second and third main themes of debate : the role of artisan skills and the diffusion of new techniques. Artisan skills were discussed here in the light of their close relation to the development of an export of machinery. It was argued that models of machinery or even the new machines themselves could not be successfully introduced without the artisan skills needed to erect them, adapt them, and repair them. This reason was originally put forward for political expediency. For those who worried about the question of justice in limiting the movements of artisans, it could be suggested that there were higher economic priorities to be considered.

One finds this theme expressed in analyses of continental competition. A characteristic argument was that foreigners were unable to make a machine from plans which 'led only to perplexity and confusion'. But if the machinery was available, 'they could make models of it and come at the principle at once'.[29] Others pointed out that such models were

---

Knitters, 1831, reprinted London, 1970, p. xvii. For more on Henson's role in this and other Parliamentary committees see R. A. Church and S. D. Chapman, 'Gravenor Henson and the Making of the English Working Class', in E. L. Jones and G. E. Mingay, eds., *Land, Labour and Population during the Industrial Revolution*, London, 1967.

[27] *Select Committee of the Artisans of Great Britain. Report at Bolton Public Meeting*, 13 January 1824.

[28] Select Committee on Combination Laws, Artisans and Machinery, *P.P.* 1824, v, Testimony of Richard Needham, 543.

[29] Robinson, *A Treatise*, p. 17.

insufficient unless combined with a base of artisan skills. The distinctive characteristic of England was her milieu of enterprising mechanics and manufacturers ('themselves mechanics and inventors'), and her systematic division of labour.[30] Success in new techniques depended on the subdivision of many branches of an industry.[31] One commentator formulated the situation aptly when he argued that he who emigrated took the knowledge he had, but could not carry the principle of improvement and growth: 'Those left behind advanced', he 'remained stationary'.[32] Much depended, however, on the institutional setting of these artisan skills. The 'moral' or 'mental' capital given such great significance by Torrens and Senior was here analysed into two components: the theoretical knowledge that went into skill and the practical 'know how' acquired through experience.

The point was often raised in these debates that if machinery was freely exported, there would be little emigration of mechanics, and thus the very important artisan skills would not be lost to the continent. However, the concept of the machine repair man seemed an adequate answer from the opponents of repeal. The mechanic who repaired machinery was conceived as having much more general and more highly developed skill than those who worked on single processes in a machine factory.[33] John Kennedy and the memorial of the Manchester Chamber of Commerce elaborated on the process by which the machine repair man became the machine manufacturer:

> The exportation of machinery absolutely compels the foreign
> manufacturer to possess the means of becoming his own machine
> maker; and the more machines you send abroad, the greater
> the number of mechanics become necessary to keep their parts
> in order. Hence again arises a demand for those tools which are
> necessary to mechanics, the mechanics with their tools are sure
> to be ultimately employed, not merely in repairing the existing
> machines, but in the making of new ones.[34]

30 *P.P.* 1824, v, Testimony of J. R. McCulloch, 596.
31 *P.P.* 1824, v, Fairbairn's Testimony, 568.
32 *The Globe and Traveller* (7 December 1826). It is likely that this correspondent was Robert Torrens.
33 This was believed even as late as 1841. Peter Fairbairn argued that repairs 'required a more skilful man than I would employ in my own works; because in my works a subdivision of labour takes place; I require a good many very superior men, but I can do by subdividing the works with some inferior men'. *P.P.* 1841, VII, 211.
34 Kennedy, *On the Exportation of Machinery*, p. 17.

A fourth theme was the division of labour among machine makers. There was contemporary distinction made between the London and the northern engineers. The London engineer viewed himself as more theoretical and more flexible than his less versatile, but more practical, northern counterpart. John Kennedy, however, doused the distinction in sarcasm : 'machine makers as they are called in this country, but engineers as they style themselves in London'.[35] If the London engineers regarded themselves as more versatile, they were also confident about their sources of labour. They were able to tap the underemployed skills of London handicraftsmen. Henry Martineau reported : 'I have known instances where watch-makers and mathematical instrument makers have become extremely useful, and these are a description of workmen who do not receive a very high rate of wages in London, and of whom I could get a very considerable quantity if required.'[36] Both Martineau and Henry Maudslay also argued that the division of labour, better tools, and the greater number of goods produced would allow for the introduction of more common workmen and for a greater diversity of hands.[37] If there was a lack of skilled men, this was blamed on demand conditions which had discouraged the training up of apprentices. Galloway, for example, argued that he had been for several years 'negligent in taking apprentices, and creating proper nurseries for workmen'.[38]

The importance of the division of labour within the machine making industry had been brought into discussions of skill. As has been pointed out, the extent to which the division of labour was carried out determined the types of skill needed. The division of labour was seen to be one of the reasons why the production of textile machinery seemed to be the preserve of the northern manufacturers. Highher wages and costs dominated the London trade, with its concomitant less practical and less extensive division of labour.[39] Neither Maudslay nor Galloway could, however, find a great deal to praise in the Manchester methods. As Galloway put it :

> that division of labour is of great advantage in articles of great consumption; but while it makes cheap goods, it does not

[35] Kennedy, *On the Exportation of Machinery*, p. 20. For a discussion of the London and Lancashire engineers see the Report of the Select Committee on The Export of Tools and Machinery, *P.P.* 1825, v, 10–11.
[36] *P.P.* 1825, v, Martineau's Testimony, 21.
[37] *P.P.* 1825, v, 20, 21.
[38] *P.P.* 1825, v, Galloway's Testimony, 39.
[39] *P.P.* 1825, v, pp. 40, 41.

make general workmen; a too great division of labour circum-
scribes the power and intelligence of the workman, which is
the great mischief of abstract employments; it makes men mere
machines, and we find that the Manchester and other country
workmen who are brought up to abstract employments, can
do little else, and are inferior workmen until they have worked
some years in a shop where general work is made.[40]

It was this concept of the 'general workman', able to make the connections between his activities and to perceive the principles behind his
toil, which was so important at this time to the rhetoric of the Mechanics
Institute Movement.

As I have shown, those who opposed the emigration of artisans in
the 1824 debates shifted the terms of debate about artisan skills from
the artisan to machinery. In 1841, however, the political effect of the
repeal of the laws on the emigration of artisans was to transfer the
terms of debate on skill back to the artisan.

This change in language was the ploy not of those opposed to repeal
but of the supporters of the abrogation of restrictions on the machine
making industry. They did this because they believed that the repeal
of restrictions had not gone far enough. They could argue, however,
that a technology was dependent on skilled artisans, and yet the
Committee had chosen to remove its protection of these. Surely then,
it ought to go further and remove restrictions on the machines which
were of such small significance when compared to a country's supply
of skilled artisans. This turn in the argument was certainly the immediate reaction of those seeking licences for the export of their
machinery.[41] It was also carried over, to some extent, into parliamentary debate on the export of machinery as late as 1841.[42]

Much earlier, in the 1824–5 debates, some discussion was directed
to the employment-generating effects of machine making. This led into
the fifth theme of debate – the role of the capital-goods sector. Techniques were embodied in artisan skills. Machines, in turn, embodied
these artisans.[43] Economists and certain policy makers fully recognised

40 *P.P.* 1825, v, Galloway's Testimony, p. 41.
41 See B. T. 1–96. Petition to Export Machinery from Alexander
   Galloway, 19 June 1824; and *P.P.* 1825, v, 37.
42 *P.P.* 1841, vii: see testimonies of Thomas Aston, Granville Withers,
   Thomas Marsden, and William Jenkinson, 22–3, 54, 89, 105–6.
43 *P.P.* 1824, v, Testimony of Phillip Taylor, cf. pp. 30 and 163; and *P.P.*
   1824, v, McCulloch's Testimony, 592–3, 598.

that much of the dispute was over the establishment of a new branch of industry. McCulloch and Hume condemned the laws for depriving Britain of 'an additional branch of manufacture'.[44] This was formulated more explicitly as early as 1825 by William Ellis, one of the Philosophic Radicals, who considered that the manufacture of machinery could become a staple industry itself.[45] Subsequently, Nassau Senior discussed the ease of transferring capital by decomposing it into its degree of 'manufacture' or 'fixedness'; the most easily transferred was 'mental capital' or 'knowledge and education'.[46] The ubiquitous Charles Babbage anticipated the development of science-based techniques with the progressive expansion of this capital-goods sector.[47]

The interest in the capital goods sector was founded on both fears of continental advance and the vision of new industrial expansion. The peril to the country was not to be measured by present competition, but by the 'magnitude of the preparations' and the 'germ of progress in the rapid increase of machine making establishments' abroad.[48]

Discussion of the capital-goods sector was broken down into some detail. It was not only skill or machines but also machine tools which were important in facilitating the diffusion of techniques. The discussion of tools became a major preoccupation for the 1841 Committee. It was an anomaly that neither steam engines nor tools were restricted from export. A petition from the Manchester machine makers in 1841 argued that these tools 'by supplying the deficiencies of inferior workmen' had 'surmounted the chief obstacle to machine making abroad'. But the tool industry was also an important contribution to the limitless possibilities of an English capital-goods industry. England could become the machine centre for the world. It would offer foreigners the largest and most profitable markets for their inventions. 'From the skill of our artisans and the advance of our mechanical arts, their crude ideas would be most likely to be perfected and brought into operation.'[49]

44 *P.P.* 1824, v, McCulloch's Testimony, 596, and J. Hume, Speeches, 5 May 1826 and 12 February 1824, *Hansard*, xv, col. 909 and x, col. 145.
45 William Ellis, 'The Exportation of Machinery', *Westminster Review*, III, April 1825.
46 Senior, *An Outline*, p. 220.
47 Charles Babbage, 'Introduction' to Barlow, *A Treatise*, p. 80.
48 J. C. Symons, *Arts and Artisans at Home and Abroad*, Edinburgh, 1839, p. 173.
49 Committee of Machine Makers, *Facts and Observations Illustrative of the Evils of the Law which Prohibits the Exportation of Machinery*. Manchester, 1841.

It was also widely recognised that the development of a capital-goods sector could have important social implications. A final theme of debate took up these implications in discussion of the structure of the labour force. The development of a capital-goods sector brought with it important implications for the structure of the working classes. Mechanics and engineers were to be important elements in an emerging labour 'aristocracy'. Charles Babbage envisaged this in 1836 when he linked the growth of this branch of industry with the class of mechanics who were more skilled and more highly paid than the class who used the machinery. The export of machinery would allow for the expansion of this 'higher and more valuable class'.[50] Some, like Torrens, were less sympathetic to this class. When Parnell raised the usual complaint of the injustice of preventing mechanics from freely exercising their industry, Torrens replied in the *Globe*: 'but the machine makers have embarked in a branch of industry, subject at the time to certain restrictions, which have been rather relaxed than increased, they have no reason to complain when those restrictions are not entirely removed'.[51] The controversy over the export of machinery acted, in ways similar to the rhetoric of the Mechanics Institute Movement, to promote a controlled and disciplined labour force formally divided into its skilled and unskilled sections. The new and 'higher class' of mechanics would defuse the threat posed by the 'mass' nature of the working class. The prospects for industry at home and the reasons for limited diffusion abroad of new techniques were reinforced by factors other than skilled labour and capital. The notion of a labour 'aristocracy' was connected with ideas of a systematic approach to production. The labour 'aristocrat' though accorded distinct status by industrialist and middle-class reformer was still subject to the discipline of the labour force.

Those involved in the debates also made explicit reference to the advantages England had over her competitors in the organisation of production and the discipline of the labour force.

Organisation, precision and discipline were fundamental to 'systematic' production. Babbage's key variable was the 'domestic economy of the factory'.[52] Fairbairn argued that the French were 'deficient' in the 'arrangements and method' of their factories and 'more confused in their operations'.[53] The French were 'less attentive to that economy of

---

50 Charles Babbage, 'Introduction' to Barlow, *A Treatise*, p. 80.
51 Place Collection of Newspaper Cuttings, vol. LVII, p. 15.
52 Babbage, *Machinery and Manufactures*, 1st edition, p. 295.
53 *P.P.* 1824, v, Testimony of William Fairbairn, 568.

manual labour', and the English had special advantages in 'those economical arrangements – the results of practical experience which are of so much importance in the management of large concerns'.[54] Even as late as 1841, J. G. Marshall expressed his fears of allowing foreigners to look at 'the mode of using the machines'.[55]

The debate over the export of machinery and the emigration of artisans only takes on its special meaning in the context of the intellectual terms of analysis, and in relation to its economic and social situation. The object of the next section will be to define more closely these economic and social influences.

Cyclical change and allegiances

Among the major influences on this debate must be counted the economic conditions during 1824–5, the commercial crisis of 1825–6, and the depression of 1841–2. The major social influences were the interests of various groups represented in the course of debate, and represented in the practical implementation of policy.

An investment boom in the north in 1824–5 operated to separate the interests of London and northern engineers. Sudden increases in the demand for machinery affected only the northern machine makers, and it was the northern mills that 'stood idle for want of machines'. William Fairbairn described the situation: 'I do not think in two, three, or four years hands can be trained to supply a greater quantity than is now in demand . . . they would not be able to supply orders from the French.'[56]

The 1826 depression threatened both machine makers and manufacturers. The question, furthermore, became linked with that of the labourers rioting in Lancashire. The fears over social disorder and machine breaking were compounded with fears of foreign competition. Foreign competition was held up as the spectre to those who sought the elimination of distress in the destruction of machinery. It was this that Edward Baines, son of the editor of the *Leeds Mercury*, stressed in his *Letter to the Unemployed Workmen of Yorkshire and Lancashire*. Francis Place and Archibald Prentice re-stated the fear in the *Trades Newspaper* and the *Manchester Gazette*.[57]

---

[54] Ross, 'Artizans and Machinery', p. 398; and Justitia, 'Letter to the Editor', *Manchester Guardian*, 28 February 1824.

[55] *P.P.* 1841, VII, Testimony of J. G. Marshall, 195.

[56] *P.P.* 1824, V, 569–70.

[57] Francis Place, 'Breaking of Machinery and Breaking of the Corn Laws', *Trades Newspaper*, 7 May 1826; and Archibald Prentice, series of leaders in the *Manchester Gazette*, April and May 1826.

By 1841–2 there was another depression. Manufacturers no longer complained of a shortage of machinery, and at least one of the major witnesses to the Select Committee had changed his opinions on the export of machinery.[58] There was, however, no concerted mobilisation of industrial opinion. Holland Hoole explained the apathy of the Manchester manufacturers and the Chamber of Commerce by the depressed trade conditions: 'the master manufacturers are almost desponding as regards the state of our trade, and the general expression of feeling is, that the legislature may do whatever they please, they cannot make things worse'.[59] John Foster explains the apathy of the Oldham manufacturers as a 'loss of will to oppose changes which still cut across their basic interests'.[60]

Economic conditions could thus render expedient certain policy actions, and did influence the quantitative impact of certain arguments. But social interests were at least as important. It seemed quite apparent to contemporary spectators that this issue was one of conflict between various interest groups. The *Morning Chronicle*, in introducing the issue, expected that those involved in metal work would want to have the laws removed, while those involved in manufactured goods would oppose repeal.[61] The issue was seen as very similar in nature to the celebrated eighteenth-century debate over the export of cotton twist. 'Liberalis', a correspondent to the *Manchester Guardian*, compared the two issues and concluded that manufacturers again sought to protect their own interests against those of machine makers.[62] The old debate was also frequently invoked during the course of the 1824 Select Committee. At least one manufacturer, Peter Ewart, was hard put to explain the difference between the two debates. He feebly argued that in exporting cotton yarns one did not export the means of making them; forgetting that yarn was also the 'means of making piece goods'.[63]

The conflict of interests between manufacturers and engineers raised the question of the extent of the social and economic differentiation of the machine makers. The Nottingham lace and stocking trades were

[58] Thomas Ashton admitted changing his views with the new economic conditions. Select Committee on the Export of Machinery, *P.P.* 1841, VII, 22.
[59] *Ibid.* p. 52.
[60] Foster, *Class Struggle*, pp. 187, 206.
[61] *Morning Chronicle*, 17 February 1824.
[62] *Manchester Guardian*, 17 April 1824.
[63] *P.P.* 1824, V, 259.

vertically integrated. There could be no conflict of interest simply because practically all manufacturers made their own machinery.[64] Lucy Brown has argued that the central conflict in these debates was between the interests of the machine makers and the interests of the spinners. And Redford argued that the debate witnessed an alliance of cotton spinners and merchants against a new class of machine makers. Musson, most recently, has argued that the real disagreement was between the country and the London engineers – that Manchester's representatives were a united front before the Commons Committee.[65] There thus appears to be little agreement among current commentators on the core of the dispute.

What is most striking about these debates is the very lack of clarity in the economic position and social composition of the opposing groups. If one looks at the engineers in Manchester, one finds some machine makers very closely tied in social composition to the manufacturers. Many carried on both trades, or had done so at some time.[66] Equally, the provincial engineers in this period were characterised by fragmentation. There were multiple groups within the machine making industry, and each followed his own trade. Throughout these years, they were seldom involved in local politics, and tended to act as a stabilising force.[67] Oldham's engineers formed an autonomous craft élite : in this period they operated a local closed shop which supported other engineering unions which together guaranteed benefits and high wages.[68] In spite of this 'united front' from Manchester one finds Joseph Hume presenting petitions from Manchester machine makers in 1826 in opposition to petitions from Manchester manufacturers in the same year. In spite of the interests of spinner against machine maker, one finds divisions in the opinions among spinners themselves, as for example that between the Glasgow cotton spinners and John Marshall, the Leeds flax spinner.[69] One group of Staffordshire iron masters opposed repeal, and another supported it.[70] Birmingham small-wares manufacturers as

[64] *P.P.* 1841, vii, William Felkin's Testimony, 141–3.
[65] See Brown, *The Board of Trade*, pp. 161–7; Redford, *Manchester Merchants*, p. 131 ; and Musson, 'The Manchester School and the Exportation of Machinery'.
[66] Examples are Peter Ewart, John Kennedy, Henry Houldsworth and Thomas Ashton.
[67] Gattrell, 'The Commercial Middle Classes', Ph.D. Thesis, pp. 95–9.
[68] Foster, *Class Struggle*, p. 225.
[69] *P.P.* 1824, v, 380–1, 601.
[70] *P.P.* 1824, v, 126, 129.

well as Norwich worsted manufacturers also opposed repeal.[71] The case
for repeal of the laws against the export of machinery was, however,
upheld by Committee members, by economists, and by the liberal
middle-class press. These latter groups were those most closely involved
with actual policy formation.

Despite the support for repeal in the circles close to policy makers,
and the divided opinion in the industrial classes, the laws remained
intact. One reason for the inertia over the laws may have been just
because, as we have seen, the restrictions on export did not present pressing practical problems. Widespread smuggling networks were a non-
legalised social convention, and were even institutionalised in manufacturing circles through various insurance arrangements. An even
greater limit on the 'interests' behind this debate was the small extent
to which these foreign exports were felt to be a problem by the northern
manufacturers. Most had the impression that if machinery was in short
supply, foreign orders were either not filled at all, or at least had to wait
until orders in the more secure home market were met. It therefore
appears to be quite impossible to align dispute on the issue with defined
social and economic interests, the definition of which must be arbitrary.
The evidence we have of 'interests' is derived only from the position of
those few groups who organised themselves to create the issue.

The only evidence that seems to exist of a politically organised and
active lobbying group is that of a small group of Manchester manufacturers. This group can be defined by its actions – constant petitioning
to Parliament and lobbying in the Board of Trade to enforce vigilance
on the laws. Analysis of actual Board of Trade decisions reveals much
more liberal licensing in 1825 and the first part of 1826 than at any
other period up to 1835. The Board generally refused between 20 and
30 per cent of applications, and this proportion did not decline even
though applications rose from 14 in 1825 to 133 in 1835. In 1825
licences were granted for printing blocks and flax spinning machinery.
Serious consideration even went to a trade of 500 mule jennies for 500
French jacquard looms.[72]

Between April and July 1826 a test case emerged which resulted in
stricter licensing on the grounds of 'manufacturing interests' : this was
the licensing of the export to France of 50 cases of machines for preparing spinning cotton. The intervention of a group of interested manu-

[71] *P.P.* 1824, v, 154, 310–11.
[72] B.T. 5–34–35 and P.R.O. Board of Trade, Machinery Book, 1827–
41.

facturers and a flurry of petitions led to such a tightening up of discretion that after 1826 all machines used in preparatory processes for the textile industry were refused. In addition refusals were now imposed much more rigorously on turning lathes, engraving machinery, machines for making bar iron, and other engineering tools.[73]

Empiricism and policy

The debates on the export of machinery and the emigration of artisans represent something more than another example of that imperialist reality behind free trade rhetoric which is held to have dominated the thinking of cotton men in this period, and right through until their overt endorsement of Palmerston's programme of imperialism and protection in the election of 1857. That they have a very much wider intellectual significance is to be found in the way this imperialist practice and the many other diverse economic interests I have noted were formulated in terms of a theoretical discussion on skill and the gen-eration of a capital-goods industry. Crude opinion became submerged on a platform which brought the enlightened provincial industrialist together with the metropolitan policy maker and economist. Witnesses to committees, writers of pamphlets, and local journalists participated in their own critical intellectual milieu. The rhetoric of their Mechanics Institutes, scientific societies, and statistical societies provided them with the cultural and intellectual tools for an intrinsic and often empirical criticism of strict classical political economy. They took pride in this culture which removed them from the sphere of the mere practical man, and yet prevented them from falling into the grip of doctrine. They saw themselves as the founders of a new critical spirit.

> Before political economy can have any pretensions to be classified among the sciences, it must be greatly simplified ... axioms must be laid down and rest on facts and experiment ... we naturally feel gratified to find that our ministers ... are at length 'beginning at the right end', by instituting inquiries among experienced men, who can alone be competent to decide how practice squares with theory. We anticipate more benefit to the cause of truth and knowledge from such

[73] On the test case see B.T. 5–34–35–36, B.T. 5–35 Minutes 19 July 1826, p. 155. On refusals to licence, see B.T. 5–35–36 for 1827 and Machinery Book for 1828.

> investigations as those now in progress in the Select Committee
> ... on artisans and machinery than from the writings of the
> whole tribe of jurists and political economists.[74]

The image of the artisan inventor and the self-made entrepreneur featured in the schemes of economic progress of those mechanics institutes and popular industrial histories which captured the imagination of middle-class members of factory towns. The Manchester factory was regarded as the natural companion of the London trades. The principles behind both were smoothed into one – the division of labour. Kennedy's idea of the origins of the cotton factory in the division of labour and small improvements in the cottage industry illustrates this idea of the continuum between workshop and factory production.[75]

Both the London trades and the Manchester factory, however, came together to demand a novel investigation of the logic of free trade. An empirical view of the process of technical change led to ideas on the dynamic of economic progress, ideas much closer to everyday concerns than theoretical speculation on the international specialisation of free trade. Adam Smith, a long time before this, had made the point that many inventions were piecemeal developments. 'The division of labour no doubt first gave occasion to the invention of machines', but furthermore, 'We have not, nor cannot have, any complete history of the invention of machines, because most of them are at first imperfect, and receive gradual improvements and increase of powers from those who use them.'[76] Such ideas demanded closer investigation of the structure of capital, and the analysis of labour into its skilled and unskilled components. The logic of free trade was challenged to meet new sectoral complexities and the real disaggregation of the factors of production. For the economically interested and intellectually aware industrialist, a policy debate like this one was simply a different platform for a new unification of concerns which dominated his culture and practice in everyday life.

Such debates, however, were just as significant for political economy. I have shown the enduring preoccupation of political economists with the process of technical change in all its manifold aspects. A political

---

[74] *Liverpool Mercury*, 16 April 1824.
[75] Kennedy, 'Observations on ... the Cotton Trade'. cf. chap. 8 above, p. 195.
[76] Adam Smith, *Lectures* quoted in N. Rosenberg 'Adam Smith on the Division of Labour: Two Views or One', *Economica*, XXXII, 1965, pp. 129, 132.

controversy over technical change such as this one was a rare opportunity for learning.

The debates were, for many, another opportunity to apply their ideas on free trade. For just as many others, however, the range of issues was tantalising and stimulated them to extend and modify their theories of capital and skill. The debates were constantly used as a source of evidence to support these new ideas. Many economists, McCulloch, Senior, Scrope, Babbage, quoted freely from the evidence. McCulloch appealed to the debates to support his analysis of the impact of high wages.[77] Furthermore, along with Malthus, he was called on in a consultancy capacity by the Select Committee of 1824.[78] Some, like Say, benefited from a post under Napoleon as inspector of foreign factories. Say regarded capital as incapable of restraint, but noted the advantages an immigrant artisan brought with him. The immigrant not only added to the population but also brought an 'accession to the profits of national industry and an acquisition of capital'.[79] Others, like Torrens, were firmly entrenched from the beginning in their opposition to repeal of the restrictions. Place, in 1826, had sneered at Torrens talking 'like a silly old woman' about the advantages of preventing export of machinery.[80] Indeed, Torrens, the honourable member for Ipswich, was introduced to the House by Baring in 1826, in the context of a debate on the export of machinery, as an economist 'who yet dissented from the modern doctrine of political economy'.[81] Nassau Senior, too, found cause in 1830 to take up the issue and to justify, under certain circumstances, restrictions on the export of machinery.[82] John Stuart Mill, in the same year, found the export of machinery to be a possible source of disadvantage until all restrictions on trade were abolished. Until then, the export of machinery was a 'proper subject for adjustment with other nations, on the principle of reciprocity'.[83]

The debate on the export of machinery and the emigration of artisans

[77] McCulloch, *Principles*, 1825, pp. 322–3.
[78] *P.P.* 1824, v, 592, 598.
[79] Say, *A Treatise*, vol. II, p. 184.
[80] Graham Wallas, *The Life of Francis Place, 1771–1854*, London, 1898, p. 179.
[81] House of Commons Debates, *Hansard*, XVI, 6 December 1826, col. 296. Cf. Robert Torrens, *Letters on Commercial Policy*, London, 1833.
[82] N. W. Senior, *Three Lectures on the Cost of Obtaining Money and Some Effects of Private and Government Paper Money*, London, 1830, p. 26.
[83] J. S. Mill, 'Of the Laws of Interchange Between Nations', in J. S. Mill, ed., *Essays on Some Unsettled Questions*, London, 1844, pp. 31–2.

was a vivid illustration of the way in which an issue of economic policy could help to generate new ideas in economic thought. An issue, which on the surface appeared to be another variant of economic policy discussion on international trade, actually provoked a wide ranging discussion of the source and impact of technological change. The intellectual terms of this debate also shifted in much the same pattern as did those of the wider economic debate on technology and industrialisation. The earlier interest in the nature and role of artisan skills gave way to an emphasis on the capital-goods sector. These ideas were raised, criticised and reformulated in the complex political interaction of regional and industrial interest groups, an incipient civil service, politicians, and political economists. The diversity of the industrial and class interests both behind and opposed to the restrictive measures make it impossible to align any particular social composition with any specific economic position. The unsystematic perspectives of many local groups of manufacturers and workers and the general confusion on the issue at the national level created, consequently, an undogmatic atmosphere of discussion. The challenge of the export-of-machinery debate provided a very fruitful point of intersection for economic policy and economic thought.

10

The handloom weavers

The debate on the export of machinery revealed the fear among industrialists that Britain would lose the machine to other nations. Another parliamentary debate, the controversy over the handloom weavers, demonstrated that not only was the machine being taken by foreign rivals but it was being repulsed at home. The export-of-machinery debate reminded political economists and industrialists that, though the machine and its makers had given Britain her lead, these could also go to other countries. New industrial nations would soon come to challenge Britain's old superiority. With foreign economic advance presenting such a threat, the idea that the progress of the machine was being resisted and undermined even on the inside gave the Machinery Question a pressing urgency. The debate on the handloom weavers was a stark testimony to the fear of and antipathy towards the machine in many parts of British society. The distress and dissension in the working class seemed directly associated with the spread of machinery. It contributed to a wider discord over the extent to which the machine disrupted old ways of life, created unemployment, and disfigured the landscape. Within the very framework of economic and scientific advance, the weavers cast a permanent and painful shadow. If the first Industrial Revolution was an experience of excitement and prospects for many living through the rapid transformation, never far from this was the consciousness of a massive and lingering case of technological unemployment. David Landes has put the situation of these years thus :

The middle and upper classes were convinced by the marvellous inventions of science and technology ... that they were living in the best of all possible worlds ... For these Britons, science was the new revelation; and the Industrial Revolution was the proof and justification of the religion of progress. The 'labouring poor', especially those groups bypassed or squeezed by machine industry, said little but were undoubtedly of another mind.[1]

The weavers, of course, had many parallels both in their own time and before. But their plight was seemingly one of unprecedented extent. While political economists and others compared them with previous cases of labour displacement and spoke of labour mobility and the creation of new employment opportunities, the weavers of a generation lingered, unemployed. Such new jobs were for others, not for them; and, while they lingered on, they voiced an eloquent challenge to the free development of industrialisation. They themselves were the subject of parliamentary enquiries, pamphlets, journals, newspapers, and economic tracts. Unlike the interests involved in the export of machinery and emigration of artisans, the weavers evoked consciousness and commitment : their's was a constant, everyday resistance to mechanisation. It was one characteristic of the workplace in most industries, craft or factory. The weaver, however, became the most apparent example of this fight to keep control in the place of production. The most outstanding feature of this struggle against mechanisation, a struggle concerned also with skill, the organisation of production, and the discipline and place of work, was the constant and pressing fear of technological unemployment.

This debate, though such a contrast with that on the export of machines, particularly in its ideological and political overtones, did share with it certain common features. The first feature, of course, was a common concern with technology, a concern with its generation and the inevitability of its diffusion. The second was that the weavers, like many provincial manufacturers, regarded their major enemies to be doctrinal political economy and the cold logic of free trade, and, like them they also gathered allies from unlikely circles. Several political economists, local and national middle-class politicians, magistrates, and manufacturers came to their support. The ideological significance of an optimistic political economy and a scientific culture cannot be under-

[1] Landes, *The Unbound Prometheus*, p. 123.

estimated as the key to the dominant middle-class vision of these years. Yet it is important to remember that not all whig-radical politicians and manufacturers fitted the picture of the 'liberal canting mill owners'.

At the basic economic level, most cotton masters took a conservative or at least cautious attitude to the introduction of the power loom, which took forty years to become the representative method of weaving. Such attitudes are easily explained by the range and number of purely economic constraints on the diffusion of this new technique.[2] Many mill owners, outside their purely economic interests, had traditional views of community and religious feeling, or even radical political views which they took beyond the realm of their class interest. Indeed, the way the weavers conducted their agitation showed that they realised this. Perhaps to their own detriment, they never renounced their 'respectable masters'.

The debates on the weavers also conveniently paralleled the debates on the export of machinery in their timing. A parliamentary agitation was organised in both cases at least twice during the twenties and thirties, including one in the early 1830s culminating in the Select Committee Reports of 1834 and 1835. Another agitation resulted in a full scale Royal Commission, starting in 1837, but not reporting until 1841. The weavers appearing as witnesses at these committees were nearly all appointed delegates of weaving associations or weaving localities. They had a background in radical politics or long years of petitioning and they made use of their sympathetic intermediaries in the middle classes. Most had some knowledge of the language of their opponents, acquired in places like the Mechanics Institutes, as well as a consciousness of their own aims and culture. Their language of negotiation in these debates reflected the process of translation. The issues raised were ones common to debates within political economy: overproduction, taxation, speculation and competition, the efficiency of machinery, and unemployment.

Early agitation

Others have sketched the details of the weavers' labour market, industrial organisation and politics. Here I will say something only of the historical foundations of the weavers' struggle against machinery.[3]

[2] See Maxine Berg, 'The Introduction and Diffusion of the Power Loom 1789–1842', M.A. Thesis, University of Sussex, 1972.

[3] See E. P. Thompson, *The Making of the English Working Class*, Harmondsworth, 1968, chap. 9, and Duncan Bythell, *The Handloom Weavers*, Cambridge, 1969.

Wage cutting took place from the earliest days of this period. The first demand of the weavers from 1790 onwards was for a legal minimum wage, and distress was spoken of even earlier. For example, Thomas Barnes, an early liberal dissenter, also addressed himself to the weavers when he denounced the destruction of early spinning machinery : 'What mean those *riotings* and *tumults*, which we saw a few months ago? What mean the petitions to parliament, to *suppress* or *tax* the machines? The wisdom of Parliament will not certainly regard such petitions.'[4] Barnes elaborated on the benefit of innovation in the language of his Unitarian faith in progress. He identified, however, with the interests of the poor and stressed the key role of the artisan labourer, but his understanding of the dread of innovation in his time did not deter him from emphasising the impact of this innovation on family incomes. Looms had 'improved continually in simplicity, usefulness, and conveniency', especially 'the stocking loom at Nottingham and the Dutch or swivel loom at Manchester'. The new spinning machinery had increased the incomes of females, 'if it is true that the weaver gets less, the wife gets more, and the family does not suffer'.[5]

The woollen weavers were speaking of their decline as early as 1803 and calling for a stop to the factory system in spinning.

> Coarse and middling cloth has undeniably become a most miserable occupation. No men living perhaps toil so hard and reap so little benefit as the clothiers of the present day. But they know no other business, nor have they capitals to turn to any other; they must therefore struggle on. Wanting the aid of their sons as early as their strength will allow, they are all very generally also doomed to the same fate, and must become cloth weavers or workers in their turn.[6]

The militancy of weavers increased, particularly under the expansion of factory weaving in the 1820s. This expansion proceeded in the 1820s and 1830s along with a sub-contract network, acting in effect as a type of 'symbiotic exploitation of labour'. The system allowed the manufacturer to set up his steady trade on the produce of power loom sheds, and to use handloom weavers as a response to fluctuations. In good

---

[4] Thomas Barnes, *Thoughts on the Use of Machines in the Cotton Manufacture Addressed to the Working People in that Manufacture … by a Friend of the Poor*, Manchester, 1780, p. 19.
[5] *Ibid.* pp. 7–8, 14.
[6] *Observations on Woollen Machinery*, Leeds, 1803, p. 16.

years they could be employed without any higher fixed cost to the manufacturer; in bad years they could be cast off.[7] Such brutal manipulation naturally provoked hostility. The riots among the Blackburn and Burnley weavers in 1826 earned extensive publicity.[8] There were more riots in the Manchester area in 1829. The year 1831 was another time of distress among the weavers,[9] but they no longer rioted and even showed disapproval of disturbances in some southern agricultural areas. Papers such as the *Blackburn Gazette* found the time convenient to run a series on the 'Advantages of Machinery'.[10] The *Bolton Chronicle* compared the far away 1831 agricultural riots with the local riots of 1826.[11]

Riots, in fact, gave way to two new types of organisation generated in the 1820s. In the cotton industry, there were those who sought an alliance with the big capitalists against the small. They saw the source of their distress in the 'grinder's system'. As William Longson, the Stockport weaver, argued time and again :

> The grinding system owes its existence to a comparatively
> small number of employers . . . 'Those who undersell the well
> disposed masters by underpaying the workman's labour' . . .
> There is in the trade such a number of well disposed masters,
> as forms a decided majority, and want nothing but a legal
> sanction . . . to enable them to abolish the grinding system.[12]

The Bolton Weavers' Committee conducted a correspondence with Huskisson, calling for boards of trade to fix a legal minimum wage. Huskisson's only reply was : 'Their plan involves . . . calling in the aid

7 Landes, *The Unbound Prometheus*, pp. 118–19, describes the interactions between factory work and outwork. Also see Berg, 'The Introduction and Diffusion of the Power Loom', M.A. Thesis, pp. 46–54, for specific instances of how this was carried out in the weaving sector.
8 Detailed reporting on these riots can be found in the *Blackburn Mail*, 3 May 1826, the *Leeds Mercury*, 6 May 1826, the *Manchester Gazette*, 29 April and 6 May 1826, and the *Manchester Guardian*, 31 March 1826.
9 Archibald Prentice, *Historical Sketches and Personal Recollections of Manchester 1792–1832*, Manchester, 1851, pp. 343–7.
10 *Blackburn Gazette*, 26 January and 2 February 1831.
11 *Bolton Chronicle*, 26 February 1831.
12 William Longson, *An Appeal to the Masters, Workmen and the Public Shewing the Cause of the Distress of the Labouring Classes*, Manchester, 1827. Also see his many letters to the editor in the *Bolton Chronicle*, 1827–9.

of that authority, to check the progress of those improvements, in mechanical and chemical science, by which manual labour is so often abridged and superseded.'[13] A debate on the disadvantages of the power loom and machinery in general featured in the northern papers over the course of this year. Francis Place's well-known letters on machinery were relayed along with many bitter replies through the pages of the *Bolton Chronicle*.[14] Pathetically, some of the weavers seemed already to be defeated when they wrote to Peel of a new epoch in manufactures: 'while every new discovery in the art of reducing manual labour, tends only to enrich those by whom the improvement was introduced and to prevent an *equal proportion of poverty* among the working classes, we cannot refrain from protesting against such innovations.'[15] At the other pole were those who called for unionisation. The Quilting Weavers' Association gave clearest expression to the difficulties of unorganised labour:

> our masters ... still refuse to make any additions to the price of our labour ... The name of the weaver is become almost synonomous with that of the vagrant ... The 'poor weavers' are not allowed to occupy a place in decent society ... Under all these circumstances the necessity of forming ourselves into a strong union for the purpose of removing these pressing evils, must be evident to every thinking mind.[16]

This polarisation allowed for two types of reaction by the middle and upper classes. On the one hand, Tory radicals and humane employers

---

13 *Blackburn Mail*, 13 September 1826; *Bolton Chronicle*, 30 September 1826.
14 See Place Collection of Newspaper Cuttings, vol. LVII. The relevant issues of the *Bolton Chronicle* no longer exist. For discussion on the power loom see *Manchester Guardian*, 31 March 1826, *Manchester Gazette*, 1 July 1826, *Blackburn Mail*, 12 April 1826, *Leeds Mercury*, 6 May 1826, *Blackburn Mail*, 12 April, 26 July, and 23 August 1826. See also John Kennedy, 'Observations on the Influence of Machinery upon the Working Classes of the Community' (read 10 February 1826), *Memoirs of the Manchester Literary and Philosophical Society*, 2nd series, v, 1831.
15 'The Weavers Address', from the Weavers Union Society to Peel, *Blackburn Mail*, 12 April 1826.
16 Webb Papers (British Library of Political and Economic Science), vol. XXXVII, 'Cotton Weavers', pp. 31–2. The Manchester Weavers' Association of 1824 also voices appeals to uphold the union.

could identify the weavers' cause with the attack on factory abuses.[17] On the other, mill owners organised to resist the weavers' unions.[18]

Agitation and alliances in the 1830s

The weavers' agitation of the 1830s continued the grievances and national petitioning that had become traditional to the trade. A new political context did, however, change the formal expression and politics of these demands. The language and personnel of the vanguard in the handloom weavers' debates now emerged with the Ten Hours Movement. This movement was a confused assortment of Tories, working-class radicals, and humanitarian liberals. In the factory movement and the handloom weavers' debates, Richard Oastler, Michael Sadler and the Reverend G. S. Bull were all evangelical Tories. Fielden, the radical, co-operated with E. S. Cayley, another Yorkshire Tory, and John Maxwell, the whig representative for Lanarkshire. The Cobbetts and Owen were also able to count on Fielden's alliance. The radical agitation among weavers and factory workers was indeed partly built up on the clearly opportunistic use by wokrers of any avenue or platform open to them to air their grievances. The politics of their allies was irrelevant. The working classes sought to use the platforms and political power of any sympathetic M.P. or mill owner in order to forward their own claims.

Tory allies, at least, became enthusiastic supporters of working-class grievances, which gave them another way of expressing their own deep-seated emotional values. The abuses of industrialism were drawn out in lurid detail by Sadler, Shaftesbury, Oastler and Bull. Within the factory movement, an older Tory paternalism became combined with a disappointed romanticism. Oastler's romantic Toryism brought him to advocate industrial and agricultural protection, taxation of machinery, and measures to reduce unemployment. This economic policy was united with Tory views of the family. The family-based domestic industry of the weavers was regarded as the best school of moral virtue. Furthermore, the impact of the introduction of machinery on the male

---

[17] For example, the woollen manufacturers and merchants of the Forest of Rossendale met in 1823 to demand protection for manual labour and a tax on the produce of the power loom. See *Observations on the Use of Power Looms by a Friend to the Poor*, Rochdale, 1823.

[18] S. J. Chapman, 'An Historical Sketch of the Masters' Associations in the Cotton Industry', *Transactions of the Manchester Statistical Society*, 13 February 1901, p. 69.

labour market was regarded as unnatural, and dilution through an unprecedented sexual division of labour was keenly felt. One public meeting in Oldham denounced the use of machinery, which had 'taken employment out of the hands of men and put it in those of women, whose province is in the house and home'.[19]

There were many personal links between the Ten Hours Movement and the handloom weavers' agitation. The number of reform leaders over the various movements of the 1830s was small. Such middle-class leaders as came to the fore had a cultural ancestry in Tory paternalism or in the service and good works of liberal dissent. When John Maxwell presented his bill on the condition of the weavers in 1835, he had the active and long-established support of many northern M.P.s, several of them from manufacturing families. John Fielden for Oldham, W. Bolling, Robert Torrens and Ainsworth for Bolton, Hesketh Fleetwood for Preston, and Joseph Brotherton for Salford all agitated for the weavers both nationally and locally.[20]

Issues were also common to both movements. The involvement of Tory radicals did not preclude great popular support for the Ten Hours Movement, which was at root a struggle over the length and control of the working day. Factory hands and domestic workers found a fundamental unity in terms of struggle within the workplace. Reformers in Bradford proclaimed that the Ten Hours legislation and taxation of machinery must be obtained together.[21] A broadside from Bradford, in fact, called for a check to the competition of machinery by a 'direct tax' on its use or by an 'indirect tax' on the period of using it : 'Unrestrained machinery must 'ere long be the ruin of the Country. Restrain it then. Time it and tax it both. Cry out aloud for a Ten Hour Bill and a Tax upon Machinery, or we shall soon all be ruined together!'[22] It was, in fact, during the official inquiry into the demands of the Ten Hours Movement that Oastler drew up the details and gave publicity to John Sadler's new 'pendulum loom', hoping this more efficient handloom would enable the weaver to compete with the power-driven factory.[23] Oastler gave evidence to the 1834 Committee, and both he and Bull

19 *Report of the Proceedings of a Public Meeting Held in ... Oldham on ... Factories,* Oldham, 1836, p. 25.
20 *Bolton Chronicle,* 15 August 1835.
21 J. T. Ward, *The Factory Movement, 1830–1855,* London, 1962, p. 125.
22 *Unrestrained Machinery must Ere Long be the Ruin of the Country,* Bradford Broadside, 1834.
23 J. H. Sadler, *The New Invention of Double and Quadruple or British National Looms,* London, 1831.

helped the Bradford weavers with their pamphleteering.[24] The Spital-field weavers asked Oastler's friend, William Atkinson, to represent them, and he wrote a tract on their behalf.[25] In 1835, G. S. Bull's *Cause of Industry* appealed for support in alleviating the 'misery of the industrious human machines' by restricting machinery: 'The small Manufacturers or Employers of Handloom Weavers are the only remaining hope of this community – they form a link between labour and independence.'[26]

Both reformers in the Ten Hours Movement and those in the hand-weavers' debate conceived their major enemy to be the rhetoric of political economy. Hesketh Fleetwood, though supporting the weavers, advised them that they would have little chance of success: 'Shew to Parliament that there are means of relieving your difficulties without fettering wages, or abandoning improvements in machinery – that those means are practicable in themselves and not dangerous to the com-munity.'[27] John Maxwell also reported the opposition of the House of Commons because of 'prejudice on free trade and sound currency', saying that many recognised that machinery was the cause of distress, but that it could not be taxed because this 'would be contrary to free trade'.[28] The reformers associated this intransigence with the unified oppression of mill owners and political economy. A broadside from Bradford at this time played on this doctrinal use of political economy. The ideological differences between working-class comber and middle-class mill owner were expressed through a debate between George Hadfield as the mill owner and Charles Comber as the comber.

> *George Hadfield.* I'm against all monopolies.
> *Charles Comber.* It's queer – are you against Big Bens?[29]
> Before two years the Bradford combers will have to seek work in vain.
> *Hadfield.* They must *emigrate*.
> *Charles.* We like old England best.

[24] Oastler and Bull helped in the preparation of the exchange with G. P. Scrope in *Political Economy versus the Handloom Weavers*, Bradford, 1835.

[25] William Atkinson, *Principles of Political Economy . . . being the Substance of a Case delivered to the Handloom Weavers' Commission*, London, 1840.

[26] Noted in Ward, *The Factory Movement*, p. 135.

[27] *Preston Chronicle*, 19 April 1834.

[28] *Bolton Chronicle*, 13 September 1834.

[29] A Big Ben was the popular name for a combing machine.

Hadfield. Would you fetter 'Capital and Ingenuity?'
Charles. Would *you* fetter Industry?
Hadfield. I am against all taxes on machinery.
Charles. If we do not 'fetter' and 'tax' machinery, it will fetter and tax our backs and bellies.
Hadfield. I'm for Free Trade.
Charles. And 'Coarser Food'.
Hadfield. I'm a Dissenter.
Charles. So was Lucifer.
Charles. Off steam looms, off Big Bens, off Hadfield and his poor law bill, and all his Scotch crew by the next ship.[30]

An inquiry into the sources and incidence of distress over several sectors of the economy, including the weavers, was conducted by the Select Committee on Manufactures, Commerce and Shipping in 1833. It made no recommendations.[31]

It was, however, succeeded by agitation in the north for wage regulation. Meetings were called in Bolton in late 1833 and petitions were ready by January 1834.[32] Glasgow's weavers also met to petition for boards of trade in January.[33] By early March Robert Torrens, the Bolton representative, was presenting three petitions to Parliament – one from the weavers, one from the borough representatives, and one from forty-five master manufacturers.[34] This was followed by similar moves to petition Parliament from other northern towns. Preston's weavers met in March 1834,[35] as did Blackburn's,[36] and Bradford's.[37]

Not only petitioning but also meetings with sympathetic M.P.s were carried on in several towns prior to John Maxwell's success in obtaining a select committee in June. Maxwell met many weavers' delegations during this interval. Others, like Hesketh Fleetwood and W. Bolling, acted as go-betweens for the weavers and the House of Commons. Bolling gave an account of his interview with Poulett Thompson on Maxwell's pending motion, reporting that Thompson thought the

30 *A Conversation between George Hadfield and Charles Comber*, Bradford Broadside, 1834.
31 Select Committee on Manufactures, Commerce and Shipping, *P.P.* 1835, VI.
32 *Bolton Chronicle*, 5 October 1833, 25 January 1834.
33 *Glasgow Herald*, 17 January 1834.
34 *Hansard*, XXI, col. 1144.
35 *Preston Chronicle*, 15 March 1834.
36 *Manchester Guardian*, 1 March 1834.
37 *Bradford Observer*, 13 March 1834.

committee would be granted, though with an inquiry wide enough to 'ascertain how far the wages of other artisans affected the wages of weaving'.[38]

Parliament and the weavers

A committee of fifty was appointed in June 1834, after John Maxwell succeeded at last with his motion for an inquiry. It was headed by Maxwell, and other principal members were Fielden, Parnell, Bowring, Peel, Poulett Thompson, Stanley and Torrens. In fact, the Committee carried many of the same members as that on Manufactures, Commerce and Shipping in 1833, with Parnell, Poulett Thompson, and Fielden as principal members of both Inquiries. The background of those who led the Handloom Weavers' Committe was diverse. Fielden, the radical, Maxwell, the whig, and Cayley, the Tory, directed proceedings.

Fielden, aside from his activities in the Ten Hours Movement and the National Regeneration Society, had also been involved in 1827 in the General Association, set up to bring in a bill for taxing all machinery. The 'Machinery and Protection of Labour Bill' gave substance to the ideas expressed in the 1820s for the taxation of machinery.[39] The handloom weaver, it was argued, was placed under heavy disadvantage by the system of indirect taxation. A tax on power looms would equalise competition, and remove some of the burden from consumption goods. The petitions of the General Association were referred to the Select Committee on Emigration of 1832 which responded : 'Your committee cannot express too strong an opinion against the idea of regulating the rate of Wages under any conceivable modification.'[40] John Maxwell, too, stressed the contrast between untaxed machinery and the heavily taxed weavers in his supporting pamphlet *Manual Labour versus Machinery*. His later writing revealed a prejudice against free trade and the emigration of operatives, and maintained in his faith that manual labour generated more taxation revenue than machinery.[41] Maxwell continued the whig reform position of his father in Lanarkshire. E. S.

[38] *Preston Chronicle*, 2 and 19 April 1834.
[39] Cf. Select Committee on Combination Laws, Artisans and Machinery, *P.P.*, 1824, v.
[40] G. W. Hilton, 'The Controversy Concerning the Relief of Handloom Weavers', *Explorations in Entrepreneurial History*, 2nd series, I, Winter 1964, p. 170.
[41] See John Maxwell, *Manual Labour versus Machinery*, London, 1834, and *Suggestions Arising out of the Present Want of Employment for Labour and Capital*, London, 1852.

Cayley was known for his opposition to Ricardian land policies,[42] his *On Commercial Economy in Six Essays* of 1830 developed an elaborate theory of over-production, gluts, and machinery.

For the first investigation in 1834, Maxwell called witnesses in favour of wage regulation along three different lines. The first system was proposed by the Bolton weavers and asked for legislation of wage scales arrived at by local boards of trade composed of masters and weavers. The Glasgow weavers proposed a nationwide system of wage regulation via boards of trade. Finally, John Fielden's own proposal was for a bill to make weaving rates dependent on the past costs of the largest masters, and for these average rate to be the minimum ones for the region.[43] The already activated weavers' committees of each town sent their most articulate and well-known representatives as delegates. The Bolton Committee, for example, selected Thomas Myerscough, Richard Needham, and John Makin, all known to previous committees, and active in the propaganda of the weavers' case.[44] But this investigation resulted in no recommendation by the Select Committee, though it did express favour for some form of parliamentary relief for weavers. The second report of the Committee, after an investigation of those opposed to the measures, recommended Fielden's proposals, together with protection against embezzlement for masters and a cheaper legal form of indenture for apprentices.[45] A bill along these lines was introduced on 28 July 1835 by John Maxwell, but was rejected by 129 to 41. It was raised again in 1836, repeatedly postponed and finally dropped.

Agitation continued in the immediate aftermath of the 1834 Committee. An august deputation on behalf of the weavers visited Alexander Baring and Viscount Lowther at the Board of Trade. The members of this included Lord Francis Egerton, D. Stuart, E. Stuart, Admiral Adam, and Messrs. Maxwell, Turner, Brotherton, Bolling, Fleetwood, Lawson, Forbes, Gillon, Ainsworth, Fielden, R. Osward, E. Tennent, Brocklehurst, R. Wallace, and Cayley.[46] Local weavers' agitation also continued: the Paisley Harness Union, the Glasgow Harness Union,

---

42 See E. S. Cayley, *Corn, Trade, Wages, and Rent*, London, 1826.
43 Select Committee on Handloom Weavers' Petitions, *P.P.* 1835, XIII, p. xx.
44 *Bolton Chronicle*, 12 July 1834.
45 A discussion of the limitations and biases of this Select Committee can be found in Bythell, *The Handloom Weavers*, pp. 162–4. Edward Baines in his *History of the Cotton Manufacture of Great Britain* attacked the Committee for bias on the side of the weavers, p. 487.
46 *Preston Chronicle*, 14 March 1835.

and the Glasgow General Protecting Union all resolved to petition Parliament for a law to regulate wages again in October 1835.[47] Government inaction rankled deeply when the story leaked out that William Ashworth, a Quaker manufacturer, after the Report of 1835 had written to Chadwick, the Poor Law Secretary, asking him to send agricultural labourers from the south to the north, as 'more handloom weavers are needed at Bolton'.[48]

Fielden moved to introduce another bill in December 1837, and he persisted until he gained a Royal Commission. Russell brought in a Commission of four for an inquiry which was to be rather a different affair than that of 1834–5; those appointed were Nassau Senior, S. Jones Loyd, W. E. Hickson and John Leslie. The inquiry was to be a wide-ranging one into the state of the handloom weavers generally, and not just into their employment situation.[49] The commissioners were not expected to visit the weavers' districts, but rather to rely on assistant commissioners for fact gathering.[50] The spokesmen for the weavers attacked the composition of the committee. Senior had acquired odious distinction on the New Poor Law Bill and his opposition to the Ten Hours Bill. S. Jones Loyd as a banking theorist and classical economist was expected to support Senior. John Leslie was a West End tailor who became a convinced advocate of the New Poor Law, on which he published three pamphlets in 1834.[51] W. E. Hickson, however, was a rather different member, he identified with the evangelical christian and early co-operative movement. In 1826 he edited the first co-operative magazine, and in 1831 attacked the Society for the Diffusion of Useful Knowledge.[52] He had also served on commissions for juvenile delinquency, industrial schools, and repeal of the taxes on the press. Although regional investigations were left to assistant commissioners, Hickson visited all the regions to produce an overall report. But the investigations took two years and accumulated into five volumes of 1,400 pages. The slowness of the inquiry provoked Fielden into moving a resolution on

[47] *The Weavers' Journal,* 31 October 1835.
[48] *The Champion,* 18 November 1837.
[49] S. M. Phillips to Senior, 26 December 1837, H. O. 74/1, pp. 118–19. (Copy in Senior Papers, National Library of Wales.)
[50] J. Russell to Senior, H.O. 74/1, p. 89. (Copy in Senior Papers.) Senior had, however, toured the factory districts in 1837 with Lord Fitzmaurice to ascertain 'the right as to the factory question'. Senior to Howick, 3 May 1837, Senior Papers.
[51] See Hilton, 'The Controversy Concerning the Relief of Handloom Weavers', pp. 174–5.
[52] See W. E. Hickson, *The Rights of Industry,* London, 1831, p. 3.

the handloom weavers on 21 December 1837. But the resolution had to await the report. The report and proposals were drafted by Senior, who saw the condition of the weavers as an inevitable result of excess supply of labour in the trade and made proposals to reduce their number.[53] Education and outlawing restrictive union practices in other trades were his major solutions. He viewed the impact of power loom weaving and technological unemployment as inevitable. However, he did make some remote suggestions to alleviate conditions. The repeal of the Corn Laws would help to reduce the cost of consumer goods for the weavers. Furthermore, the foreign demand for cloth could be improved by measures to develop better fabric designs. Both measures were far removed from any possible practical policy question: the weavers and their supporters faced the immediacy of technological unemployment. For the introduction of the new technology of the period involved a fundamental restructuring of the economy, forcing a recomposition of the workforce. Such a recomposition could only be brought about through a painful period of readjustment and large-scale unemployment among these hand workers. The intellectual validity of the weavers' demands, grievances and responses must be judged against their genuine realisation that technological change involved loss of jobs and unknown social changes as much as mechanical modification. The expression of these demands by Tory radical, weaver, or liberal mill owner reached back to a traditional language.

Political economy and weavers' resistance

The major issues in the debates over the condition of the weavers were fairly limited. The weavers struggled over two main issues: the maintenance of the handloom via a tax on machinery, and wage regulation and the elimination of internal competition. The two areas of struggle were not necessarily exclusive, but many who took up the second issue denied the decisive impact of the power loom.

It was the benefit of the power loom, or of machinery generally, which most interested political economists. Maxwell proposed a tax on machinery as early as 1820. This evoked a sharp rebuke from Ricardo,

[53] George Stigler sees Senior's analysis in this report as superior because it resembled neoclassical allocation solutions. His assessment, however, is forced. He could just as easily have identified such elements in Smith, and indeed in many of the much earlier pamphleteers on the weavers. See 'The Classical Economists: An Alternative View', in *Five Lectures on Economic Problems*, London, 1949, pp. 34–6.

who argued that it was the duty of government to give the greatest possible encouragement to the development of industry. Furthermore, he saw the proposal as a violation of the 'sacredness of property which constituted the great security of society'.[54] T. P. Thompson, McCulloch and in particular Francis Place were obsessed with drumming into the weavers, and into the working classes generally, their views of the benefits and the inevitability of technical progress. Place wrote a notable series of letters on this to the *Bolton Chronicle* in 1826, and was subsequently asked by the Royal Commission to submit a memorandum on the condition of the weavers.[55] McCulloch raised the question a number of times in the pages of the *Edinburgh Review*, but was most explicit in his views on the weavers in his review of Babbage in 1833. T. P. Thompson wrote to various provincial newspapers, but carried on his longest and most significant exchange in the *Leeds Times* of 1840. Bowring and Scrope maintained inflexible doctrinal positions in their exchanges with the weavers' committees.[56]

Scrope argued that machinery itself was the produce of labour – that goods produced by the power loom rewarded one set of labourers rather than another.[57] McCulloch maintained that the weavers could not complain about an innovation which could never cause injury.[58] The power loom had obviously increased employment by bringing more opportunities for work to the weaver's family,[59] and McCulloch, as noted

---

[54] *Hansard*, new series, II, 29 June 1820, 122.

[55] See Place Letters in the Place Collection of Newspaper Cuttings, vol. XVI. Place also deceived the Bolton Weavers Association in 1827 by offering to help them gain a committee of the House. On Place's own account, he regarded such a committee as an ideal platform for instilling in the work people the 'true' principles of machinery. Place Newspaper Cuttings, xvi.

[56] J. R. McCulloch, 'Effects of Machinery and Accumulation', *Edinburgh Review*, XXXV, 1821, and 'Babbage on Machinery and Manufactures', pp. 315–16; T. P. Thompson, 'Letters to the Leeds Times on Machinery' (March 1840), in *Exercises, Political and Others*, vol. v, London, 1842. Sir J. Bowring, *Copy of Correspondence between Dr. Bowring and the Associated Weavers' Committee, Kilmarnock*, Kilmarnock, 1835. Scrope, *Political Economy versus the Handloom Weavers*.

[57] Scrope, *Political Economy versus the Handloom Weavers*, p. 4. See also T. P. Thompson, who argued that for every group losing on the introduction of machinery two gained, 'Machinery and the Labour Question', Letter to the Editor of the *Leeds Times*, No. 1, March 1840, or in *Exercises, Political and Others*, vol. v, p. 2.

[58] J. R. McCulloch, 'Employment of Machinery – Cause of Gluts', *The Scotsman*, 6 October 1824.

[59] McCulloch, 'Babbage on Machinery and Manufactures', p. 316.

already, despised the domestic system.[60] Senior argued that the power loom was of great advantage to working-class consumption by reducing the cost of clothing.[61] Place simply reiterated his obsessive counsel on population.[62]

The weavers' associations were of a different mind. John Makin, one of the Bolton weavers' representatives, feared the intervention of the economist : 'We have a fear that the opinions of theorists will have too great an operation against the practical opinion of the trade.'[63] J. M. Cobbett advised Fielden as to how he should use the evidence of the 1834 Committee Reports and declared : 'I do really look upon this body of evidence coming just at this moment as something calculated to check the mad economists in their career.'[64] The Bradford weavers saw the power loom as 'the great screw' both to handloom employers and weavers. The power loom masters could undersell the handloom masters 'by three or four shillings in a piece'.[65] Even if the power loom was not used on every type of cloth, it affected the competitive position and price of cloth produced by the handloom.[66] The weavers believed that technical progress had to be accompanied by redundancy of some classes of workpeople, and they quoted the radical Wade, 'the direct tendency of them [mechanical improvements] is to substitute cheap for dear labour'.[67]

The extent of the influence of the power loom could be disputed. It was profitable only for certain fabrics and required a very large investment in fixed capital.[68] It was quite clear to many that the productivity of the power loom was not its greatest asset. Consistent

60 J. R. McCulloch, 'Evidence to the 1825 Committee on Emigration', quoted in O'Brien, *J. R. McCulloch*. See above chap. 3.
61 Senior, *Three Lectures on the Rate of Wages*, p. xvi.
62 See Francis Place, 'Handloom Weavers and Factory Workers', in J. A. Roebuck, ed., *Pamphlets for the People*, 1, London, 29 September 1835, pp. 6–7.
63 Select Committee on the Handloom Weavers, *P.P.* 1834, xiii, 391.
64 Fielden–Cobbett correspondence, 27 July 1834, John Rylands Library.
65 The Handloom Worsted Weavers' Central Committee, *The Report and Resolutions*, Bradford, 1835, pp. 1–7.
66 *The Weavers' Journal*, 30 January 1836.
67 *Bolton Chronicle*, 1 March 1834.
68 Select Committee on the Handloom Weavers, *P.P.* 1834, x, Testimony of Hugh Mackenzie and William Buchanan, Glasgow weavers, pp. 77 and 150. Thomas Myerscough, a Bolton delegate, argued that the power loom had taken over most of the traditional Bolton cloth. Also see the testimony of Kirkman Finlay, a Glasgow manufacturer in the Select Committee on Manufactures, Commerce, and Shipping, *P.P.* 1833, vi, 39. Finlay agreed with Mackenzie and Buchanan.

production time, and control and supervision over manufacturing processes in the factory were rather its most powerful attractions to the manufacturer.[69] Working-class discipline also had something to do with the differing labour conditions between the two techniques. The Bolton Committee was aware of this: 'The chief advantage of power looms is the facility of executing a quantity of work under more immediate control and management, and the prevention of embezzlement, and not in the reduced cost of production.'[70] The power loom master had to keep his machinery running and had a greater interest in keeping on good terms with his power loom weavers.[71]

The competition of the power loom with the handloom was nevertheless regarded as unfair. The remedy was a tax on machinery, a demand not unreasonable to the worker carrying a heavy burden of indirect taxation. R. M. Martin, brought to the 1834 Committee in his capacity as the author of a work on taxation, argued that 'The cloth made by machinery contributes less to the resources of the country than cloth produced by handlooms.' It was 'just and politic that this inequality be removed'.[72] And Edward Baines, member of the Committee, presented a petition from the Leeds weavers: 'It [the power loom] ought to be made more available to local rates, but it unfortunately happens that the persons who have the power to lay the taxes are mostly interested in machinery . . . the handloom weavers think that their labour ought to be protected as well as the farmers' corn, by a tax on power looms.'[73]

The *Weavers Journal*, voicing the interests of the Glasgow and Paisley Harness Unions and the Glasgow General Protecting Union, held the position that the increase of wages due to rising taxation on provisions inevitably put the handloom weaver out of employment, and the untaxed power loom in his place.[74] Senior still scoffed at the proposals. A tax on the power loom would throw the power weavers back on the handloom. The tax would be a premium to the foreign manufacturer and take the place of his tariffs.[75]

[69] Select Committee on the Handloom Weavers, *P.P.* 1834, x, Testimony of John Makin, p. 407.

[70] Committee of Manufacturers and Weavers of Bolton, *A Letter Addressed to the Members of both Houses of Parliament on the Distresses of the Handloom Weavers*, Bolton, 1834.

[71] *P.P.* 1834, x, Testimony of James Turner, cotton yarn dresser of Manchester, p. 621.

[72] *P.P.* 1834, x, p. 310. Testimony of R. M. Martin.

[73] Select Committee on Handloom Weavers' Petitions, *P.P.* 1835, XIII, 230.

[74] *The Weavers' Journal*, Glasgow, 30 January 1836.

[75] Report of the Royal Commission on Handloom Weavers, *P.P.* 1841, x, 50.

The demand for a tax on machinery was certainly not a bizarre notion raised by a few cranks. Its expression in ballad form is indicative of the extent to which it entered the tradition of the weavers' agitation. An 'Operative of Keighley' wrote in 1834:

> Draw near honest people of every degree
> And listen a little, I pray unto me.
> While I attempt to unfold in my tale,
> A few of the tricks which in England prevail.
>
> Then, first for the weavers, a set of poor souls
> With clothes on their backs much like riddles for holes,
> With faces quite pale, and eyes sunk in the head
> As if the whole race were half famished for bread . . .
>
> For now the rich person, who once knew the poor,
> Has grown quite a stranger, and knows him no more,
> But keeps at a distance, like some mighty God,
> And won't own acquaintance by even a nod . . .
>
> Then seeing, my friends, that you now live in times
> When pride and oppression are no longer crimes,
> Why should you not boldly of both take your fill,
> And grind down the labouring class at your will?
>
> A class which was never designed, it is plain,
> To form any link in society's chain,
> Excepting the part of a mere public hack,
> To bear the whole weight of the rest on his back . . .
>
> For there let machinery, untaxed and free,
> Bear down their tax'd labour to such a degree,
> That all competition themselves to maintain,
> Would prove an attempt both ridiculous and vain.[76]

There were some, such as the representatives of the Bolton weavers, could not concur with this position. It would have been inconsistent with their alignment with the 'respectable manufacturer'. They considered the effects of home competition, and the interests of the power loom weavers and the market for cloth generally. Such an action as the tax on power looms would only increase still more the export of yarn,

[76] *The Weavers' Complaint*, Keighley, 1834, pp. 1, 10, 32, 37.

and thus contribute to a reduction in the weavers' employment, and reduce the wages of those attending the machines. It would repress innovation, and 'it is only through improvements in machinery that our manual labour can be lightened'.[77] Fielden, too, changed his views on the taxation of machinery. He used both types of machine in his mills, and defended his position. But he now had greater hope for agitation on lower taxes, a Ten Hours Bill, and a minimum wage.[78]

While many feared that a tax on machinery would lead to greater foreign competition, others made an explicit connection between their ideas on the export of machinery and the power loom. William Longson of the Bolton weavers dismissed the connection between wages and population, and blamed foreign competition which had been encouraged by 'the export of machinery and by starving our most ingenious mechanics out of the country'.[79] Robert Torrens, true to his views of 1824–5, argued that the export of cotton twist at low or nominal duties would 'extinguish handloom weaving in England, and cause power to be universally introduced'.[80]

Many of the economists came at least to acknowledge a massive problem of transitional unemployment among the weavers. It was probably the attention given to the weavers by parliamentary and provincial statistical inquiries which brought even some economists of extreme views, like McCulloch, to recognise frictional unemployment. Not only McCulloch, but Babbage, T. P. Thompson, Bowring and Scrope reached some conception of the problems of mobility.[81] Bowring argued that machinery was a formidable rival and that weavers should prevent their children going into the trade.[82] Scrope went as far as suggesting that the government should provide some means of coping with these transitional difficulties.[83] But only Babbage in 1832 and

[77] *P.P.* 1834, x, Testimonies of Thomas Myerscough, John Makin and William Longson, pp. 358, 414 and 546.
[78] Letter to the Editor, *The Champion,* 24 February 1838, and Fielden–Cobbett Correspondence, 28 December 1838.
[79] William Longson, 'Wages, Competition, Population', *Bolton Chronicle,* 22 August 1826.
[80] *Bolton Chronicle,* 5 January 1833.
[81] T. P. Thompson, 'Machinery and the Labour Question', Letter to the Editor of the *Leeds Times,* No. 2, March 1840, in *Exercises, Political and Others,* vol. v, p. 7. Charles Babbage, *On the Economy of Machinery and Manufactures,* London, 1832, pp. 229–30.
[82] Bowring, *Correspondence,* p. 10.
[83] G. P. Scrope, *Principles of Political Economy,* pp. 192–3.

Travers Twiss in 1844 made the effort to explain the survival of the headweavers' trade. They analysed the nature of outwork, drew attention to the subcontracting network, and explored the greater flexibility given to capitalist production through the maintenance of large pools of sweated labour.[84]

Torrens, while petitioning the House on behalf of the Bolton weavers in 1834, argued: 'When the introduction of new machinery increased production and augmented the wealth of the country, the country was bound in some shape or other to afford assistance to those classes who were reduced to destitution by the change.'[85] Senior, inevitably, did not mention that part of his colleague W. E. Hickson's report which challenged the assumptions of the inquiry. Hickson saw great harm in the social impact of machinery, and felt that it made 'mere machines of human beings' and the extreme division of labour alienated men and degraded the skilled labourer. He threatened that unless some reform was undertaken, political radicalism and Chartism would succeed: 'in the People's Charter the working classes have a rallying cry which will give energy and concentration to their efforts'. Hickson predicted that the Chartist programmes, which included one for a tax on machinery and capital, would 'break up the whole framework of society'.[86]

The second major issue discussed in the handloom weavers' debate was wage regulation and internal competition. The possibility of a minimum wage was not conceived of by political economists, but it was consistently demanded by weavers as well as many manufacturers. Behind demands for wage regulation and the weavers' boards of trade was the theory of the 'slaughterhouse' grinding system, of the 'dishonourable' employer, and of 'unprincipled competition'.[87] This faith in the philanthropy of the large manufacturer and inherent ill-will of the small manufacturer was not universal. There was some suspicion that small

84 Charles Babbage, *Machinery and Manufactures*, pp. 181–6. and Travers Twiss, *Two Lectures on Machinery*, Oxford, 1844, pp. 33–8, 54–6.

85 Torrens, 'Speech', *Hansard*, 11 July 1834, cols. 377–8. Torrens's speeches during this period cannot, however, always be said to have attracted serious consideration. In 1833 Macaulay reported: 'The other day Colonel Torrens made a tipsy speech about rent and profits, and then staggered away, tumbled down a staircase and was sick as a dog in the Long Gallery.' Thomas Pinney, ed., *The Letters of Thomas Babington Macaulay*, Cambridge, 1974–, vol. II, p. 232.

86 Report of W. E. Hickson, Appendix to the 1841 Report . . . on Handloom Weavers, *P.P.* 1840, XXIV, 44, 71.

87 See *The Weavers' Journal*, 31 December 1835.

owners were used by the larger to cushion economic fluctuations and that the larger owner could just as well be responsible for triggering reductions. Placing the power of wage regulation in the hands of the greater master was in that master's interest, and would be a way of eliminating much of his competition.[88] But the weavers' associations banded together to secure stable price lists. William Thompson spoke for the Glasgow General Protecting Union of Handweavers: 'We are the cheap machinery of our employers, we cost them nothing, and therefore, we can undersell one another . . . but their capital is not materially injured.'[89]

The weavers regarded this competition of capital as the theft of their former rank in the industrial world. They spoke of a 'war of capital' which 'exists to a certain degree every day'.[90] The Owenite *New Moral World* analysed the emergence of a 'reserve army of labour'. It argued that consumption depended on the value of labour, and that labour was now depreciated in value by technological progress. 'In this state of things with the increase and increasing perfection of machinery and a limited home consumption, there will obviously always remain a redundant proportion of manual labour which capital and competition may work with as it wills.'[91]

The state, the poor, and the weavers

The official response to the weavers' critique of technology and the direction of the total economy was ambivalent. However, discussion of a policy towards technology as well as economic development was a fundamental aspect of politics, and this is clearly reflected in the differing procedures of investigation behind the Committees of 1834–5 and 1837–9. The 1834–5 Committee assumed there should be some measure of control over economy and technology. Questioning proceeded along the lines of the reasoning produced by Tory and working-class groups over the previous decade. Witnesses were grouped into supporting and opposing sides and interviewed in turn. Testimonies were used to modify the views of the Committee. The 1837–9 Commission, on the other hand, was set up as a social science project

[88] *P.P.* 1834, x, see Testimonies of Kingman and Thomas Myerscough, 26 and 347.
[89] *Glasgow Herald*, 29 August 1834. Cf. William Pilling's statement for the Bolton Weavers' Association, *Bolton Chronicle*, 25 January 1834.
[90] William Thompson, *Glasgow Herald*, 29 August 1834.
[91] *The New Moral World*, 6 January 1828.

on the model of the Poor Law Commission Inquiry.[92] Senior issued guidelines to the Commissioners for classifying grievances and identifying areas of distress, and used the recommendations of the previous Committee in 1834–5 as hypotheses to be tested and disproved.

The 1834–5 Committee addressed itself to questions about the impact of development in the wider economy on the weaving workforce : the impact of steam looms, home competition and speculation, foreign competition, heavy taxation, monetary instability. The final report emphasised home competition and recommended local boards of trade. It attributed little distress to the impact of power looms, and so gave little support to the long-standing call for a tax on machinery.[93] The 1837–9 Commission accepted the directions of the wider economy and did not challenge the tendencies of industrialisation and growth. It addressed itself instead to the individual conduct of the workmen. Senior instructed assistant commissioners carefully to investigate the extent of unionisation and strikes in the trade. They were to investigate the 'population problems' of the trade, and the level of 'diligence and frugality' of the weavers.[94] Senior argued in his *Report* that the cause of distress was the excess number of weavers in unskilled branches of the trade, and that education in 'diligence and frugality' would help the weavers, as it would the rest of the working classes. The suspension of all union barriers to entry in other trades, and the elimination of union wage demands would give the weavers greater opportunities for leaving their trade.[95]

The Report on the condition of the handloom weavers was not an outstanding document for its time. The context of Senior's assessments

92 Public Record Office, Home Office Papers 73/63, Senior to Russell, 19 August 1837. (Transcribed in Senior Papers.)
93 *P.P.* 1835, XIII, 15–30.
94 See 'Instructions from the Central Board of Handloom Weavers' Inquiry Commission to the Assistant Commissioners', Appendix to the Report of the Royal Commission on Handloom Weavers, *P.P.* 1841, X, 129.
95 Report of the Royal Commission on Handloom Weavers, *P.P.* 1841, X, 98–119. Senior's views on trades unions can be assessed from his involvement in A Report on Combinations by N. W. Senior and Thomas Tomlinson presented to Rt. Hon. Lord Viscount Melbourne, Secretary of State, 20 August 1832. This went as far as a survey of certain anonymous manufacturers to ascertain among other things, 'the way in which existing habits of combination affect the manufacturing population, and disturb the division of labour, the improvement of machinery, and manufacturing processes'. Senior Papers.

and the whole approach of the inquiry were not those of the 1834 Committee, but of the statistical investigations of the time carried on in many of the new provincial statistical societies. The surveys of Glasgow, Nottingham and Miles Platting set out the massive poverty of the domestic outworkers before Senior even wrote up his report.[96] Senior's report, in addition, affirmed some of the prejudices these earlier reports had tried to escape. Education and the evils of unionisation were still the major interest of Nassau Senior.[97] But William Felkin, for example, by no means a radical, had told the British Association in 1837 that the problems of the working classes were not questions of 'morals' but questions of the distribution of income: 'Many from amongst the working classes have exhibited vast mental and imaginative power, and have attained to a high moral elevation. When the mind is at ease on account of worldly circumstances, there is much in the nature of their ordinary employments to facilitate the exertions of the mind.'[98] Later, Felkin even challenged the superiority of the factory. He added in his *Account of the Machine Wrought Hosiery Trade*: 'At present, I do not see reason for deciding that all labour in connection with weaving machinery, must be subject to the uniform, automatic, system of operation which obtains within the gates of a factory, in order to secure good work, fair wages, or reasonable profit.'[99] However, Senior's conclusions, delivered in his scientific prose, had a tone of finality:

> the unequal race continues till the handloom weaver, finding
> the united wages of himself and his family unequal to support
> life is gradually ground out of the market and forced to
> endeavour to find some other employment . . . The cause of
> the low earnings of the handloom weavers is the disproportion
> between their numbers and the demand for their labour . . .

96 See Reports in the *Journals of the London Statistical Society*, 1834–9. These reports, too, had many limitations. See below, chap. 13.

97 Senior's lack of imagination and prosaic demeanour were remarked during an evening at Holland House. Macaulay reported; 'There was Senior the political economist, who sate very quiet, and who, as soon as he had departed, was pronounced a bore by Lady Holland.' Pinney, ed., *The Letters of Thomas Babington Macaulay*, vol. II, p. 169.

98 William Felkin, *Remarks upon the Importance of an Inquiry into the Amount and Appropriation of Wages by the Working Classes. Addressed to the Statistical Section of the British Association, Liverpool, 13 September, 1837*, London, 1837, p. 15.

99 William Felkin, *An Account of the Machine Wrought Hosiery Trade. Extent and Conditions of the Framework Knitters, Read in the Statistical Section of the Second York Meeting of the British Association, 18 September, 1844*, 2nd edition, London, 1845, p. 39.

it follows that no measure can effectually raise their earnings except by getting rid of that disproportion.[100]

Maxwell's bill for wage regulation in 1835 had been rejected. The possibility of wage regulation was not even considered by the Royal Commission which reported in 1841. Between these periods the weavers turned to the union. The *Weavers Journal* of 1836 argued that the union increased the value of labour and secured it against reductions. It advanced social and economic independence and protected the capital of the honourable employer. But the weavers' unions were generally short lived and died out in bad trade.[101] The Kilmarnock weavers despaired 'in our case so great a body cannot well unite in their defence – any upstart . . . can be the means of reducing wages and . . . compelling all others to follow'.[102] The Carlisle weavers concurred with this,[103] and Baird found the Glasgow unions to be very weak.[104] John Scott, a Salford weaver, reiterated the difficulties of the hand-loom weavers' circumstances – a large pool of labour that thwarted the success of any strike, and the scattered and isolated nature of the work which made communication and organisation difficult.[105] But the situation was not impossible in all places. The Paisley fancy weavers established a scale of prices in 1829 and maintained it for some time; their strikes were effective until the mid 1830s.[106] Such unionisation was not possible in places of specialised production.

From the point of view of many political economists, the weavers acted out the drama of the movement from workshop to capital and machinery based production. They were degenerating artisans, the 'poor outworkers', who became replaced by the factory hand. However, the economists' prediction was uncertain enough in these fragile years of change for the weavers to raise a powerful and impressive critique of machinery, a critique that carried a genuine belief that technical

100 *P.P.* 1841, x, 25, 124.
101 *The Weavers' Journal*, Glasgow, 1 March 1836.
102 Bowring, *Correspondence*, Letter IX, p. 12.
103 J. Barr, Secretary to the Carlisle Weavers' Commission, quoted in *P.P.* 1840, xxIV, R. M. Muggeridge's Report on the Condition of the Handloom Weavers of Lancashire etc., 594.
104 C. R. Baird, 'Observations on the Poorest Class of Operatives in Glasgow', *Journal of the Statistical Society of London*, I, 1838, 171.
105 *P.P.* 1840, xxIV, Report of Muggeridge, Assistant Commissioner, 599–600.
106 Bowring, *Correspondence*, pp. 17–20.

change was not a 'given' but could be tempered and directed to match the requirements of social ideals. This critique was all the more provocative for its 'exposure' of technical change, its attempt to find an underlying connection between the techniques of production and the total economy and society.

The weavers survived after the 1830s, not because they had managed to withstand the ideological barrage of the factory men, but because they were part of a system more complicated than that seen by the mill owner and economist. The weaver continued his domestic work, not in many cases because he wanted to, but because, as Peter Gaskell argued, factory work for the adult male was hard to obtain.[107] Small-scale industry continued, as Babbage pointed out, because it provided special conveniences to large-scale industry. It survived, too, because with every advance in technique manufacturers with inferior machinery sought some compensating mix of techniques.[108] Here the domestic worker had a very great advantage: he was cheap. The inevitability of the weaver's decline was not pre-determined. His sub-contracted labour was hardier and more efficient than was expected. It dragged on, as Landes points out, in those trades where the technological advantages of power machinery were small (as in certain types of weaving),[109] and it survived in symbiosis with the factory. The expansion of outwork in many other trades was integral to the process of technical change and industrialisation in the nineteenth century. The technological advance which bewitched the early nineteenth-century economist created more craft and traditionally organised industry than he and many present-day historians have cared to admit.

The condition of the handloom weavers impressed the middle classes as the most obvious case of suffering from industrialisation. Many industrialists and political economists used the condition of the weavers as a contrast to the superior standards of factory workers. They predicted all-encompassing benefit from industrialisation, and viewed the immobility of the weavers in face of the competition of the power loom as irrational. The policy controversy in the 1830s over the weavers did, however, bring some understanding of, if little action on, the ambivalent nature of economic transition. The weavers, however, were fitted all too easily into the philanthropic concerns of the middle

107 Peter Gaskell, *Artisans and Machinery*, London, 1836, p. 331.
108 Babbage, *Machinery and Manufactures*, pp. 183–6. Also see Twiss, *Two Lectures on Machinery*, p. 43.
109 Landes, *The Unbound Prometheus*, pp. 118–19.

Source: R. Seymour, *Heaven and Earth* (detail), 1830, reproduced by courtesy of the Trustees of British Museum.

classes for the 'poor'. At the disposal of the statistics societies and parliamentary commissions, they were investigated as the 'poor'. Great attention was paid to their morals, health, education and family life, and little to the organisation of their work and their wages. The weavers themselves consistently drew attention to piece rates, home competition, and the specific technical and market conditions for the introduction of power looms. They demanded a policy on technology. However, the middle classes were all too ready to have these difficulties which clouded 'improvement' shunted off into the 'problem of poverty'.

Policy debates on the weavers, unlike the debates on the export of machinery and the emigration of artisans, did not generate new and questioning attitudes. The export of machinery problem generated wide-ranging debate on all aspects of technical change. The exceptions it seemed to raise to generally accepted doctrines stimulated new ideas. The handloom weavers' proposals of a policy on technology did not stimulate much more than philanthropic concern. But the handloom weavers were an example to the middle classes of their own failure to bring harmony over the enduring issue of machinery and labour. During the Industrial Revolution, a period of rapid technical trans-formation, a central base for class struggle, was the very point of production. These debates have indicated how the weavers fought the dilution and mechanisation which took their craft and their jobs. It is little wonder that the middle classes looked to the political economist and to their scientific culture to enforce the inevitability and neutrality of their own threatened 'improvement'. The everyday struggle between master and worker over the very techniques of production was central to the formation of both middle-class and working-class consciousness during the first Industrial Revolution.

Tories

The handloom weavers' debates exposed a widespread reaction against machinery in society. This reaction was many sided. A staunchly Tory outlook spurned industrial society altogether. Radicals and workers, on the other hand, attributed poverty and unemployment to the machine in the hands of capitalist employers, but hoped to harness its benefits to themselves in a co-operative society. Finally, middle-class social reformers were stirred to investigate the recesses of poverty, and discovered the social effects of mechanisation. In the following three chapters I will analyse these three types of opposition to machinery, to be found in the upper classes, the radical working classes, and the reforming middle classes.

I will indicate the extent to which resistance to machinery was related to an opposition towards political economy in all three groups. The revulsion among Tories and radicals against the contemporary road to industrialisation was simultaneously a revulsion against the political economy which justified it. The response of the social reformers was to defend political economy by creating a separate field of inquiry for the social effects of industrialisation. In dealing with the 'Tory' outlook I will argue that, though individual responses among the Tories varied, the resistance to machinery was the unifying principle of their social and economic perspectives. This chapter will first survey the 'reviews' and other literature which expressed Tory opinion. It will then outline the various political sects within Toryism with their distinguishing characteristics: liberal Tories, country Tories, Young Englanders and Tory radicals. After this I will examine the common attitude among these Tories to social policy and the threat of revolution, and, finally, I will investigate Tory attitudes and actions which bore directly on the machinery question.

Tory social and political perspectives were brought to the governing classes by the Tory periodicals and by the romantic writers who inspired the reviewers. Journals such as the *Quarterly Review, Blackwood's Edinburgh Magazine, Fraser's Magazine, The British Critic,* and the *Oxford and Cambridge Review* acquired a large readership; the circulation of the *Quarterly* and *Blackwood's* reached 10,000 in the 1830s and this was rivalled by *Fraser's* in the 1840s.[1] Tory economic perspectives had a wider context in the literary and political writings which made up the Tory culture. Burke, Scott, Coleridge, Wordsworth and Southey inspired the intellectual outlook of the Tory reviewers, who showed a predilection for a paternalist and even feudal society, one that was hierarchic, authoritarian and organic, based on land and the church.[2]

The established, adaptable Toryism purveyed by writers in the *Quarterly Review* was increasingly challenged by new factions. The younger Tories behind *Blackwood's* and *Fraser's* conveyed the spirit of a rejuvenated, uncompromising Toryism far to the right of those who wrote for the *Quarterly Review.* They soon became the voice for the country party Tories. All the reviews commented extensively on economic issues and sported their own self-styled political economists. The *Quarterly Review* challenged the political economy endorsed by the *Edinburgh Review,* but did so largely on the basis of appeals to politics and emotion. Southey, for example, wrote : 'As for political economists, no words can express the thorough contempt which I feel for them.'[3] However, the *Quarterly* also published the work of main-line political economists who, though critical of Ricardian economics, evidently supported whig politics. These included Malthus, Senior, Whately, and Scrope. William Maginn was a major propagandist for *Fraser's Magazine. Blackwood's* gathered together what almost amounted to a school of anti-political economy : Sir Archibald Alison was its most prolific economic commentator, and Thomas De Quincey its most analytical economist. William Johnston, John Wilson, William

---

[1] David Roberts, 'The Social Conscience of Tory Periodicals', *Victorian Periodicals Newsletter,* x, no. 3, September 1977.
[2] *Ibid.*
[3] See F. W. Fetter, 'The Economic Articles in the *Quarterly Review* and their authors, 1809–1852', *Journal of Political Economy,* LXVI, February 1958.

Stevenson, David Robinson, and Edward Edwards provided the back-up in presenting the Tory readers of *Blackwood's* with a guide to the economic issues of the day.

This literature legitimated several different arms of Toryism in the early nineteenth century. The ascendancy of the liberal Tories after 1815 was complemented by the emergence of other groups – the country Tories, the Young Englanders and the Tory radicals. The so-called liberal Tories formed the faction which dominated economic policy during Lord Liverpool's administration between 1815 and 1830. This group took the line that the economy should not be allowed to regress, but they sought to keep economic growth within legitimate bounds, for they saw society in terms of a 'stationary, self-acting and unprogressive model whose beneficent workings would illuminate the wisdom and glory of the creator'. They accepted Ricardian economic theory because it justified their preference for inaction and passivity in matters of economic policy.[4]

The political and economic values of the liberal Tories were condemned by the country party men. Their arguments were presented with enthusiasm and wit. William Maginn wrote in *Fraser's* that the Tory leadership was losing its values – the values of a country, paternal Toryism.[5] David Robinson in *Blackwood's* denounced the 'degraded liberal Tory' who 'must servilely echo all the whig advances' and endorse a 'creed of national destruction'.[6] To the country party men the true Tory upheld the constitution and believed that stability was the virtue of monarchies:[7] he would have society remain aristocratic, community-spirited and religious. Yet he was now forced to live in a reality torn by the conflict of oligarchy against democracy, a reality increasingly individualistic, competitive, urban and irreligious.[8]

The liberal Tories could accept political economy, even the extremes of Ricardianism; the country Tories detested it. *Blackwood's* conveyed the frustration felt by Tories who complained that in the House of Commons the most decisive proofs were 'laughed down by the simple assertion – they are contrary to Political Economy'.[9] William Johnston

---

4 Hilton, *Corn, Cash, Commerce*, p. 312.
5 [William Maginn], 'The State and Prospects of Toryism', *Fraser's Magazine*, IX, January 1834, p. 25.
6 [David Robinson], 'Political Economy No. IV', *Blackwood's Magazine*, XXVII, January 1830, p. 41.
7 [Maginn], 'The State and Prospects of Toryism', p. 25.
8 Geoffrey Best, *Shaftesbury*, London, 1964, p. 83.
9 [Robinson], 'Political Economy No. I', *Blackwood's Magazine*, XXVI, September 1829, p. 510.

and John Wilson discussed the methods and conclusions of political economy :

> What do the economists here give us as their foundations? Instead of self evident truth, self evident fictions; instead of demonstration, confession of error. They disagree touching the meaning of terms, and admit that they call things what what they are not.[10]

> A history of the general laws of population would afford a rich treat to the lovers of the inconsistent, the contradictory and the irreconcilable.[11]

Between 1824 and 1826 William Stevenson and David Robinson wrote several articles on various theoretical and policy issues. The point of these was to show that political economy had made few advances since Adam Smith, that Ricardian theories were inconsistent, and that present economic policy was damaging to social harmony. William Stevenson denounced the social implications of the discipline : 'There is still wanting the clear and full evidence that Political Economy is not a cold, unfeeling and worldly science, and that the conclusions to which the science leads on the subject of the poor are the conclusions of comprehensive and enlightened benevolence.'[12]

Two other factions of Toryism developed in the 1830s and 1840s, and addressed themselves to the problems of urbanisation and industrialisation. Unlike the liberal Tories, neither the Young Englanders nor the Tory radicals were prepared passively to allow industrialisation to take its course. But they did not wish to escape into the old ways of country Toryism. The problems of the industrial cities, they believed, should not be left to mill owners and radical workers to solve by themselves. The two groups had a sense of mission to bring their Toryism to the towns. Disraeli voiced the doctrine of the rejuvenated Toryism of the Young Englanders. He seized on nostalgia for a feudal past and on a feeling of humane sympathy for the poor to forge a doctrine which claimed a place both for the industrial capitalist and for the people. The principal spokesman of Tory radicalism was Richard

10 [William Johnston], 'State and Prospects of the Country', *Blackwood's Magazine*, XXVI, September 1829, pp. 510, 513.

11 [John Wilson], 'The Factory System', *Blackwood's Magazine*, XXXIII, April 1833, Part I, p. 439.

12 [William Stevenson], 'The Political Economist', No. II, Part II, *Blackwood's Edinburgh Magazine*, XVI, July 1824.

Oastler, who took an overtly anti-capitalist line in his pursuit of an alliance between its two elements. Appealing to a working class whose political energies were still fluid, he found fertile soil in backward-looking sentiments and a yearning for the old deferential relationships: 'The Tory whose little world of rank and station was being overturned in the march of progress, and the Radical whom the march of progress had rendered desperately hungry, together looked to the past, to a half legendary paradise where there was no machinery, no Political Economy, no Huskisson and no Ure.'[13]

On the issue of social policy, liberal Toryism stood on a limb, opposed to the country party, the Young Englanders, and the Tory radicals. One of the most fundamental divisions between liberal Toryism and these other three strands of Toryism was on the question of social policy. The liberal Tories denied the efficacy of state intervention to help cushion the social disruption caused by industrialisation. The unresponsiveness of Lord Liverpool's government towards weavers' riots and the demands made by other workers for some assistance in overcoming the difficulties of technological unemployment has already been encountered. By contrast, other elements of Toryism constantly proclaimed their responsibilities to the poor. They argued furthermore that the hard-hearted policies of the liberal Tory administration and the similar strategies of the whigs were due to their endorsement of political economy.

Blackwood's condemned the economists for regarding the poor as animals: 'The working classes are set down as animated machines, from the use of which it is sound policy to draw the greatest amount of profit at the least cost.'[14]

Fraser's, responding to the Swing Riots, vigorously proclaimed the need for a rejuvenated social conscience, it argued that they were not caused by the march of education but by poverty. They had not been inspired by cheap tracts, but by poor fare, not by a deficiency of information, but by lack of employment and sufficient subsistence: 'The pauper is treated like a locomotive machine, as if he had neither feelings nor attachments, nor any sense of human life or animal indulgences.'[15] The proprietors of the soil in the southern and midland

---

13 Hill, *Toryism and the People*, p. 31.
14 [Edward Edwards], 'The Influence of Free Trade upon the Condition of the Labouring Classes', *Blackwood's Magazine*, XXVII, April 1830, p. 564.
15 [William Maginn], 'The Burnings in Kent and the State of the Labouring Classes', *Fraser's Magazine*, II, December 1830, p. 574.

counties were responsible. They had acted with total disregard to the condition of the people, and consequently the people had been driven to distraction.[16] It was an abiding principle of Tory paternalism to care for the poor : 'But the real friend of the industrious poor . . . will, as the first step to civilisation, morality and education, exert all his energy to give employment to the bulk of the people, and ensure an adequate reward for their labour.'[17]

The Young Englanders cemented to this principle their vision of social harmony among the industrial and rural classes. An effective social policy would join a philanthropic, paternal, mill-owning class to the rural aristocracy, and the nobility would be fused once again with the people. The wealthy would regain the confidence of the poor : they would recover the moral leadership they had lost and thereby reimpose their benevolent authority.[18] Disraeli used Egremont, the hero of the new Toryism in *Sybil*, to pronounce on his social programme :

> The new generation of the aristocracy of England are not tyrants, not oppressors, Sybil, as you persist in believing. Their intelligence, better than that, their hearts, are open to the responsibility of their position. But the work that is before them is no holiday work. It is not the fever of superficial impulses that can remove the deep fixed barriers of centuries of ignorance and crime. Enough that their sympathies are awakened; time and thought will bring the rest. They are the natural leaders of the people, Sybil; believe me, they are the only ones.[19]

The aristocracy would lead but it would bring the people with it.

> The mind of England is ever with the rising race. Trust me, it is with the people. I live among these men; I know their inmost souls . . . I know the principles which they have imbibed, and I know, however hindered by circumstances for the moment, those principles must bear their fruit. It will be a produce hostile to the oligarchical system. The future principle of English politics will not be a levelling principle, not a principle adverse to privileges, but favourable to their extension.

16 [Maginn], 'The Burnings in Kent', p. 574.
17 [Edwards], 'The Influence of Free Trade', p. 564.
18 L. Cazamian, *The Social Novel in England, 1830–1850* (1903), translated by Martin Fido, London, 1973, pp. 98–9.
19 Disraeli, *Sybil*, p. 282.

> It will seek to ensure equality, not by levelling the few, but by elevating the many.[20]

If fundamentally similar in a vital respect, the social perspectives of Tory radicalism went much further than those of either the country party or the Young Englanders. For in Tory radicalism ideas were linked to action. The agitation of Richard Oastler, Michael Sadler, J. R. Stephens and G. S. Bull helped to create the factory movement, the anti Poor Law protest and the controversy on the condition of the handloom weavers. Religious enthusiasm combined with radical militancy inspired a large number of followers to transform these campaigns into social movements, each of which was in turn a challenge to the policy prescriptions of political economy and its endorsement of the uncontrolled development of industry. The factory movement fought for restrictions on hours; the handloom weavers sought curbs on machinery and regulation of wages. Political economy propounded unrestrained labour markets and a 'natural' check to population increase. The campaigners against the new Poor Law wanted state intervention in order to care for and control the poor and unemployed. In each of these movements Tory radicals and their allies found themselves in collision with the doctrines of political economy.

These movements along with the political unrest of the 1830s in the Reform Bill and Chartist agitations impressed upon the Tories a sense of impending revolution. Only the Tory radicals believed that they could swim with and channel the revolutionary tide. Oastler, Sadler, Stephens and Bull swept ahead on a wave of discontent which their incendiary speeches, mass meetings and marches did much to inspire.

The other Tory groups, in contrast, were afraid. Carlyle defined the meaning of Chartism and the 'Condition of England Question': 'Chartism means the bitter discontent grown fierce and mad, the wrong condition therefore, or the wrong disposition, of the working classes of England.'[21] The Tory reviews did not attempt to conceal their fear of the urban working class and the rural poor. David Robinson set out the threat from the first in the 1820s.

> To look at all this and not to expect a fearful future is an impossibility. History shows that the fiend of revolution will walk the earth till the end of time, what country this fiend will next voyage, is not to be revealed by us; but we fear that

20 *Ibid.* p. 300.
21 Carlyle, 'Chartism'.

the things necessary for tempting it, and enabling it to triumph, will soon be far more abundant in our own than in any other.'[22]

Thomas De Quincey, writing in the 1830s, added to this the threat of the rural poor. He conveyed an ominous and pervasive sense of discontent: 'One voice is heard, too often not loud and clamorous, but deep and muttering, and pretty nearly the same emphatic words may be caught up by the attentive ear in every street and alley of our crowded towns – in every field and farmyard of our unhappy land.'[23] *Fraser's* echoed the sense of anarchy held by all branches of Toryism. By 1834 it could declare that reform had only kept the people in a 'state of delusive hope'. The application of the principles of political economy had entirely disrupted all social organisation.

> All the alarms of our situation in 1830 – quieted for a short
> period only – now revive in full force. Incendiarism reigns
> through half our counties – combination disorganizes our
> larger towns – all is perplexity, alarm and fearful foreboding.
> Nor is there hope behind, for the old Tory principles are
> banished, and the economists bear sway.[24]

It was this threat of revolution which inspired many of the benevolent sentiments among the Tories. Their fine pronouncements on social policy were not, however, followed up by concrete proposals.[25] Among the Tory reviewers philanthropic tendencies were confined to approving individual benevolence dispensed in small communities. Their dislike for a generalised philanthropy was combined with an implacable aversion to the growth of a centralised state. Their alarm at the New Poor Law arose rather from a dislike of the centralised organisation created by the Law than from disapproval of what it could do. They praised the social mission of the Church of England, but refused to entertain the projects of the Nonconformist sects. Ultimately, poverty

---

22 [David Robinson], 'Combinations' [of Workmen], *Blackwood's
   Edinburgh Magazine*, XVIII, October 1825, p. 478.
23 [Thomas De Quincey], 'The Prospects of Britain', *Blackwood's
   Edinburgh Magazine*, XXXI, April 1832, p. 587.
24 [Maginn], 'The State and Prospects of Toryism', p. 25.
25 See Jennifer Hart, 'Nineteenth Century Social Reform: A Tory
   Interpretation of History', in M. W. Flinn and T. C. Smout, eds.,
   Essays in Social History, Oxford, 1974.

did not disturb them as much as did heresy, centralisation and social conflict.[26]

Many of the Tory social prescriptions may have been disingenuous – provoked, as they were, by the need to check the threat of social revolution. But Tory economic and social perspectives had a more deep-seated foundation, an intense and ever present anti-industrial and anti-machinery sentiment. Behind all the divisions within Toryism in the period there was one common principle of unity over the machinery issue : none of the groups expressed enthusiasm over technical progress. Even the liberal Tories believed that such progress should be held within legitimate bounds. They expressed concern over the disruptive impact of mechanisation, though they were seldom prepared to do anything about it. Other Tory groups mounted a much more overt campaign against technical progress. The anti-political economy in reviews such as *Fraser's* and *Blackwood's* was the Tory theoretical attack on industrialisation and its social effects, and the Tory bias against the middle class was not just a matter of class antagonism, it was a deep protest against the whole mechanism of industrial society.[27]

This dissension from all that industrialisation meant found its literary expression in Southey and Carlyle, who in turn inspired the Tory anti-machinery economics of their time. Southey found Thomas More a convenient figure through whom to express his challenge to the facile belief in improvement. He provoked his readers : 'The spirit which built and endowed monasteries is gone. Are you one of those persons who thinks it has been superseded for the better by that which erects steam engines and cotton mills?'[28] He ascribed an apocalyptic significance to the machine.

> A new principle, . . . a novum organum has been introduced, . . . the most powerful that has ever been wielded by man. If it was first *Mitrum* that governed the world, and then *Nitrum*, both have had their day, . . . gunpowder as well as the triple crown. Steam will govern the world next, . . . and shake it too, before its empire is established.[29]

He goes so far in convincing his listener, the character Montesinos, that he too concedes the harmful implications of the machine :

26 Roberts, 'The Social Conscience', pp. 159–61.
27 Hill, *Toryism and the People*, pp. 11, 174.
28 Robert Southey, *Colloquies on Society* (1829), London, 1887, p. 158.
29 *Ibid.* pp. 198–9.

Steam has fearfully accelerated a process which was going on already, but too fast. Could I contemplate the subject without reference to that providence which brings about all things in its own good time, I should be tempted to think that the discovery of this mighty power had come to us, like the possession of a great and dangerous wealth to a giddy youth, before we knew how to employ it rightly.[30]

Carlyle proclaimed the mighty impact of the Industrial Revolution and all it brought in its wake :

But God said, let the iron missionaries be; and they were.
Coal and iron, so long close unregardful neighbours, are
wedded together; Birmingham and Wolverhampton and the
hundred Stygian forges, with their fire throats and never-resting
sledge-hammers, rose into day. Wet Manconium stretched out
her hand towards Carolina and the torrid zone, and plucked
cotton there; who could forbid her, that had the skill to weave
it ? Fish fled thereupon from the Mersey River, vexed with
innumerable keels. England, say, dug out her bitumen-fire,
and bade it work; towns rose, and steeple-chimneys; –
chartisms also, and parliaments they named Reformed.[31]

Carlyle, as we saw at the beginning of this book, extended his analysis of mechanisation from industry into politics and society. Men had grown mechanical in head and heart, and society was a new machine. It was 'by the mere condition of the machine, by pursuing it untouched, or else by restructuring it, and oiling it anew, that man's salvation as a social being . . . [was] to be ensured'.[32]

These attitudes pervaded country Tory opinion. For those such as the Reverend Thomas Mosley of the parish of Cholderton in Wiltshire, the factories were 'houses of bondage' and the steam engine 'a new and enormous calamity', one destructive of the 'moral units of society'.[33] Anti-industrial sentiments among the reviewers can be partly explained by their social backgrounds. In David Roberts's survey of the Tory reviewers, he found that all but two of the sixty-nine covered came from the upper classes and of these most had gone to university and had been

[30] *Ibid*. p. 201.
[31] Carlyle, 'Chartism', p. 311.
[32] Carlyle, 'Signs of the Times', p. 68.
[33] From the *British Critic*, 1840, cited in David Roberts, 'The Social Conscience', p. 159.

raised or educated in the countryside. The urban industrial situation was not one of which they had ever had much experience.[34]

General anti-machinery perspectives among Tories were also connected to particular arguments about specific events. Several of the Tory commentators explained the results of machinery with reference to the differing economic climates before and after the peace of 1815. While many technical improvements had been introduced during the Napoleonic Wars to compensate for a scarcity of labour, the peace brought a radically different situation. The time came when the government no longer needed the people's labour, yet there had been an increase in population. It was discovered during the war that machine labour was cheaper than that of men. Capitalists resorted to machinery and left the population idle.

The *Blackwood's* school of political economy offered its own analysis of technological improvement : 'never until now did human invention devise such expedients for dispensing with the labour of the poor; and the first and most important duty which the legislature could have entered upon, was to consider the means of remedying the evil, and alleviating the misery, which such a moral condition of society must occasion'.[35] The legislature, however, did not accept this Tory duty. The representatives of liberal Toryism stated their powerlessness before the inevitable mechanisation. After the rioting and machine breaking of 1826, Liverpool several times affirmed his belief in inaction : things must be allowed to take their course.

> Is not the *London Silk Manufacture* on the decline, and must not those engaged in it seek employment elsewhere? . . . There is no prospect of the hand-looms ever being able to compete again with the power-looms. This must throw an immense population out of employment, and be the cause of appalling distress, till the individuals interested shall have been dispersed and engaged in other pursuits.[36]

The benefits of a machine which had brought such unemployment in its wake were questionable and other Tories were more prepared to denounce machinery. William Johnston in *Blackwood's* declared it

> curious to find even the warmest panegyrists of all the effects of machinery admitting that some extraordinary new vent

34 Roberts, 'The Social Conscience', p. 164.
35 [Johnston], 'State and Prospects of the Country', p. 467.
36 Cited in Hilton, *Corn, Cash Commerce*, pp. 83–4.

for manufactures, some wonderful extension of trade is
necessary to prevent the country from sinking . . . where, then,
is the improvement? Of what advantage *to us* these prodigious
means of extending our manufactures without the aid of men,
when so many of our own population are thereby left to idleness
and starvation?[37]

Edward Edwards ascribed the 'condition of England' to 'mechanical
discoveries, by which the call for human labour is continually
abridged'.[38] In this condition England's lower orders, who had gone
'as low as tyranny can tread them down' were 'in many places as much
parts of machinery as are spindles. Thousands are but cogs.'[39] Peter
Gaskell, with all the empirical material he could draw to hand on the
weavers, rebuked those who maintained that the economising on human
labour was a blessing to the operative. They overlooked the fact that
the operative who could not dispose of his labour must perish, and
that every improvement in machines reduced the value of his subsistence.[40] Tories found their sharpest weapon against the new industrial
society in the many instances of technological unemployment occurring
in the period. And they generalised on the basis of this:

> Machinery which renders labour more productive is not a good,
> but a mighty evil, if it diminish employment. If it does this,
> it of necessity diminishes the means of subsistence. It takes
> from these means far more on the one hand by destroying work,
> causing a glut of labour, and lowering wages, than it adds
> to them on the other by reducing the prices of commodities.[41]

Tory commentators were interested not only in the impact of machinery on employment but also in its wider social effects – on the family
and on class structure. The Tory viewed the appearance of women and
children in the mills as anathema. Many were so ignorant of labour
conditions as to suppose that female and child employment was something new, while others disparaged its appearance outside the domestic
setting. *Blackwood's* responded to the invention by Roberts of the self-
acting mule with an analysis of the way in which it would reduce the
requirement for skilled and adult labour.

[37] [William Johnston], 'Domestic Policy, No. III : The Condition of the
Lower Orders', *Blackwood's Edinburgh Magazine*, xxvii, January 1830,
p. 92.
[38] [Edwards], 'The Influence of Free Trade', p. 582.
[39] [Wilson], 'The Factory System', p. 424.
[40] Peter Gaskell, *Artisans and Machinery*, London, 1836, p. 325.
[41] [Robinson], 'Political Economy No. ii', p. 681.

At present every improvement in machinery tends, and has
invariably tended, to the exclusion, more and more, of the
adults hands from operations which formerly could only be
managed by them, but now can be equally well attended to,
and at a much lower rate of wages, by children. The result
threatens to be their entire exclusion from manufacture . . .
accompanied as that is with the invention of more finished
machines for simplifying the processes of skilled labour, such
as the self-acting mule of De Jong and Roberts.[42]

Peter Gaskell took alarm at the prospects envisaged by Andrew Ure
and feared the disappearance of the valued artisan class in society. He
argued that mechanisation reduced the value of human labour, even
to the point of its destruction. The expectation of 'machines making
machines' led him to deplore the effect of mechanisation :

upon the higher qualities of the operative, namely his skill,
emulative pride, and respect for his own position . . . The
term artisan will shortly be a misnomer as applied to the
operative; he will no longer be a man proud of his skill and
ingenuity, and conscious that he is a valuable member of
society; he will have lost all free agency, and will be as much
a part of the machines around him as the wheels on cranks
which communicate motion.[43]

Gaskell's vision of the future picture of the fully mechanised
economy was a calamitous one : 'The time, indeed, appears rapidly
approaching, when the people, emphatically so called, and which have
hitherto been considered the sinews of a nation's strength, will be
even worse than useless; when the manufactures will be filled with
machinery, impelled by steam, so admirably constructed as to perform
all the processes required in them.'[44]

Such visions also inspired the Tory radicals to virulent polemics
against the machine. This 'Hydra of the present day' was also an 'insatiable Moloch' with a 'heart of steel, jaws as wide as the grave, teeth
of iron and claws of brass'. Its horrific presence was announced in glit-

---

42 [Alfred Mallalieu], 'The Cotton Manufactures and the Factory System',
    Part II, *Blackwood's Edinburgh Magazine*, XL, July 1836, p. 11.
43 Gaskell, *Artisans and Machinery*, pp. 355, 358.
44 *Ibid.* p. 361.

tering letters as 'Improvement'.[45] Tory radicals demanded the '*right* of the working classes to redress, protection and compensation on account of the increase of machinery'.[46] Tory radicals hoped to slow down the rate of mechanisation through such policies as the tax on machinery. The argument in favour of taxing the machine was based on the belief that there was unequal competition between capital and labour. It was argued that a heavy burden of indirect taxation hit the consumption patterns of the working class more than that of any other class :

> For there let machinery untaxed and free,
> Bear down their tax'd labour to such a degree,
> That all competition themselves to maintain;
> Would prove an attempt both ridiculous and vain.[47]

A tax on the machine was also the platform of some of the high Tories. Maginn deplored capitalist evasion of equal taxation :

> His living labourers were taxed tooth and nail, back and front, blood and sinews, bones and marrow ... But on the machine which superseded their labour, and converted them into paupers, there is no tax ... capital should be equally protected and equally taxed whether found in the ten fingers of the husbandman or artisan, or in the latest furnaces ... or the steam loom of the large capitalist.[48]

But the purpose of this demand was not just to seek more equitable income opportunities for the worker or even more equal technical prospects for hand processes. It was also linked to the Ten Hours Movement as a part of the strategy for curtailing the machine and destroying factory production. Factory reformers in Bradford and Glasgow announced that machinery was to be 'timed' or 'tax'd : chained by a direct tax on its use or an indirect tax on the period of using it'.[49]

---

45 Reported in *Voice of the West Riding*, vol. 1, no. 15, 14 September 1833, cited in John Halstead, 'Capital's Car', *Bulletin for the Society of Labour History*, Autumn 1976.
46 *The Advocate or Artisans' and Labourers' Friend*, No. 1, 16 February 1833.
47 *The Weavers' Complaint*, Keighley, 1834, p. 37.
48 [William Maginn], 'Machinery and the Manufacturing System', *Fraser's Magazine*, vol. 2, November 1830, pp. 425, 427.
49 See *Unrestrained Machinery Must Ere Long be the Ruin of the Country*, Bradford Broadside, 1834, and *Voice of the West Riding*, vol. 1, no. 15. 14 September 1833.

Lancashire factory reformers, declaring existing factory legislation to be useless because it was not enforced, turned their energy to directing the regulation to the machines rather than to the hands that operated them; in other words, to control the hours during which the engines might be run. Their slogan became 'Ten hours a day and restriction on motive power'.[50] The tax on the machine was the only Tory policy on machinery which gained any popular support in the period. A few half-hearted attempts to invent intermediate techniques were very short-lived. J. H. Sadler's pendulum loom was one which allegedly increased the productivity of the handloom weaver. It was said to be able to work silk, cotton, linen and wool, and to produce all textures and widths of cloth. One weaver could run two looms in his own home. The productivity of the hand weaver could thus be substantially increased, but the system still provided for much more employment than power loom weaving. It was also stated that this gave the handloom weaver a viable alternative to accepting the working conditions of factory life.[51]

Tories of all shades of opinion lamented the distortions produced by the machine on their image of the harmonious deferential, hierarchical, but philanthropic society : 'How strange that machinery should have an inverted and continually diverging effect on society, rendering the condition of those attendant upon it worse while others were reaping its amazing productiveness in pernicious luxury.'[52] This Tory prejudice in favour of a stable landed society undisturbed by the disruptive effects of steam power and machinery became another factor stimulating the intellectual and cultural offensive of political economy and middle-class ideologues. Political economists responded to this Tory critique of mechanisation by engaging in special pleading in favour of the advance of machinery and the industrial system. This was particularly evident in their dogmatic statements in the handloom weaver debates. But it was also evident in attacks by those such as McCulloch on programmes sometimes appealed to by Tories, for example, domestic industry. Political economists not only defended their views on technological progress from this Tory onslaught, but also sought to defend the existence of their discipline from the Tory anti-political economy of the period. This defence was especially evident among the early

---

[50] Cecil Driver, *Tory Radical, The Life of Richard Oastler*, New York, 1946, p. 149.

[51] Sadler, *The New Invention of Double and Quadruple or British National Looms*.

[52] Richard Oastler, 'Humanity Against Tyranny', cited in Driver, *Tory Radical*, p. 106.

Drummond Professors, and in particular Richard Whately who defended the compatibility between political economy and religion. Political economy was not just on the defensive against Tory critics. It also faced a barrage of criticism from radicals and the working class. The next chapter will turn to this radical critique.

12

Radicals

Question. *What is the effect of machinery?*
Answer. *To do that labour which must otherwise be done by hand, and to do it more perfectly and expeditiously.*
Question. *To whom then ought the machinery to belong?*
Answer. *To the men whose work it does – the labourers . . .*
Question. *Who are the inventors of machinery?*
Answer. *Almost universally the working men.*
Question. *But why do not the working men use machinery for themselves?*

No Answer!!![1]

The Tories who condemned the cold calculations of political economy and the dislocation produced by the machine were not alone in their protests. Radical thinkers and labour leaders proclaimed their own critique of political economy and their own hostility to the machine. In many ways they echoed the sentiments of the Tory reaction. Where political economy's analysis of poverty revolted the Tory social conscience, it appeared to radical critics to be a blatant apology for increasing inequality. Where Tories blamed the machine for rising unemployment and the disappearance of the skilled artisan, radicals saw it as a tool of industrial exploitation which ad brought only suffering to the poor. In fact, the Tory radical polemic against the capitalist industrial order can be seen directly to have inspired many strands of Owenite, trade unionist, and political radical thought in the years between 1820 and 1848.

1 *The Pioneer*, I, no. 4, 28 September 1833.

The last chapter indicated the way in which the Tory radicals had whipped up virulent polemics against the machine, describing it as the 'Hydra of the present day', or as the 'insatiable Moloch' named 'Improvement'.[2] But the Owenites could match the Tories in the extremity of their vituperation when they articulated their feelings about steam. *The New Moral World* described the steam engine as 'like a thing of life, a monstrous something that awakens in the imagination the might and vastness of pre-Adamite animals; *that* as though instinct with vitality works without pause unerringly on, an iron monster with a pulse of steam'.[3]

Tories found a cause in their anti-machinery opinions by contributing to the factory movement and the handloom weavers' controversy. Working-class radicals addressed themselves to the spontaneous events of workers' resistance to machinery: to such large-scale events as the weavers' riots of 1826 and the Swing Riots of 1830, and to smaller more localised day-to-day resistance to the machine in other branches of the textile industry and in the London trades. But the reaction of radicals to this spontaneous working-class activism was a complicated one. For, though they often joined the Tories in anti-machinery rhetoric, they also saw a positive side to the machine. Many of the radicals did not, therefore, enthusiastically endorse events of machine breaking. Rather, they explained working-class hatred for the machine in the terms of their own radical political economy of exploitation; and by taking appropriate measures they hoped to harness both the machine and working-class activism to the founding of a new society. Owenites and co-operators argued that if machinery was used in a co-operative social context it would be a benefit to man, since it would liberate him from labour. Political radicals conceived of great gains in productivity consequent on mechanisation, which needed only to be redistributed effectively to bring benefit to the working classes.

The differences of opinion among liberal and other Tories over the possibilities of stopping the machine were mirrored in the differences among radicals about the importance of the machine. Because they were participating in a very wide-ranging debate, the views of the radicals were complicated, and often apparently contradictory. Their response ranged from the straight anti-machinery rhetoric of Tory-radical journals such as *The Advocate*, *The British Labourers' Protector and Factory Child's Friend*, or *Voice of the West Riding* to Robert Owen's

[2] Reported in *Voice of the West Riding* (see chap. 11, note 45).
[3] *The New Moral World*, vol. v, no. 3, 18 May 1839, p. 470.

wondrous excitement over the machine. Not only was radical opinion diverse, but distinctions between positions taken up were by no means clear. Anti-machinery arguments often overlapped, even within the same journal or same radical speech, with positions in favour of the machine, as radicals tried to offer both a critique of the present society and an alternative for the new. This confusion of positions was also partly the result of the political and social character of the radical and working-class movements of the early nineteenth century. There was a mingling of the many movements for factory reform, trade unionism, Owenism, freedom of speech, workers' education and political reform. Cecil Driver has described the situation thus :

> Many a Northern operative professed to be a trade unionist, a radical, an Owenite co-operator, and a Ten Hours man all at the same time, actively serving (like John Doherty) in all four movements. There was thus a bewildering tendency for the various organisations to fade into one another : sometimes to vanish altogether and then reappear in another guise.[4]

In so far as movements and systems of ideas among these radical groups can be distinguished, it appears that Owenites and political radicals in particular tried to take up platforms on machinery which reflected the discernible differences in their wider political and social perspectives. This chapter will not deal with all radical movements of the period, but only with Owenism and political radicalism. Both groups disputed the uncompromising anti-machinery attitudes latent in the Tory-radical position and in much working-class radical thinking. Robert Owen and the early Owenites were very critical of the mechanisation around them, but they also offered a millennial vision of the transformation of the machine. They described at length the way in which machinery used in the context of the wage bond had degraded labour into a dispensable commodity. If extracted from the social arrangements in which it had been developed, however, technical progress could be adapted to the needs of co-operative production, and ways could be discovered of avoiding the minute division of labour.[5] Adopting quite another perspective, political radicals such as O'Brien,

---

4 Driver, *Tory Radical*, p. 261. Prothero also argues this in his *Artisans and Politics*. (This book, which also bears on other issues in this chapter, appeared after mine had gone to press.)

5 Owen, *A New View of Society*, pp. 12–13, 210, 211–15, 251; and *The Life of Robert Owen Written*; Harrison, *Robert Owen*; Hollis, *The Pauper Press*, p. 421.

Hetherington and Lovett were concerned to challenge all anti-machinery sentiments and to shift the interests of the working man away from machinery and production arrangements towards demands for political democratisation and changes in distribution.[6]

These two radical factions supported their particular positions by appealing to a radical or popular political economy whose concepts and terms of debate had become relatively commonplace in radical circles by the 1830s. The next section will outline the contents of this political economy, and examine the way in which the radical economists both presented a critique of political economy and had a positive perspective on the machine.

Popular political economy

Just as Tory opinion possessed its own school of anti-political economy in some of the ideologues of *Blackwood's* and *Fraser's*, radical thinkers espoused the doctrines of an alternative 'popular' or co-operative political economy.

Radical political economists rejected the economic theory of the middle-class establishment on several grounds. They argued that the economist should study not only the production but also the distribution of wealth. They rejected Malthusianism and all its implications, including doctrines that wages would always tend to a minimum because of workers' fecundity and that economic growth was determined by a strict division between wages and profits. They also dismissed contemporary views that the economy was self-regulating and stable, refusing to believe in Say's Law, that is, that supply could never exceed demand either because of overproduction or underconsumption. The purpose and definition of political economy should not, radicals contended, be confined to the narrow sphere of wealth and increasing wealth, but should concern itself with creating social happiness.

It was said that middle-class political economists had 'brought the subject into disrepute by siding with those who call themselves the ministers of Providence and who proclaim the doctrine that the poverty of the labourer is one of its dispensations'.[7] Radical political economists dismissed the view that the present social structure was a result of the laws of nature, that extremes of wealth and poverty were necessary to the functioning of the economic system. They went on to dismiss the 'laws' of political economy which were presented to the public as if

---

6 Hollis, *The Pauper Press*, p. 421.
7 Hodgkin, *Popular Political Economy*, pp. 226–7.

they were natural laws. As Thomas Hodgskin put it, 'The distress our people suffer . . . and the poverty we all complain of, is not caused by nature, but by some social institutions . . . I can never, therefore, join with those Political Economists, who seem ever to be fond of calumniating Nature in order to uphold our reverence for the institutions of man.'[8] They added to this that the assumptions of political economy were arbitrary, and its theories blatantly contradicted the facts. A genuine political economy would be based on a careful investigation of the facts. As J. F. Bray put it, 'A rigid comparison of theory with facts should be the first great object of the productive classes and a prelude to all demands for change.'[9]

Radical economists argued that labour was the source of all value, yet workers never received in their wages the full value they had produced. They received only a subsistence wage, and the surplus was taken from them by capitalists and landlords as profits and rent. Capitalists owned the tools and machinery which they put at the workers' disposal; landlords owned the land which they put at the disposal of farmers and farm labourers. Both used this monopoly position to extort from workers all the surplus value they produced above their own subsistence needs. Landlords and capitalists were defined in radical political economy as 'unproductive'. Unlike labour, they did not add to value; they merely took away from it. They were parasitic while labour was useful.[10] Radicals refused to entertain the proposition of establishment political economists that capitalists also added to value because they provided circulating capital and created fixed capital. Thomas Hodgskin built on the analyses and definitions of Smith, Ricardo, Malthus, McCulloch, Mill, Say, Garnier and Mrs Marcet to produce radically different theories of the sources of profit and of the significance of fixed capital. His labour theory of value was not 'Ricardian' but rather, as E. K. Hunt has demonstrated, a radical extension of Adam Smith's value theory.

> He believed that as long as existing ownership rights were maintained, prices would be the summation of wages, profits and rent. But he believed that profits and rent were morally and economically unjustifiable and that labour had a moral

8 *Ibid.* p. 267.
9 J. F. Bray, *Labour's Wrongs and Labour's Remedy: or the Age of Might and the Age of Right*, Leeds, 1839, chap. 13.
10 This theory was stated in its most systematic form in Hodgskin, *Labour Defended*, and Bray, *Labour's Wrongs and Labour's Remedy*.

right to all that it produced. In a future, ideal society when only labourers received the fruits of production, and in that society alone, would prices be determined only by the labour embodied in the production of commodities.[11]

Hodgskin called circulating capital a 'fiction'. Fixed capital was the stored-up skill of past labour. Capitalists, therefore, were merely middlemen, monopolists and parasites. The aristocracy had its parallel in the millocracy and the shopocracy.[12]

The true purpose of political economy, the basis of this analysis, should not be to analyse production, but distribution. The purpose of production in turn should not be profit but use. Some of the radicals, especially the Owenites, went on from there to challenge the competitive market basis of the economy. They challenged the assumption of establishment political economy that the market system assured that supply would always equal demand, and that competition would bring about stable economic growth. On the contrary, competition and mechanisation, both integral to industrial capitalism, created overproduction and underconsumption leading to a long-term trend towards crisis and depression. The Owenites argued that the only way out of such grim economic prospects was to replace a competitive society by a co-operative one and to bring the introduction of machinery under co-operative control as a measure for increasing leisure time, and not one for reducing wages and raising unemployment.[13]

The radical political economists produced alternative views of machinery to correspond with their principles of political economy. Hodgskin was as optimistic as many of the establishment economists he vilified. Like them, he rejected the imminence of the stationary state, claiming that 'the increase of knowledge and extended division of labour' would more than compensate for the decreasing fertility of the soil. He had a positive outlook on the introduction of machinery, and made much of his argument that the machine was an aggregation of skilled labour, and needed to be worked in conjunction with skilled labour. He went to lengths to dismiss the views of those such as Mill

---

11 E. K. Hunt, 'Value Theory in the Writings of the Classical Economists, Thomas Hodgskin and Karl Marx,' *History of Political Economy*, IX, 1977, p. 338.
12 Hodgskin, *Popular Political Economy*, pp. 254–5.
13 See Eileen Yeo, 'Social Science and Social Change', D.Phil. Thesis, University of Sussex, 1972, chap. 2, discusses this Owenite underconsumptionist theory. Stedman Jones, 'Class Struggle', discusses the limitations of this early radical economic theory.

and McCulloch that fixed capital and the capitalist were indispensable to production, claiming instead skilled labour for the key ingredient.[14] Hodgskin tried to refute the idea that capital was a separate factor of production by arguing that capital was merely 'so many different aspects of the process of labouring, of the relations among labourers, and the products of labour'.[15] 'Capital is a sort of cabalistic word, like Church or State, or any other of those general terms which are invented by those who fleece the rest of mankind to conceal the hand that shears them.'[16]

Two other radical economists, J. F. Bray and William Thompson, analysed machinery as a tool of capitalism, but also added that its very existence demanded a whole change in the nature of radical thought about future social relations. Bray concluded his analysis : 'So long as machinery is thus exclusively possessed by individuals and classes, its advantages will be partially enjoyed – it will be a curse rather than a blessing to those classes of the community by whom it is not possessed; for it dooms them to be the slaves and the prey of their fellows.'[17] William Thompson declared that the state of technology had undermined the possibility of any individualistic solution : 'it is impossible in the present state of improved machinery and complicated processes of industry, to award to any *individual* labourer the whole products of his labour, in as much as . . . it would be impossible to ascertain what those products are . . . Hence the imperative necessity of the Union of the Industrious, in large numbers.'[18]

The view of these radical economists that capital, especially fixed capital, had neither a special nor a natural role in the production process underlaid their challenge to the very existence of profits and capitalists. Their critique of establishment political economy opened the way for visions of a radical change in the existing distribution of income, and of the overturning of existing social relationships. Their critique challenged political economists to rearm – to reformulate their theories of profit, capital, and technological change. The formation of a political economy orientated around the role of capital was, as I have shown earlier, partly inspired by this early socialist critique of political economy. However, political economists were not responding simply to the threats

[14] [Hodgskin], *Labour Defended.*
[15] Hunt, 'Value Theory,' p. 343.
[16] [Hodgskin], *Labour Defended*, cited in Hunt, 'Value Theory', p. 343.
[17] Bray, *Labour's Wrongs and Labour's Remedy*, Leeds, 1839, p. 39.
[18] [William Thompson], *Labour Rewarded*, p. 115. Not one of these radicals commented on Ricardo's chapter on machinery.

of a few radical but isolated intellectuals. They were responding to the working-class movements of Owenism and political radicalism which had absorbed this 'popular' political economy. Hodgskin, Thompson and Bray may not have been, in themselves, a great national influence, but the doctrines of political economy which they systematised were widespread ones in the radical leadership. Behind such doctrines there were political movements, hence the concern of political economists to meet the challenge of their critics.

Furthermore, the doctrines of popular political economy and the politics of Owenism and political radicalism were not systematic. Many different groups of workers, artisans, and small shopkeepers could find something of appeal in such doctrines and politics. This was particularly the case in Owenism.

Owenites

A great deal has been written about Robert Owen and the Owenite movement, and this is not the place to retell their histories. However, it is important to reassert the significance of Owenism in spreading a radical economic theory. With an alternative economic theory, moreover, went a radical reassessment of machinery from the point of view of the working classes. Owenism attracted a widespread and very diverse following. There was something for the factory workers in Glasgow and Manchester, and for the artisans of Birmingham and London to be found in both the political economy and approach to machinery of the Owenite radicals. For, as E. P. Thompson has reminded us, the imprecision of Owenite theory allowed for the co-existence of different intellectual traditions, and its vision of an alternative society could be modified to suit very different industrial situations.[19]

It is not surprising then to find that the Owenites were deeply ambivalent towards the machine. They could equally whip up virulent anti-machinery polemics, and present a millennial vision of the machine harnessed to the needs of labour.

The Owenites, like the Tories, emphasised the adverse implications of the machine for skilled labour and for employment more generally. They too read the worst into Andrew Ure's panegyrics, bemoaning the prospects of 'steam engines made by machinery'. 'Not long surely will Birmingham and Sheffield boast of their ingenious artisans.'[20] The

[19] E. P. Thompson, *The Making of the English Working Class*, p. 875.
[20] *The New Moral World*, vol. II, no. 84, 4 June 1836, pp. 640–1.

New harmony – all owin' – no payin'. Source : (The Comic
Almanack for 1843), *Cruikshank Reflections; The Past and Present
in Merry Tales and Humorous Verse Illustrated by George
Cruikshank*, London, 1912.

Owenites feared technological unemployment and low wages : 'Let it
be remembered that the men which in its first application it throws out
of work are thrown out of that particular work not for a few weeks, or
months, or years, but for ever.'[21] Those displaced by machinery became
'scamping workmen', a pool of dishonourable casual labour that had
the effect of reducing wages in every trade.[22] Labour was the working
man's only commodity. Machinery depreciated the value of his labour
and placed him in the power of his oppressors.[23]

The Owenites also accepted the common Tory and radical apprehension of machinery's effect on the level of demand. Under consumption and overproduction were the twin horrors of mechanisation, and
their inevitable result was a 'reserve army of labour'. 'In this state of
things with the increase and increasing perfection of machinery and
a limited home consumption, there will obviously always remain a
redundant population which capital and competition may work with

21 *Ibid.* p. 255.
22 *The New Moral World*, vol. I, no. 22, 28 March 1835, p. 173; *Ibid.*
11 April 1835, p. 192.
23 *The Crisis*, vol. II, no. 12, 7 July 1832, p. 65.

as it wills.'[24] The machine was also connected with the scourge of competition. Competition was regarded both as 'the great evil resulting from machinery' and as the force driving the capitalist to cut costs by substituting machinery for labour : 'So long as the labouring classes allow their labour to be exposed to the wholesome breezes of competition . . . so long will they be victims of capitalists and machinery.'[25] Even those prepared to admit that machinery had created surplus wealth and saved labour were quick to add that 'it had never been the means of abating one hour of labour to the labourer'.[26]

The subject which perhaps raised the greatest feelings of ambivalence among the Owenites was the steam engine. It was, as stated already, 'a monstrous something that awakens in the imagination the might and vastness of pre-Adamite animals'. But it was also a god of the state of bliss :

> At length, casting away his guise of terror, this much cursed power revealed itself in its true form and looks to men. What graciousness was in its aspect, what benevolence, what music flowed from its lips : science was heard and the savage hearts of men were melted; the scabs fell from their eyes, a new life thrilled through their veins, their apprehensions were ennobled; and as science spoke, the multitude knelt in love and obedience.[27]

But equally the steam engine was responsible for two of machinery's most disagreeable effects. It provided the power to add to the 'duration of labour' and the oppression of the many so that the 'few by whom these powers had been engrossed could live in leisure and luxury'.

The steam engine also created the means for regular mechanical control. It subjected all in the mill to its power. It was the 'impartial arbiter'.[28] The piston of the steam engine became an image of the idolatry of political economy. The Owenites were also, however, capable of seeing the steam engine as an agent of co-operation. It would contribute to the decline of individualism and competition. They regarded it as one of those economic discoveries which would 'further advance that grand and growing CO-OPERATION', and abolish the very name of *Labourer*. This would be in the 'far time of the Millen-

---

24 *The New Moral World*, vol. IV, no. 167, 6 January 1838.
25 *The Crisis*, vol. III, no. 30, 22 March 1834, pp. 246–8.
26 *The New Moral World*, vol. III, no. 13, 20 May 1837, p. 240.
27 *Ibid.* vol. V, no. 20, 18 May 1839, p. 471.
28 *Ibid.* vol. IV, no. 208, 20 October 1838, p. 424.

nium', but even now there was something in 'promise and prospect'.[29]

When Owenites voiced an anti-machinery rhetoric it was usually on the issue of unemployment. A popular approach to the issue was to make quantitative projections on the number of men who could be replaced by any particular invention. However, their estimates revealed that the Owenites lacked any concept of labour productivity, and that they did not advance further than a static conception of the impact of new technology. Examples of such projections were those produced by *The Crisis* and *The Pioneer* pronouncing that the quantity of labour displaced by machinery was rising at the rate of ten per cent every ten years, and that inventions such as the circular screw driven by horse-power could do the work of 450 men.[30] *The New Moral World* surpassed most such estimates in its discovery of three new machines in Leeds – a felting machine, Halliley's cloth-raising machine, and the Lewis machine – which it claimed would supersede one hundred thousand labourers.[31]

However, this spectre of technological unemployment was regarded as a problem only for capitalist society. The Owenites rationalised the advantages of their proposed co-operative economic system with projections of ideal combinations of labour and leisure time. They argued that machinery would displace labour under any circumstances, socialist as well as capitalist. But whether the impact of such displacement of labour was negative or positive depended simply on social arrangements. Machinery used in the co-operative society would bring relief from labour without the poverty of technological unemployment.

> But now behold the effects of machinery in a co-operative
> community. They might have their cooking done by steam
> apparatus or machinery; washing might be done by machinery;
> house cleaning might be done by machinery; sawing, grinding,
> thrashing, ploughing, weaving, spinning, lighting, watering,
> and endless labours might be performed by machinery; *and
> the more machinery they might invent the more time they
> would have to spend in amusements, or to devote to literary
> and scientific acquirements.*[32]

The Owenite idea of the impact of new technology was a static one.

[29] *Ibid.*
[30] *The Pioneer*, vol. I, no. 3, 21 September 1833, p. 20.
[31] *The New Moral World*, vol. IV, no. 195, 21 July 1838.
[32] *Ibid.*

In speaking only of the displacement of labour which would lead in a capitalist society to unemployment and in a co-operative society to leisure, they did not face the implications of rising productivity and population. Owenism, in other words, did not provide the basis for a theory of economic growth. It provided the makings of a theory of how incomes at existing levels could be redistributed, and how labour too could be redistributed from man to machine.

The Owenites enthused about machinery, but they also examined the possibilities of alternative applications for technology in their everyday lives. These alternatives were for the most part concerned with the displacement of certain types of labour in order to open new opportunities or to increase leisure. The widespread application of machinery would, some argued, open new opportunities for women to free themselves from male bondage. Henry McCormac told the Belfast Mechanics Institute,

> Let not artificial restrictions exist to prevent women from enjoying that just equality from the other sex, to which by nature and by God's word, they are in everything entitled; nor let their inferior physical strength (which now that machinery has superseded labour can make no practical difference), the original source and only pretext for their degradation, any longer afford us an unmanly pretext for its continuance . . . Let them have the same liberty to go and come, with equal independence of each other and of the other sex.[33]

The Owenites even spoke of implementing their ideas on new applications for technology in their community experiments. They spoke of using steam in the kitchen to save the labour of women. In the Orbiston community outside Glasgow they made plans to bring up provisions from below 'by means of a machine called an elevator', and they proposed that 'clothes, shoes, etcetera would be cleaned by machinery'.[34]

Most of the existing Owenite communities were agrarian, but not necessarily by design, for there were also several plans for urban experiments. They did recommend mechanisation where possible in agri-

---

[33] Henry McCormac, *On the Best Means of Improving the Moral and Physical Conditions of the Working Classes, An Address to the Mechanics Institution, Belfast*, London 1830.

[34] *The New Moral World*, vol. IX, no. 22, 25 August 1838, p. 358; Garnett, *Co-operation*.

culture, acknowledging the usefulness of threshing and reaping machines to their communities. The Queenswood settlement even erected a small steam engine to pump water for Harmony Hall. The Owenites were also keen to apply advanced scientific methods to agricultural cultivation. But here their approach to technology differed from that of their more usual discussion of machinery and labour displacement. For the technique which they chose to champion was the new 'science' of spade husbandry. This technique did not displace labour, it was instead a labour-intensive technique, using a more primitive tool. Spade husbandry illustrated the ideas latent in Owenism of using more primitive techniques as a type of 'alternative' or 'intermediate' technology which would increase employment. But the Owenites also argued that spade husbandry or intensive agriculture was, in certain cases, a more superior technique than ploughing. They argued that it actually increased agricultural productivity by loosening the subsoil, while the plough hardened it. The issue of spade husbandry challenged Owenites to extend their discussion of technology beyond issues of labour displacement into the consideration of productivity. The spade was soon venerated by the Owenites, just as the steam engine was by the middle classes: 'The introduction of the spade, with the scientific arrangements which it requires will produce far greater improvements in agriculture than the steam engine has produced in manufactures.'[35] However, the Owenites did not get very far with experimenting with this technology: spade husbandry was only introduced at the Queenswood community and the experiment was too short to assess.[36]

The case of spade husbandry illustrated one of the rare attempts of Owenites to assess the productivity potential of the techniques they proposed to employ. Such a connection between using advanced techniques and raising the productivity of a co-operative community was not widely discussed, for most Owenite plans were too vague to go this far. But there was one piece of practical Owenite planning which celebrated science, the machine and workshop organisation as methods of raising community productivity. This remarkable piece of Owenite planning was William Thompson's *Practical Directions for the Speedy and Economical Establishment of Communities*. This, unlike most Owenite propaganda, contained sensible, informed and detailed suggestions as to how a community should be run. Thompson's discussion

---

[35] *The Economist*, vol. I, no. 16, 12 May 1821, p. 253; *The New Moral World*, vol. I, no. 44, 29 August 1835, p. 351.

[36] Garnett, *Co-operation*, p. 195.

of agriculture contained detailed treatment of crop management and forward-looking suggestions on irrigation and fertilisation. However, he did express a preference for hand cultivation 'in order to promote the health of the community'. But in his discussion of manufacture he was uncompromising in his support for mechanisation and the most advanced methods, even detailing after the manner of the management manuals of the day the best ways of arranging machinery for maximum speed of production. His discussion of power included information of various types of recent engines and their comparative costs, but also looked ahead to the tapping of other sources of power : 'by the production and combustion of gas', 'by a cheap mode of decomposing water', or 'the use of dams and reservoirs'.[37]

The anti-machinery argument of greatest interest to Owenites was, as I have stated before, the connection between machinery and unemployment. But another issue which they persistently took up was the question of skill. For they found their supporters not only in the Manchester and Glasgow factory districts, but in the Birmingham and London trades. In confronting the transformation of the trades, they analysed not just the labour displaced by machinery, but the skills which were cast aside. Andrew Ure's *Philosophy of Manufactures* and Edward Baines's *History of the Cotton Manufacture of Great Britain* revealed to them the view that 'every kind of operation in hardwares or softwares, metal, wood or plastered clay which can be reduced to a series of regularly repeated actions, *ought* to be performed by machinery'. Ure blatantly asserted that the purpose of such division of labour complemented by mechanisation was 'order produced among the industrious classes, by rendering their labour no longer necessary'. *The New Moral World* reported the acrid analysis : 'If the value of human labour be reduced, the benefit must, says the intrepid Doctor, be grasped by the *masters*, who secure it – by substituting the industry of *Women and Children* for that of men, or that of ordinary labourers, for "skilled artisans". Bitter but true satire on our existing commercial and social arrangements.'[38] The Owenites thus discovered the other face of machinery. It displaced the very labour which required skill and which might thereby be meaningful work.

Complementary with this analysis of machinery was an analogous objection to the division of labour. The Owenites challenged the

---

[37] William Thompson, *Practical Directions for the Speedy and Economical Establishment of Communities*, London, 1830, pp. 136, 156, 162, 164.
[38] *The New Moral World*, vol. II, no. 84, 4 June 1836, pp. 640–1.

alienation it left. They related Adam Smith's analysis of the division of labour's potential for raising productivity to a special historical situation of labour scarcity. Science and machinery, they argued, were capable of taking over the differentiated tasks created by the division of labour, so that it was no longer necessary to subject man to its effects, which would only deteriorate his 'mental and physical faculties'.[39] The co-operative communities of the Owenites would reconstitute this fragmentation. In their workshops the labourer would not be compelled to continue his work in any branch after the sensation of weariness or dislike : 'The varied mechanical requirements of each would enable them to change their occupations at will, without the slightest interference with the interests of the community.'[40] However, the Owenites never mentioned Adam Smith's own critique of the division of labour. Neither did they add to the economic and social analysis which Smith had set out in such comprehensive terms over forty years earlier. The Owenite analysis did not extend to the authoritarian dimensions of the division of labour. It made no comment on decision making within the production process, or even on systems of norms or penalties within which production in the community was to function. It saw the division of labour as a psychological issue not a political one.

In the end one can actually conclude very little from the Owenite critique of machinery. Though it raised a whole series of interesting issues, the alternatives offered were discussed in only the vaguest of terms. Such detailed programmes as William Thompson's in fact adopted the common radical platform of promoting the most advanced techniques for the community. In an Owenite communitarianism which was characterised by rhetoric and vision, there was in fact little discussion of how the actual experience of work would differ from that in the old society.

The co-operative movement which originated in a branch of Owenism and later acquired an independent existence was much more practical in its outlook than the communitarian form of Owenism. Did this succeed in pushing beyond the limits of Owenite communitarianism to dissect the processes of production in capitalist and co-operative societies? The original interests of both movements were similar : to challenge the divisions of labour and mechanisation and to found actual communities. George Mudie, with the backing of the Co-operative and

39 *The New Moral World*, vol. II, no. 114, 2 January 1836, p. 75.
40 *The New Moral World*, vol. II, no. 83, 28 May 1836, p. 247.

Economical Society and his journal *The Economist*, was one of the earliest co-operators to counsel working men to surmount the difficulties they encountered from competition and the excessive division of labour by making and controlling their own production arrangements.[41] Later Owenites were anticipated by the Edinburgh Practical Society's dilemma that the 'rational effects' of the use of machinery conflicted with its natural effects under the present system.[42] The co-operators soon abandoned their communitarian goals for the more immediate and attainable one of producer and consumer co-operatives in their own urban environments. It was claimed that by 1831 over 300 such societies had sprung up in Derby, Birmingham, Glasgow, Leicester, Yorkshire, the Potteries, London and elsewhere. With their own tools and materials, and without employers, workmen produced shoes, stockings, tinware, brushes, razors, files, cutlery, beaver hats, cloth and garments.[43]

But the co-operators, though practical and even fairly successful in their own industrial undertakings, at least for a time, did not in the final reckoning challenge the existing techniques of production. Their products were artisanal ones and their co-operatives appeared only in those occupations requiring neither large capital investment nor more than minimal machinery. Machinery never became a theoretical problem in the co-operators' alternative vision of a society primarily because it had never been a practical problem in the functioning of their co-operatives.

Political radicalism

Political radicals and trade unionists also grappled with the machinery issue. Many of them disclaimed views that machinery was the source of political and economic oppression. In *The Voice of the People* Doherty carried on a long dispute with W. R. Greg on the impact of labour-saving machinery. He argued it was wrong for workmen to

[41] Harrison, *Robert Owen and the Owenites,* pp. 108, 198; Sidney Pollard, 'Nineteenth Century Co-operation: from Community Building to Shopkeeping', in Asa Briggs and John Saville, eds., *Essays in Labour History,* London, 1967, p. 79; *The Economist,* vol. I, no. 6, 3 March 1821, p. 81.

[42] *Second Report of the Economical Committee of the Practical Society,* 13 February 1822, Edinburgh, 1822.

[43] Harrison, *Robert Owen and the Owenites,* p. 199; also see Pollard, 'Nineteenth Century Co-operation', who argues that after the rapid spread of the movement in 1830–1, there were up to 500 societies in existence.

oppose the new machines. They should, rather, unite to ensure for themselves a full share of the products of technical progress.[44] The *Official Gazette of the Trades Union* discussed machinery at some length, but took the line that the division of labour and mechanisation were autonomous forces out with social relations. As the *Pioneer* so fittingly put the view, knowledge and machinery were 'like manure'. It suffered to 'lie in idle heaps', they bred 'stink and vermin'. If 'properly diffused they vivified and fertilised'.[45]

This line of argument was to become the dominant one in the platforms of those political radicals who deprecated all visionary communitarian strategies as premature. Appointing as their first objectives the attainment of political power by all working men and the redistribution of property, they regarded the Machinery Question as an issue of secondary importance. But they were forced constantly to confront the issue in order to divert working-class antagonism away from the machine to the political system. Though they understood the workers' hatred of machinery, they tried to harness this to their own course of political radicalism. As O'Brien, a radical economic theorist, put it, displaced artisans blamed 'the inanimate, unthinking machine instead of the Machiavellian spirit which controls its operation'.[46] Engaging with anti-machinery advocates on issues such as the taxation of machinery, the use of steam presses in radical publications, and the restriction of machinery in weaving, they deployed a London radical style, invoking all the terms and concepts of the republican tradition in their support. A good example is provided by Lovett and Hetherington at a political meeting in 1830, where they attacked the notion of a tax on machinery. Interestingly, they made use of very traditional radical language, combining gibes against religion with ridicule of the idea of taxing the machine. Lovett, first on the platform, declared:

> Instead of praying them to tax – in fact instead of praying
> at all – (applause and laughter) . . . let us . . . say 'You have
> constituted yourselves our rulers, we have created all the
> wealth by which you are surrounded, and if any are entitled to
> it, above the rest it must surely be those who produce it'
> (Hear and Applause).

[44] R. G. Kirby and A. E. Musson, *The Voice of the People, John Doherty*, p. 219.
[45] Cited in *Poor Man's Guardian*, vol. III, no. 15, 1 June 1834, p. 146.
[46] *The Poor Man's Guardian*, vol. III, no. 222, 5 September 1835, p. 655.

He was soon followed on the platform by Hetherington who joked on Lovett's behalf :

> His friend [Mr Lovett] seemed to have a great aversion for
> praying. He [Mr Hetherington] had not quite so much, for he
> had heard that praying was in some places done by machinery.
> They would soon hear, he supposed, of cast-iron parsons,
> preaching by steam. He had heard of a heathen tribe, who
> prayed by machinery. They put their prayers into the machine,
> and then sat around if smoking and regaling themselves. He
> should like such machinery, and such praying, too, as this.
> But to the point : if machinery were taxed, would it give more
> employment to the working classes ? Who would have to pay
> the tax ? The consumers. [Hear.][47]

Cobbett availed himself of a similar combination of demands and phraseology in harnessing his usual old corruption polemic against taxation to dispel resistance to machinery. In his correspondence with the *Guardian* in 1832, he contended that in America there was no complaint against machinery, 'but there were no taxes levied against the people . . . no taxed master raising produce to sell in an untaxed country'. He put it that they should 'try what could be done for them by taking off the taxes before they either taxed or broke the machines'.[48] O'Brien and Hetherington continued in such a vein in their *Guardian* editorials on the weavers' anti-machinery position :

> It is curious to observe how cautiously men of Mr. Burges'
> kidney avoid touching the sore parts of society. They will talk
> of currency, machines, taxes, corn laws, anything in short, but
> the real grievance, which is neither more nor less than the
> subjection of the labouring to the monied classes, in conse-
> quence of the latter having usurped the exclusive making of
> the laws. Rents, tithes, taxes, tolls, but above all profits; here
> is our distress explained in five words, or to comprise all in one,
> it lies in the word ROBBERY . . . Machines indeed.[49]

Political radicals hoped for success in their efforts to stamp out the anti-machinery prejudice by combining their novel demands and

---

[47] *Magazine of Useful Knowledge, Co-operative Miscellany*, London, 30 October 1830.
[48] *Poor Man's Advocate*, no. 24, 1832, p. 2.
[49] *Poor Man's Guardian*, vol. III, no. 227, 10 October 1835, p. 697.

analysis with the traditional concepts and radical programmes long familiar to workers' movements. Their efforts included the printing of long debates on the weavers between the political economist George Poulett Scrope and 'Jeremiah Dewhirst' (the pseudonym of Richard Oastler) and engaging in correspondence on their own account with the anti-machinery advocate George Burges.[50]

They also found themselves engaged in controversy of rather more immediate personal relevance. This was a long dispute with certain members of the National Union of the Working Classes over the use of mechanical and steam-powered printing presses in the production of radical journals. Hetherington and O'Brien, proprietor and editor respectively of the *Poor Man's Guardian*, did use mechanical presses and were forced to defend this.[51] In doing so they gave support to the introduction of any form of machinery, but denied that they had done or would introduce steam-powered presses. For all their rhetoric in accepting the machine but changing political arrangements, they were very confused over their response to steam power. And their confusion was noticed by at least one member of the National Union of the Working Classes who caustically urged them to make up their minds : 'Either machinery is necessary for our cause, or it is not. If it is, use all you can that our victory may be speedy; for remember that we starve while you write.'[52]

The radical dilemma between condemning machinery or adapting to its powers continued well into the 1840s, despite the efforts of political radicals to dispel the issue. Chartism, in all its diversity, contained a distinctive anti-machinery attitude and rhetoric. Elements among the Chartist leadership were well known for their anti-machinery prejudices and they certainly struck a sympathetic chord among their many followers. Feargus O'Connor, for one, saw a return to the land as a way of countering the dominance of the machine, claiming 'machinery had hitherto had the same effect on operatives as the railway had had on horses sold to the knackers for their flesh'.[53] He regarded agriculture as the 'natural employment of man' in contrast to the 'artificial labour' in 'the manufacturing halls with their long chim-

---

50 *Poor Man's Guardian*, vol. III, no. 220, 22 August 1835, pp. 640–1.
51 *Poor Man's Guardian*, vol. II, no. 97, 13 April 1833, pp. 113–15; *ibid.* vol. II, no. 99, 27 April 1833, pp. 134–5. For Bronterre O'Brien's views on machinery also see Alfred Plummer, *Bronterre, A Political Biography of Bronterre O'Brien, 1804–1864*, London, 1971, p. 87.
52 *Poor Man's Guardian*, vol. II, no. 31, 16 January 1831.
53 J. T. Ward, *Chartism*, London, 1973, p. 170.

neys'.[54] O'Connor soon found a programme for these opinions in his back-to-the-land movement which expressed his passionate dislike of the technological innovations of the Industrial Revolution.[55] Yet he also saw in the ultimate 'restoration of the land to its natural legitimate and original purposes' the 'only means of making machinery and all other national improvements and properties man's holiday instead of man's curse'.[56]

Machinery was also an issue in the *Northern Liberator*'s 'Political Pilgrim's Progress'. This adaptation of Bunyan to Chartist purposes followed the trials and tribulations of a pilgrim baptised 'Radical' in passing by all the temptations of deviation from true Chartism. In one episode, on arriving in the City of Plunder, he came upon an area called 'Quack Quadrant' where a group of projectors were experimenting with a design for renovating the species. Their scheme was based on mechanical improvements. They intended to set carriages to run on the level plains, to carry the rich at thirty miles per hour and to gratify and 'ameliorate' the poor by allowing them to look at the wonderful exhibition. Its advantages were to be that 'such a vast improvement' would fill the bellies, clothe the backs of, and shelter the millions, without any assistance, either from themselves or anyone else. 'Radical' and his companion 'Common-sense' were solicited by some of the projectors to get into some of the sliding machines. But, needless to say, they positively refused.[57]

The general strike of 1842 saw a refurbishing of anti-machinery arguments. In certain areas the argument was heard that the distress was due to the misapplication of machinery. Cooke Taylor in his tour of the manufacturing districts noticed how the block printers and hand-loom weavers of northeast Lancashire were all Chartists, but with a difference. For they united with their Chartism a hatred of machinery not necessarily shared by factory operatives. The distress of 1842 even provoked John Doherty to bitter denunciation of machinery. Though he had consistently opposed anti-machinery arguments throughout the 1820s and 1830s, the terrible distress of 1842 induced him to condemn the speed up of machinery and to sympathise with the factory children

---

54 Feargus O'Connor, 'A Treatise on Labour', *The Labourer*, III, London, 1848, p. 289.
55 McAskill, 'The Chartist Land Plan'.
56 Feargus O'Connor, 'The Land and the Charter', *The Labourer*, I, London, 1847, p. 82.
57 *The Political Pilgrim's Progress*, Newcastle upon Tyne, 1839, (originally published in the *Northern Liberator*).

'who were forced to keep pace with the monstrous power of machinery, whether it travelled ten, twenty, thirty, or even forty miles per day'. He even came to advocate compensation for cotton spinners cast off by mechanisation.[58]

Anti-machinery and co-operative programmes continued beyond this in radical thought, but they were diverted into other projects such as Feargus O'Connor's back-to-the-land movement, or the co-operative factories which were set up among the Coventry ribbon weavers and discussed in the writings of William Bray. The attempts of the political radicals to divert attention away from the machine were, however, ultimately successful. Perspectives stressing the prior importance of political power and changes in distribution soon came not only to dominate the thinking of the Chartist leadership but also to submerge any discussion of changing the nature and organisation of production. With this, the machinery question receded along with the demise of Owenite social perspectives and the phase of general unionism and co-operation. It retreated after the defeat of the anti-Poor-Law arm of Chartism. Some of the radicals of this period came later in life to develop very uncritical perspectives on machinery. Lovett, by the time he came to write his autobiography in 1876, recollected the 'errors' of his earlier views: 'I was one who accepted this grand idea of machinery working for the benefits of all, without considering that those powers and inventions have been chiefly called forth, and industriously and efficiently applied by the stimulus our industrial system has afforded.'[59]

The machinery question receded from the central place it had held in radical ideology from the time of Robert Owen's early writings before the end of the Napoleonic Wars until the latter part of the 1840s. Yet, for over a thirty-year period, it was a contentious and unresolved issue of radical thought. However much variety there was to be found in radical opinions on machinery, there was an all pervasive resistance to

---

[58] See W. Cooke Taylor, *Tour of the Manufacturing Districts*, London, 1842, p. 121; and Kirby and Musson, *The Voice of the People*, pp. 44, 112, 313.

[59] *Life and Struggles of William Lovett* (1876), London, 1976, p. 46. Lovett even came to join forces with William Ellis, a populariser of political economy, in introducing classical political economy into the curriculum of certain elementary schools. He was followed in turn by George Jacob Holyoake and Henry Solly who helped to publicise Mill's economic doctrines among working men. See N. B. de Marchi, 'John Stuart Mill and the Development of English Economic Thought: A Study in the Progress of Ricardian Orthodoxy' (PhD Thesis, Australian National University), pp. 144–9.

the continued development of the economy and technology on its existing course.

The severity and persistence of this social dissension with the mechanisms and results of industrialisation among the highest and lowest classes of society also produced questioning and doubt in the middle classes. The energy directed by certain middle-class groups towards social reform policies cannot be separated from this unceasing outraged objection to the distresses of the new industrial system.

Social reformers

The critique of political economy among Tory and radical writers went with a challenge to the process of industrialisation. The persistence of this disturbing and unharmonious reaction evoked two main types of response among the middle classes, the first of which was to look to political economy for intellectual guidance and reassurance, and the second to recognise the significance of the challenge by calling for social reform. I have shown how political economists themselves responded to this need. But the truths of political economy were also marshalled and dispensed in a popular form for an avid middle-class audience, and for the not so avid upper- and lower-class heretics who needed to be converted.

R. K. Webb in his *The British Working Class Reader 1790–1848* has gathered and summarised many of the tracts of popular economics relating to agricultural riots and machinery, the New Poor Law, and trade unions. He describes how political economy became a potent doctrine in the hands of its popularisers by constantly conveying in a simplified form six principal points. The first was a mechanistic view of political economy which presented abstractions like 'labour' and 'capital' without human or social dimensions. The second was a central concern with problems of production and with disseminating the view of the absolute benefits of machinery. The third was freedom of all markets. The fourth and the fifth were the Malthusian population principle and the 'iron law' of wages, that wages were paid out of a fixed fund. The last was class harmony between middle and working classes in order to forward the accumulation of capital. With this went the view that the middle classes supplied this capital, and therefore had a fundamental control of economic development of society. This was a political economy which could explain the triumph of British industry and its international economic supremacy.[1]

Popular political economy acquired its own institution of dissemination in the Society for the Diffusion of Useful Knowledge, which was set up by a number of the founders of the Mechanics Institute Movement. The purpose of this society was to publish cheap editions and pamphlets and to solicit popular or simplified texts on various subjects in the sciences, political economy, history and literature, for the consumption of working-class audiences. The popular presentation of economic doctrine had first been attempted in James Mill's *Elements of Political Economy* and J. R. McCulloch's *Principles of Political Economy*.[2] The attempt by James Mill to write a 'school-book' on political economy was not successful in terms of its popularity. The *Westminster Review* recommended that the *Elements* be read as Euclid and not as a novel. And McCulloch commented that 'it is of too abstract a character to be either popular or of much utility'.[3] These popularisations by Mill and McCulloch soon found a counterpart in the tales on political economy for the edification of women and children written by Jane Marcet.[4] The Society for the Diffusion of Useful Knowledge marked a new development, for it was interested in texts in political economy for the working classes. Most of its first efforts were pamphlets addressed to particular problems or events. The agricultural riots were the first major situation of this kind after the foundation of the Society, and one of the initial productions on political economy printed by the Society was a response to these riots. The Society first attempted to reprint an abridged version of Cobbett's 'Letter to the Luddites' of 1816,[5] where Cobbett had defended the use of machinery and explained distress by taxation, the debt, and the church. But Cobbett would not allow an abridged version, so the Society printed Brougham's quickly

[1] Webb, *The British Working Class Reader*, pp. 98, 99.
[2] James Mill, *Elements of Political Economy*, London, 1821; McCulloch, *Principles*.
[3] Cited in James Mill, *Selected Economic Writings*, ed., D. N. Winch, London, 1966, p. 188.
[4] Jane Marcet, *Conversations in Political Economy*, London, 1816.
[5] This was the same pamphlet criticised in 1822 by Ricardo for its views on machinery. The fact that the S.D.U.K. had considered republishing it saved Cobbett in 1831 from imprisonment or exile after he was tried for inciting the agricultural labourers.

written 'An Address to the Labourers on the Subject of Destroying Machinery'.[6] This was soon followed by Charles Knight's longer but not so popular tracts, *The Rights of Industry* and *The Results of Machinery*.[7] *The Results of Machinery* attempted to establish the inevitability of machinery by pointing out its uses and benefits in many different industrial processes.

Such apologetic tracts had their companions in the nauseating didactic tales of Harriet Martineau, who made machinery the subject of two of her stories, one of them in *Illustrations of Political Economy*. *The Rioters*, which she wrote in 1827, was suggested by an account in *The Globe* about some machine breaking. She expounded her views more fully in *The Hill and the Valley*, the second instalment of *Illustrations of Political Economy* (first edition, 1832). She chose an iron foundry as the site for an instance of the substitution of machinery for manual labour. Strikes and machine breaking followed, bringing on the ultimate closure of the works. Martineau has her manufacturer hero finish with a long and turgid sermon to his workers on the benefits of machinery:

> Labour is saved by machinery, when a machine either does what
> a man cannot do so well, or when it does in a shorter time, or
> at less expense the work which man can do equally well in other
> respects. This last was the case with our new machinery. It
> did not like the furnaces and rollers, do what man could not
> do; but it did in a quicker and cheaper manner what man had
> hitherto done. It was a saving of labour; and as all saving
> of labour is a good thing, our machinery was a good thing.[8]

But even more interesting was the popular writing of established political economists such as Richard Whately. He combined his clerical duties with the propagation of his 'sound' views on political economy by publishing *A Letter to his Parishioners on the Disturbances which have lately Occurred* in 1830 and *Village Conversations in Hard Times* in 1831. These tracts pointed out the fallacies of destroying machinery, of equal division of property, and of ascribing low wages to high rents

---

6 See *A Full and Accurate Report of the Trial of William Cobbett Esq.*, London, 1831.
7 Charles Knight, *The Rights of Industry*, London, 1831, *The Results of Machinery*, London, 1831.
8 Harriet Martineau, *The Hill and the Valley, Illustrations of Political Economy* (1832), No. II, 4th edition, London, 1833, p. 128.

and tithes.[9] Whately encouraged others to take up such popular writing, pronouncing in his Oxford *Lectures* :

> There are some very simple but important truths belonging to the science we are now engaged in, which might with the utmost facility be brought down to the capacity of a child, and which, it is not too much to say, the Lower Orders cannot even safely be left ignorant of . . . Much of that kind of knowledge to which I have been alluding, might easily be embodied, in an intelligible and interesting form, not merely in regular didactic treatises, but in compilations of history, or of travels, or in works of fiction, which would afford amusement as well as instruction.[10]

Whately himself tried such ways of introducing political economy to children and the poor in an anonymous series in the *Saturday Magazine* in 1833.[11]

Another major middle-class response was the movement for social reform which started in the 1830s.

Machinery and social reform

In 1832 James Phillips Kay published a tract on the *Moral and Physical Condition of the Working Classes Employed in the Cotton Manufactures of Manchester*, in which he revealed the bitterness of the class conflict in the new industrial conglomerations : 'A gloomy spirit of discontent is engendered, and the public are not infrequently alarmed, by the wild outbreak of popular violence, when mobs of machine breakers defy the armed guardians of the peace.'[12] The visitor to Manchester was not just impressed with the marvellous advances in technology and the wealthy exterior of the manufacturers' and merchants' establishments. He was impressed too by contradictions :

[9] Webb, *The British Working Class Reader*, pp. 109–10.
[10] Whately, *Introductory Lectures in Political Economy*, pp. 217–19, cited in R. K. Webb, *Harriet Martineau, A Radical Victorian*, London, 1960.
[11] See R. Whately to Miss Crabtree, 7 January 1833, printed in E. Jane Whately, *The Life and Correspondence of Archibishop Whately, D.D.*, London, 1866, I, p. 180.
[12] J. P. Kay, *The Moral and Physical Condition of the Working Classes Employed in the Cotton Manufactures of Manchester*, 2nd edition, London, 1832, p. 10.

When he turns from the great capitalists, he contemplates the
fearful strength only of that multitude of the labouring
population, which lies like a slumbering giant at their feet. He
has heard of the turbulent riots of the people – of machine
breaking – of the secret and sullen organization which has
suddenly lit the torch of incendiarism, or well nigh uplifted
the arm of rebellion in the land. He remembers that political
desperadoes have ever loved to tempt this population to the
hazards of the swindling game of revolution, and have scarcely
failed. In the midst of so much opulence, however, he has
disbelieved the cry of need.'[13]

The point of Kay's tract, however, was to challenge the industrial
middle class to look at the poor. It was to rouse them to new social
responsibilities and civic duties created by industrialism :

Notwithstanding these demonstrations of insensate rage, the
enlightened manufacturers of the country, acutely sensible of
the miseries of large masses of the operative body, are to be
ranked among the foremost advocates of every measure which
can remove the pressure of public burdens from the people,
and the most active promoters of every plan which can conduce
to their physical improvement, or their moral elevation.[14]

Kay thought that the new inequalities, unemployment and disease
might in part have something to do with machinery, but concluded
that the more significant underlying problem was one of restrictions on
trade. He argued that a new invention was robbed of half its rewards
since Britain deprived other nations from the power of buying its
manufactures.

Improvements in machinery diminish the cost of production;
but if the demand for manufactures be limited by arbitrary
enactments, the increased employment which would also be
their natural and inevitable result is prevented, until commerce
is able, in some other way, to compensate for the evils of
injudicious legislation. We have capital and labour – but to
obtain the greatest amount of commercial advantages, we must
also have an unlimited power of exchange.[15]

13 Kay, *The Moral and Physical Condition*, p. 77.
14 *Ibid.* p. 11.
15 *Ibid.* p. 87.

Kay's tract and the concerns it expressed were not isolated among the middle classes. Kay was one among many of the provincial middle-class élite who appeared to convey a sense of contradiction in the industrialisation of the country, who seemed to wish to alleviate the poverty and misery they admitted existed around them, and yet endorsed the main doctrines of political economy. The response of Kay and other social reformers marked a very significant development both in the middle-class culture of industrialisation and in the formation of political economy. For the social reform movement mapped out a special territory for political economy. Industrialisation, production, work and trade were all defined as economic problems. However, most of the Tory and radical critics of political economy had drawn attention to the social effects of industrialisation, to technological unemployment, and to skill degradation. The social reformers argued that these were not economic issues but social and moral ones, and they decided to deal with them themselves. By setting aside the consideration of social problems as a sphere separate from political economy, the social reformers actually acted to protect political economy from the criticisms of its methodology and its doctrines on industrialisation. Any anomalies such as poverty or unemployment which appeared to be correlated with industrialisation were therefore dealt with separately from the consideration of industrialisation. They were ascribed to a separate moral and social influence which lay outside the boundaries of political economy. Such an effective way of dealing simultaneously with the criticisms both of political economy and of industrialisation were not arrived at in a conspiratorial fashion, nor was it a sudden clever discovery of the manipulative ideologues of the middle classes. It was instead the long-term implication of developments in the institutions and rhetoric of social reform throughout the 1830s.

This chapter will develop this argument by examining the case of the statistical movement of the 1830s. It will consider the way in which this movement regarded itself in relation to political economy, and note the attitudes of political economists themselves to statistical inquiries. The chapter will then chart the development of the statistical movement over the course of the 1830s in both its metropolitan and provincial organisations. Finally, it will point out the ways in which statistics was to come to have an object of inquiry separate from that of political economy. This object of inquiry was the social and moral effects of industrialisation. The chapter will show how consideration of these social problems would by this means no longer challenge political economy but complement it.

The statistical movement which burgeoned in the 1830s, and flourished for a decade, was an important manifestation of what seemed to be a social conscience which developed in middle-class public opinion in the 1830s and 1840s. This was a conscience which recognised that along with the advance of machinery and industrialisation there was a comparable advance in poverty, disease and social discontent, a dilemma soon requiring urgent attention. A solution was necessary, for the credibility of the middle-class social and economic programme was under attack from an increasingly vociferous Tory and radical critique. Middle-class writers were therefore forced to meet the challenge of the social discontent in their industrial sittings, and to seek the source of and find the remedies for the pressing social evils of the day. The statistical movement was one of the most significant expressions of this, for it brought together the members of the provincial middle-class élite – manufacturers, merchants, financiers, doctors – in a collaborative effort to deal with the social and economic disruption which had appeared in the wake of industrialisation. These groups, in turn, saw themselves as part of a national network which included metropolitan intellectuals and politicians.

The statisticians first attempted to deal with the social problems that they had now corporatively decided to recognise and solve, by aligning themselves with political economists and their organisations. It was not, therefore, without significance that Benjamin Heywood announced the formation of the Manchester Statistical Society as a 'new political economy club' in the midst of a discussion over the extent to which the Mechanics Institutes should be directed towards philanthropic ends. This early policy of alignment was also evident in the metropolitan and national manifestations of the movement, Section F of the British Association and the London Statistical Society. These organisations seemed to be inspired both by deficiencies in the empirical basis of government economic policy, and by inductivist interests in political economy. The origins of the movement thus fitted the practice of a progressive improvement-orientated political economy which met the needs and ideals of commercial men.

The statistical movement originated in a two-sided concern with the limitations of political economy. On the one hand, middle-class critics deplored the lack of consideration given to social problems in the traditional texts of political economy. However, on the basis of their critique, they did not wish to reject political economy, but only to provide a more comprehensive framework for the discipline. On the other hand, policy makers and provincial pressure groups were critical of the lack of relevant contemporary economic and commercial data in political economy. They regarded the collection of statistics as a way of filling this gap in information – a gap which they believed severely limited political economy's effectiveness as a guide to economic policy. Statistics, therefore, became one of the tools of economic analysis. The Statistical Department of the Board of Trade, set up by Charles Poulett Thomson and directed from within the whig–liberal intelligentsia by G. R. Porter, affirmed the doctrines of economic progress and *laissez-faire*.[16] This statistical armoury was embellished by G. R. Porter's *Progress of the Nation*, J. R. McCulloch's *Statistical Account of the British Empire* and *Dictionary of Commerce* and McGregor's *Statistics of Nations*. However, the effect of all this on policy is doubtful. Lucy Brown argues there is no sign that the government in 1839 and 1842 had a firmer knowledge of the economic situation of the provincial areas than it had ten years before. Major sources of information on conditions remained individual business men such as the Gotts and the Marshalls.[17] One example of this was the case of Nassau Senior, pundit of whig economic policy. Senior did not rely on official information for his knowledge of industrial and working conditions, declaring, 'I like Blue Books, but distrust knowledge so acquired.' Instead he toured the north on a personal network of business friends.[18]

Yet Senior was one of the several economists who championed a statistical orientation in political economy itself. In 1831, he suggested a society for the improvement and diffusion of political economy, 'a society not for the discussion of theoretical and controversial writing, but a society for the collection of facts and observations . . . a legitimate

[16] An account of the growth of government statistics can be found in Brown, *The Board of Trade*, pp. 76–94, and in M. J. Cullen, *The Statistical Movement in Early Victorian Britain*, New York, 1975, pp. 19–74. A typical example of the doctrinaire approach of this work is Bowring's 'Report on the Commerce and Manufactures of Switzerland', *Edinburgh Review*, LXIV, October 1836. Porter had been a member of the S.D.U.K. and was well known, prior to his appointment to the whig–liberal circles dominating parliamentary inquiries in the 1830s. M. J. Cullen, *Statistical Movement*, p. 21.

[17] Brown, *The Board of Trade*, pp. 182–5.

[18] Richard Johnson, 'Educating the Educators: "Experts" and the State 1833–1839', in A. P. Donajgrodski, *Social Control in Nineteenth Century Britain*, London, 1977, p. 84.

and proper pursuit which has been too long neglected'.[19] This distrust of the official and other statistical information made available throughout the 1830s by a political economist so openly sympathetic to the statistical approach was probably due both to the inadequacies and the biases which Senior detected in the statistical surveys. The equal inadequacy of the provincial surveys for meeting his particular interests would become apparent only after the hopeful beginnings of the movement. Several other notable political economists looked favourably on statistical inquiries, and like Senior hoped to integrate these with economic analysis and policy. Among these was John Sinclair, who drew up a plan in his *Code of Political Economy* to indicate how his statistics would 'lay the best foundations of all useful improvements' and bypass the failings of political economy which 'by vainly attempting to do good to all, may do infinite mischief to particular nations'.[20] Sinclair argued in the 'Outline' of his *Code* that political economists had neglected to ascertain the internal structure of those communities whose situation they proposed to examine. He felt that, though he had completed the massive *Statistical Account of Scotland*, the ultimate object of his research was not yet accomplished : his real goal was to 'found a system of political economy on a minute and extensive investigation of the local facts'. The chapters of his *Code* indicate the statistician's conception of a broader political economy. The first three chapters were to cover population, individual incomes and their sources, and the nature of national wealth. The last two chapters were to be on the nature of a political community and the 'means of improving the happiness of individuals and the prosperity of a state'.[21] J. B. Say had long promoted statistical investigations.[22] Bentham himself suggested a Statistics Society in 1831. Plans and support for a Statistics Society after the suggestion of a Statistics Section within the British Association came soon after from Thomas Chalmers, G. R. Porter, Poulett Thomson, J. D. Hume, Charles Knight and Edwin Chadwick.[23]

The Statistics Section was finally set up by the Cambridge inductivists, Richard Jones, Charles Babbage, and J. E. Drinkwater, who were

19 Mallet's Diaries, 3 June 1831, *Political Economy Club, Centenary Volume*, VI, 227.
20 Sir John Sinclair, *Analysis of the Statistical Account of Scotland*, Edinburgh, 1831, p. 226.
21 John Sinclair, *A Code of Political Economy*, Edinburgh, 1821.
22 Say, *A Treatise*, vol. I, 96.
23 Cullen, *Statistical Movement*, pp. 86–7.

joined by Malthus and Quetelet at the first meetings.[24] Both the Statistics Section and the newly formed Statistical Society of London made serious attempts to connect political economy with the statistical investigation of economic improvement, and soon included among their economist members, Malthus, Jones, Babbage, McCulloch, Senior, John Sinclair, Thomas Tooke, G. P. Scrope and S. Jones Loyd.[25] The first Committee of Section F had Babbage for President and Drinkwater as Secretary, and included Malthus, Empson, Jones, and Quetelet. Later committees in 1834 and 1835 included Cleland, Whewell, John Sinclair, Dr Chalmers, Professor Longfield, Leonard Horner, John Marshall, W. R. Greg, and W. Cooke Taylor.[26]

The inclusion of such a Section within the British Association was controversial. Its consistency with the constitution was argued on the basis that science could be defined as all subjects capable of being reduced to measurement and calculation. Statistics would give the 'raw material to political economy and political philosophy', and 'lay the foundations of those sciences'. Rules of the section restricted inquiries to facts relating to communities of men, 'which are capable of being expressed by numbers, and which promised when sufficient to indicate general laws'.[27] The London Society defined its scope less narrowly. There were plans in this Society for a survey of social conditions in local areas. Fellows of the Society were to furnish suitable questions in the branches of knowledge of their interests. The questionnaire reflected the priorities of the Committee. Senior provided questions on the 'Labouring Classes', Jones on 'Rent', Whewell on 'Education and Literature', Porter on 'Crime, Savings Banks and Agriculture', J. E. Drinkwater on 'Machinery and Manufactures', and S. Jones Loyd on 'Currency'.[28]

The provincial societies soon followed with their own studies of industrial advance. Most of these societies made some inquiry into the state

---

24 The narrative of the formation of this section and the later London Society can be found in F. J. Mouat, 'History of the Statistical Society of London', in *Jubilee Volume of the Statistical Society*, London, 1885, p. 15.

25 *Annals of the Royal Statistical Society*, London, 1934, pp. 10–12.

26 *Reports of the British Association*, II, 1833, xl, 484; III, 1834, xxx; IV, 1835, x.

27 *Ibid.* II, 1833, xxviii, 5, 6.

28 *Ibid.* II, 1833, 484. Whewell kept a jealous watch on the scientific nature of the new section, complaining at intervals of the incursion of politics into the British Association. See Whewell to Murchison, 2 October 1840 and Whewell to Northampton, 5 October 1840 in I. Todhunter, *William Whewell*, London, 1876, vol. II, pp. 291, 293.

and development of various industries, and many made calculations of the increase of steam power in their particular areas. The Ulster, Liverpool and Bristol Societies all looked into the Anglo-Irish trade, and Glasgow assessed the trade between Ireland and Scotland.[29]

The statisticians hoped that by aligning themselves with political economy they could contribute to its theoretical advances both by solving internal disputes among political economists themselves and by providing statistical proofs to meet outside criticisms of economic theory. Dissension within the theoretical circles of political economy over such basic concepts as value, rent, wages and profits reached out to the active citizens of the statistical movement. This was regarded as an answer to the current lack of doctrinal agreement in political economy – 'the study of Statistics will, ere long, rescue Political Economy from all the uncertainty in which it is now enveloped'.[30] Statistics was to help to improve political economy and to set it upon a new scientific basis. It meant a new style which 'confronted the figures of speech with the figures of arithmetic' and a mood of 'distrust of mere hypothetical theory and *a priori* assumption'. Statistics was also a new methodology, 'a general conviction that, in the business of social science, principles are valid for application only inasmuch as they are legitimate inductions from facts, accurately observed and methodically classi-fied'.[31]

In one sense the statistical societies presented themselves as the bearers of a new economics, the economics of the 1830s. It has already been argued that the political economists of this decade saw themselves as offering a fundamental critique of the old doctrinaire 'Ricardian economics'. The statisticians of the decade supported them. They claimed to have identified the facts which 'disprove Ricardo's views that poverty was a check to marriage, and that profits, rent and wages moved in antagonistic directions.'[32] In another sense, however, statistics

29 *Journal of the Statistical Society of London*, 1838–42, and *Annals of the Royal Statistical Society 1834–1934* pp. 72–6.

30 J. E. Portlock, 'An Address Explanatory of the Objects and Advantages of Statistical Enquiries', Statistical Association of Ulster, 18 May 1838, printed in *Journal of the Statistical Society of London*, I, no. 5, September 1838, p. 317.

31 'Fourth Annual Report of the Council of the Statistical Society of London', *Journal of the Statistical Society of London*, I, no. 1, May 1838, p. 8.

32 Address by Professor Lawson, 'On the Connexion between Statistical Enquiries and Political Economy', *Reports of the British Association*, XII, 1843 (Notices and Abstracts), pp. 94–5.

claimed to be more than political economy. For it gave priority to the investigation of social, cultural and moral aspects of the industrial environment. Statistics was to be broader than political economy – to encompass social problems as well as economic. Thus the London and many of the provincial societies turned to an investigation of crime, education, population, disease and poverty. But in launching surveys of such issues the Statistics Societies did not actually claim to pose any threat to political economy. They did not go further than to *say* they would go beyond it. Fundamentally, they did not even regard themselves as acting in opposition to political economy, for they also claimed they existed to 'bind up the wounds' of political economy, 'till lately a bye-word and a jest'.[33]

The statisticians did not challenge the logic of political economy, nor did they attempt to reformulate the economists' categories which underlay the first questionnaires of the London Statistical Society. Instead, when they took up their social inquiries, they turned aside from the traditional interests of political economy in production, conditions of work and technology, and chose instead to concentrate on the statistics and institutions of the moral development of society. The role of James Phillips Kay illustrates the development of the split between the interests and contexts of political economy and those which soon became almost exclusively identified with statistics and other social reform writings. When the Manchester Statistical Society was founded, C. Poulett Thomson went to Manchester to advise the members to conduct a survey of employment levels, trade and wages. However, Kay rejected the suggestion and drew up a house to house survey on the religion and education of the poor.[34] These interests reflected those he had shown in his own 'statistical study' of the poor of Manchester. Furthermore, Kay had dedicated this tract to Thomas Chalmers, the Christian economist and advocate of population theory and scientific philanthropy. Chalmers's programme of ethical economics, though scorned by many established political economists,[35] did articulate many of the criticisms of political economy which had long been latent among

---

33 William Augustus Guy, 'On the Value of the Numerical Method as Applied to Science, but especially to Physiology and Medicine', *Journal of the Statistical Society of London*, II, no. 1, February 1839, p. 35.

34 See Appendix to Minutes, Manchester Statistical Society Papers.

35 See, for example, [G. P. Scrope], 'The Political Economists', *Quarterly Review*, XLIV, January 1831.

the social reformers. It also offered a way forward in creating a new path for economics which would integrate Christian philanthropy with economic doctrine.

As Chalmers himself put it, 'Political economy is but one grand exemplification of the alliance which a God of righteousness hath enlisted, between prudence and moral principle on the one hand, and physical comfort on the other.' Science had revealed the connection between 'the economy of outward nature', and 'the economy of human principles and passions'.[36] Chalmers's ethical economics addressed itself to the question of key concern to the provincial élite comprising the grass roots of the statistical movement, that of scientific philanthropy and poor law policy. His work was an inspiration to the statistical social reformers. For the problems which interested the statisticians were not the fundamental economic issues of industrialisation. They were the social and moral ones of the poor law. When the local statisticians criticised political economy because it was too abstract and because it did not go far relief. The statisticians cast aside those questions of production which focussed on production gave them no guide for managing their poor relief. The statistician cast aside those questions of production which interested the writer on economics : machinery, skills, capital, labour, unemployment and work, and instead created issues based on income distribution and social and moral problems : poverty, home, family, education and religion.

It was not just Manchester's society, but London's and most of the other provincial societies which conducted surveys based on these social problems. Philanthropy was a dilemma to many of these societies. It was first believed that a scientific philanthropy as opposed to indiscriminate charity could be based on a political economy whose terms had been broadened to include the consideration of the whole of society. The relationships between statistics and philanthropy were turgidly outlined by William Hawkes Smith: 'Their [the great bulk of the population's] condition is . . . far inferior to what it *ought to be*, speaking as philanthropists – what it *might be* speaking as statists . . . These anticipations are now very generally entertained and these opinions indulged by the soundest and most reflective political econ-

36 Thomas Chalmers, *On The Power Wisdom and Goodness of God as Manifested in the Adaptation of External Nature to the Moral and Intellectual Constitution of Man*, London, 1833, vol. II, pp. 49–50; *On Political Economy*, p. 28; *The Christian and Civic Economy of Large Towns*, vol. I, pp. 3–24; cited in Hilton, *Corn, Cash, Commerce*, p. 310.

omists.'[37] But soon this philanthropy acquired in the statistical or social investigation its own field of inquiry. Philanthropy had become a complex affair, even for those simply following Christian ideals. The Bristol Society in 1839 complained : 'In a simple state of society, a man may know tolerably well what his duties to the poor are . . . but what shall be said of the artificial and complicated state of things when a nation manufactures for half the world – when the consequence unavoidably is the enormous distance between the labourer and his virtual and subdivided employer.'[38]

The purpose of social inquiry, however, was not just the organisation of philanthropy and poor relief. It was to make the poor 'transparent' or known to the ruling class. Poverty was blamed by the social reformer for generating crime, disease, vicious habits, and limitations on investment. The Reports of the Poor Law Commission were replete with the sins of poverty : 'The industrious man is broken down by the profligate.'[39] 'The recklessness of the people in indulgence is quite frightful.'[40] 'Pauperism we consider nearly as infectious as smallpox, and without constant vigilance it would soon overspread the whole parish.'[41] 'The veracity, the frugality, the industry and the domestic virtues of the lower classes must be very nearly extinct.'[42]

The working classes were to be informed of their true position in society : 'It is high time to disabuse them of the disastrous fallacy involved in the word "Poor".' They were to be reminded that the poor man is not a pauper.[43] Crime and pauperism were concepts which went together.[44] The workhouse was conducted as a penal institution, its members referred to as inmates, to be uniformed, disciplined and

---

[37] *The Analyst, A Journal of Science, Literature, and the Fine Arts,* London, 1834–5, p. 281.

[38] *Journal of the Bristol Statistical Society,* 1839, quoted in *Journal of the Statistical Society of London,* no. 9, 1, January 1839, p. 549.

[39] *First Annual Report of the Poor Law Commissioners for England and Wales,* London, 1835, p. 184.

[40] *Extracts from the Information Received from His Majesty's Commissioners as to Administration and Operation of the Poor Laws,* London, 1833, p. 226.

[41] *Ibid.* p. 182.

[42] *Ibid.* p. 177.

[43] *Evidence of the Revd. William Stone, Rector of Spitalfields and other witnesses as to the operation of voluntary charities, etc. Extracted from a report by Edwin Chadwick, one of the Administrators Enquiring into the Operation of the Poor Law,* London, 1833, p. 51.

[44] *Second Annual Report of the Poor Law Commissioners,* London, 1836, p. 35.

classified.[45] Constant statistical comparisons were made between the treatment and conditions in prisons and workhouses.[46] Of even greater immediacy was the connection between poverty and disease. Cholera was 'created by poverty and immorality'.[47] James Phillips Kay, reporting on Manchester, revealed the awful prospects : 'The dense masses of the habitations of the poor, which stretch out their arms, as though to grasp and envelop the dwellings of the noble and wealthy . . . have heretofore been regarded as mighty wildernesses of buildings, in which the incurable ills of society rambled, beyond the reach of sanitative interferences.'[48]

Kay went further to describe how statistics would reveal the purely institutional and moral sources of poverty and disease : 'The evils here unreservedly exposed, so far from being the necessary consequences of the manufacturing system, have a remote and accidental origin, and might by judicious management, be entirely removed.'[49]

The Poor Law was the first priority. The public health movement, education and the reform of the borough police were outgrowths of the Poor Law reform. In so far as Chadwick was involved in all these reforms, he saw them as part of a common project. Not only was vagrancy a cause of crime and disease, but an adequate police force would eradicate resistance to the New Poor Law.[50] The social surveys conducted by the statistical societies showed similar preoccupations. In addition they acted as a research base and suitable platform for the doctrines of the Poor Law reformers, and as a way of involving others in local studies to buttress their reform arguments.

The statistical movement's concern with philanthropy and with excluding the poor from contact with the rest of society also took the form of promoting institutions of socialisation : school, church, and savings club were seen to play a part in advancing class harmony among employers and labourers and in creating a socialised, disciplined and efficient labour force. Fears of social discontent and of the moral effects of urbanisation on the working classes were formative to many of the

45 S. E. Finer, *The Life and Times of Sir Edwin Chadwick*, London, 1952, p. 83.
46 *Third Annual Report of the Poor Law Commissioners*, London, 1837, passim.
47 Kay, *The Moral and Physical Condition*, p. 6.
48 *Ibid*. p. 11.
49 *Ibid*. p. 15.
50 E. Midwinter, *Social Administration in Lancashire 1830–1860*, Manchester, 1969, pp. 129, 176.

societies. 'The preservation of public tranquillity' was haunted by the 'power of sansculottism, a power overlooked and forgotten in periods of tranquillity'. 'What are the influences that increase or diminish the sanguinary character of this occult power, or its capacity to do evil? May not remedies be applied which shall go far to extinguish its existence? – which shall, therefore, place a man's liberties and his honest title to the social comforts he enjoys on a much more stable foundation.'[51] A report in 1841 argued that the rich had taken the initiative in investigations which would contribute to strengthening the bond between classes, so that the labouring classes would 'cease to believe that there was no sympathy or solicitude from them in the higher ranks'.[52] Indeed, Manchester's society was in one sense philanthropically devoted to 'cementing' together the different ranks and classes of society.[53]

The societies showed their main interests in the institutions of socialisation, not only for reasons of advancing class harmony but also in order to find reasons for poverty in the deficiencies of these institutions rather than in the economy. Poverty could be solved by the more effective socialisation of labour. The Mechanics Institutes which conveyed political economy's concerns with the labour force were complemented by the statistical societies which conveyed social reform's preoccupation with home life. Political economy and statistics separated their objects of inquiry, but in so doing complemented each other. The middle-class élite had discovered the close connections between the social relations of production, and the religious, family and educational institutions which 'reproduced' these social relations.

Though statisticians claimed to expose the evils and poverty neglected by political economy, they presented these as 'social problems' which could be attributed to accidental causes. They thus provided no challenge either to the doctrinaire optimism of political economy or to the manufacturing interest. This view of the object of statistical inquiries was not only apparent in the rhetoric of the statistical movement. It was also evident in the types of inquiries undertaken by a wide range of the societies, and in the content and analysis of their surveys. Cullen has shown how Manchester's society helped to meet the 'need to provide a coherent justification of the factory system, at least in its more humane forms'. The society almost immediately constituted the brothers

---

[51] *Journal of the Bristol Statistical Society*, cited in *Journal of the Statistical Society of London*, 1, no. 9, January 1839, p. 549.
[52] *Ibid.*
[53] Cullen, *Statistical Movement*, p. 107.

Samuel and W. R. Greg, local cotton textile magnates into a committee to report on the evidence of the 1833 Factory Commission. Their evidence of 1834 vindicated the factory system and 'demonstrated' that the health of children improved when they entered the factory.[54] Yeo has shown how the Manchester Society's first surveys were consciously directed away from employment conditions, and how the surveys of other societies concentrated on home, church, school and disease rather than the workplace.[55]

A cross-section of surveys conducted by the Leeds Society in 1838 represented the typical range of interests. The survey projects in this year covered the schools connected with the manufacturing establishment of Marshall and Company, the medical statistics of public institutions, population returns, the causes of crime and the effects of punishment on criminals, the state of the chimney sweeps and the history of unions in the Leeds woollen trade from 1833 to 1834. Even at the metropolitan level the surveys conveyed the prejudices of a reforming élite convinced of the existence of a 'non-economic' poverty. Though the economists of the London Society had, at its foundation, posed survey questions on production, machinery, and the land, their influence soon receded. The Society actually only made inquiries into criminal statistics, strikes, the poor in Westminster, the value of land and other property, the London charities and hospital statistics.

It has been argued by Eileen Yeo that though the surveys of the 1830s concentrated on the moral and home lives of the poor, this did change somewhat, later in the decade. She argues that the surveyors eventually came to give more attention to the economic rather than to the moral conditions of the poor. However, such an assessment is difficult to establish on the evidence of the topics of the surveys. The following tables, in which I categorise the topics of surveys compiled from the *Journal of the Statistical Society of London*, from the records of the provincial papers reported to Section F of the British Association, and from the Manchester Statistical Society, show no trend either way.

No more does the content of the major public papers and surveys which were published reveal a shift in the explanations of poverty. The best and most sympathetic of the statistical surveys carried out were those on the conditions of handloom weavers and other domestic outworkers. Such commendable surveys were Benjamin Heywood's study of Miles Platting, C. R. Baird's study of the weavers of Glasgow, and

54 *Ibid.*; V. A. C. Gattrell, 'The Commercial Middle Classes', Ph.D. Thesis, pp. 177–80.
55 Yeo, 'Social Science and Social Change', D.Phil. thesis, pp. 121–30.

Topics of papers delivered to the London Statistical Society

	1838	1839	1840	1841	1842	1843	1844	1845	Total
Education	11	7	1	5	4	4	–	2	34
Condition of the poor	8	4	3	1	2	1	1	1	21
Economic progress	19	6	–	3	3	4	2	1	38
Criminal statistics	7	6	–	1	2	3	–	2	21
Vital statistics	1	5	4	4	3	4	4	3	28
Medicine and disease	8	2	3	–	5	7	4	8	37
Philanthropy	–	–	–	–	–	–	–	–	–
Geography	5	6	–	1	2	3	1	–	18
Unions	2	–	–	–	–	–	–	–	2
Poor Law	5	1	2	3	3	3	2	1	20
Miscellaneous	2	2	3	6	–	2	1	–	16
Total	68	39	16	24	24	31	15	18	235

Source: Compiled from *Journal of the Statistical Society of London*, 1838–45.

Topics of papers delivered to the Statistical Section of the British Association for the Advancement of Science

	1833	1834	1835	1836	1837	1838	1839	1840	1841	1842	1843	Total
Education	–	–	3	2	5	4	4	4	1	1	2	26
Condition of the poor	–	1	1	1	5	1	2	1	5	–	1	18
Economic progress	–	1	–	3	3	1	1	–	1	2	1	13
Criminal statistics	–	–	3	–	1	2	2	4	–	2	–	14
Statistics of births and deaths	–	–	3	2	–	1	–	4	–	3	2	15
Medicine and disease	–	–	–	–	1	–	1	–	1	2	3	8
Philanthropy/Poor Law	–	–	1	1	–	1	–	2	3	3	1	9
Geography	2	2	–	–	–	2	–	2	–	–	1	12
Unions	–	–	–	1	1	–	–	–	–	–	2	4
Miscellaneous	–	–	–	1	1	–	–	–	1	–	–	3
Total	2	4	11	11	17	12	10	17	12	13	13	122

Source: Compiled from *Reports of the British Association*, Statistics Section Transactions, 1833–43. The British Association published selected papers from the provincial statistical societies. These societies sent what they considered to be their most important papers, but the papers sent also had to meet the British Association's strictly enforced rules against controversial political material.

Topics of papers delivered to the Manchester Statistical Society 1833–1841

	1833	1834	1835	1836	1837	1838	1839	1840	1841	Total
Education	3	7	5	1	5	3	4	3	1	32
Condition of the poor	3	2	1	2	2	2	3	2	–	17
Economic progress	–	–	1	3	3	3	–	–	1	11
Criminal statistics	1	3	–	–	1	–	–	–	1	6
Statistics of births and deaths	1	–	–	–	–	–	1	–	3	5
Medicine and disease	1	–	–	–	1	1	–	–	–	3
Philanthropy	2	1	3	–	–	–	1	1	–	8
Geography	–	–	–	–	1	–	–	–	1	2
Unions	–	–	–	1	–	–	–	–	–	1
Total	11	13	10	7	13	9	9	6	7	85

Source: Compiled from Theodore Gregory, 'Early History of the Manchester Statistical Society', *Transactions of the Manchester Statistical Society*, session 1925–6, pp. 30–2.

William Felkin's study of the framework knitters of Nottingham. Yeo finds these studies to be sensitive inquiries into the massive poverty of the domestic outworkers. I will argue that this sensitivity was in fact illusory, and that these studies did not go beyond the prejudices that marked most of the statistical surveys of the time.

Though these studies surveyed particular groups of workers rather than geographical areas of poverty, those chosen were domestic workers. Doctrinal political economy, as shown already, was coming to recognise during this period that weavers and other domestic workers had suffered during the process of industrialisation. But this political economy regarded such workers as the last remnant of a dying handicraft civilisation, the outcasts of the Industrial Revolution, and thus suitable cases for philanthropy. It was also a useful polemical device to contrast their poverty as handworkers to the higher standards of living of factory workers. This helped to prove the political economists' case for the benefits of industrialisation, for most of them argued that the problem was only one of mobilising handworkers to shift to the sector of factory production. The statistical studies of the domestic workers in no way contradicted these doctrines of political economy.

Benjamin Heywood's study was no great departure from the norms of the survey. He did gather information on wages paid for particular types of weaving, but the main focus of his study was the religious and educational attributes of the community. He collected detailed statistics on the regularity of church attendance, reading abilities, and numbers owning bibles, prayerbooks or hymnbooks.[56]

Baird, of course, had his own inherent biases. He attained great success as a lawyer for employers' associations fighting a series of strikes, and was known for his anti-unionism and fear of revolution. His study just reaffirmed these biases: he simply repeated the aphorisms of the doctrinal political economist's view of the weavers, and blamed the conditions of the weavers on early marriage and on restrictive union practices. Though he agreed that the weavers' unions were pretty harmless, he still found reason to support the re-enactment of the Combination Laws. It is true that he generously listed all the general causes and remedies usually suggested for the weavers' condition, but when he came to choose his own remedy from among a whole range including wage fixing, repeal of the Corn Laws, repression of embezzlement, emigration, re-enactment of the Combination Laws, retraining, and moral education, Baird chose the latter. The 'education of the people to greater industry, prudence, and economy' would be a 'means of permanent amelioration'.[57]

William Felkin demonstrated similar prejudices, though he was more sanguine of the potentialities of the working classes. Felkin was a Wesleyan, a whig, a believer in classical political economy, and an opponent of chartism and unions. Unlike many of the surveyors, he did conduct studies of the conditions of work, and launched his first survey of the bobbin net and hosiery trades in 1832 in response to requests by McCulloch and the Factory Commission. However, his first reports were criticised by McCulloch and by the Commission on the basis of political economy's categories, for they lacked information on such basic questions as earnings and hours of work. The depression of 1837 prompted Felkin to turn to economic and social statistics, and he made his project the comparative study of working-class providence and the causes of poverty in Nottingham, Hyde, Norwich and London. Reports were presented to the Statistical Section of the British Association in 1837 and 1844.[58] It is certainly true, as Eileen Yeo has argued,

---

[56] Benjamin Heywood, 'Report of an Enquiry Conducted from House to House into the State of 176 Families in Miles Platting, within the Borough of Manchester in 1837', *Journal of the Statistical Society of London*, I, no. 9, 1839, pp. 34–6.

[57] Baird, 'Observations on the Poorest Class of Operatives'.

[58] Felkin, *Remarks upon the Importance of an Inquiry*, p. 15; and Felkin, *An Account of the Machine Wrought Hosiery Trade*, p. 39.

that Felkin was one of those who came to blame poverty and unemployment on trade depressions, but his work was no less full of the conventional exhortations to prudence and foresight. His statistics, he claimed, showed that unless working men were induced to practise prudence, 'Their firesides will be altogether deserted, and their domestic habits and comforts destroyed.'[59] The remedy for poverty and unemployment was to be found, not in government intervention, but in the character of the individual workman. Working men would have potential if only they could be induced to save and to think ahead : 'Many from amongst the working classes have exhibited vast mental and imaginative power, and have attained to a high moral elevation. When the mind is at ease on account of worldly circumstances, there is much in the nature of their ordinary employment to facilitate the exertions of the mind.'[60] Yet Felkin believed that such moral and mental improvement would take place only within certain limits, and few working people had much chance of changing their rank or status. They should aspire instead, he argued, to become 'an ornament to their station'.[61]

Felkin's extensive studies of the hosiery trade were much more interesting however for the remarkable blindness they demonstrated to the whole context of industrialisation in the trade. As late as 1844 he was arguing for the health and dynamism of the domestic hosiery trade, loftily pronouncing : 'At present, I do not see reason for deciding that all labour in connection with weaving machinery, must be subject to the uniform, automatic, system of operation which obtains within the gates of a factory, in order to secure good work, fair wages, or reasonable profit.'[62] As S. D. Chapman has so forcefully demonstrated, Felkin happily believed that stocking making by hand would continue indefinitely : he seemed oblivious to the increasing use of wide frames and the transfer of the work process from cottages to shops. He failed to mention the concentration of ownership or the middleman, and his collection of data on the location of the trade, though diligent, was of little relevance to the real developments of the industry. He blithely ignored the connections between the coming of the machine and the factory, and the struggles, poverty, and suffering of the framework

59 Felkin, *Remarks on the Importance of an Inquiry*, cited in Trygve Tholfsen, *Working Class Radicalism in Mid-Victorian England*, London, 1976, p. 137.
60 Felkin, *Remarks upon the Importance of an Inquiry*, p. 15.
61 *Ibid*. cited in T. Tholfsen, *Working Class Radicalism*, p. 138.
62 Felkin, *An Account of the Machine Wrought Hosiery Trade*, p. 39.

knitters.[63] Felkin, like Baird, Heywood and most of their contemporaries, saw poverty as a moral and social phenomenon disconnected from the concerns of political economy – the development of technology, the labour process, and the total economy.

In face of all the questioning, criticism, and outright rejection of the beneficent effects of the machine, it was the plight of the domestic outworker which eventually attracted the concern of middle-class reformers. The domestic outworkers were a convenient outlet for feelings of christian humanity, for they threatened neither beliefs in political economy nor those in industrial progress. Social reformers ultimately responded in a manner not far different from that of the political economists who debated on the policy issue of the weavers. Humanity could justify some measure of philanthropic and public aid to these relics of a dying civilisation. For their poverty was an anomaly – disconnected from the process of industrialisation.

There were yet, however, a few dissenting voices who used the statistical inquiry to arrive at other conclusions, for statistical inquiry was not the sole preserve of the entrenched élite. There were cases, such as Sheffield's, where a leading light of the local statistical society could make radical use of statistics to challenge the factory system. George Calvert Holland, a Sheffield doctor, used a comprehensive set of statistics on earnings, population, crime, and mortality to support his views that 'degradation, poverty, and wretchedness were the inevitable effects of mechanization', and that the craft system was superior since 'the machine cheapens to the starving point the labour of the industrious mechanic'.[64]

These few dissenters from among the social scientists of reform were exceptional. For those who took the statistician's rhetoric on confronting poverty and bringing about social reform at face value, there was little but disappointment. One such as Thomas Carlyle was to express bitter frustration with the hypocrisy of the surveyors :

> We have looked into various statistic works, Statistic Society
> Reports, Poor Law Reports, Reports and Pamphlets not a few,
> with a sedulous eye to this question of the Working Classes and

---

[63] Chapman, 'William Felkin', M.A. Thesis, p. 340.
[64] G. C. Holland has been vividly resurrected by Cullen, *Statistical Movements*, pp. 131–2. Also see G. C. Holland's journal of the early 1840s, *The Millocrat,* and his *An Inquiry into the Moral, Social and Intellectual Condition of the Industrious Classes,* London, 1839.

their general condition in England; we grieve to say, with as good as no result whatever ... When Parliament take up 'the Condition of England question', as it will have to do one day, then indeed much may be amended. Inquiries wisely gone into, even on this most complex matter, will yield results worth something, not nothing. But it is a most complex matter; on which, whether for the past or the present, Statistic Inquiry, with its limited means, with its short vision and headlong extensive dogmatism, as yet too often throws not light but error worse than darkness.[65]

As this chapter has demonstrated, however, the point of the statistical movement, both in the definitions and purposes it conveyed in its rhetoric and in the end results of its work, was not to challenge political economy or to offer a new theory and practice which would help to solve the pressing social problems of the day. The statistical movement did not therefore fail in the way Carlyle implies it did. Rather, it succeeded in defending political economy and in removing the social problems of the day from among the objects of inquiry of political economy.

The statistical movement as a whole seemed to have been eminently successful in giving some empirical foundation to ideas on the significance of industrialisation. Yet in so doing it had also placed the question of the social impact of industrialisation in a non-contradictory and complementary position in political economy's charter for the progress of wealth. But the question was not closed with this easy intellectual separation of the economic from the social. For the issue of the lingering domestic outworker was not just one for studies and surveys, but, as we have seen, one of politics. Political activism on the part of the outworkers, in particular the massive body of handloom weavers, provoked, challenged, confronted, and incited politicians, social reformers, the state, and public opinion.

The machinery question, so fruitful of intense debate between the end of the Napoleonic Wars and the depression of 1842, was left after all unresolved. Tory opinion, backward looking and paternalist as it was, offered no practical alternative. Rhetoric and romantic dreams of a return to an 'organic' society were translated in the political arena into policies for the moral improvement of labour and the poor, and

[65] Thomas Carlyle, 'Statistics', chap. 2 of 'Chartism', in *Critical and Miscellaneous Essays, Collected Works*, vol. XXIII.

for the personal relationships which would bring social order.[66] Working class radicals, too, were unable to impose their opinions, for on the machinery issue they displayed fundamental intellectual irresolution. Their anti-machinery economic theory did not constitute a fundamental and damaging critique of political economy. Nor did their social visions include many substantive clues on how production in the new society was to be structured or how that in the old was to be overthrown. Increasingly, their economic theory had turned from consideration of machinery and the production process to issues of distribution. In the 1840s neither the Tories nor the radicals, even in the direct political setting of the handloom weavers' debates and Chartism, were able to forge anew the connections, now severed by the social reformer, between industrialisation and its social effects. However, their efforts to influence or even gain a state policy on technology were not entirely in vain, whatever the outcome of parliamentary committees and commissions. For technological unemployment among domestic workers, and the unattractive conditions among factory workers had left a question mark over machinery even into the middle of the century. The imprint they left delivered its legacy in the writings of John Stuart Mill and Frederick Engels.

66 See Jennifer Hart, 'Nineteenth Century Social Reform: A Tory Interpretation of History', reprinted in M. W. Flinn and T. C. Smout, eds., *Essays in Social History*, Oxford, 1974, p. 208; A. P. Donajgrodski, ' "Social Police", and the Bureacratic Elite: A Vision of Order in the Age of Reform', in A. P. Donajgrodski, ed., *Social Control in Nineteenth Century Britain*, London, 1977, p. 60.

14

Engels and Mill

The machine question was a national issue particular to the early nineteenth century. Though it cannot be said to have died away by the mid nineteenth century, both its context and significance had changed. Machinery certainly remained an issue in individual industries, especially as the hand techniques still dominant in many industries were gradually replaced by mechanical ones. But there was little generalisation on the basis of these experiences, and the various social groups no longer singled out machinery per se to attack or to extoll in quite the same way. For the great Victorian boom brought not just mechanisation, but expansion in all ways. The intensive employment of manual and skilled labour was as much a hallmark of the mid-Victorian economy as was large-scale capital formation and rapid mechanisation.

The Machinery Question can be said to have reached its culmination in political economy and radical theory in the 1840s. The debate on industrialisation had arisen in a specific economic situation, for machinery made its entry and advance in the context of a series of economic crises which recurred throughout the period from 1815 to 1848. The stability and prosperity of the mid-Victorian economy resolved the contradictory juxtaposition of industrialisation and economic depression. The social antagonisms which had called the benefits and directions of this industrialisation into question no longer took on such spontaneous and apocalyptic forms, as workers and employers became organised into trade unions, the anti Corn Law League, and other intermediating bodies. The formulation of the machinery question and more general debates on Britain's road to economic development were no longer needed as the central rationale for the discipline of political economy. By the mid nineteenth century the intellectual dominance of political economy was irrevocably established. Tory and radical critiques no longer constituted a potential threat to political economy's formerly precarious, but now comfortable, public credibility.

The legacy of the connection between the machinery question and the formation of political economy can be seen in the work of two major social thinkers and political economists who spanned both the generation of the early nineteenth century and that of the mid to late nineteenth century. Frederick Engels and J. S. Mill represented and articulated the contradictory directions left by the economic and social debates between 1815 and the mid 1840s, resuming the main themes of the machinery question during these years. Each inherited one of the two major intellectual traditions sprawned by this issue : Mill the tradition of classical political economy, and Engels the radical working-class critique. Frederick Engels's *Condition of the Working Class in England*, written in 1844 and published in Germany in 1845, and J. S. Mill's *Principles of Political Economy*, first published in 1848, summed up the debates and traditions with which this book has been concerned. In addition, Mill and Engels brought the inheritance of these issues and traditions of political economy's formation forward into the new and immensely influential political economy which Mill was to dominate until the 1890s, and the potent critique of political economy which the figures of Marx and Engels dominate even to today. These two works by Engels and Mill therefore represent the culmination of the problem that had formed political economy in the early nineteenth century. But equally, the interpretation of Engels and Mill in their own right should include this context of the machinery question, for the new paths of political economy which they helped to create showed the inspiration of earlier debates on the machinery question.

It must also be stressed that at the time of the first publication of their works, both Mill and Engels were highly idiosyncratic thinkers. In his *Principles*, Mill did not carry forward the liberal middle-class political perspectives of his father and other classical economists. It was an avenue for moderate socialist perspectives which carried the support of progressive circles, but not that of the middle-class establishment. However, the *Principles* was to be a major intellectual authority for the whole of the last half of the nineteenth century, and Mill's reformulation of classical economics has been of great importance in the history of economic thought. Engels was also idiosyncratic for, not only was he foreign, but his study of the working class in England emanated from an alien intellectual tradition, and was available only in German until the first English translation at the end of the nineteenth century. Furthermore its extreme radical perspectives were not to acquire a following among the radical working classes in England until some years later. But Engels's empirical study of English industrial capitalism was to inspire Marx's own economic analysis and the significance of Engels's work was to lie with the intellectual and political future of Marxism.

Engels's *Condition of the Working Class in England* encapsulated the conclusions of the radical social and political thinkers of Owenism and Chartism. It absorbed, too, both the passion of the Tory denunciations of industrialism and the social reformers' feelings of revulsion at the inadequacy of housing, sanitation, education and family life among the poor. Engels's work was thus unique not for any particular analysis or observation it made but for the way it unified the several strands of the critique of political economy. This unity in turn provided the basis for a vision of the integral dynamics of capitalist crisis and industrial and technological advance, and for a new concept of the working class.

Mill's *Principles of Political Economy* summed up the state of political economy over the generation between the 1820s and the late 1840s. It presented a reformulated Ricardian model which took into account the positions of Ricardo's critics of the 1820s and 1830s. Like Engels's *Condition of the Working Class*, however, Mill's *Principles* is interesting for the ambivalence it displayed towards the machine, and its negative judgement on the period of rapid technological change which Britain had just been through.

Engels's study of the Manchester working classes was not, as Hobsbawm has noted, an isolated literary inquiry, for it had its parallels in the work of French social surveyors such as Villermé and Buret.[1] There were also, as my previous chapter has indicated, a number of English social–industrial surveys in the 1830s and 1840s, and Engels drew on several of these. Engels himself acknowledged his debt both to Chartist writers and to Thomas Carlyle. Mill's *Principles* did not find its parallel elsewhere, for it was the first comprehensive study of

---

[1] E. J. Hobsbawm, 'Introduction', to Frederick Engels, *The Condition of the Working Class in England* (1845), ed. E. J. Hobsbawm, London, 1969.

economic principles since Ricardo's. It was, furthermore, unique to its period for the generality of its analysis and its detailed reconsideration of classical political economy. But Mill's *Principles*, too, was an aggregation of all the criticisms which had been made of Ricardo, not only by other political economists, but by radical and Tory critics as well. It revived the Ricardian approach by broadening the terms of this analysis, and on this inclusive basis answered the critics. Mill's economics was, in effect, a new Ricardianism made relevant for modern times.[2]

Both Engels and Mill brought an historical approach to their works which involved setting their analysis of technological change in a broad temporal context. Mill's historical and comparative approach revealed his absorption of Comte's methodology of the social sciences. But it was more obviously a synthesis of the Smithian method and of the more empirical and historical perspectives of Ricardo's critics of the 1820s and 1830s.[3] Mill, on the basis of the ideas of his predecessors John Rae and Nassau Senior, distinguished civilised societies from savage ones by the extent of their possession of 'instruments'.[4] Savage societies were characterised by equality of poverty. Inequalities in income first appeared in shepherd and agricultural communities, and it was this early state of inequality which formed the basis for specialised markets and ultimately for the emergence of manufacturing. The eventual transition from a feudal to a commercial and manufacturing Europe had also involved the transfer of the surplus from the aristocracy ('a squandering class') to the burghers ('a saving class'). Mill used this historical introduction to substantiate his claim that the political economy of pre-industrial societies was based on coercion and an arbitrary extraction of the surplus. Production in commercial and manufacturing societies, by contrast, was based on economic laws. It was these laws which Mill set out to investigate in his *Principles*.

Engels likewise used an historical approach in his analysis of the industrialisation process, but it was one much more closely aligned with the perspectives of Thomas Carlyle and other social critics such as Peter Gaskell. The historical approaches of radical German idealism may also have been present in the work, but it has been argued that this

---

2 N. B. de Marchi, 'J. S. Mill and the Development of English Economic Thought: A Study in the Progress of Ricardian Orthodoxy', Ph.D. thesis, Australian National University, Canberra. Also see Pedro Schwarz, *The New Political Economy of J. S. Mill*, London, 1968.

3 J. S. Mill, *Principles of Political Economy*, pp. xcii, xciv.

4 *Ibid.* pp. 3–10.

particular study also represented 'an unlearning' and escape on the part of Engels from these philosophical–historical principles.[5] In Carlyle the approaches of German literature and English romanticism were fused to produce an historical perspective on the present crisis and the 'condition of England'. In Carlyle's *Past and Present* Engels found the historical significance of the 'condition of England' cast as it was by Carlyle in the light of ancient Greece and Rome, of the medieval abbots, and of St Edmund. Both in Carlyle and in Peter Gaskell he found a sense of history in the outrage at the inhuman severing of all former personal and social networks. The stability and social harmony of rural and handicraft production in earlier centuries were in stark contrast to the present struggles and crises brought on by competition and machinery. Engels praised Carlyle as a 'Germano-Englishman' who stood 'wholly isolated' even among the critics of English society. He described Carlyle's *Past and Present* as the only one of the many books and pamphlets published in England in the previous year which 'touches upon human stirrings, which expounds upon human circumstances, which develops a sign of a human point of view'.[6] Carlyle and Gaskell provided an alternative historical approach to that of political economy. Engels could therefore bypass political economy's definitions of the stages of production, as agrarian, commercial, and manufacturing societies, and base his analysis of present conditions in England upon 'a history of English industrial development in the past sixty years, a history which has no counterpart in the annals of humanity'. This history was also the history of how the proletariat was called into existence by the introduction of machinery.[7] This was a history which had created the circumstances producing not Carlyle's 'condition of England' question but Engels's question of the condition of the working class.

> Since the Reform Act of 1832 the most important social issue has been the condition of the working classes, who form the vast majority of the English people. The problems are these : what is to become of these property-less millions who own nothing and consume today what they earned yesterday? What fate is

---

5 See Gareth Stedman Jones, 'Engels and the Genesis of Marxism', *New Left Review*, no. 106, November–December, 1977.

6 Frederick Engels, 'Condition of England : Carlyle', *Collected Works*, vol. II, London, 1975, p. 444.

7 Engels, *The Condition of the Working Class*, ed. Henderson and Chaloner, p. 9.

in store for the workers who by their inventions and labour have laid the foundations of England's greatness? What is to be the future of those now daily becoming more and more aware of their power and pressing more and more strongly for their share of the social advantages of the new era?[8]

A number of the essential concepts of Engels's economic and historical analysis of the evolution and dynamic of capitalism and industry had already appeared in his 'Outline of a Critique of Political Economy': private property, the critique of the separate existence of capital and labour, the constant and pervasive struggle of competition, the alternation of boom and crisis in economic fluctuations, and the advance of science and technology.[9] None of these concepts was new, for Engels had gleaned them all in conversation and reading from the English radicals. While he was in Manchester, Engels became involved with the Chartists, attending their meetings and reading their newspapers and tracts. He became friendly with James Leach, a leading Manchester Chartist, and drew heavily for his *Condition of the Working Class* on Leach's 'Stubborn Facts from the Factories by a Manchester Operative'. He also attended Owenite meetings in the Hall of Science, debated there with James Watts, wrote for *The New Moral World* and met George Julian Harney, sub-editor of the *Northern Star*.[10]

Engels's 'Outline of a Critique' amounted to a loose compilation of the criticisms of political economy and the analysis of industrialisation long popularised in the Owenite and unstamped press. The analysis of science and technology presented the standard contradictions of the working-class radical position. Science had brought great material rewards to man, but the capitalist and the economist took for granted the spiritual element of invention. The progress of science, furthermore, was at least as rapid as that of population, and utterly discredited any

8 *Ibid.* p. 25.
9 F. Engels, 'Outline of a Critique of Political Economy' (1844), in Karl Marx, *The Economic and Philosophical Manuscripts of 1844*, ed. Dirk J. Struik, New York, 1964, pp. 210, 214, 217, 222, 225.
10 [James Leach], *'Stubborn Facts from the Factories by a Manchester Operative'*, *published and dedicated to the Working Classes by William Rashleigh, M.P.*, London, 1844. See Steven Marcus, *Engels, Manchester and the Working Class*, London, 1974, pp. 94–5. More details on Engels's period in Manchester and the Manchester of his day can be found in W. O. Henderson, *Frederick Engels*, 2 vols., London, 1976, and W. H. Chaloner, 'Frederick Engels and Manchester', *History Today*, vol. IV, 1956.

Malthusian laws. Engels presented this argument favourable to the machine which was very familiar in English radical circles. He also repeated the negative approach to mechanisation which was just as important among Owenite radicals. He echoed the familiar horror at Andrew Ure's revelation that machinery was introduced to subdue and displace labour. Competition combined with such labour displacement created a poverty stricken surplus of labour, and thereby revealed the illusory nature of the so-called benefits of machinery.[11]

Engels analysed the Industrial Revolution in terms of the permanence of both a surplus population and the inherent tendency to technical progress, arguing that the basis for their contradictory co-existence was the trade cycle, or the constant boom and crisis fluctuations in capitalism. The position which Engels gave to technology indicated the extent to which his work stands as a culmination of the machinery question. For he made technology and the conditions of production central to his economic analysis. He argued that the origins of both the Industrial Revolution and the emergence of the working class were technological : 'The history of the English working classes begins in the second half of the eighteenth century with the invention of the steam engine and of machines for spinning and weaving cotton. It is well known that these incentives gave the impetus to the genesis of industrial revolution.'[12] He generalised, perhaps unduly, from the rapid advances of textile invention to present a picture of the rapid encroachment of mechanisation over domestic industry.

> These inventions have been improved from year to year and
> have brought about the victory of the machine over the hand
> worker in the main branches of British industry. The history
> of the handworkers has been one of continued retreat in face
> of the advance of the machine. The results of this process were
> a rapid fall in the prices of manufactured articles, the expansion
> of commerce and industry, the conquest of virtually all unpro-
> tected foreign markets, the rapid expansion of capital and
> national wealth.[13]

Engels regarded this rapid process of mechanisation as characteristic of industry generally. The machine had spread throughout the textile

---

[11] Engels, 'Outline of a Critique of Political Economy', pp. 208, 222, 225–6.

[12] Engels, *The Condition of the Working Class*, ed. Henderson and Chaloner, p. 9.

[13] *Ibid*. p. 14.

industry to lace and stocking knitting and calico printing. Furthermore, science and machinery had transformed iron and steel, the potteries and agriculture, and transportation. The old economic order had been overthrown by the division of labour, the use of water power and steam power.

The demand made by mechanisation on industrial organisation created the conditions for the emergence of the working class. Small masters who could not compete with big factories sank to the position of mere workers.

> The disappearance of the old independent small masters and the large amount of capital required to start a factory made it impossible for the worker to rise out of his social class. The proletariat now became a definite class in the population whereas formerly it had been only a transitional stage towards entering into the middle classes.[14]

The most striking result of the process of mechanisation was the emergence of a working class as a class with common experiences: 'At the present time virtually the whole of the industrial proletariat supports the workers' movement. This is not surprising because practically all the wage earners have been absorbed in large-scale industry and the different groups of workers face very similar problems.'[15]

Thus far, Engels echoed the issues of debate in the machinery question. His analysis of surplus population, fluctuations and the tendency to technical progress was an old one to Owenism. The central focus he gave to technology and production was, of course, already integral to classical political economy. But it was also apparent in Owenite political economy and in Tory radicalism. It cannot be argued that Engels accomplished a shift in focus in radical thought from a concern with competition to production. For the Owenites had managed to keep both in the fore, and Engels did so too in a very similar way. As Engels put it himself,

> We have seen . . . how competition created the proletariat at the very beginning of the industrial movement, by increasing the wages of weavers, so inducing the weaving peasants to abandon their farms and earn more money by devoting themselves to their looms. We have seen how it crowded out the small farmers

14 *Ibid.* p. 24.
15 *Ibid.* p. 27.

by means of the large farm system and reduced them to the rank of proletarians ...; how it further ruined the small bourgeoisie in great measure and reduced its members also to the ranks of the proletariat; how it centralised capital in the hands of the few, and population in the great towns. Such are the various ways and means by which competition, as it reached its full manifestation and free development in modern industry, created and extended the proletariat.[16]

Engels's analysis of the incursion of machinery on domestic industry was also a common enough one in Tory and radical circles. The debate on the handloom weavers had been replete with such observations. The degradation of the small artisan into the proletariat had also been described before both by political economists such as Say and Senior, and by Tory radicals such as G. S. Bull. Engels's innovation was not any of these arguments, but that the common experience of mechanisation had created a single unified working class.

Engels went beyond the Owenites and Chartists in the breadth of his analysis of the connections between technological change and the emergence of new class dimensions. He did not just look into the attributes of labour or the situations of particular groups of workers. His was not a sectional study of industrial and working conditions, but a broad analysis of the working class as a whole. Engels's broad survey of many sections of the working class offered a comparative perspective over its different parts – the people's living conditions and the types of exploitation to which they were subject. His purpose in doing this was to draw together the common threads of this experience, to show how modern industry aggrandised all sectors of the economy and subjected not some but all workers to the intensive exploitation which could be achieved through mechanisation, the division of labour, and harder work through longer hours and a faster pace of production. The recognition of the common exploitation of the labouring and artisan classes would create the basis for a unified working-class movement.

Engels achieved this unitary concept of the working class, not only by linking together the common elements of exploitation in many different types of labour and industrial settings, but also by linking the economic and the social characteristics of the labouring population. For he was both versed in the Tory and radical critiques of industrialisation and well read in the literature of middle-class social reform.

[16] *Ibid.* pp. 92–8.

Engels used the statistical journals, the works of W. P. Alison, James Phillips Kay, Dr Southwood Smith, J. C. Symons, and several reports from the 'Blue Books', including Chadwick's 'Report on the Sanitary Condition of the Labouring Classes' and the 'Report of the Children's Employment Commission'.

These social reformers had tried to separate the consideration of the social effects of industrialisation in areas such as housing, education, disease and family life from the economics of industrialisation. Engels fully reintegrated the two. He demonstrated vividly how capitalist exploitation at the level of the social relations of production was carried through to and reinforced by exploitation at the level of the relations of 'reproduction' in the home, the family and the urban community. This sphere of life, too, was under the control of competition and capital :

> It is only the industrial age that has made it possible for the
> owners of these shacks, fit only for the accommodation of
> cattle, to let them at high rents for human habitations. It is
> only modern industry which permits these owners to take
> advantage of the poverty of the workers, to undermine the
> health of thousands to enrich themselves. The workers have been
> caged in dwellings which are so wretched that no one else will
> live in them, and they actually pay good money to see those
> dilapidated houses fall about their ears. Industry alone has been
> responsible for all this and yet this same industry could not
> flourish except by degrading and exploiting the workers.[17]

It was in thus drawing on three traditions – the Tory and the radical critiques of industrialisation and the statistical and other surveys of social reform – that Engels was able to forge his novel unitary concept of the working class.

The significance which Engels attached to the spread of mechanisation did not end with an acknowledgement of the existence of rapid technical change. Political economists and social reformers had already gone this far. What Engels did was to integrate the economic with the social analysis of technical change, which, through its impact on the old economic order, gave rise to a new social order. He first repeated Owenite and Tory arguments on the economic effects of the machine. Just as technical change had destroyed the economic basis for the artisan, so it also dictated the continued degradation of the working classes. Capitalism, especially modern industrial capitalism, created a

[17] *Ibid.* p. 64.

pool of unemployed labour, 'the surplus population' of England, in order to maintain a flexible and competitive labour market. Technical change, at the command of capitalism, was of no public benefit, for the gains from using machinery were engrossed by the few while the many only suffered unemployment.

Engels made use of James Leach's statistics on the connections between mechanisation and unemployment to demonstrate conclusively that 'every improvement in machinery leads to unemployment, and the greater the technical improvement the greater the unemployment'.[18] He denounced the middle classes for their dismissive attitude to the critics of technical change. Their stock answer that the result of technical change must be lower prices, increased demand and re-employment of those originally made redundant, was simply inadequate.

> The middle classes coolly ignore the fact that it takes years before the decline in prices of the manufactured goods leads to the opening of new factories. Moreover, the middle classes fail to mention the fact that every technical innovation shifts more and more of the physical labour from the worker to the machine. Consequently, tasks once performed by grown men are no longer necessary.[19]

Mechanisation produced either unemployment or lower wages. Drawing on Ure, Baines and J. C. Symons, Engels re-emphasised the workers' claims that machinery led to wage reductions by unduly lowering piece rates.[20] The self-acting mule and the power loom were his special targets. Engels also commented on the old issue of the displacement of skill by machinery. He pointed out that mechanisation so changed the various branches of industrial activity that a whole new matrix of skills was required.[21] But the skills needed were manual ones easily acquired by women and children. Engels concluded, as did many conservatives and radical writers, that mechanisation would introduce to the factory a sexual division of labour which would be a complete reversal of the family division of labour.[22]

Engels pushed his analysis of the impact of the machine beyond the economic sphere and into the social in considering also the impact of

[18] *Ibid.* p. 151.
[19] *Ibid.* p. 153.
[20] *Ibid.* p. 155.
[21] *Ibid.* p. 153.
[22] *Ibid.* p. 159.

mechanisation on the psychological condition and health of workers and its connection with industrial accidents.[23] Middle-class social reformers had ignored this issue. Engels saw the factory worker as one who must intensely dislike his job, for, compounded with his long hours, was the unceasing monotony of his task.

> The division of labour has intensified the brutalising effects of forced labour. In most branches of industry the task of the worker is limited to insignificant and purely repetitive tasks which continue minute by minute for every day of the year . . . The introduction of steam power, and machinery has had the same result. The physical labour of the worker has been lightened, he is spared some of his former exertion, but the task itself is trifling and extremely monotonous.[24]

To sum up Engels's analysis, it can be argued that what he accomplished was an integration of the economic and the social analysis of the machine. He brought together the three traditions of the critique of machinery – the Tory, the radical and the social reform analysis. On the basis of this he came to see the machine as a necessary determinant of the characteristic fluctuations of an industrial economy. From this economic analysis of the interaction of capitalist crises and technological progress, Engels moved on to a social analysis of the impact of this on workers. Moving beyond the analysis of the social effects of the machine on individual groups of workers he saw that technology in the context of capitalism affected all labourers at some time or another. The correct concept was therefore not labour, nor even the worker, but the working class. New technology arose out of the extreme competitiveness of the capitalist order. The result was a bitter but justified anti-machinery feeling in the working class.

Engels's summation of many of the attitudes of social reformers and radicals had a strange counterpart in John Stuart Mill's analysis of the impact of technical change. Engels carried forward and provided a framework for all the anti-machinery sentiments of the preceding decades. Mill brought forward and revitalised earlier traditions of political economy, in particular Ricardianism. But he disclaimed any attachment to the efforts of earlier political economists to present a purely optimistic picture of the impact of machinery. Mill developed

23 *Ibid.* pp. 185, 199.
24 *Ibid.* p. 134.

very different traditions arising out of the machinery question from those taken up by Engels : he reassessed, by and large, all the internal debate in political economy over the period from 1815 to the late 1840s. These traditions were exposed in his lengthy discussions of the concepts of labour and capital.

The very different origins of Engels's and Mill's ideas on the economic development of capitalism were apparent in their contrasting approaches towards integrating labour into their economic systems. Engels studied the working class as a part of a capitalist economy which expanded and contracted with the trade cycle and technical change. Mill studied the attributes of labour in an evolving commercial industrial system, and extended the traditional analysis of labour supply in classical economic theory. He reiterated the basic classical propositions on productive and unproductive labour, but amended these to take into account the technical and social determinants of labour productivity to which economists of the prior generation had drawn attention. Babbage's mark was in evidence in Mill's careful attempts to distinguish labour from skill, and both from the machine. Labour was 'solely employed in putting objects in motion'. The skill and ingenuity of man was 'exercised in discovering movements, practicable by their powers and capable of bringing about the effects they desire'. Labour could be replaced by animal power or the powers of nature.

> This service is extorted from the powers of wind and water
> by a set of actions, consisting like the former in moving certain
> objects into certain positions in which they constitute what
> is termed a machine; but the muscular action necessary for
> this is not constantly renewed, but performed once for all, and
> there is on the whole a great economy of labour.[25]

Skill could be accumulated, and was to be counted as part of the national wealth : 'The skill, the energy and perseverance, of artisans of a country, are reckoned part of its wealth, no less than their tools and machinery.' To objections that skills were embodied in human beings, and therefore could not be regarded as part of wealth, Mill had a positive barrage of replies.

> It seems to me, however, that the skill of an artisan (for
> instance) being both a desirable possession, and one of a certain
> durability (not to say productive even of national wealth),

25 J. S. Mill, *Principles of Political Economy*, p. 28.

there is no better reason for refusing to it the title of wealth because it is attached to a man, than to a coal pit or manufactory, because they are attached to a place. Besides, if the skill itself cannot be parted with to a purchaser, the use of it may; if it cannot be sold, it can be hired; and it may be, and is, sold outright in all countries whose laws permit that the man himself should be sold along with it. Its defect of transferability does not result from a natural but from a legal and moral obstacle. The human being himself (as formerly observed) I do not class as wealth. He is the purpose for which wealth exists. But his acquired capacities, which exist only as means, and have been called into existence by labour, fall rightly, as it seems to me, within that designation.[26]

If skills could be counted as part of national wealth, the even more intangible attributes involved in invention and discovery could be understood as part of productive labour.

The labour of Watt in contriving the steam engine was as essential a part of production as that of the mechanics who build or the engineers who work the instrument . . . In the national, or universal point of view the labour of the savant, or speculative thinker, is as much a part of production in the very narrowest sense, as that of the inventor of a practical art; many such inventions having been the direct consequence of theoretic discoveries, and every extension of knowledge of the powers of nature being fruitful of applications to the purposes of outward life.[27]

Mill gave further consideration to the question of skill in his remarkable revision of the analysis of the division of labour and the sources of gains in labour productivity. He placed great store in the impact of what he referred to as the greater energy of Anglo-American labour as opposed to the indolence of 'savage' peoples. Mill wrote in the manuscript of his *Principles*, but later discarded, a comment that Anglo-Americans had the distinguishing characteristic of seeing the whole of their life in their work – that they had the desire of growing richer and getting on in the world.

[26] *Ibid.* p. 48.
[27] *Ibid.* p. 42.

This last characteristic applies chiefly to those who are in a condition superior to day labourers; but the absence of any taste for amusement, or enjoyment of repose, is characteristic of all classes. Whether this or anything else be the cause, the same steadiness and persistence of labour is common to the most improvident of the English working classes – those who never think of saving, or improving their condition. It has become the habit of the country, and life in England is more governed by habit, and less by personal inclination and will, than in any other country except perhaps China or Japan. The effect is that when hard labour is the thing required, there are no labourers like the English; though in natural intelligence, and even in manual dexterity, they have many superiors.[28]

The problem with the English labourer was not his ability to work hard, but his lack of appreciation of why he was working so hard. The English labourer needed to be taught not the desire for wealth, but the use of wealth, 'and an appreciation of the objects of desire that wealth cannot purchase'.[29]

Mill's unorthodox opinion that English workmen needed not to work harder but to recognise that there was more to life than labour was, however, paralleled by his equally strong views on the moral qualities of the good worker. English workers worked without reason, and they conducted their personal lives without reason. Mill condemned the average worker's domestic economy as 'improvident, lax, and irregular'. His lack of 'practical good sense' made him fit only for 'a low grade of intelligent labour'. The uneducated English workman needed to be disciplined constantly to remind him of his place: 'As soon as any idea of equality enters the mind of an ordinary English working man, his head is turned by it. When he ceases to be servile he becomes insolent.'[30]

Mill's low opinion of the bulk of the English working classes was even more vividly expressed in his reassertion of the Malthusian principle of population. The base natures of ordinary working people would prevent the economist from rejecting the Malthusian principle whatever the advances in technology. I will deal with this in greater detail below.

28 *Ibid.* p. 104.
29 *Ibid.*
30 *Ibid.* p. 109. This was added by Mill in 1852.

When Mill came to make his critique of the effectiveness of the division of labour, by contrast, he chose to side with the critics of political economy. He was very critical of the emphasis placed by both Adam Smith and Charles Babbage on the time-saving advantages of the division of labour. Where Smith was dismissive of the country labourer's efficiency because of his lack of specialisation, Mill defended his skill and energy. He says of Smith :

> This is surely a most exaggerated description of the inefficiency of country labour, where it has any adequate motive to exertion ... Many of the higher description of artisans have to perform a great multiplicity of operations with a variety of tools. They do not execute each of these with the rapidity with which a factory workman performs his single operations; but they are, except in a merely manual sense, more skilful labourers, and in all senses whatever more energetic[31]

Mill regarded the relief from the monotonous routine of a single occupation as much more conducive to gains in productivity than spurious attempts to save time by 'dividing labour'.

> The habit of passing from one occupation to another may be acquired, like other habits, by early cultivation and when it is acquired there is none of the sauntering which Adam Smith speaks of, after each change; no want of energy and interest, but the workman comes to each part of his occupation with a freshness and a spirit which he does not retain if he persists in any one part ... beyond the length of time to which he is accustomed.[32]

However, Mill did accept Babbage's principle of the economic distribution of labour. This was the really great advantage of the division of labour : the classification of work people according to their capacities and of tools according to their utilities produced unquestioned gains.

Mill rejected orthodox opinion on issues as closely related to the machinery question as was the division of labour. He also doubted traditional creeds on the scale of enterprises, and rejected Babbage's claim that the cause of large factories was the introduction of new technical processes requiring expensive machinery. Not regarding such fixed capital investment to be necessarily beneficial, he also went on to

[31] *Ibid.* p. 125.
[32] *Ibid.* p. 127.

challenge the economies of scale claimed by large enterprises. Alluding to Ricardo's Chapter On Machinery (which he dealt with at much greater length in another part of the *Principles*) Mill claimed that the gains in productivity from using machinery in large-scale units could be outweighed by the initial cost to the community in loss of employment and wages.[33] If it was argued that large-scale production in and of itself could be said to save labour, Mill pronounced that it was only the labour of capitalists that was saved, and he did not attach much importance to this type of saving : 'For this labour, however, the small producers have generally a full compensation, in the feeling of being their own masters, and not servants of their employer.'[34]

Mill took great pains to apply his unorthodox opinions on scale of industry to farming enterprises. He wrote extensively on the peasant and co-operative farming arrangements, which he regarded as satisfactory alternatives to the English system of large-scale landed proprietorship. He defended vigorously the productivity potentials of small farms, and dismissed the usual English criticism of Irish cottier farming and French *petite culture*. Lower productivity in these nations was due, not to the system of small-scale farming, but in Ireland's case to property arrangements which denied to the cultivator even the rights of secure tenure, and in France's case to the lower national average of industrial skill and energy.[35]

The questioning which lay behind Mill's analysis of the sources of higher productivity and his critique of traditional ideas on the division of labour must also have affected the approach he took to the issue of the social and economic impact of machinery. Mill did not accept the stream of criticism from political economists which had followed upon Ricardo's chapter on machinery. He dismissed as spurious a number of the claims of the apologists for the machine. To the claim that capital reproduced itself, he replied that circulating capital might do so, but not so necessarily fixed capital : 'Since machinery is not wholly consumed by one use it is not necessary that it should be wholly replaced from the product of that use.' If increases in fixed capital took place at the expense of circulating capital there had therefore to be, at least for a time, an adverse impact on the working class.[36]

The other main argument made by apologists was that machinery

---

[33] *Ibid.* p. 134.
[34] *Ibid.* p. 135.
[35] *Ibid.* p. 148.
[36] *Ibid.* p. 93.

so cheapened production that it created a new surplus, and with this new employment for any labour originally displaced by machinery. Mill was not impressed, and replied :

> But if this capital was drawn from other employments, if the
> funds which took the place of the capital sunk in costly
> machinery, were supplied not by any additional saving con-
> sequent on the improvements, but by drafts on the general
> capital of the community; what better were the labouring
> classes for the mere transfer? In what manner was the loss
> they sustained by the conversion of circulating into fixed capital
> made up to them by a mere shifting of part of the remainder
> of the circulating capital from its old employments to a new
> one?[37]

Mill condemned all the apologists outright for their dismissive attitudes to Ricardo's chapter on machinery : 'All attempts to make out that the labouring classes as a collective body *cannot* suffer temporarily by the introduction of machinery, or by the sinking of capital in permanent improvements, are, I conceive, necessarily fallacious.'[38]

Yet Mill, like Ricardo, was unwilling after assessing a generation's writing on the costs and benefits of technical progress, to regard the dislocations caused by technical change as a really pressing problem. Like Ricardo, he believed that most technical improvements were made gradually, and that they were seldom made at the cost of withdrawing circulating capital from production. He was prepared to admit that there was usually some suffering during the process of technical change, and believed that the state should, therefore, try to moderate the rapidity of innovation : 'There cannot be a more legitimate object of the legis-lator's care than the interests of those who are thus sacrificed to the gains of their fellow citizens.' But Mill judiciously concluded on an optimistic note :

> The quantity of capital which will, or even which can be
> accumulated in any country, and the amount of gross produce
> which will, or even which can, be raised, bear a proportion
> to the state of the arts there existing; and that every improve-
> ment, even if for the time it diminish the circulating capital and
> the gross produce, ultimately makes room for a larger amount
> of both, than could possibly have existed otherwise. It is this

[37] *Ibid*. p. 96.
[38] *Ibid*.

which is the conclusive answer to the objections against machinery; and the proof thence arising of the ultimate benefit to labourers of mechanical inventions even in the existing state of society will hereafter be seen to be conclusive.[39]

Mill gave further consideration to the significance of technical change in the wider context of economic growth when he came to examine capital accumulation, population increase, diminishing returns, and, finally, the stationary state.

In his analysis of capital accumulation, which he regarded as proceeding alongside and allowing for technical change, Mill deployed the same type of sociological reasoning which had so impressed him in the work of John Rae. Like Rae he cited numerous instances of improvidence and of an underdeveloped sense of future among 'savage' nations, including the natives of Paraguay, the North American Indians, and the Chinese.[40] But Mill was equally critical of what he regarded as the excessive spirit of accumulation in the English middle classes. The English bourgeois seemed to possess an almost infinite capacity to save, for he desired not mere wealth, but rank, that is the ability not only 'to have a large income while in business, but in order to retire from business'. Mill did not have to await Weber for the explanation of this. He argued himself that such attitudes had been nurtured in England 'by the extreme incapacity of the people for personal enjoyment which is characteristic of countries over which puritanism has passed'.[41]

Mill envisaged little possibility of growth being limited in the English economy by insufficient capital accumulation. However, he did find a limit to growth in the land. Unlike nearly the entire generation of Ricardo's critics who had dismissed the immediate prospect of limitations on growth due to diminishing returns in agriculture, Mill clung firmly to a belief in the combination of Malthusian population growth and limits on land. As he put it, it was

> commonly thought . . . that for the present all limitation to production and population from this source is at indefinite distance and that ages must elapse before any practical necessity arise for taking the limiting principle into serious consideration.

[39] *Ibid.* pp. 99, 98.
[40] *Ibid.* p. 104.
[41] *Ibid.* p. 171.

> I apprehend this to be not only an error, but the most
> serious one to be found in the whole field of political economy.
> The question is more important and fundamental than any
> other; it involves the whole subject of the causes of poverty, in
> a rich and industrious community.[42]

After detailing all the countertendencies to the law of diminishing
returns to be found in technological, agricultural, industrial, legal,
trade, and government improvements, Mill still asserted the domination
of the limitations of land and excessive population growth : 'the necessity
of restraining population is not peculiar to a condition of great inequality of property – a greater number of people cannot in any state
of civilization be collectively so well provided for as a smaller.'[43] Even
though the repeal of the Corn Laws could be said to be analogous to a
technological improvement in agriculture, it did not allay 'the necessity
of restraining population'.[44]

In Book II of his *Principles*, when he considered the laws of distribution, Mill again asserted in no uncertain terms his belief in the
population principle. Again a generation of critics and social reformers
he chose a determined and 'rational' course.

> Unhappily, sentimentality rather than common sense usually
> presides over discussion of these subjects; and while there is a
> growing sensitiveness to the hardships of the poor, and a ready
> disposition to admit claims in them upon the good offices of
> other people, there is an all but universal unwillingness to face
> the real difficulty of their position, or advert at all the con-
> ditions which nature has made indispensable to the improve-
> ment of their physical lot. Discussions on the condition of the
> labourers, lamentations over its wretchedness, denunciations of
> all who are supposed to be indifferent to it, projects of one kind
> or another for improving it, were in no country and in no time
> of the world so rife as in the present generation; but there is a
> tacit agreement to ignore totally the law of wages, or to dismiss
> it in parenthesis, with such terms as 'hard-hearted Malthusian-
> ism'; as if it were not a thousand times more hard-hearted to
> tell human beings that they may not, call into existence swarms
> of creatures who are sure to be miserable, and most likely to be

[42] *Ibid.* p. 173.
[43] *Ibid.* p. 189.
[44] *Ibid.*

depraved; and forgetting that the conduct, which it is reckoned so cruel to disapprove, is a degrading slavery to a brute instinct in one of the persons concerned, and most commonly, in the other, helpless submission to a revolting abuse of power.[45]

Mill's harsh words on the barbarian sexual appetites of the human race determined his final assessment of the growth and prospects of the British economy. Like many of his contemporaries, he expressed excitement and satisfaction over the enormous range of technological improvements that seemed to come in endless succession.

> Our knowledge of the properties and laws of physical objects shows no sign of approaching its ultimate boundaries : it is advancing more rapidly, and in a greater number of directions at once, than in any previous age or generation, and affording such frequent glimpses of unexplored fields beyond, as to justify the belief that our acquaintance with nature is still almost in its infancy. This increasing physical knowledge is now, too, more rapidly than at any former period, converted by practical ingenuity, into physical power. The most marvellous of modern inventions, one which realises the imaginary feats of the magician, not metaphorically but literally – the electro-magnetic telegraph – sprang into existence but a few years after the establishment of the scientific theory which it realises and exemplifies . . . there is no difficulty in finding or forming, in a sufficient number of working hands of the community, the skill requisite for executing the most delicate processes of the application of science to practical uses. From this union of condition, it is impossible not to look forward to a vast multiplication and long succession of contrivances for economising labour and increasing its produce; and to an ever wider diffusion of the use and benefits of those contrivances.[46]

Mill, however, believed that whatever the extent of scientific and techno-logical progress, the Malthusian law of population growth might still remain a real practical problem. For though there might be an increase in national prosperity, and even a better distribution so that both rich and poor could get richer, still the very poorest might 'increase in numbers only, and not in comfort nor in cultivation'.[47]

45 *Ibid.* pp. 352–3.
46 *Ibid.* p. 706.
47 *Ibid.* p. 708.

With this reassertion against the critics of Ricardo and Malthus of the continuing significance of the Malthusian population principle, Mill added his belief that technological progress in agriculture would never be sufficient to outweigh diminishing returns. Mill observed that technological progress in agriculture was very different in character from that in manufacturing. In agriculture skill and knowledge increased only gradually and spread more slowly, inventions and discoveries took place only very occasionally. There was, in effect, little prospect of agricultural improvements ever acting to reduce rents, for population and capital were more likely to increase faster.[48]

These limitations of land and population, acting together, would ultimately drive the rate of profit down to the point where there would be no further incentive to capital accumulation. This was the stationary state. But these were the limitations imposed by scarcities and need, and the approach to this gloomy prospect could therefore be held back by improvements in production and trade. There was, however, another force which could drive an economy to a stationary state : a high accumulation of capital, such that opulence itself could prove to be a limitation.

> When a country has long possessed a large production, and a
> large net income to make savings from, and when therefore the
> means have long existed of making a great annual addition
> to capital . . . it is one of the characteristics of such a country,
> that the rate of profit is habitually within the minimum and
> the country therefore on the verge of the stationary state.[49]

The approach of this stationary state was to be prevented only by wasting capital through commercial crises, or by exporting it to colonies and other nations.[50] It was indeed just as much a prospect for rich nations as for poor. In rich, populated and highly cultivated countries it was not capital which was deficient but fertile land. The legislature needed to promote not savings but greater return to savings through improvements in agriculture and the cultivation of more fertile land. In a society rich in capital, the introduction of machinery could not bring any loss to the working class, but only benefit. Where capital was abundant, as in the days of the railway mania, the conversion of cir-

[48] *Ibid.* pp. 727, 729.
[49] *Ibid.* p. 738.
[50] *Ibid.* pp. 742–6.

culating into fixed capital would not be likely to reduce gross produce or the level of employment.[51]

Mill, unlike Ricardo, believed that a stationary state was quite likely to come to the British economy. Though recognising the range and impact of technological and scientific progress, he was not so ready as his predecessors to see in the machine the great social and economic panacea to all the economy's strains and stresses. Like Ricardo he was ambivalent towards the idea of the universal benefits of mechanising in a capital scarce economy. But he envisaged no fears from the machine in the British economy of the late 1840s and 1850s, for the problem now was not the scarcity but the excess of capital.

A more telling indication of Mill's ambivalence towards the great spirit of technological improvement in the mid-Victorian economy is to be found in his critique of the division of labour. Mill was not impressed with the disciplined alienated labour produced by the factory system and the division of labour. The end of economic growth would, he hoped, produce more than this. He therefore welcomed the advent of the stationary state and demurred from the predisposition of all previous economists 'completely to identify all that is economically desirable with the progressive state, and with that alone'.

> I cannot, therefore, regard the stationary state of capital and wealth with the unaffected aversion so generally manifested towards it by political economists of the old school. I am inclined to believe that it would be, on the whole, a very considerable improvement on our present condition. I confess I am not charmed with the ideal of life held out by those who think that the normal state of human beings is that of struggling to get on; that the trampling, crushing, elbowing, and treading on each other's heels, which form the existing type of social life, are the most desirable lot of human kind, or anything but the disagreeable symptoms of one of the phases of industrial progress.[52]

The constant improvements of the progressive state of society did not necessarily include, and indeed generally excluded, the mental, moral and social improvements which civilised a nation. Mill regarded America as the epitome of the philistinism of economic progress.

[51] *Ibid.* p. 751.
[52] *Ibid.* p. 752.

> The northern and middle states of America are a specimen of
> this state of civilization in very favourable circumstances;
> having, apparently, got rid of all social injustices and inequal-
> ities that affect persons of Caucasian race and of the male sex,
> while the proportions of population to capital and land is such
> as to ensure abundance to every able-bodied member of the
> community who does not forfeit it by misconduct. They have
> the six points of Chartism, and they have no poverty : and all
> that these advantages do for them is that the life of the whole
> of one sex is devoted to dollar hunting, and of the other to
> breeding dollar hunters.[53]

Mill idealised the stationary state as the time to look forward to improvements in the 'Art of living'. This would be the time when minds
would no longer be 'engrossed with the art of getting on'. The industrial
arts could be cultivated for a new purpose : not that merely of increasing
the wealth of a few individuals, but of reducing labour and increasing
leisure.

> Hitherto it is questionable if all the mechanical inventions
> yet made have lightened the day's toil of any human being.
> They have enabled a greater population to live the same life
> of drudgery and imprisonment, and an increased number of
> manufacturers and others to make fortunes. They have in-
> creased the comforts of the middle classes. But they have not
> yet begun to effect those great changes in human destiny,
> which it is in their nature and in their futurity to accomplish.[54]

The machinery question reached its culmination as a major issue of
economic thought in the 1840s. The disputes of a generation were
summed up, but not resolved, in the contrasting legacies of classical
political economy – the writings of Frederick Engels and John Stuart
Mill in the 1840s. While the period of remarkable economic growth
which constituted the Industrial Revolution had been attributed by a
generation of economic and social commentators to the machine, the
final assessment of this revolution and of machinery's economic and
social impact was not an enthusiatic one. Both Engels and Mill recognised that the modern economic and social system was founded on the
machine, and that the machine contained within it wonderful possi-

[53] *Ibid.* p. 754.
[54] *Ibid.* pp. 755–6.

bilities to help create a better future. But Engels linked the impact of the machine to the expansion of capitalism. However much technical progress added to economic growth, it was used only for the aggrandisement of capital and the degradation of labour. In the context of capitalism, the machine had not brought relief from labour but greater intensity of labour, lower wages and unemployment. Nor was Mill very sanguine as to the machine's universal benefits. It could not be said to have improved the lot of the very poor. Where Engels attributed this misallocation of the gains from technical progress to capitalism, Mill attributed it to the pressures of economic growth. He awaited a stationary state which would bring reassessment, redistribution, and revival of moral and mental cultivation.

Political economy between the end of the Napoleonic Wars and the 1840s did not carry the messages of gloom and pessimism generally associated with the 'dismal science' in these years. It was, rather, a literature of improvement, singing the praises of the great technological advances of the time. But these optimistic economists and the many layers of middle-class apologists who vulgarised their message were missionaries come to spread the gospel of the machine in a land of heretical anti-machinery attitudes. The actual lingering distress experienced by the handloom weavers encouraged writers of radical and reactionary persuasion, social reformers, and even some economists and manufacturers to challenge the advance of the machine. The struggle over how far, how fast, and for whose benefit the machine should be allowed to advance was not resolved before the onset of the mid-Victorian boom. In one sense the anti-machinery critics of political economy won their point, for J. S. Mill, who was to hold sway as the leader of middle-class political economy for almost the rest of the century, passed on to the establishment their criticisms and dissatisfaction with the great benefits brought by the machine. In another sense the critics lost, for there was to be no policy on technology, no redistribution of the gains of increased productivity, and no state or private means of providing for those displaced, if even for a time, by the machine. But in the final analysis it was, after all, technological change which had given economists the possibility of disclaiming the prospect of the stationary state, and it was only in an economy that had experienced its technological revolution that Mill could envisage the possibility of a beneficient stationary state.

There was ultimately a more important end to the machinery question than the success or failure of either of its antagonistic intellectual traditions. For in its total configuration it was the dynamic principle of Marx's concept of the phase of 'modern industry'. In 'modern industry' the drive to increase surplus value found its most complete and most powerful support in the tendency to revolutionary technological change. This phase was defined by Marx to distinguish the role of the machine and automatic processes of production. Machinery was a new subjective force 'with a soul of its own in the mechanical laws acting through it'.[55] The introduction of machinery required 'the substitution of natural forces for human force, and the conscious application of science, instead of rule of thumb'.[56] Marx predicted that the most complete form of machinery was its automatic system of machinery – 'this automaton consisting of numerous mechanical and intellectual organs, so that the workers themselves are cast merely as conscious linkages'.[57] Moreover, Marx analysed the way in which this road to the automatic system of machinery was based on the division of labour.

> This road is, rather, dissection ... through the division of labour, which gradually transforms the workers' operations into more and more mechanical ones, so that at a certain point a mechanism can step into their places. .... Thus, the specific mode of working here appears directly as becoming transferred from the worker to capital in the form of the machine, and his own labour capacity devalued thereby. Hence the workers' struggle against machinery. What was the living worker's activity becomes the activity of the machine. Thus the appropriation of labour by capital confronts the worker in a coarsely sensuous form; capital absorbs labour into itself – 'as though its body were by love possessed'.[58]

This book has demonstrated how these images of science, technology, and the automatic system of machinery which we find in Marx were created by political economy. Marx was not the originator of this vision of the future impact of the machine, nor was he only developing the perceptions of his socialist ancestors in English radicalism. He took this conception of technology and the focus on production as the centre

[55] Karl Marx, *The Grundrisse* (1857–8), trans. Martin Nicolaus, Harmondsworth, 1973, p. 693.
[56] Marx, *Capital*, p. 386.
[57] Marx, *The Grundrisse*, p. 692.
[58] *Ibid.* p. 704.

of the economic dynamic of the capitalist system from his major antagonist, English political economy. It was Ricardo who demonstrated the limitless potential in machinery to carry the economic system beyond the threat of a stationary state. It was Senior, Jones, Babbage and Ure who translated the abstract concept of technological progress into a practical but all embracing means of power and control. It was from these sources, from this political economy 'made' by the machinery question, that Marx drew his inspiration to write of a new era where :

> The production process has ceased to be a labour process in the sense of a process dominated by labour as its governing unity. Labour appears, rather, merely as a conscious organ, scattered among the individual living workers at numerous points of the mechanical system; subsumed under the total process of the machinery itself, as itself only a link of the system, whose unity exists not in the living workforce, but rather in the living (active) machinery, which confronts his individual, insignificant doings as a mighty organism.[59]

But this new technological era would also be a new era for class formation. Here Marx, through Engels, drew on the critique of machinery and political economy in English radicalism, Tory romanticism and social reform to describe the degradation of labour under the capitalist development of technology. He describes, as did the Owenites, the process by which labour was divided, and then transferred to the machine. Capital absorbed labour into itself, 'as though its body were by love possessed'. Marx drew not only on the images of the degradation of labour conjured up by the Owenites but also on their apocalyptic predictions of the revolutionary potential in a degraded class that had been itself created by the technological revolution. He incorporated Engels's concept of a unitary working class created by a common experience of exploitation under the new industrial and technological system. Yet he went beyond Engels, for the systematic concept of modern industry which he built out of political economy contained within it the conception of an ultimate technological future without labour. It was not a big step to take English radicalism and Engels to their limits, and to declare that modern industry contained not only the conditions for the creation of the working class but also the conditions for the destruction of capitalism itself.

[59] *Ibid.* p. 693.

Capital itself is the moving contradiction, ... In the one side, it calls to life all the powers of science and of nature, as of social combination and of social intercourse, in order to make the creation of wealth independent (relatively) of the labour time employed on it. On the other side, it wants to use labour time as the measuring rod for the giant social forces thereby created, and to confine them within the limits required to maintain the already created value as value. Forces of production and social relations – two different sides of the development of the social individual – appear to capital as mere means, and are merely means for it to produce on its limited foundation. In fact, however, they are the material conditions to blow this foundation sky high.[60]

[60] *Ibid.* p. 706.

BIBLIOGRAPHY

Manuscript sources

Birkbeck College, London.
  London Mechanics Institution, Minute Books of the Committee, 1824–39.
The British Library.
  Babbage Papers
  Peel Papers
  Place Collection of Newspaper Cuttings
  Place Papers
British Library of Political and Economic Science.
  John Barton, Manuscript Notebooks
  Webb Papers – Trade Union Collection
Brotherton Library, University of Leeds.
  Benjamin Gott Papers
  Marshall Papers
Houghton Library, Harvard University.
  Letters from Harriet Martineau
Lambeth Palace Library.
  Correspondence of Richard Whately
Leeds Public Library.
  Baines Papers
Manchester Public Library.
  Lancashire Commercial Clubs Association Minutes 1834–64
  Manchester Chamber of Commerce Annual Reports 1820–45
  Manchester Chamber of Commerce Minutes 1821–41
  Manchester Statistical Society Appendix to the Minutes
National Library of Scotland.
  Letters from Joseph Hume
National Library of Wales, Aberystwyth.
  Senior Papers
Nuffield College Library.
  Cobbett Papers

T.M.Q.—M

Public Record Office.
  Board of Trade Papers
  Home Office Papers – Handloom Weavers' Petitions
Royal Statistical Society, London.
  Minutes of the London Statistical Society
John Rylands Library, Manchester.
  Fielden–Cobbett Correspondence 1834–48
Trinity College, Cambridge.
  Whewell Papers
University College, London.
  Brougham Papers – Letters to H. Brougham Concerning Mechanics' Institutions
  1826

Unpublished theses

Berg, Maxine, 'The Introduction and Diffusion of the Power Loom 1789–1842',
  M.A., University of Sussex, 1972.
– 'The Machinery Question : Conceptions of Technical Change during the
  Industrial Revolution c. 1820–40', D.Phil., University of Oxford, 1976.
Chapman, S. D., 'William Felkin', M.A., University of Nottingham, 1962.
De Marchi, N. B., 'J. S. Mill and the Development of English Economic Thought :
  A Study in the Progress of Ricardian Orthodoxy', Ph.D., Australian National
  University, Canberra, 1970.
Dobson, J. L., 'The Contribution of Francis Place and the Radicals to the Growth
  of Popular Education 1800–1840', Ph.D., University of Newcastle upon Tyne,
  1959.
Foster, J. C. O., 'Capitalism and Class Consciousness in Earlier Nineteenth Century
  Oldham', Ph.D., University of Cambridge, 1967.
Gattrell, V. A. C., 'The Commercial Middle Classes in Manchester 1820–1857',
  Ph.D., University of Cambridge, 1972.
Hilton, A. J. B., 'The Economic Policies of the Tory Governments 1815–1830',
  D.Phil., University of Oxford, 1973.
Morris, R. J., 'Organization and Aims of the Principal Secular Voluntary Organiza-
  tions of the Leeds Middle Class 1830–1851', D.Phil. University of Oxford, 1970.
Yeo, Eileen, 'Social Science and Social Change', D.Phil., University of Sussex, 1972.

Printed sources – Primary

PARLIAMENTARY PAPERS (P.P.)

Report from the Select Committee Appointed to Inquire How Far it May be
  Practicable to Compel Persons Using Steam Engines and Furnaces to Erect Them
  in a Manner Less Prejudicial to Public Comfort, 1819 (574), VII; 1820 (244), II.
Report of the Select Committee on Combination Laws, Artisans and Machinery,
  1824, V.
Report from the Select Committee on the Laws Relating to the Export of Tools
  and Machinery, 1825, V.
Report from the Select Committee on Manufactures, Commerce and Shipping,
  1833, VI.
Report from the Select Committee on Handloom Weavers, 1834, X.
Report from the Select Committee on Handloom Weavers' Petitions, 1835, XIII.
Report of the Select Committee on Arts and Manufactures, 1835, V.
Report of the Select Committee on Education in England and Wales, 1835, VII.

A Return of the Number of Powerlooms used in Factories in the Manufacture of Woollen, Cotton, Silk, and Linen in each County of the U.K. respectively, so far as they can be collected from the Returns of the Factory Commissioners, 15 February 1836 (24), XIV.

Reports from the Assistant Handloom Weavers Commissioners, 1840, part iv, XXIV.

Report of the Royal Commission on Handloom Weavers, 1841, X.

Report of the Select Committee Appointed to Inquire into the Export of Machinery, 1841, VII.

Report of the Select Committee on Public Libraries, 1849, XVII.

NEWSPAPERS

The Advocate or Artisans' and Labourers' Friend
Birmingham Advertiser
Blackburn Gazette
Blackburn Mail
Bolton Chronicle
Bradford Observer
Caledonian Mercury
The Champion
The Chartist Circular
The Crisis
The Economist
Glasgow Chronicle
Glasgow Herald
Glasgow Weavers' Journal
The Globe and Traveller
Herald of the Rights of Industry
Herald of the Trades Advocate and Co-operative Journal
The Journeyman and Artisans' London and Provincial Chronicle
Leeds Intelligencer
Leeds Mercury
Liverpool Mercury
Manchester Gazette
Manchester Guardian
Manchester and Salford Advertiser
The Morning Chronicle
The New Moral World
Pamphlets for the People
The Pioneer
The Political Magazine
Poor Man's Advocate
Poor Man's Guardian
Preston Chronicle
The Scotsman
Sheffield Independent
Sheffield Iris
The Times
The Trades Newspaper and Mechanics' Weekly Journal
Voice of the West Riding
The Weavers' Journal

PERIODICALS

The Analyst
Blackwood's Edinburgh Magazine
The British Critic
The Edinburgh Review
Fraser's Magazine
The Glasgow Mechanics Magazine
Journal of the Statistical Society of London
The London Mechanics Magazine
Magazine of Useful Knowledge, Co-operative Miscellany
Mechanics Gallery of Science and Art
Mechanics Weekly Journal and Artizans Miscellany
Memoirs of the Manchester Literary and Philosophical Society
The Millocrat
Proceedings of the London Statistical Society
Quarterly Review
*Reports and Transactions of the British Association for the Advancement of
    Science*
Transactions of the Glasgow and Clydesdale Statistical Society
Transactions of the Philosophical and Literary Society of Leeds
Westminster Review

BOOKS AND ARTICLES

*Advice to the Labouring Poor with Especial References to Tumultous Assemblages
    and the Breaking of Machinery*, n.p., 1831.
[Alison, Sir A.], 'Social and Moral Condition of the Manufacturing Districts of
    Scotland', *Blackwood's Edinburgh Magazine*, 1841.
Allin, Thomas, *A Lecture Delivered on the Opening of the Sheffield Mechanics
    Institution on the 14th of January, 1833 by the Reverend Thomas Allin*, Sheffield,
    1833.
[Americus Curiae, pseud.], *A Word to the Manufacturers of Great Britain on the
    Prospects of the Cotton Trade*, 1840.
*Analysis of the Evidence taken before the Factory Commissioners as Far as it
    Relates to the Population of Manchester . . . Read before the Statistical Society
    of Manchester*, March 1834.
Annual Reports of the Poor Law Commissioners for England and Wales, London,
    1835, 1836, 1837.
*Second Annual Report of the Literary, Scientific and Mechanical Institution of
    Newcastle upon Tyne*, Newcastle upon Tyne, 1826.
*Third Annual Report of the Literary, Scientific and Mechanical Institution of
    Newcastle upon Tyne*, Newcastle upon Tyne, 1827.
[Arrowsmith, J. H.], *Essay on Mechanics Institutes with Particular Relation to the
    Institution Recently Established in Bolton*, Bolton, 1825.
Atkinson, W., *Principles of Political Economy . . . being the Substance of a Case
    delivered to the Handloom Weavers' Commission*, London, 1840.
Babbage, C., 'Account of the Great Congress of Philosophers at Berlin', *Edinburgh
    Journal of Science*, x, 1829.
– *Reflections on the Decline of Science in England*, London, 1830.
– *On the Economy of Machinery and Manufactures*, London, 1st, 2nd and 3rd
    editions, 1832, 4th edition, 1835.
– *Passages in the Life of a Philosopher*, London, 1864.

'Mr. Babbage and the Useful Arts', *Cobbett's Magazine*, II, December 1833.

[Bailey, S.], *Essays on the Formation and Publication of Opinions*, London, 1821.

[–] *A Critical Dissertation on the Nature, Measures, and Causes of Value: Chiefly in Reference to the Writings of Mr. Ricardo and his Followers*, London, 1825.

[–] *A Letter to a Political Economist Occasioned by an Article in the Westminster Review on the Subject of Value*, London, 1826.

Baines, Edward, jun., *Letter to the Unemployed Workmen of Yorkshire and Lancashire on the Present Distress and on Machinery*, London, 1826.

– *History of the Cotton Manufacture of Great Britain*, London, 1835.

– *On the Moral Influence of Free Trade and its Effects on the Prosperity of Nations; Read before the Leeds Philosophical and Literary Society*, Leeds, 1830.

Baird, C. R., 'Observations on the Poorest Class of Operatives in Glasgow', *Journal of the Statistical Society of London*, I, 1838.

Barlow, Peter, *A Treatise on the Manufactures and Machinery of Great Britain to which is Prefaced an Introductory View of the Principles of Manufactures by Charles Babbage*, London, 1836.

Barnes, Thomas, *A Discourse Delivered at the Commencement of the Manchester Academy*, Warrington, 1786.

– *Thoughts on the Use of Machines in the Cotton Manufacture Addressed to the Working People in that Manufacture . . . by a Friend of the Poor*, Manchester, 1780.

Barton, John, *An Inquiry into the Causes of the Progressive Depreciation of Agricultural Labour in Modern Times*, London, 1820.

– *Observations on the Circumstances which Influence the Condition of the Labouring Classes of Society*, London, 1817.

Bolton County Borough Manufacturers and Weavers Committee, *Letter to Parliament*, Bolton, 1834.

Bowring, Sir J., *Copy of Correspondence between Dr. Bowring and the Associated Weavers' Committee, Kilmarnock*, Kilmarnock, 1835.

– 'Report on the Commerce and Manufactures of Switzerland', *Edinburgh Review*, LXIV, October 1836.

Bray, J. F., *Labour's Wrongs and Labour's Remedy: or the Age of Might and the Age of Right*, Leeds, 1839.

[Brewster, David], 'Charles Babbage, Reflection on the Decline of Science in England', *Quarterly Review*, XLIII, October 1830.

[–]'Whewell's History of the Inductive Sciences', *Edinburgh Review*, LXVII, 1838.

Brontë, Charlotte, *Shirley* (1849), Everyman, London, 1970.

[Brougham, H.], *Address of Henry, Lord Brougham to the Members of the Manchester Mechanics Institution*, Manchester, 1835.

[–] *An Address to the Labourers on the Subject of Destroying Machinery*, London, 1830.

[–] *A Discourse on the Objects, Advantages, and Pleasures of Science*, London, 1827, printed in The Library of Useful Knowledge, London, 1829.

[–] 'Lord Lauderdale's Inquiry into the Nature and Origins of Public Wealth', *Edinburgh Review*, IV, July 1804.

[–] *Practical Observations upon the Education of the People Addressed to the Working Classes and their Employers*, London, 1825.

Burges, G., *Unrestrained Machinery Must Ere Long be the Ruin of the Country*, Bradford, 1834.

Burnet, Richard, *A Word to the Members of Mechanics Institutes*, Devonport, 1826.

Burns, David, *Mechanics Institutions; Their Objects and Tendency*, Glasgow, 1837.

Burrows, G. C., *A Word to the Electors. Letters to the Present Generation on the*

Unrestrained Use of Modern Machinery, Norwich and London, 1832.

Carlyle, Thomas, *Collected Works*, 17 vols., London, 1885–91.

Cayley, E. S., *On Commercial Economy in Six Essays*, London, 1830.

Cazenove, John, *Considerations on the Accumulation of Capital*, London, 1822.

[–] *Outlines of Political Economy*, London, 1832.

[Chalmers, Thomas], *The Christian and Civic Economy of Our Large Towns*, 3 vols., Glasgow 1821–6.

– *On Political Economy in Connexion with the Moral State and Moral Prospects of Society*, Glasgow, 1832.

– 'State and Prospects of Manufactures', *Edinburgh Review*, XXXIII, May 1820.

[Chenevix, R.], 'Comparative Skill and Industry of France and England', *Edinburgh Review*, XXXII, October 1819.

[–] 'History and Prospects of British Industry', *Quarterly Review*, XXXIV, June 1826.

Cleland, J., *Statistical Facts Descriptive of the Former and Present State of Glasgow*, Glasgow, 1837.

Coates, Thomas, *Report on the State of Literary, Scientific and Mechanics Institutes in England*, Society for the Diffusion of Useful Knowledge, London, 1841.

Cobbett, W., *Rights of Industry*, London, 1833.

– 'A Letter to the Luddites', *Cobbett's Weekly Political Register*, London, 30 November 1816.

[–] *A Full and Accurate Report of the Trial of William Cobbett, Esq.*, London, 1831.

Colquhoun, P., *A Treatise on the Wealth, Power, and Resources of the British Empire*, London, 1814.

Committee of Machine Makers, *Facts and Observations Illustrative of the Evils of the Law which Prohibits the Exportation of Machinery*, Manchester, 1841.

Committee of Manufacturers and Weavers of Bolton, *A Letter Addressed to the Members of both Houses of Parliament on the Distresses of the Handloom Weavers*, Bolton, 1834.

'Condition of the Labouring Classes', *Quarterly Review*, XLVIII, November 1831.

A Conversation between George Hadfield and Charles Comber, on Machinery, Emigration, and Free Trade, Bradford, 1834.

Corbet, D., *An Address Delivered to the Members of the Worcester Literary and Scientific Institution*, Worcester, 1833.

Cotterill, C. F., *An Examination of the Doctrines of Value*, London, 1831.

[Coulson, E.], 'McCulloch's Principles of Political Economy', *Edinburgh Review*, LII, January 1831.

Craster, T., *A View of Manufactures, Money and Corn Laws ... with Observations on the National Worth of Machinery*, London, 1840.

Davis, John, *An Appeal to the Public on Behalf of the Manchester Mechanics Institution*, Manchester, 1831.

[De Quincey, T.], 'Dialogues of the Three Templars on Political Economy', in *Works*, ed. David Masson, London, 1897, IX.

[–] 'The Prospects of Britain', *Blackwood's Edinburgh Magazine*, XXXI, April 1832.

Detrosier, Rowland, *An Address Delivered at the New Mechanics Institution, December 30, 1829*, Manchester, 1829.

– *An Address Delivered to the Members of the New Mechanics Institution on the Necessity of an Extension of Moral and Political Instruction among the Working Classes*, Manchester, 1831.

– *An Address on the Advantages of the Intended Mechanics Hall of Science*, Manchester, 1831.

– *The Benefits of General Knowledge, more especially the Sciences of Mineralogy,*

*Geology, Botany, and Entomology in an Address delivered at the Opening of
the Banksian Society*, Manchester, 1829.

*A Dialogue on Rick-burning, Rioting etc. between Squire Wilson, Hughes his
Steward, Thomas the Bailiff and Harry Brown a Labourer*, n.p. 1830.

Dickens, Charles, *Hard Times* (1854), Harmondsworth, 1969.

Disraeli, Benjamin, *Sybil; or the Two Nations* (1845), London, 1926.

Dodd, George, *Days at the Factories, or The Manufacturing Industry of Great
Britain Described*, London, 1843.

Dupin, F. C., *Voyages dans la Grand Bretagne*, Paris, 1824.

[Duppa, B. F.], *A Manual for Mechanics Institutions*, London, 1839.

[Edwards, Edward], 'The Influence of Free Trade upon the Condition of the
Labouring Classes', *Blackwood's Edinburgh Magazine*, XXVII, April 1830.

The Effects of Machinery on Manual Labour, London, 1831.

Eliot, George, *Middlemarch* (1861–2), Harmondsworth, 1965.

Ellis, E. E., *Memoir of William Ellis*, London, 1888.

Ellis, William, *Conversations upon Knowledge, Happiness and Education*, London,
1829.

[–] 'Effects of the Employment of Machinery upon the Happiness of the Working
Classes', *Westminster Review*, V, January 1826.

[–] 'Exportation of Machinery', *Westminster Review*, III, April 1825.

[Empson, William], 'Mrs Marcet, Miss Martineau', *Edinburgh Review*, LVII,
January 1833.

Engels, Frederick, *The Condition of the Working Class in England* (1845),
trans., and ed. W. O. Henderson and W. H. Chaloner, Oxford, 1958.

– *The Condition of the Working Class in England* (1845), trans. Institute of
Marxism–Leninism, Moscow, ed. E. J. Hobsbawm, London, 1969.

[–] 'Condition of England: Carlyle', *Collected Works*, vol. III, London, 1975.

[–] 'Outline of a Critique of Political Economy' (1844), in Karl Marx, *The
Economic and Philosophical Manuscripts of 1844*, ed. Dirk J. Struik,
New York, 1964.

An Essay on the Political Economy of Nations, London, 1821.

*Extracts from the Information Received from His Majesty's Commissioners as to
Administration and Operation of the Poor Laws*, London 1833.

Fairbairn, William, *A Treatise on Mills and Millwork*, 2 vols. (1861), 2nd edition,
London, 1865.

Farey, J. H., *A Treatise on the Steam Engine, Historical, Practical and Descriptive*,
London, 1827.

Felkin, William, *An Account of the Machine Wrought Hosiery Trade. Extent and
Conditions of the Framework Knitters, read in the Statistical Section of the
Second York Meeting of the British Association*, 2nd edition, London, 1845.

– *A History of the Machine Wrought Hosiery and Lace Manufactures*, London,
1867.

– *Remarks upon the Importance of an Inquiry into the Amount and Appropriation of
Wages by the Working Classes. Addressed to the Statistical Section of the British
Association*, London, 1837.

A Few Observations on Some Topics of Political Economy, London, 1825.

Fielden, John, *The Curse of the Factory System*, London, 1836.

*First Report of the Directors of the School of Arts of Edinburgh for the Education
of Mechanics in such Branches of Physical Science as are of Practical Application
in their Several Trades*, May 1822.

First Report of the Mechanics Institute of Darlington, Darlington, 1826.

Gaskell, Elizabeth, *Mary Barton* (1848), Everyman, London, 1967.

Gaskell, Peter, *Artisans and Machinery*, London, 1836.
– *The Manufacturing Population of England*, London, 1833.
Gaskell, W. P., *An Address to the Operative Classes, being the Substance of a Letter Explanatory and in Defence of the Nature and Objects of the Cheltenham Mechanics Institution*, Cheltenham, 1835.
Glasgow Literary and Commercial Society, *List of Essays Read by Members, 1806–1830*, Glasgow, 1831.
Glasgow Stastistical Society. *Constitution, Regulations and Transactions,* Glasgow 1836.
Gray, Simon, *The Essential Principles of the Wealth of Nations in Opposition to Some False Doctrine of Dr. Adam Smith*, London, 1797.
– *The Happiness of States or an Inquiry Concerning Population*, London, 1815.
– (pseud. George Purves), *All Classes Productive of National Wealth or the Theories of M. Quesnai, Dr. Adam Smith and Mr. Gray*, London, 1817.
Greg, Samuel, *Two Letters to Leonard Horner on the Capabilities of the Factory System,* London, 1840.
Gregory, Theodore, 'Early History of the Manchester Statistical Society', *Transactions of the Manchester Statistical Society*, session 1925–6.
Grinfield, E. W., *A Reply to Brougham's 'Practical Observations'*, London, 1825.
Hamilton, Robert, *The Progress of Society*, London, 1830.
'The Handloom Weavers' Inquiry Commission', *Westminster Review*, XXXVI, 1841.
Handloom Worsted Weavers' Central Committee, *The Report and Resolutions of a Meeting of Deputies from the Handloom Worsted Weavers*, Bradford, 1835.
Henson, Gravenor, *The Civil, Political and Mechanical History of the Framework Knitters,* Nottingham, 1831, reprinted London, 1970.
Heywood, Benjamin, *Addresses Delivered at the Manchester Mechanics Institution*, London, 1843.
– 'Report of an Enquiry Conducted from House to House into the State of 176 Families in Miles Platting, within the Borough of Manchester in 1837', *Journal of the Statistical Society of London*, I, London, 1839.
Hickson, W. E., *The Rights of Industry*, London, 1831.
Hindley, Charles, *Address Delivered at the Establishment of the Mechanics Institution*, Ashton-under-Lyne, 22 June 1825.
[Hodgskin, Thomas], *Labour Defended against the Claims of Capital*, London, 1825.
– *The Natural and Artificial Rights of Property Constrasted. A Series of Letters Addressed . . . to H. Brougham, Esq., M.P.*, London, 1832.
– *Popular Political Economy*, London, 1827.
Hole, James, *An Essay on the History and Management of Literary, Scientific, and Mechanics Institutions*, London, 1853.
Holland, G. C., *An Inquiry into the Moral, Social and Intellectual Condition of the Industrious Classes*, London, 1839.
Hopkins, Thomas, *Economical Enquiries Relative to the Laws which Regulate Rent, Profit, Wages, and the Value of Money*, London, 1822.
– *On Rent of Land and its Influence on Subsistence and Population*, London, 1828.
– *Wages, or Masters and Workment*, Manchester, 1831.
Horton, R. J. W., *Correspondence between the Right Hon. R. Wilmot Horton and a Select Class of the Members of the London Mechanics Institution*, London, 1830.
– *Lectures Delivered at the London Mechanics Institution*, London, 1831.
Hume, A., *The Learned Societies and the Printing Clubs of the U.K.* (1847), 2nd edition with supplement, London, 1853.
Speeches of the Rt. Hon. William Huskisson, 3 vols., London 1831.
An Inquiry into those Principles Respecting the Nature of Demand and the

Necessity of Consumption Lately Advocated by Mr. Malthus, London, 1821.

[Jeffrey, Francis], 'Political Economy by J. R. McCulloch', *Edinburgh Review*, XLIII, November 1825.

[Johnston, William], 'Domestic Policy, No. III: The Condition of the Lower Orders', *Blackwood's Edinburgh Magazine*, XXVII, January 1830.

[–] 'State and Prospects of the Country', *Blackwood's Edinburgh Magazine*, XXVI, September 1829.

Jones, Richard, *An Essay on the Distribution of Wealth, I, Rent*, London, 1831.

– *Literary Remains, Consisting of Lectures and Tracts on Political Economy*, ed. William Whewell, London, 1859.

Kay, J. P., *The Moral and Physical Condition of the Working Classes Employed in the Cotton Manufactures of Manchester*, 2nd edition, London, 1832.

Kennedy, John, 'Observations on the Influence of Machinery upon the Working Classes of the Community' (1826), *Memoirs of the Manchester Literary and Philosophical Society*, 2nd series, V, 1831.

– 'Observations on the Rise and Progress of the Cotton Trade in Great Britain', *Memoirs of the Manchester Literary and Philosophical Society*, 2nd series, III, 1819.

– *On the Exportation of Machinery*, Manchester, April 1824.

Knight, Charles, *The Results of Machinery*, London, 1831.

– *The Rights of Industry: Capital and Labour*, London, 1831.

Labour and Capital. Common Sense to the Working Classes on the Division of Labour and Profits, London, 1836.

Lauderdale, Lord, *An Inquiry into the Nature and Origin of Public Wealth*, Liverpool Statistical Society, *Proceedings*, vol. I, part I, Liverpool, 1838.

Lloyd, W. F., *A Lecture on the Notion of Value*, London, 1834.

– *Two Lectures on the Justice of the Poor Laws and One Lecture on Rent*, London, 1837.

London Debating Society, *Laws and Transactions*, London, 1826.

Longfield, Mountifort, *Lectures on Political Economy*, Dublin, 1834.

Longson, W., *An Appeal to the Masters, Workmen and Public Shewing the Cause of the Distress of the Labouring Classes*, Manchester, 1827.

Lucock, J., *Moral Culture*, London, 1817.

[Lyell, W.], 'Scientific Institutions', *Quarterly Review*, XXIV, 1826.

McCormac, Henry, *On the Best Means of Improving the Moral and Physical Conditions of the Working Classes* (Belfast Mechanics Institution), London, 1830.

McCulloch, J. R., 'Arkwright', *Encyclopædia Britannica*, 7th edition, vol. III.

[–] 'Babbage on Machinery and Manufactures', *Edinburgh Review*, LVI, January 1833.

[–] 'Combination Laws – Restraints on Emigration', *Edinburgh Review*, XXXIX, January 1824.

[–] 'Cottage Systems', *Encyclopedia Britannica*, 6th edition, Supplement, vol. III.

– *A Dictionary of Commerce and Commercial Navigation*, London, 1832.

– *A Discourse Delivered at the Opening of the City of London Literary and Scientific Institution, 30 May, 1825*, London, 1825.

– *A Discourse on the Rise, Progress, Peculiar Objects and Importance of Political Economy*, Edinburgh, 1824.

[–] 'Effects of Machinery and Accumulation', *Edinburgh Review*, XXXV, March 1821.

– *An Essay on the Circumstances which Determine the Rate of Wages and the Condition of the Labouring Classes*, Edinburgh, 1826.

[–] 'Jones on the Theory of Rent', *Edinburgh Review*, LIV, December 1831.

[McCulloch, J. R.], 'On Cottage and Agrarian Systems', *The Scotsman*, 1 March 1817.

[–] 'On Economic Distress and Pauperism', *The Scotsman*, 22 July 1826.

– 'On the Effects of the Employment of Machinery in Manufacturing', *The Scotsman*, 19 April 1817.

[–] 'The Opinions of Messrs. Say, Sismondi, and Malthus on the Effects of Machinery and Accumulation', *Edinburgh Review*, xxxv, March 1821.

[–]'Philosophy of Manufactures', *Edinburgh Review*, lxi, July 1835.

– 'Political Economy', *Encyclopedia Britannica*, 6th edition, Supplement, vol. iii.

[–] 'Present State of Manufactures, Trade and Shipping', *Edinburgh Review*, lviii, October 1833.

– *Principles of Political Economy*, London, 1825, 2nd edition, 1830.

[–] 'Ricardo's Political Economy', *Edinburgh Review*, xxx, June 1818.

[–] 'Mr. Ricardo's Theory of Exchangeable Value Vindicated from the Objections of R', *Edinburgh Magazine*, November 1818.

[–] 'On the Rise, Progress, Present State and Progress of the British Cotton Manufacture', *Edinburgh Review*, xlvi, June 1827.

– *A Statistical Account of the British Empire*, London, 1837.

Machinery versus Manual Labour, London, 1830.

[McIniscon, John, pseud. of J. C. Ross], *Principles of Political Economy and Population*, London, 1825.

MacKinnon, W. A., *On the Rise, Progress and Present State of Public Opinion in Great Britain*, London, 1828.

[Maginn, William], 'The Burnings in Kent and the State of the Labouring Classes', *Fraser's Magazine*, ii, December 1830.

[–] 'The State and Prospects of Toryism', *Fraser's Magazine*, ix, January 1834.

Maitland, James (Lord Lauderdale), *An Inquiry into the Nature and Origins of Public Wealth*, Edinburgh, 1804.

[Mallalieu, Alfred], 'The Cotton Manufactures and the Factory System', Part ii, *Blackwood's Magazine*, xl, July 1836.

Mallet, J. L., 'Diary', *Political Economy Club*, vi, Centenary Volume, London, 1921.

Malthus, T. R., *Definitions in Political Economy*, London, 1827.

– *The Measure of Value Stated and Illustrated*, London, 1823.

– 'Political Economy', *Quarterly Review*, xxx, January 1824.

– *Principles of Political Economy Considered with a view to their Practical Application*, (1820), in P. Sraffa, ed., *Works and Correspondence of David Ricardo*, ii, Cambridge, 1951.

Marcet, Jane, *Conversations in Political Economy*, London, 1816.

Martineau, Harriet, *The Hill and the Valley, Illustrations of Political Economy*, (1832), No. ii, 4th edition, London, 1833.

Marx, Karl, *Capital*, vol. i, trans. Samuel Moore and Edward Aveling, New York, 1967.

– *The Grundisse* (1857–8), trans. Martin Nicolaus, Harmondsworth, 1973.

– *The Poverty of Philosophy*, Moscow, 1947.

– *Theories of Surplus Value*, 3 vols., London, 1969.

Matthews, William, *A Sketch of the Principal Means which Have been taken to Ameliorate the Intellectual and Moral Conditions of the Working Classes at Birmingham*, London, 1830.

Maxwell, John, *Manual Labour versus Machinery*, London, 1834.

[Mercator, pseud.], *A Letter to the Inhabitants of Manchester on the Exportation of Cotton Twist*, Manchester, 1800.

[Merivale, Herman], *An Introductory Lecture on the Study of Political Economy*, London, 1837.

– 'Definitions and Systems of Political Economy', *Edinburgh Review*, LXVI, October 1837.

Mill, James, *Commerce Defended*, London, 1804.

– *Elements of Political Economy*, London, 1821.

– *History of India*, London, 1817.

– *Selected Economic Writings*, ed. D. N. Winch, London, 1966.

Mill, J. S., *Autobiography*, London, 1873.

– *Essays on Some Unsettled Questions of Political Economy*, London, 1844.

[–] 'The Measure of Value of T. R. Malthus', *Morning Chronicle*, 5 September 1823.

[–] 'The Nature, Origin and Progress of Rent' (1828), *Essays on Economics and Society, Collected Works*, vol. IV, Toronto, 1967.

[–] 'Notes on N. W. Senior's Political Economy', *Economica*, XII, 1945.

[–] 'On the Definition of Political Economy and the Method of Philosophical Investigation in that Science', *London and Westminster Review*, XXVI, October 1836.

– *Principles of Political Economy with Some of their Applications to Social Philosophy* (1848), *Collected Works of J. S. Mill*, vols. II and III, Toronto, 1965.

[–] 'The Quarterly Review on Political Economy', *Westminster Review*, III, 1825.

Montgomery, James, *The Theory and Practice of Cotton Spinning; or the Carding and Spinning Master's Assistant*, 2nd edition, Glasgow, 1833.

A Narrative and Exposition of the Origin, Progress, Principles, Objects, etc. of the General Association Established in London for the Purpose of Bettering the Condition of the Manufacturing and Agricultural Classes, London, 1827.

Nasmyth, James, *Autobiography*, ed. Samuel Smiles, London, 1883.

Nicholson, William, *An Abstract of Such Acts of Parliament As Are Now in Force for Preventing Export of Wool and Other Commodities, Tools, and Implements Used in the Manufacture Thereof*, n.p. 1786.

Observations Addressed to all Classes of the Community on the Establishment of Mechanics Institutes, Derby, 1825.

Observations on Certain Verbal Disputes in Political Economy, Particularly Relating to Value and Demand and Supply, London, 1821.

Observations on the Cotton Weavers Act, n.p. 1804.

Observations on the Use of Power Looms by a Friend to the Poor, Rochdale, 1823.

Observations on Woollen Machinery, Leeds, 1803.

O'Connor, Feargus, 'A Treatise on Labour', *The Labourer*, III, London, 1848.

– 'The Land and the Charter', *The Labourer*, I, London, 1847.

'On the Decline of Science in England', *The Athenaeum*, January 1831.

The Opinions of the Late Mr. Ricardo and Adam Smith on Some of the Leading Doctrines of Political Economy. Stated and Compared, London, 1824.

Owen, Robert, *The Life of Robert Owen Written by Himself*, ed. John Butt, London, 1971.

– *A New View of Society and Report to the County of Lanark*, ed. V. A. C. Gattrell, Harmondsworth, 1969.

Partington, C. F., *Account of Steam Engines and Other Models of Machinery Illustrative of Improvements in Railroads, Steam Navigation, and the Arts and Manufactures, with an Historical and Descriptive Account of the Steam Engine*, London, 1840.

Pettman, W. R. A., *An Essay on Political Economy*, London, 1828.

Place, Francis, 'Handloom Weavers and Factory Workers; A Letter to James Turner, Spinner', in J. A. Roebuck, ed., *Pamphlets for the People*, 29 September 1835.

[–] *Notes of Mr. McCulloch's Lecture on the Wages of Labour and the Condition of the Labouring People*, London, 1825.

Plain Sense and Reason. Letters to the Present Generation on the Unrestrained Use of Modern Machinery, Norwich and London, 1831.

Political Economy Club, Minutes of Proceedings, vols. I–VI, London, 1860–1921.

The Political Pilgrim's Progress (first published in the *Northern Liberator*), Newcastle upon Tyne, 1839.

Porter, G. R., *The Progress of the Nation*, London, 1851.

Prentice, Archibald, *Historical Sketches and Personal Recollections of Manchester 1792–1832*, Manchester, 1851.

– 'On the Causes and Cure of the Present Distress', *Manchester Gazette*, 15 and 22 July 1826.

The Present Condition of British Workmen, n.p. 1834.

Prevost, J., 'Diary', *Political Economy Club, Centenary Volume*, VI, London, 1921.

Radcliffe, W., *Origin of the New System of Manufacture*, Stockport, 1828.

Rae, John, 'Essay on Education' (1843), in C. W. Mixter, ed., *The Sociological Theory of Capital*, London, 1905.

– *New Principles of Political Economy*, Boston, 1834.

Ramsay, Sir George, *An Essay on the Distribution of Wealth*, London, 1830.

[Rathbone, W.], *Suggestions Regarding the Objects and Management of Mechanics Institutes*, Manchester, 1830.

Read, Samuel, *An Inquiry into the Natural Grounds of Right to Vendible Property or Wealth*, Edinburgh, 1829.

Reeve, H., ed., *Greville Memoirs, A Journal of the Reigns of King George IV and King William IV*, 3 vols., London, 1875.

A Reply of the Journeyman Bookbinders, to Remarks on a Memorial . . . on the Effects of a Machine to Supersede Manual Labour, London, 1831.

Report of the Proceedings of a Public Meeting Held in . . . Oldham on Friday 11 November, 1836 on the Subject of Shortening the Time of Labour in the Cotton, Woollen, Silk and other Factories, Oldham, 1836.

Ricardo, David, *Works and Correspondence of David Ricardo*, ed. P. Sraffa, 11 vols. Cambridge, 1951.

Robertson, George, *Essays on Political Economy in which are Illustrated the Principal Causes of the Present National Distress*, London, 1830.

[Robinson, David], 'The Combinations of Workmen', *Blackwood's Magazine*, XXXI, April 1832.

[–] 'Political Economy No. I to IV, To the Heads of the University of Oxford', *Blackwood's Magazine*, XXVI–XXVII, September 1829 – January 1830.

Robinson, Thomas, *A Treatise on the Injurious Effects of the Free Trade System and the Export of Machinery*, Leeds, 1830.

Ross, Charles, 'Artizans and Machinery', *Quarterly Review*, XXXI, March 1825.

Royal Statistical Society, *Annals of the Royal Statistical Society*, London, 1834–1934.

[S.P.], [Alsop], *On Machinery to All*, London, 1831.

Sadler, J. H., *The New Invention of Double and Quadruple or British National Looms by 'A Practical Master Weaver of Manchester'*, London, 1831.

Say, J. B., *De L'Angleterre et des Anglais*, 2nd edition, Paris and London, 1816.

– 'Letters to Mr. Malthus on Various Subjects of Political Economy Particularly on the Causes of the General Stagnation of Commerce', *The Pamphleteer*, vol. XVII, no. 34, London, 1821.

– *Des Principes de l'Economie Politique et de l'Impôt, par M. David Ricardo, avec Notes par M. Jean Baptiste Say*, 2 vols., Paris, 1819.

– *A Treatise on Political Economy*, trans. of 4th edition by C. R. Prinsep, London, 1821.

[Scrope, G. P.], 'Dr. Chalmers on Political Economy', *Quarterly Review*, XLVIII, October 1832.

[–] 'Jones on the Doctrine of Rent', *Quarterly Review*, XLVI, 1831.

[–] 'The Political Economists', *Quarterly Review*, XLIV, January 1831.

– *Political Economy versus the Handloom Weavers*, Bradford, 1835.

– *Principles of Political Economy, Deduced from the Natural Laws of Social Welfare*, London, 1833.

[–] 'Rights of Industry and the Banking System', *Quarterly Review*, XLVII, July 1832.

Second Report of the Economical Committee of the Practical Society, 13 February 1822, Edinburgh, 1822.

Senior, N. W., 'Ambiguous Terms in Political Economy', Appendix to Richard Whately, *Elements of Logic*, London, 1826.

– *Introductory Lecture on Political Economy delivered before the University of Oxford*, London, 1827.

– *Letters on the Factory Act*, London, 1837.

– *An Outline of the Science of Political Economy*, London, 1836.

[–] 'Report on the State of Agriculture', *Quarterly Review*, XXV, July 1821.

– *Three Lectures on the Costs of Obtaining Money and on Some Effects of Private and Government Paper Money*, London, 1830.

– *Three Lectures on the Rate of Wages*, London, 1831.

– *Two Lectures on Population*, London, 1829.

Sinclair, Sir John, *Analysis of the Statistical Account of Scotland with a General View of the History of that Country and Discussions on Some Important Branches of Political Economy*, Edinburgh, 1831.

- *A Code of Political Economy Founded on the Basis of Statistical Enquiries, Sketch of the Introduction and Chapter I*, Edinburgh, 1821.

Sismondi, J. C. L. Simonde de, *De La Richesse Commerciale*, Geneva, 1803.

– *Nouveaux Principes d'Economie Politique* (1819), 2nd edition, Paris, 1827.

- 'Review of John Barton's *Observations* and *Inquiry*', from *Annales de Legislation et d'Economie Politique*, November 1822, in J. Sotiroff, *John Barton, Economic Writings*, Regina, Sask., 1962.

Sketch of an Association for Gathering and Diffusing Information on the Condition of the Poor, London, 1833.

Smiles, Samuel, *Industrial Biography: Iron Workers and Tool Makers*, London, 1863.

Smith, Adam, *An Inquiry into the Nature and Causes of the Wealth of Nations*, (1776), 2 vols. Oxford, 1976.

Smith, W. Hawkes, *Birmingham and its Vicinity as a Manufacturing and Commercial District*, Birmingham, 1836.

– 'On the Tendency and Prospects of Mechanics Institutes', *The Analyst*, II, 1835.

Sotiroff, J., ed., *John Barton, Economic Writings*, 2 vols., Regina, Sask., 1962.

Southey, Robert, *Colloquies on Society* (1829), London, 1887.

[Stevenson, William], 'The Political Economist', No. II, *Blackwood's Magazine*, XVI, July 1824.

Stewart, Dugald, *Lectures on Political Economy, Collected Works of Dugald Stewart*, ed. Sir William Hamilton, vol. VIII, Edinburgh, 1855.

Summary of the Report of a Select Committee of Artizans Appointed to Enquire into the Causes Leading to Extensive Depression or Reduction in Remuneration of Labour in Great Britain, London, 1824.

Symons, J. C., *Arts and Artisans at Home and Abroad: With Sketches of the Progress of Foreign Manufactures*, London, 1839.

Taylor, W. Cooke, *Tour of the Manufacturing Districts*, London, 1842.

Third Annual Report of the Literary, Scientific and Mechanics Institute of Newcastle-upon-Tyne, Newcastle upon Tyne, 1827.

[Thompson, T. P.], *A Catechism on the Corn Laws with a List of Fallacies and The Answers*, London, 1827.

– *Exercises, Political and Other*, 6 vols., London, 1842–3.

[–] 'Machine Breaking: A Review of *The Life and History of Swing the Kent Rickburner written by Himself*, 1830', *Westminster Review*, xiv, January 1831.

Thompson, W., *An Inquiry into the Principles of the Distribution of Wealth*, ed. W. Pare, London, 1830.

[–] *Labour Rewarded. The Claims of Labour and Capital Conciliated by One of the Idle Classes*, London, 1827.

– *Practical Directions for the Speedy and Economical Establishment of Communities*, London, 1830.

Torrens, Roberts, *The Economists Refuted*, London, 1808.

– *An Essay on the External Corn Trade*, London, 1815, 3rd edition, 1826.

– *An Essay on the Production of Wealth*, London, 1821.

– *Letters on Commercial Policy*, London, 1833.

[–] 'Mr. Owen's Plans for Relieving the National Distress', *Edinburgh Review*, xxxii, October 1819.

– *On Wages and Combinations*, London, 1834.

– *A Paper on the Means of Reducing the Poor Rates and of Affording Effectual and Permanent Relief to the Labouring Classes*, London, 1817.

[–] 'Strictures on Mr. Ricardo's Doctrine respecting Exchangeable Value', *Edinburgh Magazine*, October 1818.

Tozer, John, 'Mathematical Investigations into the Effect of Machinery on the Wealth of the Community', *Transactions of the Cambridge Philosophical Society*, 1838.

Tuffnell, E. C., *Objects and Effects of Trades Unions*, London, 1834.

Twiss, Travers, *Two Lectures on Machinery*, Oxford, 1844.

[–] *View of the Progress of Political Economy in Europe, since the Sixteenth Century*, London, 1847.

Unrestrained Machinery must Ere Long be the Ruin of the Country, Bradford, 1834.

Ure, Andrew, *The Cotton Manufacture of Great Britain*, London, 1836.

– *A Dictionary of Arts, Manufactures and Mines* (1839), 3 vols., 5th edition, ed. Robert Hunt, London, 1863.

– *The Philosophy of Manufactures*, London, 1835.

Wade, John, *History of the Middle and Working Classes*, 3rd edition, London, 1835.

Wakefield, E. G., *Swing Unmasked; or the Causes of Rural Incendiarism*, London, 1831.

The Weavers' Complaint, or a Bundle of Plain Facts . . . by an Operative of Keighley, Keighley, 1834.

Whately, E. Jane, *The Life and Correspondence of Archibishop Whately, D.D.*, London, 1866.

Whately, Richard, *Introductory Lectures on Political Economy*, London, 1831.

[–] *A Letter to his Parishioners on the Disturbances which have lately Occurred*, London, 1830.

[–] 'Oxford Lectures on Political Economy', *Edinburgh Review*, xlviii, 1828.

[–] *Village Conversations in Hard Times*, London, 1831.
Whewell, William, *A History of the Inductive Sciences*, London, 1837.
– 'Mathematical Exposition of Some Doctrines of Political Economy', *Transactions of the Cambridge Philosophical Society*, III, 1830.
– 'Mathematical Exposition of Some of the Leading Doctrines in Mr. Ricardo's Principles of Political Economy and Taxation', *Transactions of the Cambridge Philosophical Society*, IV, 1833.
– 'On the Use of Definitions', *Philological Museum*, II, 1832.
– *The Philosophy of the Inductive Sciences*, London, 1840.
– 'Political Economy as an Inductive Science', in *The Philosophy of Discovery, Chapters Historical and Critical*, London, 1860.
[–] 'Review of An Essay on the Distribution of Wealth by Richard Jones', *British Critic*, X, 1831.
[Wilson, John], 'The Factory System', *Blackwood's Edinburgh Magazine*, XXXIII, April 1833.

Printed sources – Secondary

Abrams, P., *The Origins of British Sociology*, Chicago, 1968.
Armytage, W. H. G., *A Social History of Engineering*, London, 1961.
Ashton, T. S., *Economic and Social Investigations in Manchester*, London, 1934.
Aspinall, A. M., 'The Circulation of Newspapers in the Early Nineteenth Century', *Review of English Studies*, XXII, 1946.
– *Lord Brougham and the Whig Party*, London, 1927.
– *Politics and the Press. 1780–1850*, London, 1949.
Badham, Charles, *Life of James Deacon Hume*, London, 1859.
Barber, William, *British Economic Thought and India*, Oxford, 1975.
Barton, D. B.,*The Cornish Beam Engine*, Truro, 1966.
Beach, E. F., 'Hicks on Ricardo on Machinery', *Economic Journal*, LXXXI, December 1971.
Bellot, H. H., *University College, London 1826–1926*, London, 1929.
Bendix, R., *Work and Authority in Industry* (1956), 2nd edition, Berkeley, Calif., 1974.
Beresford, M. W., *The Leeds Chamber of Commerce*, Leeds, 1951.
Berman, M., 'The Early Years of the Royal Institution', *Science Studies*, II, 1972.
Black, R. D. C., *Economic Thought and the Irish Question*, Cambridge, 1960.
– 'Parson Malthus, the General and the Captain', *Economic Journal*, LXXVII, March 1967.
– 'Smith's Contribution in Historical Perspective', in Thomas Wilson and A. S. Skinner, eds., *The Market and the State*, Oxford, 1976.
Blaug, Mark, 'The Classical Economists and the Factory Acts – A Reconsideration', *The Quarterly Journal of Economics*, LXXII, 1958.
– *Economic Theory in Retrospect*, 2nd edition, London, 1958.
– 'The Empirical Content of Ricardian Economics', *Journal of Political Economy*, LXIV, 1956.
– *Ricardian Economics, A Historical Study*, New Haven, Conn., 1958.
Blyth, E. K., *Life of William Ellis*, London, 1892.
Bottomore, T. B., 'Social Stratification in Voluntary Organizations', in D. V. Glass, ed., *Social Mobility in Britain*, London, 1954.
Bowley, Marian, *Nassau Senior and Classical Economics*, London, 1937.
– *Studies in the History of Economic Theory before 1870*, London, 1973.

Braverman, H., *Labour and Monopoly Capital*, New York, 1974.

Briggs, Asa, 'The Background of the Parliamentary Reform Movement in Three English Cities', *Cambridge Historical Journal*, x, 1952.

– 'The Language of Class in the Early Nineteenth Century', in Asa Briggs and J. Saville, *Essays in Labour History in Memory of G. D. H. Cole*, London, 1967.

– *Press and Public in Early Nineteenth Century Birmingham*, Dugdale Society Occasional Papers, no. 8, Oxford, 1949.

Brown, Lucy, *The Board of Trade and the Free Trade Movement*, Oxford, 1958.

Bukharin, N., *The Economic Theory of the Leisure Classes*, London, 1937.

Burrow, J. W., *Evolution and Society*, Cambridge, 1970.

Bythell, D., *The Handloom Weavers, A Study in the English Cotton Industry during the Industrial Revolution*, Cambridge, 1969.

Cannan, E., *A History of Theories of Production and Distribution, 1776–1848*, 2nd edition, London, 1903.

Cannon, W. F., 'History in Depth: The Early Victorian Period', *History of Science*, III, 1964.

– 'Scientists vs. Broad Churchmen: An Early Victorian Intellectual Network', *Journal of British Studies*, IV, December 1964.

Cardwell, D. S. L., *The Organization of Science in England*, London, 1957, revised edition, 1972.

Cazamian, L., *The Social Novel in England, 1830–1850* (1903), trans. Martin Fido, London, 1973.

Chaloner, W. H., 'Frederick Engels and Manchester', *History Today*, IV, 1956.

Chapman, Dennis, 'William Brown of Dundee 1791–1864: Management in a Scottish Flax Mill', *Explorations in Entrepreneurial History*, IV, February 1952.

Chapman, S. J., 'An Historical Sketch of the Masters' Associations in the Cotton Industry', *Transactions of the Manchester Statistical Society*, 13 February 1901.

Checkland, S. G., 'The Birmingham Economists, 1815–1850', *Economic History Review*, I, 1948.

– 'Economic Attitudes in Liverpool, 1793–1807', *Economic History Review*, V, 1952.

– 'Growth and Progress: The Nineteenth Century View in Britain', *Economic History Review*, 1959.

– 'The Propagation of Ricardian Economics in England', *Economica*, XVI, February 1949.

Church, R. A. and Chapman, S. D., 'Gravenor Henson and the Making of the English Working Class', in E. L. Jones and G. E. Mingay, eds., *Land Labour and Population during the Industrial Revolution*, London, 1967.

Clark, E. K., *History of One Hundred Years of the Leeds Philosophical Society*, Leeds, 1924.

Clark, M. P., 'The Board of Trade at Work', *American Historical Review*, XVII, 1912.

Clements, R. V., 'British Trade Unions and Popular Political Economy', *Economic History Review*, 1951.

Clive, John, *The Scotch Reviewers: The Edinburgh Review, 1802–1815*, London, 1957.

Coats, A. W., 'Changing Attitudes to Labour in the Mid Eighteenth Century', *Economic History Review*, XI, August 1958.

– 'The Role of Authority in the Development of British Economists', *Journal of Law and Economics*, VII, October 1964.

Cooper, Charles, 'Choice of Techniques and Technical Change as Problems in Political Economy', *International Social Sciences Journal*, XXV, 1973.

– 'Science, Technology and Production in Underdeveloped Countries', *Journal of Development Studies*, October 1972.

Copeman, W. S. C., 'Andrew Ure', *Proceedings of the Royal Society of Medicine*, 1951.

Corry, B. A., *Money, Saving and Investment in English Economics 1800–1850*, London, 1962.

Cullen, M. J., *The Statistical Movement in Early Victorian Britain*, New York, 1975.

Curtin, Philip, *The Image of Africa*, London, 1965.

Davis, R., 'The Rise of Protection in England, 1669–1786', *English Historical Review*, LXXXI, 1966.

Deane, Phyllis and Cole, W. A., *British Economic Growth*, 2nd edition, Cambridge, 1969.

De Marchi, N. B., 'The Empirical Content and Longevity of Ricardian Economics', *Economica*, XXXVII, 1970.

– 'Malthus and Ricardo's Inductivist Critics', *Economica*, XL, 1973.

– 'The Success of Mill's Principles', *History of Political Economy*, VI, 1974.

Dickinson, H. W., *A Short History of the Steam Engine*, Cambridge, 1938.

Dobb, Maurice, *Theories of Value and Distribution since Adam Smith*, Cambridge, 1973.

Dobbs, A. E., *Education and Social Movements*, London, 1919.

Driver, Cecil, *Tory Radical, The Life of Richard Oastler*, New York, 1946.

Facts and Observations Illustrative of the Evils of the Law which Prohibits the Exportation of Machinery, Manchester, 1841.

Farrar, W. V., 'Andrew Ure', *Notes and Records of the Royal Society of London*, XXVII, February 1973.

Fay, C. R., *Huskisson and His Age*, London, 1951.

Feinstein, C. H., 'Capital Formation in Great Britain', *Cambridge Economic History of Europe*, VII, Cambridge, 1978, p. 88.

Ferguson, C. E., 'The Specialization Gap : Barton, Ricardo and Hollander', *History of Political Economy*, V, Spring 1973.

Ferricelli, Jean, 'Malthus, Théoreticien de la Croissance', *Revue d'Histoire Economique et Sociale*, 1966.

Fetter, F. W., 'The Authorship of Economic Articles in the Edinburgh Review 1802–1847', *Journal of Political Economy*, LXI, June 1953

– 'The Economic Articles in the Quarterly Review and their Authors, 1809–1852', *Journal of Political Economy*, LXVI, February 1958.

– 'The Economic Articles in the Westminster Review and their Authors, 1824–1951', *Journal of Political Economy*, LXX, December 1962.

– 'Economic Controversy in the British Reviews 1802–1850', *Economica*, XXXII, November 1965.

– 'The Rise and Decline of Ricardian Economics', *History of Political Economy*, I, Spring 1969.

– 'Robert Torrens : Colonel of the Marines and Political Economist', *Economica*, XXIX, May 1972.

Finlayson, G. B., 'Joseph Parkes of Birmingham, 1786–1865, A Study of Philosophic Radicalism', *Bulletin of the Institute of Historical Research*, XLVI, November 1973.

Foote, G. A., 'The Place of Science in the British Reform Movement 1830–1850', *Isis*, XLII, 1951.

Forbes, Duncan, 'James Mill and India', *The Cambridge Journal*, V, October 1951.

Foster, John, *Class Struggle and the Industrial Revolution*, London, 1974.

Foucault, M., *Discipline and Punishment, the Birth of the Prison*, trans. A. Sheridan, London, 1977.

Fraser, Derek, 'Edward Baines', in Patricia Hollis, ed., *Pressure from Without in Early Victorian England*, London, 1974.

Gallagher, J. and Robinson, R., 'The Imperialism of Free Trade', *Economic History Review*, VI, 1953.

Garnett, R. G., *Co-operation and the Owenite Socialist Communities in Britain 1825–1945*, Manchester, 1972.

Gattrell, V. A. C., 'Labour, Power, and the Size of Firms in Lancashire Cotton', *Economic History Review*, XXX, February 1977.

Geilkie, A., *Life of Sir Roderick I. Murchison*, London, 1875.

Gellner, E., *The Legitimation of Belief*, Cambridge, 1974.

Gilmour, R., 'The Gradgrind School : Political Economy in the Class Room', *Victorian Studies*, XI, December 1967.

Gordon, B. J., 'Criticism of the Ricardian Views on Value and Distribution in the British Periodicals, 1820 to 1850', *History of Political Economy*, I, Fall 1969.

– 'Say's Law, Effective Demand, and the British Periodicals, 1820 to 1850', *Economica*, XXXII, November 1965.

Gourvitch, A., 'Survey of Economic Theory on Technological Change', Mimeo, 1940.

Grampp, William, *The Manchester School of Economics*, Stanford, 1960.

– 'Politics of the Classical Economists', *Quarterly Journal of Economics*, LXII, 1947.

Gregson, T. E. G., *Early History of the Manchester Statistical Society*, 1925.

Haber, F., 'Fossils and the Idea of a Process of Time in Natural History', in B. Glass, O. Tenkin, and W. R. Strauss jun., eds., *Forerunners of Darwin*, Baltimore, 1959.

Halévy, Elie, *The Growth of Philosophic Radicalism* (1928), 2nd edition, London, 1934.

– *Thomas Hodgskin*, trans. A. J. Taylor, London, 1956.

– *J. C. L. Simonde de Sismondi*, Paris, 1933.

Halstead, John, 'Capital's Car', *Bulletin for the Society of Labour History*, Autumn 1976.

Hamburger, Joseph, *Intellectuals in Politics. John Stuart Mill and the Philosophic Radicals*, Yale, 1965.

Harrison, Brian, 'Two Roads to Social Reform : Francis Place and the "Drunken Committee" of 1834', *Historical Journal*, XI, 1968.

– 'Philanthropy and the Victorians', *Victorian Studies*, IX, 1965–6.

Harrison, J. F. C., *Learning and Living, 1790–1960*, London, 1961.

– *Robert Owen and the Owenites in Britain and America*, London, 1968.

– 'The Steam Engine of the New Moral World : Owenism and Education 1817–1929', *Journal of British Studies*, VI, 1967.

Harrison, W. W., *The Founding of the British Association*, London, 1881.

Hart, Jennifer, 'Nineteenth Century Social Reform : A Tory Interpretation of History', in M. W. Flinn and T. C. Smout, eds., *Essays in Social History*, Oxford, 1974.

Helm, E., *Chapters in the History of the Manchester Chamber of Commerce*, London, 1902.

Henderson, W. O., *Frederick Engels*, 2 vols., London, 1976.

Hey, W., *Sketch of the York Founders of the British Association*, York, 1881.

Hicks, J. R., *Capital and Time*, Oxford, 1973.

– 'A Reply to Professor Beach', *Economic Journal*, LXXXI, December 1971.

– *A Theory of Economic History*, Oxford, 1969.
– 'Capital Controversies : Ancient and Modern', *American Economic Review, Papers and Proceedings*, LXVI, 1974.
Hill, R. L., *Toryism and the People*, London, 1929.
Hilton, A. J. B., *Corn, Cash, Commerce; The Economic Policies of the Tory Governments 1815–1830*, Oxford, 1977.
Hilton, G. W., 'The Controversy Concerning the Relief of Handloom Weavers', *Explorations in Entrepreneurial History*, 2nd series, I, Winter 1964.
Hobsbawm, E. J., *Labouring Men* (1964), New York, 1967.
Hobsbawm, E. J. and Rudé, George, *Captain Swing* (1968), New York, 1975.
Hodgkinson, R. C., 'Social Medicine and the Growth of Statistical Information', in F. N. L. Poynter, ed., *Medicine and Science in the 1860's*, London, 1968.
Hollander, Samuel, 'The Development of Ricardo's Position on Machinery', *History of Political Economy*, III, Spring 1971.
– *The Economics of Adam Smith*, London, 1973.
– 'Malthus and the Post Napoleonic Depression', *History of Political Economy*, I, Fall 1969.
– 'The Reception of Ricardian Economics', *Oxford Economic Papers*, XXIX, July 1977, No. 2.
– 'Ricardo and the Corn Laws : A Revision', *History of Political Economy*, IX, 1977.
– 'Ricardo's Analysis of the Profit Rate 1813 to 1815', *Economica*, XL, August 1973.
– 'Some Technological Relationships in the *Wealth of Nations and Ricardo's Principles*', *Canadian Journal of Economics and Political Science*, XXXII, May 1966.
Hollis, Patricia, *The Pauper Press: A Study in Working Class Radicalism of the 1830's*, Oxford, 1972.
Houghton, W. E. and Houghton, Esther, *The Wellesley Index to Victorian Periodicals 1824–1900*, Toronto, 1965.
Howarth, O. J. R., *The British Association for the Advancement of Science: A Retrospect 1831–1921*, London, 1922.
Hunt, E. K., 'Value Theory in the Writings of the Classical Economists, Thomas Hodgskin and Karl Marx', *History of Political Economy*, IX, 1977.
Hutchinson, T. W., 'James Mill and the Political Education of Ricardo', *The Cambridge Journal*, VII, 1953.
Hyde, C. K., *Technological Change and the British Iron Industry 1700 to 1870*, Princeton, 1977.
Inkster, I., 'Science and the Mechanics Institutes 1820–1850 : The Case of Sheffield', *Annals of Science*, September 1975.
James, E. W., 'The Life and Work of John Rae', *Canadian Journal of Economics and Political Science*, XVII, May 1951.
Jefferys, J. B., *The Story of the Engineers 1800–1945*, London, 1946.
Jeremy, David, 'Damming the Flood : British Government Efforts to Check the Outflow of Technicians and Machinery 1780–1843', *Business History Review*, 1977.
Johnson, L. G., *General T. Perronet Thompson*, London, 1957.
Johnson, Richard, 'Educational Policy and Social Control in Early Victorian England', *Past and Present*, no. 49, November 1970.
– 'Educating the Educators : "Experts" and the State 1833–1839', in Donajgrodski, A.P., ed. *Social Control in Nineteenth Century Britain*, London, 1977.

Kaldor, N., 'Alternative Theories of Distribution', *Review of Economic Studies*, XXIII, 1955–6.

Kelly, Thomas, *George Birkbeck, Pioneer of Adult Education*, Liverpool, 1957.

– *A History of Adult Education in Great Britain*, 1970.

Kennedy, W. F., 'Lord Brougham, Charles Knight and the Rights of Industry', *Economica*, XXIX, February 1962.

Kirby, R. G. and Musson, A. E., *The Voice of the People, John Doherty 1798–1854, Trade Unionist, Radical and Factory Reformer*, Manchester, 1975.

Koolman, G., 'Say's Conception of the Role of the Entrepreneur', *Economica*, XXXVIII, August 1971.

Landes, David, *The Unbound Prometheus*, Cambridge, 1969.

Lantz, P., 'De la Richesse des Besoins à la Richesse des Nations', *Revue d'Histoire Economique et Sociale*, 1968.

Lees, Lynn, 'The Irish in London', in S. Thernstrom and R. Sennett, eds., *Nineteenth Century Cities*, New York, 1969.

Linglebach, A. L., 'The Inception of the British Board of Trade', *American Historical Review*, XXX, 1925.

– 'William Huskisson as President of the Board of Trade', *American Historical Review*, XLIII, 1938.

Lutfalla, M., *L'Etat Stationnaire*, Paris, 1964.

McAskill, Joy, 'The Chartist Land Plan', in Asa Briggs, ed., *Chartist Studies* (1959), London, 1965.

McGregor, O. R., 'Social Research and Social Policy in the Nineteenth Century', *British Journal of Sociology*, VIII, 1963.

McKindley, E. W., 'Ricardo Sulle Machine', *Rivista Internazionale di Science Economiche a Commerciale*, XIII, 1963.

Marcus, Steven, *Engels, Manchester and the Working Class*, London, 1974.

Marglin, Steven, 'What Bosses Do,' in André Gorz, ed., *The Division of Labour*, London, 1976.

Marx, Leo, *The Machine in the Garden*, Oxford, 1964.

Mathias, Peter, *The First Industrial Nation*, London, 1969.

– 'Skills and the Diffusion of Innovation from Britain in the Eighteenth Century', *Transactions of the Royal Historical Society*, XXV, 1975.

– 'Who Unbound Prometheus? Science and Technical Change 1600–1800', in Peter Mathias, ed., *Science and Society, 1600–1900*, Cambridge, 1972.

Meek, R. L., 'The Decline of Ricardian Economics in England', in R. L. Meek, ed., *Economics and Ideology and Other Essays*, London, 1967.

– 'Physiocracy and Classicism in Britain', *Economic Journal*, LXI, March 1951.

– 'Physiocracy and the Early Theories of Underconsumption', *Economica*, XVIII, August 1951.

– *Social Science and the Ignoble Savage*, Cambridge, 1975.

– *Studies in the Labour Theory of Value* (1956), 2nd edition, London, 1973.

Menger, Anton, *The Right to the Whole Produce of Labour*, London, 1899.

Midwinter, E., *Social Administration in Lancashire 1830–1860*, Manchester, 1969.

Mitchell, B. R., *Abstract of British Historical Statistics*, Cambridge, 1962.

– 'Statistical Appendix 1700–1914', *Fontana Economic History of Europe*, IV, London, 1971.

Morrell, J. B., 'Individualism and the Structure of British Science in 1830', *Historical Studies in the Physical Sciences*, III, 1971.

– 'Science and Scottish University Reform: Edinburgh in 1826', *British Journal of the History of Science*, VI, June 1972.

Mouat, F. J., 'History of the Statistical Society of London', *Jubilee Volume of the Journal of the Royal Statistical Society*, 1885.

Musson, A. E., 'An Early Engineering Firm : Peel, William and Company of Manchester', *Business History*, III, 1960.

– 'The Manchester School and the Exportation of Machinery', *Business History*, XIV, January 1972.

Musson, A. E. and Robinson, E., *Science and Technology in the Industrial Revolution*, Manchester, 1969.

Myint, Hla, 'The Classical View of the Economic Problem', *Economica*, May 1946.

Nesbitt, G. L., *Benthamite Reviewing: The First Twelve Years of the Westminster Review 1824–1836*, New York, 1934.

Norris, J. M., 'Samuel Garbett and the Early Development of Industrial Lobbying in Great Britain', *Economic History Review*, X, 1957.

O'Brien, D. P., *The Classical Economists*, Oxford, 1975.

– *J. R. McCulloch: A Study in Classical Economics*, London, 1970.

Opie, R., 'A Neglected British Economist : George Poulett Scrope', *Quarterly Journal of Economics*, 1930.

Orange, A. D., 'The British Association for the Advancement of Science; The Provincial Background', *Science Studies*, I, 1971.

– *Philosophers and Provincials: The Yorkshire Philosophical Society 1822–1844*, York, 1973.

Paglin, M., *Malthus and Lauderdale: The Anti Ricardian Tradition*, New York, 1961.

Pasinetti, L., 'From Classical to Keynesian Dynamics', in L. Pasinetti, ed., *Growth and Income Distribution*, Cambridge, 1974.

– 'A Mathematical Formulation of the Ricardian System', *Review of Economic Studies*, XXVII, 1959–60.

Perkin, H. J., 'Middle Class Education and Employment in the Nineteenth Century : A Critical Note', *Economic History Review*, XIV, 1961–2.

Pinney, Thomas, ed., *The Letters of Thomas Babington Macaulay*, Cambridge, 1974–.

Plummer, Alfred, *Bronterre, A Political Biography of Bronterre O'Brien 1804–1864*, London, 1971.

Pocock, J. G. A., *Politics, Language and Time*, London, 1972.

Pole, W., ed., *Life of Sir William Fairbairn*, London, 1877.

Pollard, Sidney, *The Genesis of Modern Management*, Harmondsworth, 1965.

– 'Industrialization and the European Economy', *Economic History Review*, XXVI, November 1973.

– "Nineteenth Century Co-operation : from Community Building to Shopkeeping', in Asa Briggs and John Saville, eds., *Essays in Labour History*, London, 1967.

Porter, Roy, 'The Industrial Revolution and the Rise of the Science of Geology', in M. Teich and R. M. Young, eds., *Changing Perspectives in the History of Science*, London, 1973.

Poynter, J. R., *Society and Pauperism, 1795–1834*, London, 1969.

Protheroe, Iorwerth, *Artisans and Politics in Early Nineteenth Century London*, London, 1979.

Prouty, R., *The Transformation of the Board of Trade 1830–1855*, London, 1957.

Rauner, R. M., *Samuel Bailey and the Classical Theory of Value*, London, 1961.

Read, Donald, *Peterloo, the Massacre and its Background*, London, 1958.

– *Press and People 1790–1850: Opinion in Three English Cities*, 1961.

Redford, A., *Manchester Merchants and Foreign Trade 1794–1858*, Manchester, 1934.

Rimmer, G., *Marshalls of Leeds, Flax Spinners, 1788–1886*, Cambridge, 1960.

Robbins, Lionel, *Robert Torrens and the Evolution of Classical Economics*, London, 1958.
– *The Theory of Economic Policy in English Classical Political Economy* (1952), 1965.
Roberts, A. J., 'Robert Owen, Cotton Spinner : New Lanark', in Sidney Pollard and John Salt, eds., *Robert Owen Prophet of the Poor*, London, 1971.
Roberts, David, 'The Social Conscience of Tory Periodicals', *Victorian Periodicals Newsletter*, x, September 1977.
Roberts, John, 'Engineering, Consultancy, Industrialization and Development', *Journal of Development Studies*, October 1972.
Robinson, E., 'The Diffusion of Steam Power', *Journal of Economic History, Papers and Proceedings*, 1974.
– 'The Derby Philosophical Society', *Annals of Science*, ix, 1953.
Roll, Eric, *An Early Experiment in Industrial Organization*, London, 1930.
Rolt, L. T. C., *Tools for the Job. A Short History of Machine Tools*, London, 1965.
– *Victorian Engineering* (1970), Harmondsworth, 1974.
Rosenberg, Nathan, 'Adam Smith on the Division of Labour : Two Views or One', *Economica*, xxxii, 1965.
– 'Economic Development and the Transfer of Technology : Some Historical Perspectives', *Technology and Culture*, xi, 1970.
– 'Science, Invention and Economic Growth', *Economic Journal*, lxxxiv, March 1974.
– 'Technological Change in the Machine Tool Industry 1840–1910', *Journal of Economic History*, 1963.
Rowe, D. J., 'Francis Place and the Historians', *Historical Journal*, xvi, 1970.
Royle, Edward, 'Mechanics Institutes and the Working Classes, 1840–1860', *Historical Journal*, 1971.
Rubel, N., 'Actualité de Sismondi', *Revue d'Histoire Economique et Sociale*, 1972.
Rudé, George, *The Crowd in History*, New York, London, Sydney, 1964.
Rudwick, M. J. S., 'Poulett Scrope and the Volcanoes of Auvergne : Lyellian Time and Political Economy', *British Journal for the History of Science*, vii, March 1974.
– 'Uniformity and Progression : Reflections on the Structure of Geological Theory in the Age of Lyell', in D. H. D. Roller, ed., *Perspectives in the History of Science and Technology*, Norman, Oklahoma, 1971.
Samuel, Raphael, 'The Workshop of the World', *History Workshop*, No. 3, 1977.
– ed., *Village Life and Labour*, London, 1975.
Sanderson, M., 'Literacy and Social Mobility in the Industrial Revolution in England', *Past and Present*, no. 56, August 1972.
Schumpeter, J. A., *History of Economic Analysis*, London, 1954.
Schwarz, Pedro, *The New Political Economy of J. S. Mill*, London, 1968.
Seligman, E., 'On Some Neglected British Economists', *Economic Journal*, xiii, 1903.
Semmel, Bernard, *The Rise of Free Trade Imperialism: Classical Political Economy, the Empire of Free Trade 1750–1850*, Cambridge, 1970.
– ed., *Occasional Papers of T. R. Malthus*, New York, 1963.
Sexton, A. H., *The First Technical College: A Sketch of the History of the Andersonian and the Institution Descended from it. 1796–1894*, London, 1894.
Shairp, J. C., Tait, P. G. and Adams, A., *Life and Letters of James David Forbes*, London, 1873.
Shapin, Stephen, 'The Pottery Philosophical Society 1819–1835, An Examination of the Cultural Uses of Provincial Science', *Science Studies*, ii, 1972.

- 'Phrenological Knowledge and Early Nineteenth Century Edinburgh', *Annals of Science*, 1975.
Shapins, S. and Barnes, B., 'Science and Nature : Interpreting Mechanics Institutes', *Social Studies of Science*, VII, 1977.
Skinner, A. S., 'Say's Law : Origin and Content', *Economica*, XXXIV, 1967.
Skinner, Quentin, 'The Limits of Historical Explanation', *Philosophy*, July 1966.
- 'Some Problems in Political Thought and Action', *Political Theory*, II, 1974.
Smart, W., *Economic Annals of the Nineteenth Century*, 2 vols., London, 1910 and 1917.
Smith, R. E., *A Centenary of Science in Manchester*, London, 1883.
Sorenson, L. R., 'Some Classical Economists, Laissez-Faire and the Factory Acts', *Journal of Economic History*, 1952.
Sraffa, Piero, 'Malthus on Public Works', *Economic Journal*, LXV, 1955.
Stedman Jones, G., 'Class Struggle and the Industrial Revolution', *New Left Review*, No. 90, March–April 1975.
- 'Engels and the Genesis of Marxism', *New Left Review*, No. 106, November–December 1977.
Stigler, G. J., 'The Classical Economists : An Alternative View', in *Five Lectures on Economic Problems*, London, 1949.
- 'Ricardo and the 93 per cent Labour Theory of Value', in *Essays in the History of Economics*, Chicago, 1965.
Street, R. and Walter, A. C., 'The Beginning of the Manchester Chamber', *Manchester Chamber of Commerce Monthly Record*, XXXII, 1921.
Tann, Jennifer, *The Development of the Factory*, London, 1970.
- 'The Textile Millwright in the Early Industrial Revolution', *Textile History*, V, October 1974.
Thackray, A., 'Natural Knowledge in Cultural Context : The Manchester Model', *American Historical Review*, LXXIX, 1974.
Thomas, W. E. S., 'Francis Place and Working Class History', *Historical Journal*, V, 1962.
- 'Philosophic Radicalism in the 1830's', in Patricia Hollis, ed., *Pressure from Without in Early Victorian England*, London, 1974.
Thompson, E. P., *The Making of the English Working Class*, Harmondsworth, 1968.
- 'Time, Work Discipline and Industrial Capitalism', *Past and Present*, no. 38, 1967.
- 'The Moral Economy of the English Crowd in the Eighteenth Century', *Past and Present*, no. 50, 1971.
Todhunter, I., *William Whewell*, London, 1876.
Tribe, Keith, *Land, Labour and Economic Discourse*, London, 1978.
Tucker, G. S. L., 'The Origins of Ricardo's Theory of Profits', *Economica*, XXI, 1954.
- *Progress and Profits in British Economic Thought 1650–1850*, Cambridge, 1960.
Tunzelman, G. N. von, *Steam Power and British Industrialization to 1860*, Oxford, 1978.
Tylecote, Mabel, *The Mechanics Institutes of Lancashire and Yorkshire Before 1851*, Manchester, 1957.
Tyrrell, A., 'Political Economy, Whiggism and the Education of Working Class Adults in Scotland 1817 to 1840', *Scottish Historical Review*, XLVIII, 1967.
Vernon, Sally, 'Trouble up at T'Mill : the Rise and Decline of the Factory Play in the 1830's and 1840's, *Victorian Studies*, Winter 1977.
Vigier, F., *Change and Apathy, Liverpool and Manchester during the Industrial Revolution*, 1970.

Vincent, L. A., 'Progress Technique et Progress Economique', *Revue Economique,* 1961.

Von Schulze-Gavernitz, G., *The Cotton Trade in England and on the Continent,* London, 1895.

Wallas, Graham, *The Life of Francis Place, 1771–1854,* London, 1898.

Ward, J. T., *Chartism,* London, 1973, p. 170.

– *The Factory Movement, 1830–1855,* London, 1962.

Watson, R. S., *History of the Philosophical and Literary Society of Newcastle upon Tyne,* London, 1897.

Webb, R. K., *The British Working Class Reader 1790–1848,* London, 1955.

– *Harriet Martineau, A Radical Victorian,* London, 1960.

Weber, Gay, 'Science and Society in Nineteenth Century Anthropology', *History of Science,* xii, 1974.

Williams, Gwyn, 'Roland Detrosier: A Working Class Infidel', *Borthwick Papers,* xxviii, 1965.

Williams, L. Pearce, 'The Physical Sciences in the First Half of the Nineteenth Century', *History of Science,* i, 1962.

Williams, Raymond, *The Country and the City,* St Albans, Herts., 1973.

– *Culture and Society 1780–1950,* Harmondsworth, 1961.

– *Keywords,* Glasgow, 1976.

Winch, D. N., *Classical Political Economy and Colonies,* London, 1965.

Yeo, Eileen, 'Robert Owen and Radical Culture', in Sidney Pollard and John Salt, eds., *Robert Owen Prophet of the Poor,* London, 1971.

Young, A. 'Increasing Returns and Economic Progress', *Economic Journal,* xxxviii, 1928.

Young, R. M., 'The Historiographical and Ideological Context of the Nineteenth Century Debate on Man's Place in Nature', in M. Teich and R. M. Young, eds., *Changing Perspectives in the History of Science,* London, 1973.

– 'Malthus and the Evolutionists. The Common Context of Biological and Social Theory', *Past and Present,* no. 43, May 1969.

INDEX

DATE DUE